OFFICIALLY DISCARDED BY
UNIVERSITY OF PITTSBURGH LIBRARY

THE GLOBAL POLITICS
OF ARMS SALES

LIBRARY GRADUATE SCHOOL OF PUBLIC
AND INTERNATIONAL AFFAIRS
1G12 FORBES QUAD
UNIVERSITY OF PITTSBURGH
PITTSBURGH, PA 15260

COUNCIL ON FOREIGN RELATIONS
BOOKS

The Council on Foreign Relations, Inc., is a non-profit and nonpartisan organization devoted to promoting improved understanding of international affairs through the free exchange of ideas. The Council does not take any position on questions of foreign policy and has no affiliation with, and receives no funding from, the United States government.

From time to time, books and monographs written by members of the Council's research staff (like this book) or visiting fellows, or commissioned by the Council, or written by an independent author with critical review contributed by a Council study or working group are published with the designation "Council on Foreign Relations Book." Any book or monograph bearing that designation is, in the judgment of the Committee on Studies of the Council's board of directors, a responsible treatment of a significant international topic worthy of presentation to the public. All statements of fact and expressions of opinion contained in Council books are, however, the sole responsibility of the author.

LIBRARY GRADUATE SCHOOL OF PUBLIC
AND INTERNATIONAL AFFAIRS
1G12 FORBES QUAD
UNIVERSITY OF PITTSBURGH
PITTSBURGH, PA 15260

The Global
Politics of
ARMS
SALES

Andrew J. Pierre

Princeton University Press
Princeton, New Jersey

Copyright © 1982 by Princeton University Press

Published by Princeton University Press, Princeton, New Jersey
In the United Kingdom: Princeton University Press, Guildford,
Surrey

All Rights Reserved

This book has been composed in APS-5 CRT Caledonia

Clothbound editions of Princeton University Press books are
printed on acid-free paper, and binding materials are chosen for
strength and durability

Printed in the United States of America by Princeton University
Press, Princeton, New Jersey

Designed by Laury A. Egan

CONTENTS

List of Figures   ix
List of Tables   ix
Preface   xi

PART ONE   DILEMMAS   1

Trends in Transfers   8

Uncertain Rationales for Arms Sales   14
  Influence and Leverage   14
  Security and Stability   19
  Economic Benefits   24

Competing Foreign Policy Aims   28
  Nuclear Proliferation and Conventional Arms Sales   29
  Human Rights and the Sale of Arms to Repressive
    Regimes   31
  Standardization of Arms within the Atlantic Alliance
    versus Exports to the Third World   34
  Arms Purchases—A Diversion from Economic
    Development?   36

PART TWO   SUPPLIERS   39

UNITED STATES   45
  Criticism of Arms Sales   45
  The Role of Congress   50
  The Carter Policy   52
  Evaluation of the Carter Policy   54
  The Reagan Difference   62
  The Economic Dimension   68
  Public Opinion   71

CONTENTS

SOVIET UNION   73
   Second Largest Supplier   74
   Improved Logistical Capability   77
   The Economic Dimension   78
   A Balance Sheet   80

FRANCE   83
   Growth in Sales   83
   Policy of Independence and Autonomy   85
   The Military-Industrial Complex   87
   Decision-Making Process and Policy   89
   Public and Political Debate   91
   The Mitterrand Approach   93
   An Uncertain Future   97

UNITED KINGDOM   100
   Arms Sales Rationales   101
   Defense Industry and Export Production   102
   Policy and Politics   105

THE RESTRICTORS: WEST GERMANY, JAPAN,
SWEDEN, AND SWITZERLAND   109
   West Germany   109
   Japan   116
   Sweden and Switzerland   120

NEW, THIRD WORLD SUPPLIERS   123

PART THREE   RECIPIENTS   129

MIDDLE EAST   136
   *Role of the Superpowers (I): The Soviet Experience in
      Egypt and Syria*   138
   *Role of the Superpowers (II): The American Experience
      in Iran*   142
   Arms and Influence   154
   Israel   156
   Egypt   164
   Jordan   172
   Saudi Arabia and North Yemen   175
   Syria and Iraq   189
   Libya   197
   Arms Restraint in the Middle East   199

CONTENTS

ASIA   210
 South Korea   210
 North Korea   213
 Taiwan   214
 Japan   218
 Southeast Asia   218
 India and Pakistan   221
 People's Republic of China   225

LATIN AMERICA   232
 Security Concerns and the Military   234
 Brazil   237
 Peru   239
 Argentina and Chile   241
 Cuba   244
 Venezuela   245
 Central America   247
 Mexico   248
 American Arms Sales Policy and Human Rights   249

SUB-SAHARAN AFRICA   255
 Soviet and Cuban Designs   256
 Changing American Perspectives   259
 French, British, and Chinese Roles   263
 South Africa   264
 East-West Competition and Arms Restraint   268

PART FOUR   RESTRAINTS   273

New Significance of Arms Sales   275

The Need for International Management   278

Past Approaches to International Restraints   281

The Conventional Arms Transfer Talks
  with the Soviet Union   285

Forms of Multilateral Regulation   291

Priority to the European-American Dimension   296

East-West "Rules of the Game"   301

Third World Arms Industries—A Limited Role
  as Suppliers   303

CONTENTS

Recipient Perspectives and Regional Approaches   306

Notes   313

Index   337

About the Author   353

LIST OF FIGURES

1. World Arms Exports, 1977   8
2. World Arms Imports, 1977   9
3. United States Arms Sales, 1970–1980   47

LIST OF TABLES

1. Imports of Arms by Developed and Developing
Nations, 1969–1978   11
2. Weapons Delivered to the Third World by
Category, 1972–1978   12
3. 25 Largest Third World Major-Weapon Importing
Countries, 1977–1980   133

PREFACE

Writing this book has been both challenging and frustrating.

The role of arms sales in world politics has grown greatly over the past decade, yet it has received little serious and systematic attention. The literature on the global diffusion of conventional arms is sparse indeed, in comparison with the extensive bookshelf on strategic arms and nuclear proliferation. Yet the importance of arms sales is increasingly evident—in the foreign policies of supplier and recipient nations, in regional politics and balances, and in the East-West competition as in North-South relations. The opportunity to undertake a comprehensive and sustained study, seeking to bring some analytic order to this amorphous phenomenon, has been the challenge.

The frustration has arisen from several sources. One is the sheer complexity of the global politics of arms sales. We are dealing with the political motives, economic incentives, and security perspectives of practically all nations of the world. Because the sale of arms is a political act, whatever the other incentives, it affects both bilateral and multilateral relationships among states. In addition to the complexity of the phenomenon is its scope. Arms sales have become a daily occurrence. Hardly a day has gone by in the past years when I have not clipped some relevant item from the newspapers. Yet the organized data on the transfer of weapons are very limited, most governments choosing not to release information on their sales or purchases, and what does exist is often inconsistent. The availability of data is discussed in the first note in the back of the book. Suffice it to say here that I have not found the problem such as to impede analysis of principal trends in the transfer of arms or the political consequences of weapons sales.

Perhaps the most challenging *and* frustrating aspect of my task has been the circularity of the arguments involving arms sales. For every pro or con there is likely to be a fair amount of validity in the counter-argument. Answers must be tentative and conditional. They will be greatly influenced by the weight that one gives to competing considerations. Intuition rather than accepted wisdom must often serve as guide. Much will depend upon the time frame involved. In part, this is because the politics of arms sales is now being played out mainly in the Third World, which is marked by internal instability and external fluidity in relationships with outside arms suppliers. Moreover, there is a lack of norms by which to assess the requirements of international security. The criteria for restraint in the proliferation of conventional arms, for example, are far more difficult to establish when one is moving from the East-West to the North-South context. Nevertheless, I have not hesitated to offer my own preferences and policy judgments throughout this book.

A few words about what this book does not seek to do may be appropriate. This is not primarily an analysis of United States policy, although American practice is discussed in some detail, including the early approach of the Reagan administration. Most of what has been written on arms sales has concentrated on the United States, giving insufficient attention to broader aspects of the issue, and I have therefore chosen to undertake a global examination. This is not an exposé of wheeling and dealing or of the "merchants of death" in the underworld of the arms trade. Much of that involves small arms and does not have the impact upon world politics of the government-sponsored arms sales discussed in this volume. (The reader will nevertheless find a few spicy vignettes.) Nor is this book an exercise in abstract theory or model-building. The subject remains too inchoate to be amenable to such methods; an overly theoretical approach runs a high risk of being divorced from political reality. What I have attempted to do, simply stated, is to increase our knowledge of a very complex but not well-understood phenomenon. The organization of the book, part functional and part geographical, has been chosen as the best way to accomplish this end. A discussion

PREFACE

partially rooted in regional and national perspectives is essential,
in my view, to achieving true insight.

Writing this book has taken me to twenty countries in five
regions of the globe. It has been a fascinating and instructive
experience, giving me the opportunity to deal more fully with
political and security issues in the Third World, after having long
concentrated on East-West and European-American relations.
Along the route the number of people who have been of assistance are legion. I have also received support from a number of
foundations and institutions, for which I am grateful.

A Rockefeller Foundation Fellowship in its Conflict in International Relations Program enabled me to take a year's leave of
absence from the Council on Foreign Relations. During 1977–78
the Atlantic Institute for International Affairs in Paris provided
me with an office and an intellectual home. A grant from the
Ford Foundation made it possible for me to undertake research
in five countries in Latin America. Travel assistance provided by
the Council on Foreign Relations allowed me to speak with scores
of individuals in eight countries in the Persian Gulf and the Middle East. An invitation from the Institute for the Study of the
United States and Canada in Moscow gave me the opportunity
to learn more about Soviet perspectives on arms sales. Pen was
first put to paper during a productive month at the Bellagio
Study and Conference Center of the Rockefeller Foundation in
Italy. Earlier, during the summer of 1976, a NATO Research
Fellowship first gave me the opportunity to explore this question
in a number of European capitals.

I have benefited from visits to many institutions, among them
the International Institute for Strategic Studies and the Royal
Institute for International Affairs in London, the Institut Français
des Relations Internationales in Paris, the Stockholm International Peace Research Institute, the Center for Political and Strategic Studies of Al Ahram in Cairo, the Iranian Institute of Political and Economic Studies and the Iranian Institute for
Communications and Development in Teheran, the Shiloah Center on the Middle East and Africa and the Center for Strategic
Studies in Tel Aviv, the Leonard Davis Institute for International

xiii

Affairs in Jerusalem, the Institute of International Studies in Santiago, the Instituto Rio Branco in Brazilia and IUPERJ in Rio de Janiero, the Centro de Estudios Militares and the Institute for Peruvian Studies in Lima.

I attended conferences whose discussions contributed to my thinking about conventional arms sales at the Ditchley Foundation in the United Kingdom, at the Aspen Institute in Berlin (for the United Nations Association of the United States), at the Centre Quebecois des Relations Internationales in Quebec and one organized by the Carnegie Endowment for International Peace and the Arms Control Association in Talloires, France.

Literally hundreds of conversations have given me guidance, many of them with senior officials in ministries of foreign affairs and defense, as well as with the foreign affairs staffs of heads-of-state. In a number of countries I also spoke with representatives from the arms manufacturing industries. An assurance of confidentiality does not allow me to name all. For the sake of brevity I will not list the scores of Americans, in and out of government, with whom I have talked about arms sales over the years. I would, however, like to give special thanks to a number of persons in Europe, the Middle East, and Latin America who willingly spoke to me.

In London: Christoph Bertram, Shahram Chubin, Julian Critchley, François Duchêne, John Edmonds, Martin Edmonds, Lawrence Freedman, Denis Healey, Arthur Hockaday, Kenneth Hunt, Mary Kaldor, Jenny Little, James Meacham, Andrew Palmer, William Rodgers, John Roper, Anthony Sampson, Ian Smart, Dan Smith, John Stanley, Sir Lester Suffield, John Thompson, Christopher Tugendhat, and Valerie Yorke. In Paris: Christian d'Aumalle, Jean Louis Gergorin, Gerald Hibbon, Jacques Huntziger, Jean Klein, Jacques Martin, André Mistral, Thierry de Montbrial, Pierre Morel, Yves Pagniez, Gabriel Robin, Walter Schutze, and Jacques Vernant. In Bonn: Peter Corterier, Helga Haftendorn, and Walther Stützle. In Stockholm: Nils Andren, Frank Barnaby, Karl Birnbaum, Bjorn Hagelin, Ron Huisken, and Signe Landgren-Backstrom.

In Cairo: Mohammad Sid Ahmad, Tahseen Basheer, Ali Dessouki, Major-General Hassan El-Badry, Lufti Khouli, Samy Mansour, and El Sayed Yassin. In Damascus: Ahmed Iskander Ahmed, Rafik Atassi, Adnan Baghajatti, Khalid Fahoum, Safwan Ghanem, Abdulillah Mallah, and Hamoud Shoufi. In Teheran: Abbas Amirie, Shaul Bakhash, Darius Bayandor, Dara Chehrazi, J. Nadim, General Toufanian, and Manouchehr Zelli. In Amman: Crown Prince Hassan, Abnan Abu Odeh, Lieutenant-General Sharif Zeid bin Shaker, and Sharif Abdul Hamid Sharaf. In Jerusalem and Tel Aviv: Mordechai Abir, Yeheskel Dror, Abba Eban, Boaz Evron, Yair Evron, Shlomo Gazit, Galia Golan, Yosef Govrin, Yehoshofat Harkabi, Shelom Keital, David Landau, Avraham Lif, Yaacov Lifschitz, Moshe Maoz, Matityahu Mayzel, Nissan Oren, Shimon Peres, Mosker Raviv, Eli Rekhess, Gideon Samet, Zeev Schiff, Shmuel Segev, Amnon Sella, Haim Shaked, Shimon Shamir, Zvi Sussman, Major-General Israel Tal, General Ahron Yariv, and Moshe Zak.

In Brasilia and Rio de Janiero: Walter de Amusatogui, Rubens Antonio Barboso, Sergio Bath, Fernando Henrique Cardoso, Colonel Luiz Francisco Ferreira, Jose Nogueria Filho, Walter de Goes, Ivan Zanoni Hansen, Helio Jaguaribe, Candido Mendes, and Hugo Scolnick. In Buenos Aires: Victor Beauge, Mario Corti, General Ubaldo Diaz, Claudio Escriviano, Aldo Ferrer, Ezequiel Gallo, General Juan Guglialmelli, Fernando Petrella, Louis H. Sales, and Torcuato di Telli. In Santiago: Enrique Inglesias, Alejandro Magnet, Anibal Pinto, Walter Sanchez, and Colonel Ernesto Videla. In Lima: Alberto Tamayo Barrios, Jose Coz Botteri, Julio Cutler, Jose Antonio Encinas, Mercado Jarrin, Jose Matos Mar, and Vice Admiral Ricardo Zevallos Newton. In Caracas: Gene Bigler, Nava Carillo, Antonio Casas Gonzalez, Carlos Gueron, Juan Carlo Puig, and Carlos Rangel.

In each country I spoke with the American ambassadors and their staffs and often with their European counterparts. The assistance received from them, especially in opening doors and arranging meetings, was invaluable.

A study group of the Council on Foreign Relations, chaired by Paul Warnke, which met in Washington in 1976–77 represented a first cut into the subject. The papers prepared for it have been published in Andrew J. Pierre, editor, *Arms Transfers and American Foreign Policy* (New York: New York University Press, 1979). Looking at the arms sales question initially from an American policy perspective reinforced my conviction that more attention had to be given to the global context.

A special debt of gratitude is owed to a number of persons who read the manuscript and offered comments (or evaluations). The manuscript as a whole was read by Richard Betts, Barry Blechman, Peter Dawkins, Edward Kolodziej, Robert Osgood, and Richard Ullman. Others read the regional sections: Harold Saunders (Middle East), Alan Romberg and Michael Blaker (Asia), Robert Bond (Latin America), William Foltz and Jennifer Whitaker (Africa). The above bear no responsibility for the final product but each contributed toward its improvement.

Winston Lord and my colleagues on the Studies Staff of the Council on Foreign Relations were unflagging in their encouragement of a book that never seemed to be finished. Special thanks is due, and warmly given, to those who helped me directly with the manuscript, in one way or another, at various stages: Kay King, Tami Bauer, Betty Bradley, Pat Berlyn, and Rob Valkenier. The incomparable Grace Darling Griffin, true friend of remarkable abilities, assisted the book with every means at her command.

At Princeton University Press, Sandy Thatcher recognized the timeliness of the subject and with his professional skill managed to shepherd the book through the usual publication process with unusual dispatch. At home Clara, my writer-wife, was quick to respond to such questions as: "Is this a sentence?"

New York, N.Y.   A. J. P.
August 1981

THE GLOBAL POLITICS
OF ARMS SALES

PART ONE

DILEMMAS

A rms sales have become, in recent years, a crucial dimension of international affairs. They are now major strands in the warp and woof of world politics. Arms sales are far more than an economic occurrence, a military relationship, or an arms control challenge—*arms sales are foreign policy writ large.*

The dramatic expansion in arms sales to the developing world during the 1970s is by now widely known. Less clear is what judgment to make of this important phenomenon.

To some observers, the arms delivered feed local arms races, create or enhance regional instabilities, make any war that occurs more violent or destructive, and increase the tendency for outside powers to be drawn in. The arms received are often seen as unnecessary to the true needs of the purchasing country and as a wasteful diversion of scarce economic resources. The remedy often proposed is drastic curtailment of arms sales, with tight international controls as the best means for achieving this.

To others, the recent increase in arms sales is no cause for particular concern. Sovereign nations have every right to the weapons that they deem necessary. By giving or selling arms the supplier country acquires political influence or friendship. It receives economic benefits. Regional peace and stability may be advanced rather than hindered by the transfer of arms. In any case, there is little that can be done about the international trade in arms. If one country does not sell the weapons, some other state will be only too happy to oblige. Accordingly, seeking international restraints is a will-o'-the-wisp.

Neither judgment is fully right or wrong. In order to be better understood, the arms trade phenomenon must be viewed in the wider context of the transformations under way in world politics.

Arms sales must be seen, essentially, in *political* terms. The world is undergoing a diffusion of power—political, economic, and military—from the industrialized, developed states to the Third World and the so-called Fourth World (poor and without

3

oil). The acquisition of conventional arms, often sophisticated and usually in far greater quantities than the recipient state previously had, is a critical element of that diffusion.

Arms are a major contributing factor to the emergence of regional powers such as Israel, Brazil, South Africa, or, until recently, Iran; their purchase makes a deep impact upon regional balances and local stability. The diffusion of defense capabilities contributes at the same time to the erosion of the early postwar system of imperial or hegemonic roles formerly played by the major powers around the globe. Thus the superpowers, and even the medium-sized powers such as Britain and France, are losing the ability to "control" or influence events in their former colonies or zones of special influence. And the transfer of conventional arms is only one element of the diffusion of military power. Another, of prime importance, is the trend toward nuclear proliferation. As we shall see, the relationship between the two is intricate and complex.

Arms sales must also be seen in the context of North-South issues. They constitute a form of redistribution of power whose significance in certain cases may be equal to or greater than that of some of the well-recognized economic forms. Certainly the withholding or granting of arms can have a great political and psychological impact. Arms transfers can also be a form of transfer of technology; an increasing number of states do not want the weapons fresh out of the crate but the technology that will enable them to build, or "co-produce," them at home.

Finally, arms sales remain a key element of the continuing East-West competition. Indeed, they may now be the prime instrument available to the Soviet Union, and a significant one for the United States, in their rivalry for the allegiance of much of the world. The condition of mutual deterrence at the nuclear level, and the risk that a conventional conflict could quickly or uncontrollably escalate to the nuclear level, make a direct military confrontation between the two superpowers unlikely—hence the tendency toward competition by "proxy" in the Third World, with the superpowers supporting friendly states or regimes, or (in the case of the Communist states) assisting "move-

4

ments of national liberation." Sometimes alliances and the identification of "friends" alter quickly, as happened in the Horn of Africa where the Soviet Union initially supported Somalia with arms and the United States supported Ethiopia, only to see their respective roles reversed. A contributing factor to the emerging importance of arms transfers as an instrument of the East-West competition has been the relative decline of ideology as an element in the continuing struggle, because of the diminishing attractiveness of both the United States and the Soviet Union as models. Yet another factor has been the declining size and role of economic and developmental assistance. Both the United States and the Soviet Union now give less in economic assistance than the value of their arms sales.

Arms do not of themselves lead to war. The causes of war are manifold and complex, but the underlying roots are usually found in political, economic, territorial, or ideological competition. Yet arms sent into a region may exacerbate tensions, spur an arms race, and make it more likely that, as Clausewitz taught us, war will emerge as the continuation of politics by other means. Once war has started, the existence of large and sophisticated stocks of weapons may make the conflict more violent and destructive. And if the arms have been acquired from abroad, often with the establishment of a resupply relationship and sometimes including the presence of technical advisers from the producing country, they may have a tendency to draw the supplier into the conflict. Yet these undesirable developments need not be inevitable. Arms may deter aggression, restore a local imbalance, and generally enhance stability. All depends upon the specifics of the case and the perceptions that exist about it.

Nevertheless, the people of the world can take little comfort from the trend toward a higher level of global armaments. Total world military expenditures have grown from $100 billion in 1960 to $500 billion in 1980. Measured in constant prices this is an increase of 80 percent. The rise in arms spending in the developing world has been especially acute. Since 1960 military expenditures in the Third World have risen over fourfold (in constant prices), while those in developed countries have gone up

5

a more modest 48 percent.[1] (Note 1, this chapter, discusses fully the data base for this study.)

For all these reasons, we need a more complete and sophisticated understanding of the global politics of arms sales. We also need to think more creatively, as well as realistically, about developing some type of international management for the process of transferring weapons.

Neither of these aims is easy to achieve. What we term the global politics of arms sales involves an enormous number of variables: the foreign affairs of close to 150 nations; their economic affairs, ranging from their industrial or development policies to questions of balance of payments and trade; their approach toward the acquisition or sale of technology; their perceptions of the threats to their national security and what must be undertaken to maintain it. This involves, in turn, a very large number of bilateral and multilateral relationships. Arms are usually sought because of the desire to maintain security vis-à-vis one's neighbors, or to enhance one's role and status within a region— hence the importance of a regional approach to both comprehending and controlling arms transfers. This regional emphasis is reinforced by the present diffusion of political, economic, and military power away from the principal postwar centers of power and influence.

Beyond the task of better understanding the arms transfer phenomenon is the need to manage or regulate it. But this is uncommonly difficult because of the lack of norms by which to measure restraints and controls, or even of agreement on the basic necessity for them. With regard to the spread of nuclear weapons capabilities, a general consensus has been reached in the world that nuclear proliferation is undesirable. There are some exceptions to this agreement but they are quite negligible. The nuclear non-proliferation debate today, significant as it is, is about the means for preventing or retarding proliferation, not about the widely accepted end goal. No equivalent consensus exists on the proliferation of conventional arms.

With regard to conventional arms three general points of view can be identified. Some persons perceive arms to be inherently

6

wasteful or even evil. They seek a maximum curtailment of their production and distribution. At the opposite end of the spectrum are those who make no moral judgment on arms and who view their sale abroad as essentially a commercial activity. They would prefer to have a minimum of regulation by governments, with the arms trade left to the forces of the marketplace. A third perspective—and the one reflected in this study—is primarily concerned with the impact of arms transfers upon regional stability and international security. Arms transfers, it is argued, should be managed so as to prevent or contain conflict and enhance the forces of moderation and stability.

But how are such laudable purposes to be achieved? Assuming that some restraints or controls over arms transfers are desirable in principle, how are they to be created in practice? Underneath the practical aspects of the problem is the difficulty in making normative judgments that have universal applicability.

A particular sale may be destabilizing, or it may restore a balance. It may promote an arms race in a region, or it may act so as to deter a potential conflict. Moreover, what is true in the short run may not hold true for the longer term. Who is to say how a weapon transferred now could be employed in ten years' time? And who can vouchsafe that the political leadership of a country will be as sober and "responsible" about the use of weapons in the future as it appears at present? Or that the alliances and foreign policy alignments of today—upon which the prospective supplier must base his decision—will be the same tomorrow?

Arms sales are fraught with policy dilemmas. There are no easy answers to the above questions. There are no "simple truths" to guide policy makers. Even when a supplier country has adopted general policy guidelines, each weapons transfer decision will involve complex judgments and trade-offs. Long-term risks must be weighed against shorter-term benefits. The prospective economic advantages of a sale may have to be balanced against potentially disadvantageous political or arms control consequences. One foreign policy goal, such as strengthening an alliance relationship or a nation's capacity for self-defense, may run counter to another goal, such as promoting human rights. As

7

the debates of recent years on individual arms transfers show, one can almost take for granted that every decision will involve competing objectives.

TRENDS IN TRANSFERS

It is, of course, the major increase in both the quantity and the quality of arms sent to the Third World that has given this problem its current salience. Complete and reliable data on arms

FIGURE 1

World Arms Exports, 1977
Shares by Suppliers

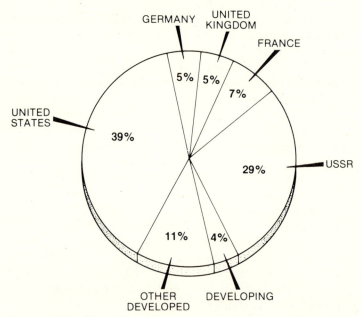

SOURCE: ACDA, *World Military Expenditures and Arms Transfers 1968–1977*, p. 10.

8

FIGURE 2

World Arms Imports, 1977
Shares by Regions

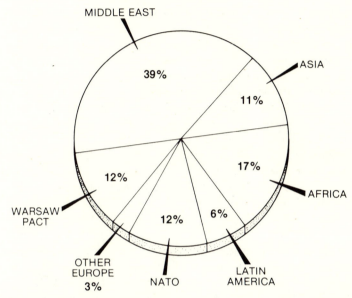

SOURCE: ACDA, *World Military Expenditures and Arms Transfers 1968–1977*, p. 8.

transfers are not readily available. Governments are not inclined to release data that could prove to be embarrassing either at home or abroad. Nevertheless, enough is known to give a reasonably accurate impression of the trends.

In worldwide terms, arms transfers have more than doubled in the past decade, having grown from $9.4 billion in 1969 to $19.1 in 1978 (in constant dollars).[2] At the beginning of the 1980s most estimates of arms sales worldwide were on the order of $21 billion per annum.

The United States has been the largest supplier of conventional arms and has had the greatest increase in sales. American foreign military sales (the accounting for these sales includes items other than weapons, such as training and logistical assistance, which can account for 40 percent of the total) totaled $1.1 billion in 1970 and rose sharply to $15.8 billion in 1975.[3] They have since remained above $10 billion per annum, with a projected all-time high for 1981 of $16 billion. As sales went up, however, there was a decline in grant aid through military assistance programs. Equally significant has been the more than quadrupling of the French and British export of arms since 1970, as well as a marked increase in the level of Soviet transfers.

Changes in the qualitative dimension of the arms trade have been as significant as its quantitative expansion. In the past, most arms transferred to less developed countries were the obsolete weapons of the major powers which they wanted to eliminate from their inventories to make room for new, more advanced ones. Often they were gifts from surplus stocks of over-age, technologically inferior equipment. Thus many of the arms transferred to the Third World prior to the 1970s were still of the World War II, or early postwar, vintage. Even in the early 1960s, the aircraft transferred to the developing world more often than not were ten-year-old American F-86s and Soviet MiG-17s rather than the first-line planes of the period (such as F-4s and MiG-21s). In contrast, today many of the arms being sold are among the most sophisticated in the inventories of the supplier states. This is strikingly evident with certain advanced fighter aircraft. The F-15, the most sophisticated plane of its type, is being sold to Saudi Arabia and Israel, and plans are in progress to have it co-produced in Japan; the Soviet MiG-23 is being exported to several nations in the Middle East, as is the French Mirage F-1. It is less evident, but equally significant, in smaller yet very advanced systems such as the TOW anti-tank missile, which was not released from the American inventory until the critical stages of the Yom Kippur War but has now been approved for sale to more than a dozen countries. As was the case with the $1.3 billion sale of the Airborne Warning and Control System (AWACS) aircraft to Iran, foreign orders have been

10

accepted while the producing country was still deciding about procurement for its own armed forces. Foreign orders have occasionally been given higher priority than domestic ones or have become the necessary element in a favorable decision to start a production run to equip the supplying country's own armed forces.

Another dimension of the qualitative change has been the significant growth in the transfer of arms through co-production agreements. These enable states to acquire through licensing arrangements the knowledge to manufacture or to assemble a weapons system. More than two dozen developing countries now participate in such arrangements. As a result of this trend, there has been a spread in sophisticated weaponry around the globe.

The acquisition of a new weapon by one country in a particular region creates strong pressures in the surrounding countries for the acquisition of comparable weapons. In 1960 only four developing nations had supersonic combat aircraft; by 1977 the

TABLE 1

IMPORTS OF ARMS BY DEVELOPED AND
DEVELOPING NATIONS, 1969–1978
Billions of Constant (1977) U.S. Dollars

Year	Developed Nations	Developing Nations	Total
1969	3.2	6.2	9.4
1970	2.7	6.4	9.1
1971	2.5	6.9	9.4
1972	4.4	10.3	14.7
1973	4.6	13.0	17.6
1974	4.1	10.2	14.3
1975	3.9	10.1	14.0
1976	4.4	12.9	17.3
1977	4.1	15.2	19.3
1978	3.6	15.5	19.1

SOURCE: Calculated from ACDA, *World Military Expenditures and Arms Transfers 1969–1978*, p. 117.

total had risen to forty-seven. There has been a similar proliferation with respect to long-range surface-to-air missiles, from two
nations in 1960 to twenty-seven by the mid-1970s.[4]

A third change has been in the direction of the arms flows.
Until the mid-1960s most weapons transferred went to developed
countries, usually the NATO allies of the United States or the
Warsaw Pact allies of the Soviet Union. It was not until the war
in Southeast Asia in the second half of the decade that the dominant portion went to the developing world. Nor was the trend
reversed by the end of the Vietnam War. During the late 1970s
the Persian Gulf and Middle East countries received by far the
largest portion of arms. Iran, Saudi Arabia, and Israel were the
major recipients of Western arms, while most Soviet weapons
were shipped to Syria, Iraq, Libya, and, a little earlier, Egypt.

TABLE 2
WEAPONS DELIVERED TO THE THIRD WORLD
BY CATEGORY, 1972–1978

Equipment Description	United States	U.S.S.R.	Major West European Nations
Tanks and self-propelled guns	6,110	8,570	2,090
Artillery	3,715	6,310	955
Armored cars and personnel carriers	9,735	6,975	2,430
Major surface combatants	83	7	17
Minor surface combatants	157	94	247
Submarines	24	9	20
Guided missile boats	0	60	15
Supersonic combat aircraft	11,160	1,990	355
Subsonic combat aircraft	925	390	35
Helicopters	1,730	575	1,180
Other aircraft	1,520	260	855
Surface-to-air-missiles (SAMs)	6,240	15,745	1,065

SOURCE: U.S., Congress, Senate, Committee on Foreign Relations, *Prospects for
Multilateral Arms Export Restraint*, Staff Report, 96th Cong., 1st sess., April
1979, p. 11.

The importation of weapons by Third World countries rose from $6.2 billion in 1969 to $15.5 billion in 1978 (in constant dollars).[5] Over three-quarters of the global arms trade now goes to the Third World. No area has not seen some growth in its imports; after the Persian Gulf and Middle East, the most notable increases have been in arms sent to Africa and Latin America.

Quite interestingly, only a very small number of countries constitute the principal suppliers of arms, thereby maintaining the pattern of the past twenty-five years. Four states accounted for 87.5 percent of the value of the major weapons transferred to the developing world during the decade of the 1970s: the United States (45 percent), the Soviet Union (27.5 percent), France (10 percent), and Britain (5 percent). When one adds a few members of the NATO alliance (West Germany, Canada, Italy, the Netherlands) and the Soviet Union's Warsaw Pact ally Czechoslovakia, the figure is raised to 94.3 percent. The largest supplier not included in one of the two alliances is the People's Republic of China, but it only accounts for slightly more than 1 percent of transfers.[6] Other industrialized countries that export arms, such as Sweden and Switzerland, are still relatively minor suppliers.

There are a number of new arms manufacturers within the so-called Third World (a misnomer for which there is no satisfactory alternative) such as Brazil, South Korea, India, South Africa, and Israel that are developing their industries and actively seeking export markets. This is a relatively recent phenomenon. Two decades ago almost none of the states in Asia, Africa, and Latin America could produce arms indigenously. Arms production in the Third World is likely to continue to expand at a steady rate and is a new dimension of world politics. But, as discussed subsequently, because these countries are mainly dealing in second-echelon technology, and in most cases cannot provide the political support the principal suppliers do, which is often part of the attraction of doing business with them, these new arms producers are unlikely to present a serious challenge to the four major suppliers. From 1969 to 1978 arms exports by developing countries grew from $276 million to $837 million (in constant dollars), but this only accounted for 4.4 percent of world arms exports.[7]

13

This configuration of the suppliers becomes significant when one considers opportunities for developing some form of arms control or international management for arms transfers, as discussed later in this book. The domination of the arms trade by the Big Four should facilitate efforts in this direction because they are but four and, in effect, have an oligopoly. Moreover, they all have experience and past involvement in the pursuit of common objectives, either in East-West arms control negotiations or in intra-Western alliance diplomacy. As much as 67 percent of arms transfers to the Third World were undertaken in 1978 by members of NATO, while the Warsaw Pact accounted for another 29 percent.[8]

UNCERTAIN RATIONALES FOR ARMS SALES

The dilemmas created by the international trade in arms, which face decision makers presented with an arms transfer request, arise from the difficulty in reaching a judgment as to whether a given transfer would be "good" or "bad." This can best be illustrated by examining some of the justifications traditionally given for making weapons sales or grants. We do this here in general terms, postulating the justifications and questioning or examining their validity, before turning in the following sections to some of the more specific situations and dilemmas that exist in particular countries and regions.

Influence and Leverage

A major political rationale for arms transfers has been the influence the supplier gains in dealings with the recipient nation. Arms can be an important symbol of support and friendly relations and thereby create influence. Arguments for the sale of weapons to China have been based not so much on the need to enhance its military capabilities against the Soviet Union, for the Chinese will remain comparatively weak under any circumstances, as to demonstrate American friendship and further the normalization of relations. After the invasion of Afghanistan,

14

pressure on the Soviet Union became an additional objective. Similarly, the Soviet Union has transferred arms to Arab states and to national liberation movements as a demonstration of ideological support or affinity. Moscow sold weapons to Peru on a long-term, low-interest basis in order to establish a base of influence in South America. American arms sales to Saudi Arabia have been justified by the need to maintain a "special relationship" with that country.

Arms may provide access to political and military elites. This has been the traditional justification for many of the U.S. military assistance programs to Latin American nations, where often there was no serious military threat or need for arms. The continuing contacts between defense establishments, which accompany arms transfers through training missions and the sending of Latin American military officers to U.S. military schools, is thought to be important because of the political role played by the military on the continent. Similarly, the Soviet Union has competed with China for access to foreign elites through the sale of weapons to countries such as Indonesia and India.

When countries are dealing with established allies, arms can give substance to treaty commitments. NATO and the Warsaw Pact are the most obvious cases. But in a more fluid situation where there is no formal alliance, and when a prospective recipient may turn to one side or the other, the argument for an arms transfer has often been made on preemptive grounds: to deny the transfer, and the influence that presumably flows with it, to the competing side. Many recipient countries have become adept at this game. Faced with American reluctance to provide a modern air defense system, King Hussein of Jordan discussed such a purchase with the Soviet Union in 1975 before being able to get from the United States the 500 Hawk surface-to-air missiles that he wanted. Preemptive selling is not limited to the East-West competition but often occurs between Western states, although the motivations in such cases are more commercial.

The most important political benefit of arms transfers may be leverage over other countries' sensitive foreign policy decisions. In the Arab-Israeli conflict, the offer of arms has been used to make difficult political and territorial decisions more acceptable.

15

Former Secretary of State Henry Kissinger, who was especially inclined to use arms transfers as an instrument of foreign policy, promised Israel substantial amounts of new weapons (including the first sale of the F-15 to another country) in exchange for its leaders' approval of the 1975 Sinai disengagement agreement. The Carter administration's decision in 1978 to sell F-5E fighters to Egypt was strongly influenced by the need to buoy up Anwar Sadat in order to dissuade him from breaking off the peace negotiations after the initiative he had launched seemed to be going nowhere. Implicit in the large-scale provision of arms to Iran and Saudi Arabia was the belief that this would make it less likely that the Shah or King Khalid would support an OPEC embargo cutting off the supply of oil.

Yet one must be very cautious in accepting some of the generalized justifications for arms transfers. Influence and leverage are transitory phenomena: they can be lost even more quickly than they are acquired. The Soviet Union developed a close relationship with Egypt when it began supplying arms in 1955; after it refurbished the Egyptian armed forces following the 1967 war it gained the use of naval facilities in Alexandria for its Mediterranean fleet and access to air bases, and greatly augmented its physical presence in the country. Still, the very existence of this arms supply relationship led to friction between Cairo and Moscow. Sadat expelled the Soviet advisers in 1972, and after the Yom Kippur War changed the orientation of Egypt's foreign policy toward close ties with the United States. To take another example, the United States brought promising military officers to the States for training as part of its Latin American military assistance programs, partially in order to indoctrinate them with the democratic values it sought for the Western hemisphere; yet the leaders of most of the military juntas that today exercise repression and violate human rights in Latin America are graduates of these programs.

The most vivid demonstration of the uncertain nature of the influence that arms can achieve is the course of events in Iran. Because the United States sold large quantities of sophisticated arms to Teheran, it was seen by many Iranians as a strong supporter of the Shah—to some he was even an "American puppet," with the arms the most visible symbol of American support. Came the revolution, the United States was thoroughly discredited. Not only did it lose all influence, but America became *the* enemy against which conflicting groups within Iran rallied so as to achieve a common goal. If arms sales have the effect of closely associating the supplier with a certain regime in a country, and that regime is overturned, the former association can have serious negative consequences. Local conditions can always change, and general assumptions that underpin the sought-after influence or leverage are always subject to being undermined.

One can also question the essence of the leverage that arms provide over specific foreign policy decisions. The United States used its arms relationships with success in deterring a war between Greece and Turkey in 1967, but in 1974 it was powerless to prevent Turkey's invasion of Cyprus. Nor, it should be noted, did the subsequent arms embargo legislated by the Congress succeed in bringing about Turkish concessions; on the contrary, Ankara responded by placing restrictions on NATO bases in the country. Western largess in making arms available to Iran (in some cases delaying the equipping of the supplier state's armed forces) did not persuade the Shah to help keep oil prices down; Iran was a consistent advocate within OPEC for higher oil prices—in part, to help pay for the weapons it was purchasing.

Indeed, the provision of arms can even give the recipient "reverse leverage" over the supplier. Perhaps the most striking example of this occurred during the Vietnam War when America's deep commitment to that country was played upon by the Thieu government in vetoing various peace proposals. A different kind of reverse leverage can exist when arms have been made available in exchange for base rights. In the Philippines, for example, Washington has been limited in the extent to which it can make known American disagreement with the internal human rights policies of the Marcos government. Washington's continued dependence on U.S. bases for its Pacific strategy encouraged Manila to demand substantial military and economic assistance in return for the use of bases on Philippine soil.

17

The transfer of arms can go so far as to make the supplier hostage to the recipient. As a 1976 report to the Senate Foreign Relations Committee on American arms sales to Iran noted, the large-scale sales to Teheran invariably involved a commitment to provide support for the weapons. The United States could not abandon its arms-support activities without provoking a major crisis in Iranian-U.S. relations (and such a crisis, were it to occur, could have a major consequence for the supply of oil). If Iran had become involved in a war then, it would have been difficult to keep American personnel uninvolved. Thus the 24,000 American personnel in Iran at the time, whose number was expected to increase substantially in the coming years as more arms were scheduled to be delivered, could physically become hostages at a moment of crisis. The report concluded that because of the political symbolism that stems from a close supplier-client arms relationship, "it is not clear *who really has influence over whom in time of an ambiguous crisis situation.*"[9] Although events did not proceed exactly as foreseen—they rarely do—the warning was prescient. Reverse leverage of another type came into play in the spring of 1981 when the level of Saudi oil production was linked to arms sales. Speaking on American television Sheik Ahmed Zaki Yamani, the Saudi oil minister, stressed the importance that his country attached to the planned sale of five AWACS planes in the context of a discussion on both the price and the future output of Saudi oil.

In short, it is clear that the provision of arms may provide influence and leverage. Arms sales can be important tools of foreign policy. As such, they are attractive to policy makers who are in immediate need of instruments to help implement their strategies.

But experience suggests that the political value of arms sales in global politics can be overrated. Creating an arms supply relationship is not sufficient to cement relations between two countries and entails certain risks. The influence acquired may be of surprisingly short duration. The amount of leverage will depend upon the alternatives available to the recipient state. If there are other suppliers, then the degree of leverage will be less than if the recipient has little or no choice. The supplier may find that there are incalculable political costs in applying leverage. The recipient may come to regret his dependence and the implicit conditions attached to a sale. In short, the transfer of arms can often create an uncertain and symbiotic supplier-recipient relationship which ends up limiting the freedom of action of both.

Security and Stability

Another traditional rationale for supplying arms is to help fulfill the security requirements of allies and friends. From the early postwar period until the mid-1970s, when most U.S. arms transfers were in the form of military grants, this was the basic reason for transferring arms to NATO and to other allies such as Japan and South Korea. As the danger thought to be posed by internal subversion in South Vietnam and elsewhere came to occupy the attention of the Kennedy administration, arms for purposes of counterinsurgency were deemed to be important. Later, the Nixon Doctrine expanded the reliance upon arms transfers by emphasizing the role of U.S. weapons for indigenous forces as a replacement for the direct presence of American military personnel. Only in recent years as arms transfers have become predominantly sales rather than grants, and the bulk of U.S. transfers has gone to the Persian Gulf and Middle East, have they become controversial and have the presumed benefits become more difficult to identify with certainty.

Providing military support for allies and friends has also been an important Soviet motivation in countries such as North Korea, North Vietnam, Syria, Iraq, Somalia, and Cuba, as well as in the Warsaw Pact countries. Arms have been transferred to Cuba to encourage and enable it to become or remain involved in conflicts in Angola and elsewhere on the African continent. France and Britain, as they withdrew from their colonies, often transferred some of their remaining arms or undertook to provide new ones for the new states; but most of their more recent sales have been essentially commercial rather than political or security related in nature.

Arms for allies are often perceived as being transferred within the context of creating, or maintaining, a regional balance of power. This is most evident in the Middle East, where additional arms from both East and West have been justified as necessary to maintain the Arab-Israeli balance. Similarly, arms for Chile and Peru, or for India and Pakistan, have been viewed in this manner in the past.

But one nation's perception of balance may be another nation's "*im*balance." The risk of a process of competitive acquisition, leading to a local arms race, is often present. Local arms races exist in the Latin American and South Asian cases just cited. In Africa, Kenya and Tanzania felt impelled to build up their own capabilities with Western assistance after Idi Amin's Uganda received arms from the Soviet Union. Sometimes the question whether or not an arms race even exists is open to interpretation. The Shah insisted that Iran's massive defense buildup was not aimed at such Persian Gulf states as Saudi Arabia and the United Arab Emirates, but was the consequence of the need to respond to, and deter, his immediate neighbors, the Soviet Union, Iraq, and Afghanistan. Saudi Arabia also disclaimed being in an arms race with Iran. Yet the Saudis were deeply concerned with the Shah's military aggrandizement, and this concern had a major impact on their decision to increase and modernize their armed forces. Moreover, as their request for the F-15 demonstrated, even if they did not intend or wish to match Iran fully, for reasons of both pride and politics they sought clear assurance of equal access to American arms.[10]

Other classical military concerns are often cited as rationales for making arms transfers. One of these is the right to establish a military base in the recipient country. As far back as 1940 President Roosevelt offered fifty destroyers to Britain in exchange for base facilities in the Caribbean. Following World War II, as the United States came to rely upon a global network of overseas bases for its bombers and for monitoring the Soviet Union, arms were often transferred as a quid pro quo for the availability of bases. The United States received base rights in Pakistan, Ethiopia, and Libya and naval facilities in Spain and the Philippines

20

with such understandings. More recently, after the Soviet move into Afghanistan, Washington promised arms to Oman, Somalia, and Kenya in exchange for access to bases. Arms were an even more important instrument for the Soviet Union as it sought to expand its strategic reach and break out of its continental isolation through achieving access to various military support facilities in South Yemen, Somalia, Syria, and Cuba, among other locations. Moscow in the late 1970s gained valuable strategic access to the American-built bases at Cam Ranh Bay and Danang in Vietnam in exchange for arms and economic aid.

Although the total number of U.S. bases abroad has declined (because of the reliance upon long-range intercontinental ballistic missiles and missile-firing submarines, new satellite observation techniques, and shifting international needs), overseas bases are likely to remain an important component of American and Soviet strategic planning. This is certainly the case in the Persian Gulf and Middle East, where both superpowers seek to improve their on-the-spot presence. Given the critical necessity of protecting the oil flow from the region, American planners would like nothing more than a military base in the area. The granting of any such facility is certain to include arms as part of the deal.

Closely related to the need for overseas military bases is the need for intelligence facilities for such activities as electronic eavesdropping and surveillance flights, as in the case of the famous U-2 flights over the Soviet Union. Here, too, the supply of arms can be an invaluable quid pro quo. In early 1980 Egypt was promised forty F-16 fighters as part of a military equipment package totaling just under $1 billion at a time when the United States began flying AWACS aircraft from Egyptian bases. But no bargain is without some risk: when the United States placed its embargo on arms to Turkey following the invasion of Cyprus, Turkey retaliated by restricting the use of American intelligence activities, saying, in effect, "no arms, no intelligence."

Another justification for arms transfers, popular with military establishments, is based on the assumption that they are more likely to be tested in combat earlier by the receiver than by the supplier. New American precision-guided anti-tank weapons

21

were first employed in conflict by Israel during the Yom Kippur War; the lessons learned and the experience gained in 1973 through their use had a profound impact upon military planners thereafter. The testing of new weapons also appears to have been one of the Soviet motivations in selling some arms to Iraq that were used in the Kurdish rebellion. The fighting in Afghanistan in 1980, in which some Soviet arms were used by regular Afghan forces, provided another opportunity to test them.

There are several possible military costs or disadvantages that any government must take into account before it sends arms overseas. Once they are in the arsenal of another country it becomes difficult, if not impossible, to control their use. Thus the arms sent may one day be transferred by the recipient country to a third party, as happened when French Mirages, sold to Saudi Arabia, found their way to Egypt. Most arms transfer agreements now have a clause forbidding re-transfer without the supplier's permission, but such prohibitions may be difficult to enforce in a crisis. This also applies to any stipulation as to the circumstances in which the arms are to be used. Washington objected at one point, but to no avail, to Morocco's use of F-5 fighters, based in Mauritania and intended for defensive purposes only, in the Western Sahara. A similar "defensive purposes only" provision was attached to the sale of F-15 fighters to Israel; their use against Lebanon in 1979, which led to the shooting down of six Syrian MiG-21s, may have violated existing agreements, according to Secretary of State Cyrus Vance. Another violation took place when Israel in 1981 bombed the Osirak nuclear reactor outside Baghdad with American-built aircraft. Moreover, there can be no guarantee that the arms will not fall into enemy hands as a result of conflict, thereby creating a boomerang effect. Here the most notable case occurred in South Vietnam when U.S. arms in the possession of the South Vietnamese army were captured by the Viet Cong and North Vietnamese and were then used against American forces. These same arms were used again in Cambodia in 1979. Israel acquired in 1973 Soviet arms that had been sent to Arab countries; some of these weapons provided valuable new knowledge on Soviet equipment for the Pentagon.

22

Another concern arises out of the fact that a nation's professional military will always want to give priority to the equipment and readiness of its own armed forces. Yet there is the risk that large arms transfers, rapidly made, may reduce the supplier state's own inventory and diminish its military preparedness. This occurred in the months immediately following the Yom Kippur War when substantial quantities of arms were taken from U.S. forces and shipped to Israel, much to the dismay of the Joint Chiefs of Staff. To judge from the Soviet Union's ability to send large quantities of arms to distant places rapidly (as demonstrated in the Horn of Africa) without any visible strain on its own armed forces, it appears to have a larger stockpile of arms permanently available for such purposes; hence this consideration may be less relevant to the Soviet Union.

There is always the danger that unforeseeable political changes may make past transfers of arms unfortunate, if not tragic, in retrospect. Who is to know where, or when, irrational leaders such as an Idi Amin or Colonel Qaddafi or Ayatollah Khomeini may suddenly seize power in a country that has received arms from abroad? Likewise, shifts in political alignments and alliances cannot be predicted. In the Horn of Africa, the United States supplied to Ethiopia, over two decades, close to half a billion dollars worth of weapons, making it the largest recipient of U.S. arms in black Africa. Similarly, the Soviet Union sent large numbers of advisers and arms to neighboring Somalia. Yet the American investment did not prevent Ethiopia's shift from a conservative monarchy to a radical socialist state with close ties to Moscow, just as Soviet military assistance to Mogadishu did not forestall its break with Moscow and its turn to the West. In the end, these arms from outside suppliers were employed in a manner completely opposite from that originally intended.

Finally, mention should also be made of the concern that the supply of arms will set off a chain of events that will ultimately drag a nation into war. This fear reflects the history of the Vietnam involvement which began with U.S. military assistance to Saigon. Entry into war is, of course, a highest-level political decision based upon broad foreign policy considerations. But there is always the risk that direct involvement through the supply of arms will encourage the creation of a parallel supplier relationship on the other side, thereby introducing an arms competition which can then become an issue of political will and resolve; or that a supplier will come to the conclusion that it must participate more directly because it cannot afford to let its partner be defeated. Concerns of this sort were part of the arguments for restraint as Washington was faced with the question of how to respond to events in Angola and whether to send military equipment to Zaire.[11] Among the arguments made in early 1981 against sending U.S. arms to El Salvador was that such a course might lead to a deeper American involvement.

Economic Benefits

The third cluster of rationales for arms transfers comprises the economic advantages they are thought to bring. Arms sales have come to be viewed as an important earner of foreign exchange and contributor to the balance of payments. This was particularly true with respect to weapons sales to the Persian Gulf following the quintupling of the price of oil. After the 1973–1974 price rise, the Nixon administration appointed an interagency task force headed by Deputy Secretary of Defense William P. Clements, Jr., the purpose of which was to stimulate exports, especially of arms. At that time the French government also adopted a new sense of urgency about weapons sales to Saudi Arabia and Iran as a way of paying for higher oil costs. And the Soviet Union took a new interest in selling arms to countries that could pay in cash from oil revenues, principally Libya and Iraq.

Arms sales are also thought to provide significant employment in the defense industries of the producers. In addition, the export of arms is seen as an excellent way to create economies of scale, thereby reducing the per-unit costs of arms to be manufactured for the armed forces of the producer country. Exports are also a way of spreading out, or recouping, some of the research and development expenses.

24

These are all important considerations, especially at a time when the Western world is in an economic slump and is faced with the prospect of higher energy costs. Defense budgets are under continuing and growing pressure, in part because of the rising expense of ever more sophisticated weapons. Such countries as France and Britain have a smaller domestic market for their arms manufactures than has the United States and are therefore more dependent upon overseas sales. Indeed, in 1977, 41 percent of French-built arms were exported, and approximately 35 percent of Britain's. Certain industries, such as naval construction and tank manufacture in Britain, or aeronautics in France, are even more export dependent than the above percentages would indicate. For these reasons the advocacy within defense establishments for new weapon systems, especially advanced aircraft such as the F-16 or the Mirage 2000, has often been phrased in terms of which system will be most successful in foreign markets.

It may be, however, that the economic importance of arms sales—the "explanation" most often given for their existence and expansion—is not so great as it is often believed to be. The widespread perception that high levels of arms sales are necessary for the national economies of the principal suppliers is based upon vague, general notions rather than on hard data. Closer investigation, as undertaken on a country-by-country basis in Part Two of this book, suggests that the economic benefits are less than is generally assumed. Accordingly, limited restraints on sales may have a relatively small economic impact, except for the particular companies or regions directly affected.

Reliable data are not available on all dimensions of this question. According to the U.S. Arms Control and Disarmament Agency, in 1978 French arms exports came to 1.7 percent of total exports, British to 1.5 percent and American to 4.7 percent.[12] A Library of Congress study estimates that arms exports accounted for 2.7 percent of France's and 2.0 percent of Britain's total exports of "machinery, transport equipment, firearms of war and ammunition" in 1975 while the American figure was 10.2 percent.[13] According to still another study, for the same year French military exports accounted for 0.9 percent of total exports, British for 0.8 percent, and American for 4.5 percent.[14] These estimates seem low for the Europeans and vary greatly for the United States. Through discussions with officials in a position to know in the three countries, the author has arrived at an estimate for 1980 of 4 to 5 percent for the United States, approximately the same for France, and 3 to 4 percent for Britain.

Two important conclusions emerge, whatever the variations in the available figures. First, arms exports are relatively small in terms of total exports, and are only a small fraction of what is needed to pay the increased oil import bill of recent years. In fact, the most rapid adjustment to the higher oil prices has been made by Germany and Japan, countries whose sales of arms are relatively insignificant. Arms exporters must also consider the risk that oil prices will be raised to pay for the purchase of costly weapons. It is no accident that the largest purchaser of arms in the late 1970s—Iran—was one of the leading advocates within OPEC of higher oil prices. Second, and contrary to accepted wisdom, the principal European suppliers are *not* more dependent than the United States is on arms exports for balance of payment purposes.

Additional economic indicators support the hypothesis that none of the major suppliers is heavily dependent upon arms exports. According to a special study completed in 1977 by the Bureau of Labor Statistics of the U.S. Department of Labor, foreign military sales provided 277,000 jobs in 1975. Since total employment in the United States came to 80 million, arms exports accounted for only 0.3 percent of national employment.[15] As to the savings generated through enlarged production runs and recoupment of research and development expenses, a Congressional Budget Office study has estimated that arms exports of $8 billion per year produce savings of only $560 million.[16] This amounted to 0.5 percent of the 1977 defense budget. A study prepared by the Department of Defense found that "there is only a loose relationship between production readiness and cost economies on the one hand, and the total dollar volume of transfers on the other."[17] A similar conclusion was reached by a parliamentary committee in Britain (discussed in Part Two).

26

In France, of a total work force of 22 million, only 90,000 are engaged in manufacturing weapons for customers abroad; in Britain it was 70,000 to 80,000 in 1975.[18] Comparable figures for the Soviet Union are unavailable—some scholars at institutes in Moscow suggest that the data do not even exist—but we do know that in the policy followed for many years of granting long-term, low-interest loans to purchasers of arms, the U.S.S.R. traditionally emphasized the political significance rather than the economic benefits of arms sales. More recently, the U.S.S.R. has sold arms at higher prices to countries that could afford to pay, such as Libya. As the Soviet Union has sought hard currencies to pay for its import of Western technology and grain, it has placed a higher reliance on weapons sales as a source of revenue.

We do not mean to conclude that the economic importance of arms exports is as trivial as some of the data seem to suggest. Arms exports for the European countries may, in some years, make the difference between a trade balance that is in deficit and one that is in surplus. The data on direct employment only tell part of the story, for they say nothing about the multiplier impact of jobs in one industry upon those in another. Specific companies may be particularly dependent on arms exports, although this is not the case for many American companies. Relatively minor economic benefits, in statistical terms, may be perceived to be of great importance by a country that is trying to climb out of a recession. Such minor benefits from exports may also be seen to be of considerable value by particular interest groups that may have a significant influence on policy. As indicated earlier, overseas markets are more important for the European suppliers than for the United States or the U.S.S.R., because the Europeans require fewer arms for their own armed forces. Moreover, the maintenance of viable national defense industries is perceived—especially in France where it is linked with images of independence and sovereignty, and to a lesser extent also in Britain—as an important political goal. Yet for none of the main suppliers do arms exports occupy as important a role in the national economy as is often assumed by those who believe that economic imperatives must overrule any attempt to restrain arms sales.

COMPETING FOREIGN POLICY AIMS

The dilemmas that arise in making decisions on arms sales are only in part a consequence of the uncertainty regarding the rationales for the transfers. Another source of difficulty is the existence of multiple foreign policy objectives, not all of which can be satisfied. Thus, difficult trade-offs present themselves, and the resulting decisions may appear somewhat inconsistent with each other, even at times contradictory.

Should the United States sell sophisticated arms to China, on the ground that it would further assist the normalization of relations? Or should it avoid a step that could strongly antagonize the Soviet Union and contribute to the erosion of East-West détente? Or yet again, would such sales be an effective way of moderating Soviet behavior or of putting pressure on Moscow to adopt a more cooperative posture toward the West?

In dealing with the Middle East, should the West sell more arms to the Arab states in order to give concrete manifestation to a policy of evenhandedness, to help assure a continuing supply of oil on which it is heavily dependent, and to put pressure on the Israeli government seriously to undertake negotiations that will eventually lead to a withdrawal from the occupied territories? Or would arms sales to the moderate Arab states have the countereffect of making Israel more cautious about its security frontiers and less inclined to negotiate withdrawals from the West Bank, while running the risk of placing advanced arms in the hands of countries that might one day be led by radical, expansionist leaders?

As part of the post–Vietnam War reappraisal of U.S. foreign policy, the Carter administration decided upon a phased withdrawal of 33,000 ground forces from South Korea. To compensate for the withdrawal and help assure the maintenance of the military balance on the Korean peninsula, the United States undertook a $2 billion modernization assistance program to include the transfer to Seoul of advanced fighters, A-10 attack aircraft, tanks, and TOW anti-tank missiles. After that, the Park regime defied the U.S. Congress's inquiry into charges of illegal

28

bribery by Korean agents on Capitol Hill, and took repressive measures against opposition leaders and student groups that clearly embarrassed the United States. Under such circumstances, should Washington have reconsidered its planned transfer of arms while still intending to reduce its military presence?

Dilemmas such as these abound in the global politics of arms sales. Many are discussed in the following sections in the context of particular supplier- and region-related questions. But before this, we now turn to four special and important dilemmas which have general applicability: nuclear proliferation and conventional arms sales; human rights and the sale of arms to regimes that violate them; the relationship between the aim of NATO arms standardization and European-American competition on arms sales to the Third World; and the question of whether arms purchases for legitimate security reasons should be condemned as a diversion from economic and social development.

Nuclear Proliferation and Conventional Arms Sales

Preventing the spread of nuclear weapons is one of the most critical elements of future world order. Are restraints on conventional arms transfers incompatible with this objective, creating a deep dilemma—sometimes referred to as the "doves' dilemma"—for those who believe in the need for working toward both objectives?

It can be argued that supplying conventional arms to a nation that feels threatened reduces its sense of insecurity, and thereby makes it less likely that the recipient will turn to nuclear weapons if that is an option available to it. In this sense, arms transfers are an alternative to nuclear proliferation. As concern that Pakistan's clandestine centrifuge program would lead to a bomb grew in 1979, the United States offered to sell Pakistan fifty F-5E fighters if Islamabad would agree to place the centrifuge facility under safeguards. When this offer turned out to be of no avail, adherents within the Washington bureaucracy of what came to be known as the "buy out" option argued that Islamabad might be dissuaded from acquiring a nuclear weapons capability by an

29

offer of the far more advanced F-16; but this was judged to be too provocative to India, with the risk that it might stimulate a heightened arms race on the subcontinent. In any transfer of arms the likely impact upon neighboring states and the region must always be carefully taken into account.

President Reagan, however, reversed the Carter decision and offered the F-16 to Pakistan. His avowed approach is to treat the "causes" rather than the "symptoms" of nuclear proliferation. To this end, the Reagan administration is far more inclined to sell arms for the purpose of reducing motivations for obtaining nuclear weapons.

There is a second, related proposition: states, such as Israel, that may already possess, or are very close to obtaining, nuclear weapons will be less likely to cross the threshold and use nuclear weapons if they can defend themselves with an adequate supply of conventional arms. Considerations such as these are of special significance to such "pariah states" as Taiwan and South Africa, which feel isolated and might be forced to defend their existence one day. In such cases, restraints on arms transfers might become an impetus to acquiring nuclear weapons, an option that is becoming increasingly available because of the diffusion of nuclear technology.

One must, however, question the proposition that conventional arms will be perceived as a substitute for nuclear weapons by nations that feel a need for them. If a nation believes that its existence is so threatened that it must base its security upon an independent nuclear weapons capability, it is unlikely to be dissuaded by an uncertain supply of conventional weapons from abroad. A clear security guarantee from a close ally might be more effective in preventing proliferation. Moreover, the nuclear decision is likely to be made in many countries for reasons quite separate from a rational calculation of security requirements. These include factors of prestige, the desire to achieve regional dominance or to catch up with another state in the area, the interests of indigenous scientific and bureaucratic communities, or the pressures of domestic politics in which nuclear issues— involving, as they do, notions of sovereignty and status—can

30

often become key ingredients of the national debate. In none of these considerations would conventional arms be viewed as real alternatives to nuclear weapons. Paradoxically, the acquisition of new, sophisticated arms might simply serve to whet the appetite of military and political leaders for further enhancing the nation's defense forces and its status by acquiring nuclear weapons. Some of the more advanced arms being transferred are in effect dual-capable delivery systems, on which nuclear as well as conventional warheads can be attached. Acquisition of these arms, coupled with a close training relationship with military officers from the nuclear powers, may well stimulate interest in a nuclear arsenal to complement the conventional forces. We can only conclude that there is no simple relationship between the two, that we should be wary of proposals to sell arms so as to forestall a nuclear weapons program—as suggested by some Reagan administration spokesmen—and that strategies designed to reduce the risk of nuclear proliferation do not obviate the need for restraints on conventional proliferation.

Human Rights and the Sale of Arms
to Repressive Regimes

A salient question today is whether the sale of arms, or its refusal, can be effectively used to improve human rights in receiving countries. Quite apart from moral considerations, which democratic governments cannot or ought not overlook, the transfer of arms can be a source of deep embarrassment to the supplier country if they are then used for internal repression and to crush dissidents. The British and, to a lesser extent, the French governments have applied arms embargoes on South Africa for this reason, in large measure as a response to public opinion at home. In the United States, military assistance to repressive Latin American regimes became an issue in the Congress before the Carter administration came into office. After evidence that severe repression by the military junta followed the overthrow of Salvadore Allende in Chile, Congress in 1974 adopted the Kennedy Amendment, which forbade all security assistance and sales to

31

that country, despite the objections of Secretary of State Kissinger that the cutoff would undermine American efforts to encourage Chile to improve its human rights practices. This was made more general in the International Security Assistance and Arms Export Control Act of 1976, which prohibits transfers to any country "which engages in a consistent pattern of gross violations of internationally recognized human rights," except in extraordinary circumstances.[19]

The same act requires that the president make an annual country-by-country evaluation for the Congress on human rights conditions to aid it in making judgments on security assistance. In the first such report, compiled by the Carter administration in March 1977, it was found that in most of the eighty-two countries that receive some form of security assistance—the exceptions being the Western European nations and a few others—human rights were being violated in some degree. The plain fact is that judged by American and, generally speaking, Western standards, a good many and perhaps a majority of countries around the globe have authoritarian regimes of one type or another. Many of these engage in practices that in Western eyes appear as violations of civil liberties. The normative evaluations about the role of the state and the rights of the individual made in these countries, which do not in most cases have democratic legal or cultural traditions, are often at variance with those made in the West. The need to deal effectively with fundamental economic, social, and ethnic problems, which subject these societies to great stress, and at the same time avoid terrorism and internal strife, is often cited as a justification for authoritarian measures.

Apart from this basic philosophical and ideological dilemma, other, more pragmatic dilemmas arise in applying human rights criteria to arms sales. Some of the most severe "violators" of human rights in the non-Communist world have been nations in which the United States has important political and security interests. Iran under the Shah had a large number of political prisoners who had been denied due process of law and allegedly were subjected to torture. Yet it was also a major exporter of oil and strongly resisted Soviet encroachment in the area. Iran was also the single largest purchaser of U.S. arms in 1977, accounting for $5.5 billion of the $11.4 billion total.[20]

Faced with some difficult choices, the Carter administration decided in its first year that arms aid to Argentina, Uruguay, and Ethiopia would be reduced because of human rights violations (Ethiopia was in fact turning to the Soviet Union at the time anyway), but that other "violators" such as South Korea and the Philippines would continue to receive planned levels of aid because of their importance to the security of the United States. Subsequently, Argentina and Uruguay announced that they wanted no American assistance at all, while Ethiopia closed some U.S. facilities and ordered American personnel to leave the country. Brazil, which had been cited in the human rights evaluation report for torture of political prisoners as well as arbitrary arrest and detention, canceled a twenty-five-year-old military assistance treaty, rejected U.S. military credits, and loudly expressed resentment against American "moral imperialism" and the "intolerable interference" in its internal affairs. This occurred, it should be added, precisely when Washington was attempting to gain Brazil's support on a nuclear non-proliferation policy that was implicitly at odds with an important new Brazil-West German nuclear accord. Not surprisingly, the criticism of human rights and the end of the arms transfer relationship (subsequently Brazil was denied even spare parts for U.S. weapons already in its inventory) had a damaging effect on U.S. non-proliferation efforts.

We find here yet another example of the competing aims with which governments must wrestle in resolving questions of arms transfers. The sending of arms to countries that violate human rights may be regrettable, and may result in an unfortunate image for the supplier, especially if the arms should at some point be used against the local population. (Of course, this may not be the case if they are used against unpopular terrorist groups.) Yet there may well be sound reasons for transferring arms in any case, as with national security considerations in South

Korea. The protection of American interests in the Pacific, through the continued availability of air and naval bases at Clark Field and Subic Bay in the Philippines, has required the continued transfer of arms despite the repressive nature of the Marcos regime. Human rights criteria are therefore unlikely to be applied with any real consistency. This leads to the important conclusion that arms transfer policy is not a very effective way of showing dissatisfaction with human rights conditions in a particular country. It may, in fact, lead to charges of hypocrisy if inconsistent standards are applied, as is inevitable. Clearly, curtailing arms transfers is not the best instrument, and should certainly not be the primary one, for promoting human rights.[21]

Standardization of Arms within the Atlantic Alliance versus Exports to the Third World

For some years it has been evident that one of NATO's major weaknesses has been its multiplicity of weapons systems. On NATO's central front alone, allied combat forces employ twenty-three different combat aircraft, seven main battle tanks, eight types of armored personnel carriers, and twenty-two different families of anti-tank weapons.[22] This multiplicity leads to a loss of military effectiveness and a tremendous waste of money. NATO's national armies maintain separate logistical and communications systems. The member nations duplicate one another's weapons development and production. It has been estimated in the widely circulated Callaghan report that over $10 billion per year could be saved by an increased standardization of arms throughout the Alliance, and that this would produce a 40 percent augmentation in effectiveness without any increase in defense budgets.[23] Accordingly, the Alliance has placed, especially since its summit meeting of May 1977, a considerable priority on the rationalization of its weapons development and procurement. This is commonly known as the quest for a "two-way" street, whereby the United States would buy many more European arms, and the Europeans would continue to purchase many of the weapons that can be most efficiently manufactured in America.

There are many who see an incompatibility between the aim of NATO arms standardization and the development of restraints on arms transfers to the Third World. According to this line of reasoning, efforts to temper arms exports to the developing world will put still greater stress on the economically hard-pressed European arms industries. Many of these industries have production capacities far in excess of national needs, and they have come to rely upon exports for their economic viability, and in the case of some companies, for their very survival. Therefore, it is argued, the economic costs of restraints on exports outside the Alliance will strongly reduce, if not totally eliminate, any willingness to standardize arms.

Yet there is another way to look at this dilemma, and it has too often been overlooked.[24] Given the rising cost of defense technology and the shrinking of domestic markets, the European arms industries face severe problems of overextension, which exports are simply masking temporarily. The day of reckoning may be ahead. At present, arms transfers, by giving a new but temporary lease on life, permit the continuation of national weapons programs which would otherwise be subject to the discipline of the market. Indeed, the potential of exports has led both France and Britain to develop weapons systems they would not otherwise have produced for their own armed forces, thereby encouraging trends that run directly counter to standardization.

Multilateral restraints on exports could create, as an additional benefit, important new incentives for an international specialization of labor among some arms-supplying nations. If each major weapons-producing country could be assured of a fair share of the total world export market, each country could concentrate on manufacturing certain items, which then would have longer production runs and lower unit costs. This would practically guarantee the maintenance of the defense industry. A "market-sharing" approach would provide savings by avoiding duplication. It would reduce the economic need to export to developing countries, while simultaneously forcing the rationalization of defense efforts—the very goal of NATO standardization.

Arms Purchases—
A Diversion from Economic Development?

A widely shared criticism of arms sales is that the recipients are purchasing arms with scarce resources which should be used for urgent economic and social needs at home. The Brandt Commission on North-South relations echoed this theme in its 1980 report.[25] The significance of this criticism is apparent when one recalls that over three-quarters of arms transfers in the past decade went to Third World countries. Of the ninety-four developing nations that imported arms in 1978, more than one-third were among the poorest nations in the world, with average annual per capita income of under $500. The basic problem for many of these countries is to ensure an adequate food supply for their growing populations. On the other hand, there are a number of oil-producing, "nouveaux riches" countries in the Third World that can afford to pay for arms, and they have been among the largest purchasers in recent years.

The relationship between arms expenditures and economic development is more complex than it is often stated to be. The developing countries increased their military spending more than three times as fast as the industrialized countries during the decade of the seventies. Nevertheless, their defense expenditures remain relatively modest, along the lines of 2 percent of the gross national product in Latin America, 3 percent in Africa, and 4 percent in Asia. Compared to the First and Second worlds, the Third World is not heavily armed. The striking exception is the Middle East, where military expenditures have averaged 14 percent of GNP since the mid-1970s. At the same time the rapid growth in arms imports has evidently canceled out most of the increases in developmental aid; arms purchases have risen twice as fast as gains in development assistance. The developing countries that are not oil exporters have had a sharply rising external debt, yet continue to invest in foreign arms. Moreover, spending on military forces, even when modest as a percentage of the GNP, is often very substantial when compared to governmental spending on other, often urgent, needs such as public health, housing, or education. There is, therefore, a solid basis for the belief that considerable amounts are being spent on the purchase of arms which could be better used for other purposes.

But would the money not spent on arms purchases then be spent on economic and social needs? There is no guarantee that the savings accrued from reducing expenditures on defense would be wisely used for the common good. It is well to remind ourselves that we are discussing the choices made by sovereign governments, many of which are authoritarian in character. In some cases the leadership has a narrowly based interest in forestalling rising expectations, which would create political demands that it is unable or unwilling to fulfill. In other cases the social and economic structure and tradition of the country may be unlikely to lend themselves to more rapid development. One cannot assume that the resources previously allocated for national security would simply be redirected into a more socially "constructive" use.

In addition, there is a view that arms transfers often have a positive impact upon development in Third World countries. Some of the activities and expenditures associated with weapons purchases involve the creation of a national infrastructure— roads, airfields, and the like—which have a wider than military application. Training for the use of arms also involves general education and the acquisition of skills that can later be used in the civilian economy. Arms purchases may therefore have important economic spinoffs. Related to this is the argument that in many developing countries the military establishment is the sector of the society most capable of undertaking the difficult but needed development tasks. In the 1960s academic theories placed great value upon the role the armed forces could play in the modernization process.[26]

The turn of many Third World countries toward authoritarian military regimes, often as a result of coups d'état, raises doubts

37

about such theories. So does the fact that many of the military governments have proved to be grossly inept in handling economic problems, as in the case of the "southern cone" states of Latin America. The experience of Iran, examined at length in Part Three, will long be significant for any discussion regarding the domestic social and economic impact of expenditures on arms. Although one must eschew any single-factor analysis, there can be little doubt that the tenfold increase in defense spending to over 25 percent of the national budget, and the related inadequacy of expenditures on housing, education, and social development, as well as the unequal distribution of benefits, helped fan the discontent and grievances that brought the Iranian revolution. Judgments about the role of the military in developing societies are difficult to make, but in any case, it is far from clear that channeling funds through defense budgets is a constructive way of pursuing economic development and meeting civilian needs.

PART TWO

SUPPLIERS

The transfer of arms, as we have seen, has become a newly important determinant of international politics. Nations supply arms to the Third World for a number of reasons. For the superpowers, in playing their global roles, making arms available to states they seek to protect or influence can be a major instrument of policy. As the political and economic disadvantages of maintaining overseas bases and forces have grown since the early postwar period, the superpowers have turned to other instruments. Economic assistance through bilateral channels has decreased, and the role of ideology ("Communists versus Free World") as a motivating force has diminished. Thus arms have become one of the best—often *the* best— available remaining instrument to support their interests. There is an inclination to use arms supplies freely to support security commitments to a nation, rather than to rely upon new formal treaty undertakings or the creation of new alliances. The principal European suppliers also have some political rationales for supplying arms, although for them economic considerations are of greater significance.

Still, most discussions of the problem usually start with a description of the growing demand for weapons. More countries want larger amounts of more advanced arms (as discussed in Part Three). Hence, as is usually argued, the way to reduce the arms trade is for the recipient countries jointly to adopt restrictions on the import of arms on a regional basis. This has also been the favored approach of governments in the one forum in which the proliferation of conventional arms has been a regular item on the agenda, the Geneva Conference of the Committee on Disarmament.

In this book we reverse the more usual approach. We are looking at the global politics of the arms trade not only to increase knowledge and understanding of it, but also to suggest ways to develop restraints so as to reduce the chances that arms transfers will have a destabilizing, conflict-inducing impact. Restraints involve the decisions of the supplier states, which thus have the

41

responsibility for examining each transfer of arms not only for the shorter-term political or economic benefits, but also in terms of its longer-term consequences. It is in this "over the horizon" perspective that the deleterious effects are usually to be found. Governments will rarely transfer weapons so as to provoke an immediate conflict. Indeed, most weapons are usually transferred with the hope, if not the expectation, that they will not be used in war but that their effect will be of a deterring or political nature. There are, of course, important exceptions: weapons can be transferred directly into a battle, as has occurred in the Middle East, or they can be sent to national liberation movements fighting for power within a country.

A conclusion that evolves out of this study is that greater and more rapid progress is likely to be made in developing international restraints from the suppliers' side than from the recipients'. There are several reasons for this. First, it is the suppliers who ultimately have the choice of whether or not to sell. Second, it is often the case that within a region the recipients are too much in competition with each other, and that on the global scale they are too diverse, to take the initiative in developing a system of multilateral restraints. Third, the fact that the major producers are few in number greatly assists the still extremely difficult task of organizing supplier restraints. (Four producers, it will be recalled—the United States, the Soviet Union, France, and Britain—account for 87.5 percent of weapons transfers to the Third World; when one adds a few of their close allies in the two principal military alliances, the figure rises to 94.3 percent.) Fourth, and closely related, competition among the main suppliers is a major factor in the arms trade.

Competition among suppliers can be of two types, political and economic. Along the East-West axis, the competition is usually highly politicized as part of their rivalry in the Third World, although the Soviet Union has been increasingly motivated by the commercial benefits of arms sales in its quest for hard currencies with which to pay for needed imports. Along the West-West axis, among the members of NATO, the competition tends to be economic, especially when sales to oil-producing countries

42

are at stake. Nevertheless, subtle political considerations have a way of intruding. Such factors include pride in national technology, the maintenance of defense industries, and the creation or continuation of special political links with certain recipient countries.

Difficult and problematic to create as it may be, multilateral management is essential if there are ever to be any meaningful restraints on arms trade. A critical reason is manifest here: even if one country unilaterally restrains itself from making a particular sale because of its potentially damaging impact, there is little assurance that a competitor will make the same evaluation and follow suit. Thus the argument, "If we do not sell, someone else will," is often the reason given for not adopting a restraint that otherwise seems commendable. Indeed, within governments this preemptive rationale is probably the most widely used justification for arms sales as the pace of transfers has grown, as their nature has changed from military assistance grants to commercial sales, and as they have become more separated from cold war alignments. At times the argument may be valid, and at other times it may not be, but because it is based on a presupposition of negative consequences—which could make one appear to have been taken advantage of—policy makers often prefer not to put it to the test and consequently decide to approve a sale. Multilateral management among suppliers might therefore create conditions whereby individual producers would accept restraints they would not feel at liberty to accept on a unilateral basis.

Supplier-side restraint would in no way diminish the critical importance of cooperation with the recipients. With the diffusion of power and the concomitant significance of North-South relations, actions that run directly counter to the preferences of major Third World countries are unlikely to be taken. Refusal to sell arms can easily be perceived as a form of paternalism and neocolonialism. Thus, successful international restraints must be based upon recipients working with suppliers in common endeavors. On occasion the initiatives may come from the recipients themselves. And even when, as is more frequently likely to be the case, they are originated by the suppliers, such initiatives will have to be worked out in consultation with the recipients within a geographical region. Indeed, because of varying world circumstances, arms restraint accords are more likely to be regional than global in character.

Here in Part Two we look at the supplier countries. We examine the role of the export of weapons in national armaments industries and national economies; the arms transfer policies and practices of governments; the political milieu in which decisions are reached, including, when relevant, the role of the parliament, political parties, the press, business and intellectual elites, and public opinion; and various perspectives on foreign policy, arms control, and international security which will shape attitudes and approaches toward managing the arms trade phenomenon. In Part Three we examine recipient perspectives in major regions of the world before turning, in Part Four, to the problems of developing international restraints.

UNITED STATES

It is in the United States that the arms transfer phenomenon has received the most attention. The nation's policy on weapons sales has become a political and foreign policy issue; the legislative branch has sought to impose controls; and the major and controversial new policy, announced in 1977 in consequence of the change of government, was the basis for overtures for some form of international restraints. Moreover, the United States has long been the world's largest supplier of arms. During the period 1950–1979 it transferred abroad over $110 billion in arms and related military services, more than half of the world total. Under the Reagan administration, with its emphasis on arms sales as an instrument of diplomacy and its tendency to sell weapons permissively, arms sales are likely to continue to grow and become still more controversial.

Criticism of Arms Sales

During the 1976 presidential election campaign candidate Carter spoke of the "almost completely unrestrained" American arms sales in past years as being a policy as "cynical as it is dangerous." Being the leading "arms merchant of the world," he contended, was "contrary to our long standing beliefs and principles." "Moral bankruptcy," his running mate Walter Mondale charged, had turned the United States into an "arsenal for the world."

Although some of this had to be discounted as campaign rhetoric, it was nevertheless the case that the charges of the president-to-be reflected a widespread criticism in the Congress and in the press, and growing malaise in the public mind, regarding

45

America's rapidly increasing arms sales. Nor was this a purely partisan issue. Former Secretary of Defense Melvin Laird, after having left office and become associated with the American Enterprise Institute, publicly deplored the enormous amount of arms being sold to foreign customers.

U.S. foreign military sales had increased fourteenfold in the previous five years to over $15 billion in new sales per year by 1975 and appeared to be heading upward. Amid newspaper headlines of spectacular new deals with Iran and Saudi Arabia, several mitigating elements were usually overlooked. The figures most often cited, as above, were in current rather than constant dollars and were thus not adjusted for inflation; the amounts cited as sales included not only weapons but supporting equipment, spare parts, and services such as construction and training (these could amount to as much as 40 percent of the total package); and military assistance *grants*, as opposed to *sales*, had declined from $2.2 billion in 1970 to a mere $265,000 in 1976.[1]

Still, even before the dramatic increase in sales starting around the time of the 1973 oil price hike (sales to Teheran actually began shooting up a year earlier), the overall trend was clearly upward. The value (in constant dollars) of completed U.S. arms deliveries rose by 150 percent within the 1968–1977 decade; more than three-quarters of these deliveries were to states classified by the U.S. Arms Control and Disarmament Agency as developing countries.[2] The surge in sales in the mid-1970s was expected to lead to another increase in deliveries in the late seventies and early eighties; well over half would be to four states in the Middle East: Israel, Saudi Arabia, Egypt, and Iran.

A good deal of the criticism was based as much on the manner in which the United States sold arms as on the amounts. To many critics, arms sales policy under the Nixon and Ford administrations had gone out of control. Indeed, it often seemed as if there was no coherent arms transfer policy at all. Decisions on sales appeared to be made capriciously, or for short-term diplomatic advantage, without any or adequate consideration of their long-term political and strategic consequences. Thus Secretary of State Kissinger had indicated to the Israelis a willingness to sell the

46

FIGURE 3

United States Arms Sales, 1970–1980

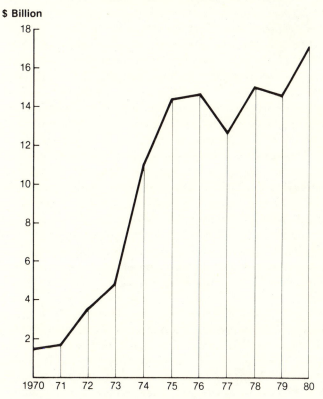

U.S. government-to-government sales agreements
and commercial arms exports (in billion current dollars)

Source: Report by the Comptroller General of the United States, *Opportunities to Improve Decisionmaking and Oversight of Arms Sales*, ID-79-22, U.S., General Accounting Office, May 21, 1979, p. 68; for 1979–1980, U.S., Department of Defense, *Foreign Military Sales and Military Assistance Facts*, December 1980, pp. 2, 26.

47

Pershing surface-to-surface missile, which could carry a nuclear warhead, without consulting the Pentagon, which eventually managed to dissuade him. The Arms Control and Disarmament Agency was regularly excluded from any participation in the decision-making process, in spite of its having statutory responsibilities.[3] Congressional hearings brought out President Nixon's personal offer to the Shah, while on a trip to Teheran in 1972, to sell any armaments short of nuclear weapons.[4] This extraordinary decision—which had the effect of predetermining subsequent ones—was made without preliminary staff-level considerations. A National Security Council staff member at the time later called it "the key sales decision of the past three years."[5] Except on routine decisions, the bureaucracy was often short-circuited. The decisions to sell the F-14 and the advanced Spruance-class destroyers to Iran had been made without full discussions within the government as to their desirability. A similar criticism could be made of President Ford's decision during the heat of the 1976 presidential campaign to sell to Israel cluster concussion bombs, laser-guided missiles, and ultramodern electronic equipment whose sale had previously been banned. One of the first steps of the incoming Carter administration was to cancel much of this sale.

Many other examples could be cited. They all point to a strong tendency to use arms sales as a diplomatic instrument for immediate gain, with a rather laissez-faire or insouciant attitude toward the longer-term implications of the transfers for regional stability or the impact upon the recipient nation.

The excesses of American arms sales—excesses in quantity, as in the Persian Gulf, and excesses in quality, as in the transfer of the most sophisticated, up-to-date weapons—were the source of much unease. But equally disturbing to many were the cascading revelations of bribery, what appeared to be an uncontrolled commercial "pushing" of U.S. arms in foreign markets without adequate restraints based on foreign policy objectives, and the corrupt and widespread meddling in the internal politics of purchasing nations, as made evident by the long succession of Lockheed and Northrop scandals.[6] In Japan, Italy, and the Netherlands, to name but a few, large sums of money had been secretly offered by American warplane manufacturers, which, when made public, badly shook the governments and, in the case of the Netherlands, the monarchy. Furthermore, American manufacturers sought to use foreign arms sales as a lever to influence purchases by the American government for its own armed forces. Evidence of this came out when it was revealed that Thomas Jones, the president of Northrop, had sought to persuade the Shah of Iran to order a land-based model of the F-18L in order to put pressure on the Pentagon to decide to produce this aircraft for the U.S. Navy.

Thus by the beginning of the Carter presidency, the momentum pushing for a reappraisal of U.S. arms transfer policy was already considerable. This is worth underscoring because of the subsequent observations at home, but especially overseas, that the "new look" of the Carter administration was the result of the president's moral rectitude. Rather than being idiosyncratic, the new policy reflected proposals and judgments that had been several years in the making. As early as October 31, 1975, 102 members of the Congress from both parties (including Senator Walter Mondale) felt moved to write to Secretary of State Kissinger because of their deep concern about the "anarchic and escalating nature of the worldwide rush to acquire new weapons." They asked that the United States initiate efforts to convene an international conference of arms-producing nations to seek some "rational control and coordination of what now seems to be pathological competition in foreign military sales."[7] Congress was also putting pressure on the executive branch to reappraise U.S. arms sales policy so as to develop greater restraints in general, and to moderate sales to the Persian Gulf in particular. But the Nixon-Ford administrations had little interest and saw even less value in such undertakings. They refused to begin multilateral discussions on arms transfers with other nations, and an internal reappraisal in the form of a National Security Council Study Memorandum was permitted to get totally bogged down in bureaucratic differences and never saw the light of day. An unofficial report sent to interested congressional leaders by Sec-

49

retary Kissinger dismissed any attempt to limit arms sales internationally as unrealistic.[8] Meanwhile, however, arms transfer
policy was the subject of lively attention in unofficial settings
such as the Council on Foreign Relations and the United Nations
Association of the United States, both of which convened study
groups on the topic.[9]

The Role of Congress

Congressional interest in arms sales grew with the rise in their
volume and reflected a lack of confidence in the executive
branch's decision-making process. Acting out of frustration with
the administration's unwillingness to impose self-restraints, the
Congress passed in 1974 the Nelson Amendment to the military
assistance bill which obligated the executive branch to give
twenty-days' advance notice of foreign military sales of over $25
million, during which time a sale could be blocked by the passage of a concurrent resolution of disapproval by both houses of
Congress. Although Congress already had authority over grant
aid, until then it had had none over government-approved sales.
But this proved to be too unwieldy a procedure to be very effective, requiring a major political mobilization by the Congress,
and was never successfully applied. More comprehensive and
flexible legislation, expanding congressional oversight, was
enacted on June 30, 1976, after President Ford had vetoed an
earlier and stronger version of the bill because of his belief that
it would seriously "obstruct the exercise of the President's con-
stitutional responsibility for the conduct of foreign affairs."[10]
   The International Security Assistance and Arms Export Control Act was the most significant piece of legislation dealing with
arms transfers since the enactment of the Mutual Security Act
more than a quarter of a century earlier. It sought to "shift the
focus of U.S. arms sales policy from that of selling arms to controlling arms sales and exports."[11] The act emphasized public dis-
closure and review procedures. All sales of over $25 million in
weapons or ancillary services to non-NATO countries were to be
handled through government-to-government rather than com-

mercial channels, thereby eliminating most of the direct or exclusive dealings between U.S. companies and foreign governments; the time during which a concurrent resolution could block a sale was lengthened to thirty days; the president was called upon to submit information to the Congress on arms transfers on a quarterly basis; U.S. military assistance advisory groups (MAAGS) in foreign countries were to be severely reduced in both number and size, and their remaining personnel were subsequently instructed to avoid any activity that could stimulate host country requests for military equipment; prohibitions were placed on arms transfers to countries that violated human rights; "agents' fees" (often, although not always, a euphemism for bribes) and political contributions related to arms sales had to be reported to the Department of State. Through this act Congress secured its role in dealing with the process of arms transfers and gave voice to its continuing interest in restraints. The act expressed the "sense of the Congress" that annual aggregate sales should not exceed then current levels.

Congress, however, cannot make U.S. policy on arms transfers. This is the job of the executive branch. Congress has given itself the right to make individual arms transfers subject to its disapproval, rather than the right to approve sales to foreign countries before they are completed. This power of rejection, which requires concurrent resolutions, will be used only sparingly as it inevitably involves judgments on foreign policy that can best be made by the president and his advisers. As of this writing, in fact, Congress had yet to use this authority, having ultimately shrunk away from it in dealing with the highly controversial "plane package" to three Middle East countries in 1978. Nor is Congress likely to vote itself the power to approve each sale, as has been recommended by some, for it is neither prepared nor equipped in time and staff to make case-by-case or country-by-country decisions. Congress has sought to make certain that arms transfers are subject to close scrutiny on Capitol Hill, and has put the executive branch on notice that prospective sales must be justifiable. In this way the Congress has served as an inhibiting factor on some prospective sales that were likely to be seen as excessive.

A former senior government official gives Congress much credit for moving the executive branch toward a more discriminating and moderate position.[12] Nevertheless, the decisive role in formulating U.S. arms sales policy can only be undertaken by the president.

The Carter Policy

On May 19, 1977, after much speculation and considerable bureaucratic infighting over Presidential Directive 13, President Carter unveiled the new administration's policy. Henceforth arms transfers were to be viewed as an "exceptional foreign policy implement, to be used only in instances where it can be clearly demonstrated that the transfer contributes to our national security interests." Cognizant of criticisms of past practice, the statement indicated that in the future "the burden of persuasion will be on those who favor a particular arms sale, rather than on those who oppose it."

To implement the policy a set of qualitative and quantitative controls was established. But these restrictive guidelines were not to apply to transfers to countries with which the United States has major defense treaties—NATO, Japan, Australia, and New Zealand. Israel presented a problem, for although Israel was not a formal treaty partner of the United States, its supporters wanted it excluded from the restraints and took their case to friends in the Congress. Special mention was therefore made of the intention to honor "our historic responsibilities to assure the security of the State of Israel." And almost complete presidential discretion and flexibility were retained with the announcement that the controls would be binding "*unless* extraordinary circumstances necessitate a Presidential exception, *or* where I determine that countries friendly to the United States must depend on advanced weaponry to offset quantitative and other disadvantages in order to maintain a regional balance."

The guidelines included the following six provisions:

1. *The United States would not be the first supplier to introduce into a region newly developed, advanced weapons systems*

52

that would create a new or significantly higher combat capability. This was intended to discourage regional arms competition based on the acquisition of higher levels of weapons technology.

2. *The United States would not sell newly developed, advanced weapons systems until they were operationally deployed with U.S. forces.* There had been occasions when weapons had been sold abroad before being delivered to U.S. forces, to the detriment of the Department of Defense's delivery schedules and the readiness of the military services. Also, foreign sales had been promoted by U.S. companies in the hope of giving them a competitive advantage, through lowered unit costs, in the competition for sales to the Pentagon.

3. *The United States would not permit development or significant modification of advanced weapons systems solely for export.* This removed incentives for U.S. industry to design and produce advanced arms whose only market was abroad.

4. *The United States would not permit co-production agreements with other countries for significant weapons, equipment, and major components.* This was intended to help limit the spread of production facilities for advanced technology and the increase in the number of arms suppliers. In particular, it sought to inhibit co-production arrangements whose economic justification rested on exports to third countries once the co-producing countries' own needs had been met.

5. *The United States would not allow U.S. weapons or equipment to be transferred to third parties without U.S. government consent.* Although this was a longstanding legal requirement, its statement as a matter of policy was designed to avoid unnecessary bilateral friction caused by the need to deny such requests. Re-transfers would be approved only when the United States would be willing to sell the article in question directly to the third party.

6. *The United States would require policy-level authorization by the Department of State for actions by agents of the United States or private manufacturers that might promote the sale of arms abroad.* Embassy and military representatives abroad were instructed not to engage in any activity that could be construed

as promoting the sale of conventional arms. This was intended to stop the "pushing" of arms sales and to provide for an early screening of potential sales requests from purchasers as well as of sales activities by commercial firms.

In addition, the statement indicated that human rights within recipient countries would be a consideration in future security assistance programs, as would the economic impact of the arms purchases for those less developed countries also receiving U.S. economic assistance. The United States would seek multilateral cooperation in reducing the "worldwide traffic in arms."

Finally, there was to be a dollar ceiling on the volume of new commitments for foreign military sales and military assistance programs, with the total for fiscal year 1978 to be less than the previous year. Officials indicated that this was to be the first of a series of annual reductions.[13]

Evaluation of the Carter Policy

How successful was the Carter policy in regulating the flow of arms sales? Was the policy as stated in principle followed in practice? The answers to these simple questions require somewhat complex judgments. They depend, moreover, upon what assumptions one makes about the intent of the policy. To those who saw in the president's 1977 pronouncements a pledge to curtail all arms sales drastically, the results were clearly disappointing. For those who regarded the principal aim as one of putting greater order into the arms transfer process, making it more certain that weapons sales would be carefully measured against overall foreign policy and national security considerations, the outcome could be seen in a more favorable light—although even here there is room for a wide spectrum of judgment. Let us look at some of the actual sales decisions made by the Carter administration, examine the quantitative ceiling which became the subject of much confusion as well as controversy, discuss the "reform" of the internal decision-making process that was undertaken, and then reach some general conclusions.

In examining the decisions made, it should be borne in mind that turndowns of requests for sales are often not publicized, for they can be embarrassing to the would-be purchaser. It is clear, nevertheless, that there were some significant decisions not to sell weapons.

In its early days the Carter administration decided against the sale of the F-18L fighter aircraft to Iran, a decision consistent with its prohibition on the development of advanced weapons systems solely for export. Teheran was also turned down later in its bid for Wild Weasel F4-G fighter-bombers equipped with highly advanced electronics designed to suppress radar because this would have introduced a new, sophisticated weapons system into the region. Pakistan was denied permission to purchase 110 A-7 fighter-bombers, on the grounds that the sale would have introduced a more advanced weapons system into South Asia and run the risk of starting a new round in a regional arms race, but it was indicated that in their place the United States would consider sympathetically the A-4 or F-5 aircraft, both of which have less range and offensive capability. On similar grounds, Sweden was prevented from selling to India the Viggen fighter which includes American components. Taiwan was refused the F-4 Phantom because its 1,000-mile range would enable it to reach deep into mainland China. Israel was prevented from exporting the Kfir fighter aircraft to Ecuador on the grounds that it contained a General Electric engine and therefore was subject to U.S. restrictions on transfers to third countries. The administration also refused Israel's request for a license to co-produce the F-16 in Israel, although it approved direct purchase of the plane. A request from South Korea for F-16s was deferred because it would have introduced a higher combat capability into the Korean peninsula, but permission was given to co-assemble the F-5 through a waiver of the co-production restriction. And in Latin America the decision to restrict, on human rights grounds, military assistance credits to Brazil, Argentina, and Uruguay had the effect, in part because of angry reactions, of curtailing arms transfers to these countries. Altogether, according to government officials, 614 requests from 92 countries totaling more than $1 billion were turned down in the first fifteen months of the new Carter arms transfer policy.

On the other side of the ledger, the administration approved a number of significant transfers. Most controversial was its $4.8 billion plane package consisting of sixty F-15 aircraft, the most advanced fighter in the U.S. inventory, for Saudi Arabia; fifty F-5Es for Egypt; and for Israel fifteen F-15s in addition to the twenty-five already sold as well as seventy-five more F-16s. This sale epitomized the central role of arms transfers in the broader issues of peace negotiations and macroeconomic (that is, oil) relations.[14] Subsequently, in early 1980, it was agreed in principle that Egypt could also buy the F-15 or F-16. Although Egypt only requested the latter, symbolic equivalence with the other two countries was clearly important for Sadat.

Also controversial was the sale to Iran for $1.3 billion of 7 sophisticated AWACS planes. This decision, which was the first major exception to the Carter policy, was significant in the signal it sent throughout the bureaucracy indicating that the guidelines would be applied loosely. Congressional opposition questioning its necessity initially delayed the sale, but it eventually went through after assurances were given regarding the protection or exclusion of sensitive electronic equipment which could be of value if it fell into hostile hands. Reflecting concern about the massive shipment of arms to Iran, the administration indicated to the Shah upon his visit to Washington in November 1977 that the sale of another 140 F-16 aircraft, to supplement the 160 already sold, would be dependent upon congressional approval, but this was not expected at the time to stem Teheran's continuing quest for arms.

In compensation for the intended phased withdrawal of American ground forces from South Korea, the administration agreed to turn over, or provide aid for the purchase of, $1.8 billion in arms, including A-10 attack aircraft, Nike-Hercules surface-to-air missiles, tanks, and TOW anti-tank missiles. Sudan became a new recipient of U.S. arms. Morocco was promised OV-10 armored reconnaissance aircraft usable for counterinsurgency missions against the Polisario in Western Sahara. And an indication of willingness to furnish arms to Somalia, once withdrawn as a result of uncertainties and shifting political alignments in the Ogaden War, was revived in 1980 as Washington sought the use of the Berbera base to support the Carter Doctrine. These were only among the most noteworthy of the hundreds, perhaps thousands, of arms transfer decisions involving qualitative criteria.

As for the dollar ceiling, which was designed to impose quantitative controls, a somewhat dubious numbers game ensued. In conformity with the announced policy, the 1978 ceiling of $8.5 billion was 8 percent lower than the 1977 volume of $8.8 billion, after adjustment for inflation, and the 1979 ceiling was set with a further 8 percent reduction in constant dollars. The ceiling was designed to impose restraint and to force a solid justification for sales. But in practice there were ways to circumvent it in intent, if not in fact. With the May 19 announcement having set the 1977 total as a high, from which the 1978 amount was to be reduced, parts of the government developed an interest in having it be as high as possible; hence accounting procedures were altered and recalculations made that created a higher ceiling so as to allow more leeway in coming years. In addition, there were three major loopholes. First, arms sales to treaty allies, eighteen countries in all, were excluded from the ceiling (about 10 percent of total sales); second, transfers that could be listed as commercial arms exports controlled by munitions-licensing procedures rather than government-to-government sales were left out entirely and these subsequently tripled (10 percent); third, the ceiling did not apply to military "services" which account for a substantial portion of what is listed as U.S. foreign military sales (20 to 40 percent). The net result was that, while the ceilings were respected, giving the appearance of reductions, in reality total U.S. arms sales actually increased. Total U.S. arms sales (including government-to-government sales and commercial arms exports) rose from $12.8 billion in 1977 to $17.1 billion in 1980, with only slightly more than half covered by the ceiling. By the end of 1979 there was a backlog of $43.5 billion, which stretched out orders that would not be delivered until as late as 1986. (The administration had inherited a backlog of $27 billion from the

57

Ford administration.) These points were not lost on the critics, who accused the Carter administration of suggesting that more was really less.

As to the implementation of the policy, the Arms Export Control Board was created under the chairmanship of the under secretary of state for security assistance, science, and technology, with ten federal agencies represented. Working groups of the board wrote new regulations and definitions for applying the controls, and developed review and clearance procedures and guidelines for industry personnel and U.S. officials dealing with foreign governments on arms sales matters. The International Traffic in Arms Regulations (ITAR) were amended so as to require prior approval from the Department of State of proposals to foreign governments for the sale of significant arms through military or commercial channels. This process was intended to prevent the recurrence of situations in which sales were approved to avoid the political embarrassment that would result from refusing to honor an agreement between a manufacturing company and a foreign government. The result of these changes was to sensitize the bureaucracy to a set of new, or heightened, concerns—particularly when it became known that President Carter personally reviewed and decided on a surprisingly large number of arms sales requests. During the 1979 fiscal year, Carter reviewed 88 out of a total of 126 significant transactions.[15]

Clearly, the reality of arms sales under the Carter administration—their overall increase rather than reduction—did not conform to the initial rhetoric of its salad days. Arms sales did not become an "exceptional" instrument of foreign policy, as promised in the May 1977 pronouncement. The overblown rhetoric promised a sea change in the practice of selling arms and implied that there would be a sharp curtailment. As it turned out, past practice was modified in important ways, but arms sales remained a continuing and important instrument of foreign policy—as is, in fact, inescapable. Some of the administration's early statements led to exaggerated expectations. And after that, its arms transfer policy was constantly buffeted by both sides. Liberal critics saw it as a sham, a policy of exceptions, and a failure

58

in the goal of cutting back on arms sales.[16] More conservative observers, and those in the defense industry, viewed the policy as naive, unworkable, and hypocritical.[17]

What the policy did accomplish was to provide a framework for an important aspect of America's foreign relations. Arms sales decisions were to be made more systematically, according to qualitative and quantitative criteria, so as to be more certain that they were congruent with the nation's political and security interests. This was an ambitious policy, comprehensive in scope and detail. Inevitably there were controversial decisions, including some that did not seem to conform to the administration's policy. Confusion over the annual ceiling, more than anything else, contributed to public and international skepticism regarding the policy. Nevertheless, the "message" was sent to prospective arms purchasers that henceforth requests for arms would be more carefully considered and scrutinized for their full implications. And the "message" was also understood by the relevant elements of the American military and civilian bureaucracy, which began showing a far greater sensitivity than it had in the past to the broader dimensions of arms transfer issues. The task was likened, by Under Secretary of State for Security Assistance, Science and Technology Lucy W. Benson, to that of turning a supertanker.

Inevitably, and often properly, exceptions were made so as to permit flexible application of the controls. The largest number of exceptions was made for the prohibition against co-production agreements with other countries for significant weapons, equipment, and major components. Most of these exceptions were made for co-production arrangements with countries friendly to the United States and involved low technology items such as grenade launchers, artillery pieces, and unsophisticated missiles. Nevertheless, South Korea is to co-assemble F-5Es; and Japan, which is exempt from the controls because it is a treaty ally, is to co-produce the F-15.

The most notable exception was to the control that prohibited the development or significant modification of an advanced weapons system solely for export. For almost two decades the

59

United States had been selling abroad various models of the Northrop F-5, a simple and fairly inexpensive fighter of good but limited capabilities. More than 1,200 of these aircraft were sold to twenty-seven countries, making it the standard fighter sold to Third World countries. But with the passage of time Northrop, supported by some U.S. officials, made a case that many countries would be looking for a somewhat more advanced fighter. Such upgrading was in keeping with the practice of the major powers, which had meanwhile developed aircraft of far more advanced design for their own forces. The problem was that the United States was manufacturing top-of-the-line F-14s, 15s, 16s, and 18s—all of which have the most sophisticated technology and a very high capability in speed, range, and weapons—but nothing of an intermediate type between these models and the F-5s. It was argued that with a number of Third World countries intending to replace their F-5s (Taiwan was the case at hand), the choice came down to either sticking by the no-arms-for-export-only principle, thereby abandoning the market to West European aircraft manufacturers and the Soviet Union, which were presumed willing to fill their order books, or permitting the development of a new, between-generation fighter. Other U.S. officials, especially from the Arms Control and Disarmament Agency, strongly disagreed. They saw no waiting market during the 1980s for an F-5 replacement, and argued that the United States should not encourage the development of a new aircraft for the export trade, which would inevitably create pressures to find markets. In January 1980, siding with Defense and State against ACDA, President Carter decided to make a waiver of his arms transfer policy in order to permit the development of the FX, an intermediate fighter aircraft for the export market. Two models of the FX are now in competition, the General Dynamics F-16/79 (a scaled-down version of the F-16) and the Northrop F-5G (a major improvement on other F-5s). In theory the FX could be sold in the hundreds, perhaps thousands, to Third World countries in the coming ten to twenty years, although its actual market remains undetermined. It will be less expensive than the first-line alternatives, of more limited range, and easier

60

to maintain. It could discourage the purchase of more sophisticated fighters from other suppliers if there is no real need for them, thereby helping to moderate regional arms rivalries.

The FX determination illustrated the need for maintaining flexibility while also having guidelines to ensure that critical decisions are carefully reached. In this case the president's decision was made after many months of interagency study. Given the considerations in the case, it did not represent the "collapse" of the Carter arms transfer policy, as was charged by some critics.

The least successful aspect of Carter's program was the dollar ceiling, which stimulated more discussion and less comprehension than any other part of the policy.[18] As noted earlier, it was circumvented in several ways so that approximately half of U.S. arms sales were to be counted outside the ceiling. When originally imposed, it could be justified as a management tool intended to force reductions. The locus of power in arms sales decisions had usually been in the Pentagon. According to Leslie Gelb, former director of the Bureau of Politico-Military Affairs in the Department of State, the existence of the ceiling "made a real difference in giving the State Department some real authority, for the first time, in the management of the sales program."[19] But a ceiling is an arbitrary instrument, unrelated to shifting international trends and security needs. If a sale is warranted on political or security grounds, it should be approved whether or not it exceeds the ceiling. An unexpected event, such as a war in the Middle East or Africa, would of necessity lead to disregarding the ceiling, while the loss of a major customer could make a ceiling unnecessarily high. The latter is precisely what occurred with the fiscal year 1979 ceiling, as Iran ended its purchases and sales to Taiwan were suspended for a year because of the normalization of relations with Peking. While the setting of an annual ceiling may have been useful for a time as a symbol of the overall shift in policy, it made less and less sense as time passed and was wisely dropped by the Reagan administration.

The Carter policy as implemented, in spite of its shortcomings, made the internal decision-making process on arms sales more rigorous and systematic. By shifting the burden of persuasion from those who opposed a sale to those who favored it, the policy added requirements for analysis and long-range planning. Ultimately, however, its success depended upon a second component: the ability of the United States to enlist other nations in a multilateral strategy for restraining arms sales. American unilateral self-policing was absolutely necessary to achieve credibility in this regard. But in the long run a multilateral effort is essential, and as we shall see in Part Four, only minimal advances were made in this direction. Altogether, therefore, the Carter administration made only modest progress in achieving its proclaimed goals.

The Reagan Difference

The Reagan administration's approach toward arms sales is one of the major differences between its foreign policy and that of preceding administrations. More than ever before, arms sales are to be actively used as a key instrument of American foreign policy. The new Under Secretary of State for Security Assistance, Science and Technology, former Senator James L. Buckley, told the Aerospace Industries Association in his first major address that the Carter Administration had adopted policies on the sale of arms that "substituted theology for a healthy sense of self-preservation."[20] In contrast, the Reagan administration would view the transfer of conventional arms as an essential element of the U.S. global defense posture and an indispensable component of foreign policy. In its first months the new administration announced its intention to make a large number of arms sales, many of which went beyond what the previous administration had been willing to do, and sought the repeal of restrictions based on human rights and non-proliferation concerns. The emphasis was less on restraints of arms sales and on the dangers posed by conflict in the Third World and more on using arms sales to respond to the Soviet global challenge.

A four-page statement on "Conventional Arms Transfer Policy," issued by the White House on July 9, 1981, made clear the new thrust of policy. In contrast to the Carter statement of four years earlier, which had begun by noting the "threat to world peace embodied in the spiraling arms traffic," the Reagan directive began by stating that challenges and hostility toward fundamental interests of the United States, and the interests of its friends and allies, had grown significantly in recent years. The United States could not defend the free world's interests alone but must be prepared to strengthen the military capabilities of friends and allies by the transfer of conventional arms and other forms of security assistance. Such transfers would complement American security commitments and serve important U.S. objectives. "We will deal with the world as it is," the policy statement concluded, "rather than as we would like it to be."

Not only was there a difference in policy emphasis and tone, but also striking was the absence of specific guidelines. The listing of restrictions on the sale of arms, which had been the centerpiece of Carter's policy statement, was replaced by a stress on the need for flexibility in arms sales so as to be able to respond promptly and adequately to requests for weapons. The Reagan administration would evaluate arms sales requests primarily in terms of their "net contribution to enhanced deterrence and defense." In reaching its decisions, it would give consideration to such factors as whether the arms transfer would "enhance the recipient's capability to participate in collective security efforts with the United States"; whether the transfer would "promote mutual interests in countering externally supported aggression"; and whether "any detrimental effects of the transfer are more than counterbalanced by positive contributions to United States interests and objectives." Such very general principles provided full freedom of action in determining arms sales on a case-by-case basis. Nowhere in the statement was there any reference to human rights considerations. As to international restraints, it made the observation that there had been "little or no interest in arms transfer limitations manifested by the Soviet Union or the majority of other arms producing nations." In the absence of such interest, "the United States will not jeopardize its own security needs through a program of unilateral restraint."[21]

63

In order to increase flexibility in the selling of arms, several important and indicative steps were taken in the first months of the administration. A Carter directive had discouraged American representatives abroad from initiating discussions on, or stimulating interest in, the purchase of weapons from the United States, unless authorized by Washington, and even from assisting American businessmen to do the same. Dubbed the "leprosy letter," this directive was quickly rescinded and replaced by one whereby representatives of American companies producing weapons were to receive assistance from U.S. embassies in marketing their products. The new arms sales approach, an editorial in *Aviation Week and Space Technology* commented, could best be characterized as a free enterprise one. The idea that the U.S. government should support military exports was back in fashion, it observed. Approvals for sales, which used to take weeks, were now coming through in a day.[22] As mentioned earlier, the annual ceiling on arms sales was dropped. Part of the sale of arms is financed by U.S. government credits, which had decreased in availability over the past decade. The Reagan administration sought to reverse this trend and asked for financing of security assistance programs totalling $6.9 billion for 1982, an increase of 30 percent over the amount proposed by the Carter administration. (At the same time, funds for development assistance were slashed by 26 percent.) It also sought a "direct credit" program whereby there would be a reduction in the interest rates which some countries must pay to finance loans for the purchase of arms. Congress, in addition, was asked for $350 million to create a special "defense acquisition fund," which would be used to purchase in advance some arms which countries were likely to request but which, due to the long lead-time in manufacturing, would not be available without considerable delay once a request was approved. This fund could be used to make available an arms-for-sale inventory. Congress was also asked to raise the dollar thresholds at which proposed military sales must be reported to it from $7 million to $14 million in weapons and $25 million to $50 million in other defense articles and services.

Further "flexibility" was sought through the request to Congress that it repeal some special legislative restrictions on the sale of arms which had been designed and enacted to enhance particular foreign policy goals. The administration asked that a ban on arms sales to Argentina, due to its human rights record, be lifted because of Argentina's strategic location along vital lines of communication in the southern Atlantic as well as its natural resources. Similar action was sought with respect to Chile. It urged the repeal of the Clark Amendment, which prohibits military assistance to the anti-Marxist faction in Angola, because it was restricting policy options, although some well-informed members of Congress felt that its repeal would adversely affect efforts to negotiate an end to the conflict in Namibia (South-West Africa) and alienate some black African countries. And Congress was also asked to repeal the Symington Amendment, which prohibits military assistance to countries that do not pledge to refrain from developing nuclear weapons. The latter change was sought to enable the immediate provision of $400 million in military aid to Pakistan with the intention of giving $3 billion in military and economic aid over five years.

A cornucopia of arms sales seemed to mark the beginning of the Reagan administration. Hardly a week went by without the announcement of an important weapons transfer. Arms sales came to have a central role in American diplomacy. "This is the currency in which foreign policy now deals," said a senior Department of State official. "We can't sign treaties anymore, we can't deploy forces abroad—so how the hell else do you do it?"[23] The Washington correspondent of Le Monde wrote home that all American diplomatic activity now seemed to be concentrated in one section of the State Department, the one dealing with security assistance.[24]

President Reagan offered to supply about $15 billion in weapons and other military help to other governments in his first three months. The impact of these sales on regional stability, and the controversies which they aroused in some cases, are discussed more specifically in the regional sections in Part Three. Saudi Arabia was to receive five AWACS early warning aircraft, aerial tankers, as well as extra fuel tanks and Sidewinder air-to-air missiles to enhance the combat capabilities of the sixty F-15s already on order. Israel was promised additional F-15 fighters and was told that restrictions on the export of its Kfir fighter, containing an American engine, would be dropped. Jordan was sold Cobra helicopters equipped with anti-tank missiles. Morocco was told that it would receive American tanks and planes; the Carter administration had insisted that Rabat "qualify" for such arms by making moves toward peace in its war with Polisario guerrillas in the western Sahara. Pakistan was offered the F-16 fighter and sophisticated radar equipment as part of the $3 billion package of military credits and economic aid over five years. The F-16 was also offered to South Korea and Venezuela. With much fanfare about the "China card," restrictions on the sale of "lethal weapons" to the People's Republic of China were removed. El Salvador was sent military aid and military advisors. Arms were sent to Guatemala for the first time since 1977 and the administration similarly sought to send military assistance to Argentina and Chile. In addition, the transfers of arms to Somalia, Sudan, Tunisia, Turkey, and the anti-Marxist element in Angola were either approved or sought from the Congress.

Although at the end of the first months of the Reagan administration it was too early to make a full and fair evaluation of its arms sales policy, nevertheless a pattern had been set about which one could make some observations. Clearly the Reagan administration was relaxing the arms sales controls which had been imposed, though not rigidly enforced, by the previous administration. The dominant perspective among its senior officials was the competition with the Soviet Union. Moscow was seen as expanding its own arms transfers in a steady manner, similar to its military build-up, by officials such as Richard R. Burt, director of Politico-Military Affairs in the State Department.[25] Under Secretary of State James L. Buckley, in the speech already noted, declared that the administration would "face up to the realities of Soviet aggrandizement" with a sober, balanced, and responsible arms transfer policy, one essential for the protection of U.S. national security interests. Accordingly, the provision of arms to friends and allies was viewed as an effective way of enhancing their military preparedness, revitalizing alliances, and fashioning an effective strategy toward the Soviet Union and its allies.

This rationale underlay the more receptive policy on arms sales to Beijing, the decisions to buttress Islamabad and to sell advance fighters to Seoul. Yet it was by no means clear that one could buy friendship or influence with weapons. These decisions, moreover, raised serious doubts about their ultimate impact upon regional security. Providing arms to Beijing could increase Soviet fears of China and tempt it to undertake some preemptive actions. Arming Pakistan was thought to be important in order to strengthen its resistance against the Soviet presence in Afghanistan, but the same weapons could be used against India, the traditional enemy. Authorizing the F-16 for South Korea could escalate the arms competition on the peninsula and force the Soviet Union to provide the more advanced MiG-23 to North Korea. Some of these sales had the effect of introducing a far higher military technology into a troubled region with potential arms race consequences.

The wisdom of the sale of F-16s to Venezuela was also open to question for the precedent that it set. This was the first time that one of the most advanced supersonic fighter-bombers had been sold to a Latin American nation, crossing a threshold that had been carefully observed up to then. If Venezuela, with no real need for such an advanced aircraft, was to be permitted to purchase the F-16, it would be hard to deny it to other nations. In Latin America alone, Argentina, Brazil, Chile, and Peru might make such a request.

The Reagan approach to arms sales also downplayed two considerations that, in the preceding years, had served to restrict the transfer of arms. One was human rights considerations; these no longer prevented actual or intended sales to Guatemala, Argentina, or Chile. The other was nuclear non-proliferation. Selling arms to Pakistan without an iron-clad commitment that it would forego the development of nuclear weapons had the effect of reducing whatever leverage the United States had on Islamabad on this very sensitive and important question. Administration officials stated, tamely, that selling conventional arms to Pakistan might take care of its security concerns, thus obviating the need for atomic bombs. But it could also be argued that the willingness of the United States to do this, coming after an explicit policy to the contrary based upon non-proliferation aims, suggested a tacit acceptance of Islamabad's quest for the bomb.

Arms sales had become a major component of the American government's approach to the competition with the Soviet Union on a global basis, perhaps *the* major instrument for action overseas, short of the direct use of U.S. armed forces. The risk was that the Reagan administration was overvaluing this instrument. Nations pursue their interests; their friendship or foreign policies cannot long be "bought" with weapons. Many problems, especially in the Third World, could best be addressed by a greater attention to other means, such as economic assistance or traditional diplomacy to deal with political conflicts. Under the Carter administration arms sales policy was inconsistent and perhaps overly restrictive in some cases. In the Reagan administration it ran the risk of becoming overly permissive.

The Economic Dimension

We now take up the economic role of American arms exports, in greater depth than in the opening part. Their assumed major importance for the economy of the United States is often cited as the fundamental reason why little can really be accomplished in the way of constraints on arms sales, even by those who would otherwise support restraints on foreign policy grounds.

In Part One it was noted that arms exports account for only 4 to 5 percent of total U.S. exports; and that these exports, according to the U.S. Bureau of Labor Statistics, provided approximately 277,000 jobs in the sample year of 1975, or approximately 0.3 percent of national employment. These figures are far less than is generally assumed and, indeed, are considerably lower than is sometimes claimed. The Defense Security Assistance Agency, which supervises the Department of Defense security assistance program, has estimated that each $1 million in foreign arms sales creates 50 new jobs and keeps 50 existing jobs active among subcontractors and vendors. Such a formula would suggest that some 1 million Americans owe their employment to $10 billion in foreign military sales.[26] But even this figure, which is surely inflated, does not make a convincing case against greater restraints because of the harmful economic consequences to the U.S. economy. The fact is that only a very few are making a serious argument for eliminating all, or even most, foreign arms sales. Most reasonable advocates of restraints would propose rather moderate reductions, and only when foreign policy considerations would support them. Such limited and tempered reductions would have relatively minor economic consequences.

The last point is supported by the first authoritative and comprehensive analysis of the significance of arms exports for the American economy, undertaken by the U.S. Department of the Treasury in response to a congressional requirement included in the International Security Assistance and Arms Export Control Act of 1976. The study used an econometric model and postulated three alternative scenarios: (1) constant annual arms sales equal to $8.5 billion per year (in 1975 dollars); (2) an immediate cut of 40 percent in the volume of new orders; (3) an annual reduction of 10 percent in the volume of new orders from the previous year's level, spread over four years so as to equal 34 percent. In each case a macroeconomic simulation was made in order to ascertain the effect of the reductions on such factors as employment, the balance of payments, and trade.

The Treasury study found that the impact on broad economic aggregates of any plausible policy curtailing arms exports is likely to be modest; and that the moderate adverse effects could be easily countered by slightly more expansionary monetary and fiscal policies. The estimated percentage decline in total employment by 1983 would be 0.1, irrespective of whether the 40 percent reduction in military sales was achieved immediately or spread over four years (resulting in a 34 percent reduction). The job displacement would be essentially limited to three industries—ordnance, aircraft, and communications equipment—and would be most strongly felt by professional and technical employees, rather than by semiskilled or unskilled workers. The effect on the balance of payments would depend upon the assumptions made regarding the behavior of the dollar exchange rate and its impact upon future nonmilitary exports and levels of imports. Small depreciations in the exchange rate, which came about because of the curtailment of arms exports, but which resulted in an increase in other commercial exports, as well as some decline in imports, could have a neutral or mildly expansionary effect. There are, to be sure, many qualifications within the Treasury study, but its general conclusion does not support the picture of an American economy heavily dependent upon the export of arms.[27]

It is often asserted that arms exports have an important, beneficial role in reducing the cost of weapons for the American defense budget. It is sometimes possible to recover a part of research and development expenses by adding a surcharge to the prices foreign customers pay. Another major source of savings is thought to be the lowered per-unit cost made possible by longer production runs. Both factors are significant; however, the extent of the benefits has been challenged by a study of the Congressional Budget Office.

This study concluded that large savings do not generally result from U.S. foreign military sales, and that the individual cases in which exports do produce substantial savings in a given weapon's total program costs tend to be exceptional. For a few weapons systems, the savings from foreign sales may come to 8 percent of total research and development costs. These savings are primarily from sales of high technology systems, which employ newly developed and specialized technology, particularly advanced fighter aircraft and missiles. However, for the great majority of sales—ships, ammunition, artillery, military equipment, and services, for which early research and development costs have already been absorbed—there appear to be little or no cost savings. The relationship between any restraints on arms sales and weapons costs to the U.S. Department of Defense will therefore depend less on the total dollar volume of sales than on what portion of sales is of newly developed, high technology items. In

70

recent years, it is precisely in this category that the internal pressure for exports has been the greatest. But the volume of exports of high technology items has not been such as to lead to a major saving for the U.S. defense budget.[28]

Of course certain manufacturing companies would be more affected by restraints on arms sales than others. It is noteworthy, however, that of the top ten contractors with the Department of Defense in 1977, only one, the Northrop Corporation, was heavily dependent upon foreign sales. The remaining nine relied on foreign military sales for only about 12 percent (on the average) of their total sales. None, with the exception of Northrop, depended on arms exports for even 25 percent of its business. As for Northrop, which sold abroad 81 percent of its defense production, it prospered for decades by concentrating on various models of the F-5, a lightweight fighter of limited range, to whose export there have been relatively few objections.[29]

A careful, albeit necessarily limited, analysis of available data and studies on American arms sales abroad as a percentage of total exports, as a source of employment, as a way of reducing unit costs for U.S. forces, as a means of recouping research and development expenses, and in terms of broad economic aggregates involving trade and balance of payments, leads to an inescapable conclusion: economic considerations are not of sufficient importance to be an overriding, or in some cases even a major, factor in overall foreign policy considerations in dealing with arms transfers.

Public Opinion

The American public, it should be noted, has been less than enthusiastic about the high level of U.S. arms sales achieved in recent years. Public opinion polls have consistently supported greater restraint. Indeed the largest portion of respondents to polls taken in the late 1970s stated fairly routinely that as a general policy the United States should not sell weapons to other countries at all. For example, a National Broadcasting Company-Associated Press poll taken in December 1978 indicated that 57

71

percent were opposed to all arms sales. Other polls taken by various national polling organizations have reported similar results.[30] Moreover, an "opinion ballot" survey taken of 50,000 persons by the respected Foreign Policy Association in its Great Decisions program found that 71 percent favored an agreement among major arms suppliers, or within the United Nations, to control the sale or transfer of conventional arms.[31] Even after the Reagan administration adopted a new approach, 67 percent opposed giving military assistance to anti-Communist allies that violate human rights. [32] These results are quite striking, particularly in light of the shift during the last decade toward more conservative views on foreign and defense affairs.

SOVIET UNION

Arms sales play a greater role in the Soviet Union's policy toward Third World countries than they do in U.S. policy. The West has more to offer the developing world than arms. There are other, often more influential instruments of foreign policy, such as the relative attraction of the Western economic system or the existence of free and democratic institutions. The Soviet economic and political model, as it exists in reality rather than in theory, has far less appeal in most of the Third World. The Soviet Union remains apart from much of the world economy; the West is better able to offer trade, investment, and the transfer of technology. Weapons, however, are one of the very few items that most developing countries can hope to receive from the Soviet Union. Soviet economic assistance to the Third World has been quite modest, and usually tied with political strings. On the other hand, Soviet military assistance has been generous, often given with speed and flexibility and on advantageous terms. Seweryn Bialer notes the "imbalance of Soviet policy resources [in the Third World], with military resources as the chief asset and all other resources playing at most a supportive role."[33] Because of the limited alternatives that exist, it is probably no exaggeration to conclude that arms transfers have been the most important instrument available to the Soviet leadership in dealing with the Third World.

For this reason the Soviet motivation in supplying arms has traditionally been far more political and ideological than economic. For the past quarter-century Moscow has carefully shaped its arms transfers to serve political purposes. Arms have been supplied to movements of national liberation actively engaged in armed struggle to demonstrate Socialist solidarity and foster their affinity with Marxist-Leninist ideology. They have

73

been given to radical or Marxist regimes as well as to other countries whose favor Moscow has wanted to court or whose political leanings it wanted to reinforce. In the case of Cuba, they have been supplied so as to enlist Castro's direct support for achieving Soviet aims in Africa and Latin America. Thus arms transfers have been—and continue to be—a major tool in the political competition with the West.

Related to this is the use of arms supplies for strategic purposes to acquire bases, usually naval facilities. As the Soviet Union has wished to expand its world role and to demonstrate full superpower status, it has sought to augment its military presence through a wider network of overseas bases.

Second Largest Supplier

Stalin was not especially interested in the Third World in the early postwar period, maintaining his essentially European perspective and being preoccupied with problems of internal reconstruction. During his years Soviet arms transfers were limited primarily to the Warsaw Pact countries and China. Khrushchev, however, was quick to see the opportunities that rising nationalism and the emergence of new nations among the less developed countries presented to the Soviet Union. Military and limited economic aid to the Third World became important components of foreign policy starting in 1954. They have been carefully designed to satisfy specific political and strategic needs, rather than humanitarian motives. According to the Central Intelligence Agency, Soviet military deliveries to the Third World were less than $1 billion per year prior to 1970, but have ranged between $2 billion and $3.8 billion for most of the years between 1970 and 1978. During the same period, economic aid was less than $1 billion for most years.[34]

The Soviet Union has been the second largest supplier of arms in the world, with approximately 30 percent of the total. During the five-year period 1973–1977 the United States exported $21.6 billion in arms to the developing states while the Soviet Union transferred $16.5 billion.[35] Military grants and sales have tended

74

to be concentrated in a few key countries and areas. The Middle East has received the most Soviet arms with Iraq, Syria, and Libya having received 50 percent of Soviet arms sent to the Third World between 1974 and 1978. Earlier, Egypt was a major recipient. Thus, by shipping the largest portion of their weapons to the Middle East, the Soviet Union and the United States mirror one another. Other major recipients during this period were Algeria, Ethiopia, and India, and in the previous decade, Indonesia. The flow of arms to Africa south of the Sahara has increased significantly, with military deliveries rising from $90 million in 1974 to over $12 billion in 1978. The Soviet Union became the largest supplier of weapons to sub-Saharan Africa during the 1970s, providing a total four times that of the United States. Weapons have been shipped to Angola, Ethiopia, Guinea, Mali, Mozambique, Nigeria, Somalia, and Uganda, among a total of eighteen countries. In Asia the largest recipient of Soviet arms during the 1970s was North Vietnam during the Indochina War. A major agreement to provide India with $1.6 billion of arms over five years was signed in May 1980. In Latin America, Peru is the sole country, apart from Cuba, that has decided to purchase weapons from the Soviet Union.[36]

We examine transfers to each region in some detail in Part Three, but several elements in the evolving pattern of Soviet arms transfers are worth noting now. Among the largest recipients in recent years have been countries able to pay in cash: Libya, Iraq, and Algeria. One of the largest Soviet sales in the 1970s was to Tripoli which in 1974 signed a contract for delivery over the following years of a vast array of arms, including MiG-23 fighters, TU-22 medium bombers, surface-to-air and Scud missile systems, and modern ground equipment; still more arms were purchased thereafter. This proved to be far more than Libya, with a population of 2.5 million and total armed forces of 29,700, was capable of absorbing. Colonel Qaddafi's army is not only small, but poorly trained and unable to employ or maintain its modern weaponry. Some of the sophisticated Soviet arms are reported to be sitting in unopened crates. Iraq, another oil-producing state, became one of the Soviet Union's largest recipients of arms in the Middle East with a 1976 agreement to purchase $1 billion in weapons. The trend in the Middle East during much of the 1970s was not only from grants to sales, but from the relatively moderate states of Egypt and Syria to the more radical ones of Iraq, South Yemen, and Libya. In 1979–1980, however, Syria again became a major recipient.

In sub-Saharan Africa the Soviet Union has used arms to develop or consolidate its presence, to support national liberation movements on the theory that they would then be more likely to adopt a socialist orientation, and to acquire military bases. Large quantities of weapons were shipped to the People's Movement for the Liberation of Angola (MPLA) in Angola, where they were in part used by Cuban forces. Arms have been supplied to Mali and the Congo partly in exchange for aircraft landing rights and to Guinea-Bissau and Somalia as payment for the use of naval facilities, in the case of the latter the strategically important base at Berbera on the Red Sea. A dramatic reversal of an arms relationship occurred in the Horn of Africa in 1977 when Russian advisers were expelled and Soviet base rights were terminated in Somalia, a country that has been well armed and equipped by the U.S.S.R. The Soviets then launched a massive effort to arm and train soldiers in neighboring Ethiopia with which Somalia was already engaged in its frontier war. Among the Soviet Union's motivations was its interest in acquiring the right to base its fleet at two Ethiopian ports on the Red Sea, Assab and Massawa, as replacement for the excellent facility it lost at Berbera.

Another noteworthy aspect of Soviet transfers is the number of advisers and technicians who accompany the weapons. Rarely are weapons sent without advisers, and their number is often greater than would appear warranted, thereby raising questions about the real purpose for sending some of them and suspicions that they are there to gather intelligence. The CIA estimated that 12,070 military advisers from the U.S.S.R. and East European countries were stationed abroad in 1978, ostensibly to assemble and maintain equipment as well as to train the forces of the host country in their operation. They were to be found in large numbers in Libya (1,750), Syria (2,580), Iraq (1,200), Ethiopia

76

(1,400), and Angola (1,300), and in smaller numbers in Peru (150) and elsewhere in the Middle East, Africa, and South Asia. As in American programs, officers from arms-recipient countries have had training in the Soviet Union. Some 52,890 military personnel from the Third World traveled to the Soviet Union or Eastern Europe for this purpose between 1955 and 1978.[37]

Improved Logistical Capability

During the 1970s the Soviet Union greatly improved its capacity to transport arms over long distances by developing long-range cargo aircraft and by expanding its maritime capabilities. In the previous decade Moscow's ability to aid Lumumba in the Congolese civil war was limited. No such logistical problems hampered the impressive capability of the Soviet Union to bring Cubans to Angola and Ethiopia or to support them with sea and airlift operations, ferrying thousands of tons of arms and military supplies. The production of the IL-76, a transport aircraft with a cargo capacity of forty-four tons—twice that of the AN-12 it is replacing—represents a major addition to the Soviet airlift capability. Roll-on, roll-off ships for carrying supplies and delivering them without the need for complicated port facilities have also been constructed.

The Soviet Union's ability, and perhaps willingness, to send arms to the Third World is also affected by the large quantity of surplus equipment available. It stocks reserve arms in large quantities, more than the West does, and these provide a cushion, obviating the need to ship operational stocks. The Soviet defense industry routinely overproduces with potential exports in mind. Large production runs are established which manufacture extra new weapons. In addition, weapons that have been phased out of the Soviet armed forces are sold. American intelligence estimates are that for both old and new arms, the average time lapse between sale and delivery of Soviet arms abroad is half that of the United States.[38]

The improvement in transport capacity, coupled with the relative availability of weapons, has considerable significance for

77

future situations in which Moscow may wish to send arms rapidly and effectively. Russia's leaders have not been prone to take risks by sending Soviet forces to distant places. They prefer indirect involvement by means of arms transfers and, when available, the employment of proxy warriors such as the Cubans in Africa. The Soviet Union is acquiring an expanded capability for intervention, both direct and indirect, in the Third World and may be more tempted than in the past to seize upon future opportunities to make what it perceives as geopolitical gains.

The Economic Dimension

For a long time the rather negligible economic benefits of Soviet arms transfers served to reinforce their fundamentally political orientation. Arms either were provided completely free, or were sold on extremely favorable conditions for the purchaser. Often the prices were set well below comparable Western prices. Some customers received "discounts" up to 40 percent. Usually the sale of arms was accompanied with long-term credits of eight to twelve years duration, at minimal interest rates of 2 1/2 percent, often repayable in soft, local currency, which was then used by the Soviet Union for the purchase of domestic goods or investment in the recipient country. Some of the largest transfers of Soviet arms in the past were at considerable cost to the U.S.S.R.: weapons sent to North Vietnam were given as grants, and Egypt and Indonesia have not repaid the large amounts that they owe.[39] Thus it was a general rule in the 1960s that Soviet weapons were offered on better terms—longer repayment periods, lower interest rates, payment in local currency, commodities, or raw materials—than could be obtained in the West. In some cases Moscow has granted moratoriums on payments when purchasers have been unable to meet their debts; Peru is an example. At other times, it has accepted payments in goods and commodities, sometimes then "dumping" these goods on the world market. When the Ethiopians could not pay for arms in 1978, the U.S.S.R. accepted coffee beans in barter; their resale on the international market lowered the price, seriously harming the Ethiopian economy. For the recipient, political rather than commercial considerations were almost always the determining factor in the choice of supplier, but the attractive terms the U.S.S.R. was prepared to give were indicative of the political role attached to arms transfers.

In the 1970s, as the Soviet Union experienced unprecedented hard-currency trade deficits because of its crop failures and the need to import grain as well as its desire to purchase Western technology, it revised its approach and came to place greater emphasis on arms sales as a source of revenue. Terms were toughened, and some of the largest sales were to oil-rich countries, such as Iraq, Libya, and Algeria, which could pay in cash, often in Western currencies. Arms sales such as these were yielding over $1.5 billion in hard currency by 1978 and, along with the sale of gold reserves, helped to reduce the national trade deficit. Total arms deliveries came to $3.8 billion in 1978. Without these sales, which account for about half of total Soviet exports to the less developed countries, Moscow's trade balance with the Third World would have been in the red. The earnings from arms exports were important in helping the U.S.S.R. pay for the sizable expansion of imports of Western technology. Roughly 10 percent of Moscow's total hard currency earnings came from arms sales to the less developed nations; many of the weapons sales required payment in convertible currencies. Outright grants of arms were proportionally smaller, although weapons are still delivered at no cost in areas of keen competition with the West, as in Africa.[40] And it is noteworthy that the terms of the $1.6 billion sale to India, signed in May 1980, are extremely generous, providing for repayment over seventeen years at a mere 2 1/2 percent interest. This may have resulted from Moscow's desire to remain on good terms with New Delhi to counter the negative image the intervention in Afghanistan gave it in the rest of South Asia. In any case, the Indian deal demonstrates that Moscow's pricing policy on weapons sold remains politically determined.

Russian weapons tend not to be quite as technologically attractive as American arms, but the Soviets attempt to overcome this

79

by promising fast delivery—without the uncertainties created by the possible disapproval of the U.S. Congress—and offering substantially lower prices. According to a U.S. government official, the price of the first U.S. F-15 fighters sold to Israel was about $12 million per aircraft, while the price of the roughly comparable Soviet MiG-23 fighter averages $6.7 million. A MiG-21 fighter lists at $2 million, while a somewhat comparable F-4 is $5.7 million.[41]

Yet the economic pressure to export is still lower than in the West. In a state-managed economy like the Soviet Union's, with its shortages of skilled manpower, maintaining levels of employment is not a factor in exports, especially in the highly favored defense industry. Nor are the lower unit production costs, attributable to exports, likely to be considered of significance. The number of weapons sent to the developing world, in relation to those produced for the armed forces of the Soviet Union and the Warsaw Pact, has not been large enough to have had a significant impact on production costs; until the mid-1960s many of these arms came from surplus stocks. Our knowledge of the inner workings of the Soviet "military-industrial complex" is quite limited, as it remains shrouded in secrecy. Yet it appears that the arms-production industry is geared to a steady rate of production, and weapons systems do not have to have promising export potential to be developed because of the large demand for arms already existing within the Warsaw Pact.[42] In sum, the Soviet armaments industry is not subject to the strong economic pressures that exist in the West.

A Balance Sheet

In the mind of the Soviets, the Third World is now the main battleground in the ideological competition with the West. As the central East-West balance has come to be partially stabilized through a combination of deterrence and arms control, the locus of the continuing struggle has shifted to the developing countries. The Third World is the prime area of opportunity in Soviet strategy, and the results of the competition there are bound to affect perceptions of the overall power relationship between East and

West. This trend has been reinforced by the emergence of China as a competitor to the Soviet Union in the Third World. The supply of arms has become a key factor—for some, the major instrument—in the intense competition for power and influence.

In the post-Vietnam era, and the period of economic recession in the capitalist countries, the West has been reluctant to intervene directly in the Third World and has relied more upon regional self-determination. The Soviet Union has been less hesitant, and has therefore considerably augmented its capabilities for quickly shipping weapons by air or sea over long distances. Thus it has become and will remain a participant, at least indirectly, in Third World conflicts. Moscow is not likely to abstain voluntarily from taking advantage of unstable situations and weak governments where they exist in areas such as Africa unless some restraining "rules of the game" are developed among the outside powers.

Whether the arms transfer instrument will be as successful for the Soviets as they clearly hope or expect is open to question. It may also be that the anxiety and alarm these sales create in the West are exaggerated. According to one study dealing with Soviet military assistance, "political penetration, the securing of strategic position, and the impairment of Western (and more recently, Chinese) influence in the Third World are its major goals. . . . The Soviet military aid program has been applied opportunistically, often taking advantage of instabilities created by international crises or regional conflicts. At the same time it has remained purposeful; it has increased steadily despite setbacks."[43] It is probably the case that the Soviets are ideologically predisposed to sending arms to the developing countries and into unstable situations in order to support the forces of movement rather than the forces of order.[44]

Yet the record suggests that the Soviets will have as many setbacks as successes in the Third World, and that the provision of arms does not easily translate into lasting influence. The transfer of $1.2 billion worth of arms to Indonesia did not inhibit Sukarno from adopting a pro-Chinese foreign policy to the dismay of Moscow. The abortive Communist coup in 1965 led to the ouster of the Soviets from Indonesia, and was a serious blow to Moscow's strategic position in Southeast Asia. Weapons for Peru did nothing to enhance Moscow's position on the South American continent as a whole. The Congo, Ghana, Guinea, and other parts of sub-Saharan Africa have witnessed a long string of Soviet failures to establish a permanent influence on that continent. The Russian navy was summarily ousted from Berbera, the Soviet Union's largest overseas naval base. Disputes over arms deliveries embittered relations with China and contributed to the final break. Arms supplied to Syria and Iraq have not made them pliable to Soviet political wishes—indeed, the adequacy of supply has been a source of tension, which has led both countries to seek diversification. Damascus has refused to give the Soviets as many military facilities as they wanted, and Baghdad condemned the Soviet invasion of Afghanistan. Perhaps the most striking Soviet failure has been in Egypt, where the Soviets had penetrated the Egyptian military as they did with no other clients. Egypt's armed forces were reorganized in Soviet style, and at the peak there were 17,000 military personnel in Egypt, some actually manning air defense sites and flying on patrols. Yet Cairo's total dependence on Soviet arms in a zone of military confrontation and the existence of a relationship extending back two decades did not prevent it from breaking ties with Moscow and sending Soviet advisers home.

Whatever leverage the shipment of arms provides, Moscow's experience confirms that it is not guaranteed to be lasting. Most of the recipients of Moscow's favors have also sought to buy arms elsewhere so as to diversify their sources. Many have resented the cultural arrogance and indifference of the advisers. The bilateral relationship between supplier and recipient will be constantly subject to new disturbances and reappraisal. The acceptance of grants of arms does not destroy a nation's freedom of action, and the outright purchase of arms may considerably enhance its ability to maneuver. In the volatile and fast-changing Third World, nations will be guided by their own perceptions of their self-interest, and considerations of arms supplies—especially at a time of eased availability of weapons—will only impose limited constraints. This is a lesson that the Soviet Union as well as other suppliers have not yet fully assimilated.

FRANCE

After the two superpowers, France ranks as the third largest supplier of conventional arms. More than one-third of its national arms production is sold abroad. Its arms sales policy generally has been considered to be the most permissive of the major suppliers, with the assumption often made that the French government is willing to sell almost any weapon to anybody. On occasion, French ministers have spoken of a policy of selling arms "without political conditions." France is also thought to reap major commercial benefits as a result of its laissez-faire attitude toward arms sales.

In reality, the situation is more complex. Arms exports do have considerable economic importance to France. But their fundamental motivation has been more political—related to French concepts of national independence and autonomy—than commercial. Moreover, despite the apparent "success" of its arms exports, the French armaments industry may be facing a crisis in the years ahead because of the troubling extent to which it has been allowed to become dependent on exports. This makes the French case all the more interesting when examined within the context of the global politics of arms sales.

Growth in Sales

French arms sales, like those of the United States, increased dramatically during the 1970s. Arms *deliveries* rose from 2,673 million francs in 1970 to 20,500 million francs in 1980 in current francs, or an increase approximately fivefold in constant francs. Most of this increase in deliveries took place after 1972, with an annual increment of about 30 percent. *Sales* abroad increased from 6,341 million francs in 1970 to a total of 25,200 million francs in 1979, with the largest annual increase—from 8,373 to 18,343 million francs—coming between 1973 and 1974 after the Yom Kippur War and the oil embargo. By 1979 foreign military sales accounted for approximately 4.9 percent of total French exports, in comparison to 2.5 percent in 1970. Overseas sales continued at a high level throughout the decade. Indeed, the export of arms grew twice as rapidly as France's total exports.[45]

Since the beginning of the 1970s there has been a change in the direction of the flow of arms. Previously, two-thirds of deliveries were to other industrialized countries, primarily members of the European Economic Community with occasional sales to the United States. During the seventies most deliveries went to the Third World, and by 1977 the developing countries accounted for 85 percent of arms purchases. The Middle East has accounted for more than half of total French arms exports in recent years, 55 percent in 1980.

There is a significant correlation between France's oil imports and its arms sales. Despite its ambitious civil nuclear program, the nation is dependent for two-thirds of its energy requirements upon oil from abroad. Over 80 percent of its petroleum imports come from the Middle East. The largest suppliers of oil are Saudi Arabia and Iraq, and those are precisely the states with which Paris has signed its largest contracts for arms since 1974. One of the biggest arms deals ever, for $3.5 billion, was made in 1980 to expand, modernize, and train the Saudi navy. Saudi Arabia's ground forces are equipped with AMX-30 tanks and Panhard vehicles, while Iraq is due to receive Mirage F-1s. Earlier, when France was more dependent upon oil from Libya, it sold Mirage fighters to Tripoli. Although arms-for-oil is never officially acknowledged as a policy, the assurance of future supplies of oil is clearly an important motivation for French leaders. Nevertheless, the income from the sale of weapons to the oil-producing Middle East states only covers a fraction, about one-fifth, of the cost of the oil imports.[46]

The statistics above give a clear indication of the growing role of arms sales in the French economy. There has been a steady increase in arms made for export compared to those made for

84

use by the French military services, from 17 percent of the total manufactured in 1971 to 41 percent in 1980. Yet this does not give the complete picture, for certain sectors of the defense industry—especially the aeronautic one—are more dependent upon exports than others. It is generally believed that exports play an important role in reducing the unit costs of research and development as well as of production. This is undoubtedly correct as overseas sales account for more than half of the production runs of some of France's most important weapons systems, and for more than 75 percent in the aeronautical industry. Finally, there are 280,000 persons employed in the arms industry, of whom an estimated 90,000 work on arms ordered from overseas. Although this may appear to be a modest number in a work force of 22 million, it does not include employment provided by the spinoff effect of subcontracting and the provision of services.

Policy of Independence and Autonomy

Yet political motivations involving a strategic concept of France's place in the world are at the root of the significance attached to the existence of the arms industry. Much of the French political leadership, including members of the principal political parties and of the permanent bureaucracy, as well as the public at large, remains attached to the concept of national independence. The encroachments upon national independence that are an inescapable fact of contemporary international relations are not unobserved. But defense is the last area in which the French are prepared to surrender their freedom of action. Thus with regard to nuclear weapons, there is wide support for the maintenance of an autonomous capability, even though it is recognized that France cannot survive a nuclear war or crisis without the assistance of allies. Similarly, France has withdrawn from the integrated command of NATO in order to maintain freedom of maneuver even though in reality it is dependent upon the other members of the Alliance.

The commitment to an independent foreign policy, many in

France are convinced, must in turn, be based upon an autonomous defense policy. This is perceived as important not only for French security but for the projection of the nation's influence in Europe and the world. And a national armaments industry is viewed as an essential characteristic of an autonomous defense policy. To the maximum possible extent France must have the capability of equipping its own armed forces without depending upon an uncertain source of supply from abroad. In order to maintain this ability to arm itself, France must export weapons abroad as the demand for arms at home is insufficient to justify the arms industry in economic terms. Arms exports, therefore, make economically possible a basic political necessity of the country.

The above characterization is perhaps more simplistic and extreme than the views held by many Frenchmen, especially by those who are more familiar with foreign and defense issues, but it does nonetheless reflect basic attitudes dominant in the French establishment as well as the symbols that continue to hold their appeal in the nation's political life. It is no accident that as recently as the presidential election of 1981, the Socialists and Communists attempted to outbid the parties of the right and center in proclaiming their allegiance to French independence in defense matters, including maintenance of the nuclear role. Neither party was critical of the notion of continuing a viable armaments industry. At the practical level the problem was well explained by Hugues de l'Estoile, the director for international affairs of the Délégation Ministérielle pour l'Armement, in opening the arms exhibit at Sartory in 1973: "Our objective is not to export, but to maintain a national and independent armament industry . . . the task is to ensure that the production plans, which are set by national purchases, be guaranteed through exports."[47]

Additional incentives for exporting arms follow from the policy of independence. By remaining outside the military structure of NATO, France puts itself at a disadvantage in selling weapons in Europe; this was certainly one of the factors in the failure to persuade Belgium, Denmark, Norway, and the Netherlands to purchase the Mirage F-1 rather than the General Dynamics

86

F-16 in the "Deal of the Century" competition of 1976. Hence, greater importance accrues to the sale of Mirage aircraft to the Third World. Similarly, by expending a substantial portion of the defense budget on the nuclear *force de dissuasion*, the funds for conventional forces are more limited; fewer weapons can be purchased for the French armed forces, and therefore more must be exported to maintain the industry or to lower unit costs. French defense doctrine has also occasionally stressed the "antihegemonic" nature of the nation's arms export policy. Thus the 1972 White Book on National Defense pointed out the benefit of being able to assist countries that do not want to be at the mercy of the two "blocs" by creating opportunities for them to purchase weapons from other than the two superpowers. Finally, much of the French establishment is proud of the technological sophistication of the armaments industry. This pride is not unrelated to the quest for prestige and independence.[48]

The Military-Industrial Complex

The structure for manufacturing and selling arms is quite complicated—a mixture of the public and private sectors, the latter still being closely tied to the state. A special government agency, the Délégation Générale pour l'Armement (DGA), formerly known as the Délégation Ministérielle pour l'Armement, is responsible for supervising the production of French arms. Within the DGA a special unit, the Direction des Affaires Internationales, is charged with maximizing the export of arms. The DGA owns and runs twenty-five arsenals (twelve for naval construction, eleven for equipment for ground forces, and two for aviation) which employ about 60,000 persons. A second category of weapons manufacturers contains the nationalized companies which employ about 70,000. These include the Société Nationale des Industries Aérospatiales (SNIAS), known also as the Société Aérospatiale; the Société Nationale d'Etudes et de Construction de Moteurs d'Avions (SNECMA); and the Société Nationale de Poudres et Explosives (SNPE). The third, and largest, category is the private companies which employ 150,000. Among the bet-

87

ter known of these are Marcel Dassault-Breguet, which manufactures Mirage and other aircraft; Matra, which produces guided missiles, electronics, and communications equipment; Thomson-Hotchkiss-Brandt, which makes artillery pieces and electronics; and Panhard-Levassor, which makes armored personnel carriers and other ground transport. (Some of these companies will be nationalized by the Socialist government.) Military armaments have a greater share in the total business of some of these companies than others; in the aeronautics industry it is quite high. Altogether, 1,300 factories can be included in the third category, of which 250 do considerable work on arms and 120 are more than 80 percent occupied with military orders. As much as 90 percent of Dassault's production was of a military nature in 1980.

Relations with the French state are extremely close at all levels, and the intervention of the state is frequent, its role extending to having a say in the appointment of key executives. Dassault-Breguet has been favored by the government; and although it successfully resisted demands from political parties on the left that it be nationalized throughout the Giscard years, as of 1979 it was 21 percent government owned. Société Aérospatiale, the major manufacturer of missiles, was created by the state as a nationalized company with a certain degree of autonomy. These are fine distinctions, however, and the line between the public and private sector is thin and even questionable in some cases. Indeed, it is far more accurate to speak of the existence of a "military-industrial complex" in France than it is in the United States.

The promotion of arms sales is also subject to this symbiotic relationship between industry and state. Four separate corporations, created for the specific purpose of expanding the export of arms, work closely with the Délégation Générale pour l'Armement. Each specializes in selling to one part of the arms market. These are "mixed corporations," with part of their capital private and part contributed by the state.[49] In addition, every other year since 1967 the DGA has organized armament fairs where equipment for sale is on view to delegations invited from all over the world; over sixty countries are usually represented by their chief arms purchasers. The fair for ground forces weapons at Sartory and the military aircraft exhibition at Le Bourget, neither of which is open to the general public, are exuberant and extravagant occasions which have little difficulty in drawing potential customers from afar. At these fairs weapons are displayed and sold as if they were no different from any other merchandise like cars or washing machines.[50]

The state has thus become *the* purveyor of French arms. This has involved large promotional efforts and, it is widely believed, dealings of questionable ethics involving considerable amounts of state funds made available for "pots-de-vin," or bribery. President Valéry Giscard d'Estaing became sufficiently uncomfortable with the situation to commission Pierre Mayer, a widely respected *inspecteur de finance*, to undertake a top-secret investigation in 1976 of the state's role as a manufacturer and exporter of arms. The central findings of the Mayer report were disputed by the Ministry of Defense, which attempted to quash it by commissioning a rival report from the inspector general of the army. The Mayer findings were leaked to the press, however, and were revealing. Mayer concluded that the French state was unwisely exposing itself by underwriting operations it should not be assuming responsibility for, and covering up transfers of money, that is, bribes, that would be subject to severe criticism should they become public knowledge. The 135-page report disclosed many instances of waste and inefficiency created by interservice rivalry and overly close relationships between the arms producers and the military services. It recommended a broad reorganization of the methods of selling arms and a sharper distinction between the role and responsibilities of the state and those of the industry.[51] Yet there is no evidence that the recommendations of the Mayer report were acted upon or led to any significant change in the French practice of selling arms.

Decision-Making Process and Policy

The actual decision-making process on arms sales is highly organized and closely controlled. A government-wide committee, the Commission Interministérielle pour l'Etude des Exportations de

Matériels de Guerre, meets every two weeks and passes on all sales on a case-by-case basis. It also decides which weapons can be sold abroad, and which cannot. Consisting of about twenty representatives, mainly of the Ministries of Foreign Affairs, Defense, Finance, and the Economy, it is chaired by the *sécrétaire général de la défense nationale* who reports to the prime minister. The committee has been in existence since 1955, and industrial interests do not normally try to circumvent it. In its early years the Defense representatives were dominant, but in recent times the Quai d'Orsay has taken a more active interest and role. On occasion, there are strong differences on prospective arms sales, not only between defense and foreign affairs representatives, but also between the Délégation Générale pour l'Armement, which seeks to maximize exports, and defense officials who oppose a sale on military grounds. In any case, there is every reason to believe that decisions on French arms transfers are carefully regulated, whatever the substance of the decisions reached.[52]

Policy on transfers—when they will be permitted and when not—is more difficult to discern. There is no single equivalent to the Carter guidelines of May 19, 1977. Occasionally, government spokesmen in the National Assembly have referred to various principles of restraint, usually in response to criticisms of particular sales. According to these principles, arms are not to be transferred to a war zone or to belligerent states engaged in open and direct conflict with each other; caution is to be exercised in sending arms to "areas of tension"; a distinction is made between arms that are likely to be legitimately used to protect the national security of a state and those that might be used internally for police action and repression; in the latter case they are not to be transferred. The chief of staff of the armed forces, General G. Méry, in a speech before the Institut des Hautes Etudes de Défense Nationale in 1976, expressed concern about the transfer of highly sophisticated arms, as well as long-range ones, and cited the need to examine not only the commercial benefits of transfers, but also the strategic and political consequences.[53] Occasionally there may be specific embargoes on arms shipments, as in de

Gaulle's total embargo on arms for Israel in 1969 or the partial embargo on South Africa because of its apartheid policy (and the French desire to stay in the good graces of francophone African states).

However laudable the criteria established, they must be judged against the reality of their application. Here the record has been weak, and sales to such states as Libya and South Africa have given French transfer policy the reputation of permissiveness. France remained, for example, Pretoria's largest supplier until 1979 and provided it with missiles, helicopters (which could well be used for internal repression), and even the ability to co-produce Mirage III and F-1 fighters as well as the Cactus surface-to-air missile. This has caused nonaligned and black African countries to make protests to Paris on a number of occasions over the years. Sales to Portugal during the war against the liberation movements in its colonies aroused criticism, as did the sale of armored cars to the Greek military junta and the sale of Mirage fighters to Libya, which were later re-transferred to Egypt and used in the Yom Kippur War of 1973. The Iraq-Iran war, begun in 1980, did not prevent Paris from continuing the delivery of Mirage F-1s and anti-aircraft missiles to Baghdad. Purchasers often find French arms attractive, not just because of their acknowledged high quality, but because of the French government's principle of selling arms without making judgments about the domestic politics of the recipients, and of not attaching to sales contracts clauses that can be viewed as imposing restrictions on the recipient's national sovereignty. The inherent incompatibility among some of the principles that are said to guide French arms sales policy, and the discrepancy between policy and practice, have led to a general air of skepticism and cynicism.

Public and Political Debate

Public debate in France concerning its arms sales has been relatively quiescent compared to the United States, but it is not lacking. Most Frenchmen are aware of the country's position as an important supplier of arms, and discussions or journalistic writings on the subject often reveal a certain sense of malaise. Yet this is more than balanced by an attitude of resignation in the face of what are assumed to be the economic and political imperatives of arms exports. Pride in such national achievements as the technology of French aircraft runs deep, as does a visceral belief that France must to the maximum extent feasible retain its autonomy on questions of foreign policy and national security.

The government, moreover, has in the past discouraged public discussion of arms exports. It publishes little on the size or direction of French arms flows so that information can only be found through a very careful reading of parliamentary debates and the press. In 1974, Minister of the Army Robert Galley ordered government officials to keep their public discussions of arms sales to a bare minimum.

Nevertheless, there has been a consistent pattern of criticism of arms sales, and its continuity over time suggests that it has deep roots. The fact that government officials attempt to foreclose the debate by keeping knowledge about French exports limited, or by occasionally feeling compelled to respond, indicates that a certain sensitivity and malaise surround the problem.[54] In the 1978 elections for the National Assembly (more than in 1981) the Socialist Party gave considerable attention in its statements on defense and disarmament to the need to develop a new approach on arms sales.

The sharpest opposition has come from religious groups, although one can question its impact. In particular the French section of the international Pax Christi movement within the Catholic church has been very active. The archbishop of Paris, Cardinal François Marty, probably the most powerful and influential ecclesiastic authority in France, created a considerable stir in 1976 when, speaking from the pulpit of Notre Dame, he criticized the government's growing arms exports. Acknowledging their economic importance, he nonetheless deplored the extent to which the selling of arms was becoming a national institution. He criticized the concept of dealing with the balance of payments by arming other nations, and called for a gradual conversion of the arms industry to other forms of production.

92

Government officials questioned the competence of the cardinal in this domain, although for a time, as the problem received renewed attention in the press and television, they were clearly on the defensive. Catholic and Protestant representatives have been involved in study groups and other forms of consultations on the arms trade in recent years, but criticisms emanating from church organizations, based as they are in some measure on the question of morality, have had only limited effectiveness.[55]

Arms sales are more of an issue on the left than on the right of French politics. They have presented an especially awkward problem for the labor unions, which are torn between condemning the "merchants of death" on ideological grounds and avoiding any course that could reduce the employment of their members. Hence the Socialist-based Confédération Française Démocratique du Travail (CFDT) has adopted resolutions deploring French arms sales, yet "recognizing" that the conversion of the arms industry to pacific purposes will be long and costly and should not be undertaken at the expense of the workers. As to the Communist Confédération Générale du Travail (CGT), it has ranted against the "arms trusts" and the transfer of arms to "reactionary and antiprogressive regimes," but has insisted that France retain the necessary means for assuring its national independence and territorial integrity. The labor unions have persistently criticized particular sales, such as those to Chile and to South Africa, or to the Greek colonels, but they have always made certain to stop short of a general condemnation of arms exports.

The Mitterrand Approach

The Socialist Party has long had a special interest in arms sales policy. Prior to the 1978 elections, François Mitterrand developed a reasonably sophisticated approach toward reforming French arms sales in a realistic manner. The Programme Commun of the Left, a joint Communist-Socialist statement, rather simplistically stated that all arms transfers to "colonialist, racist,

93

or fascist" governments should be stopped. Mitterrand noted that with 275,000 persons then employed in the arms industry, of whom 75,000 were working on arms for export, the industry could not be simply shut down from one day to the next; nor would that be desirable from the point of national security, he added, as he accepted the desirability of maintaining an auton-omous arms production capability. Rather, he suggested several long-term goals: a limitation on sales, a reorientation of the direc-tion of French exports, and a more open and controlled process of manufacturing and transferring arms.

The first Mitterrand proposal was for a series of regional con-ferences involving recipients and suppliers with the purpose of setting regional ceilings on transfers. The Middle East was sug-gested as a good place to start. This idea was later echoed by Giscard d'Estaing at the United Nations Special Session on Dis-armament in May 1978. Second, the Socialist leader called for a reorientation of French sales from the Third World, which by then absorbed three-quarters of them, to Western Europe. As models to be followed he cited joint aircraft production projects such as the French-British Jaguar and the French-German Alpha Jet. Third, Mitterrand made some fairly detailed proposals for "lifting the secrecy" and introducing "democratic control" over the various sectors—private, mixed public and private, and gov-ernmental—engaged in arms manufacture and exports. Parlia-mentary oversight and a degree of control would be institution-alized by having the defense commissions of the National Assembly and the Senate informed of all sales under 1,000 mil-lion francs and requiring their authorization for transfers above that amount. Each year a public report would be issued on French arms sales. In addition, a Secretariat of State responsible for the arms industry in its totality would be established; the Min-istry of Industry would have a section responsible for conversion of parts of the arms industry to other endeavors; and, finally, a Council for Disarmament and Security, whose responsibilities would include the limitation and reorientation of arms sales, would be created.[56]

The extent to which President Mitterrand would implement

his past proposals was far from clear in the period immediately after his election. The new government, Prime Minister Pierre Mauroy told the National Assembly, would redefine policy on arms sales in such a way as to reconcile the new principles which would guide French foreign policy with the necessities of maintaining employment and safeguarding the dynamism of industries in a particularly competitive environment.[57] One of the first decisions made was that almost all existing contracts for French arms should be honored. Within days of Mitterrand's election, before even the elections for the parliament, the President sent his brother, retired Air Force General Jacques Mitterrand, now the head of Aérospatiale, to Saudi Arabia for the purpose of assuring King Khalid that arms contracts valued at over $4 billion would not be touched.

The Socialist government was committed to giving more attention to North-South relations and to being more receptive to the economic, social, and humanitarian needs of the developing world. As to policy toward arms sales, the major new principle as enunciated by Minister of Defense Charles Hernu was that France would not sell arms to "racist and fascist" states.[58] This was expanded upon by Foreign Minister Claude Cheysson to include dictatorships that could use the arms for repression, countries whose policy menaces the liberty of other peoples, and states at war.[59] The true nature of any change in French policy depended, of course, on the changes in practice. The Mitterrand government was very unlikely to sell anything with military implications to South Africa. This was seen to be of considerable symbolic importance. It refused to deliver some previously ordered armored vehicles to Chile because they could be used to repress the population. On the other hand, the transfer of patrol boats to Argentina was permitted. Iran was allowed to receive some missile-launching ships which were on order but whose delivery had been held up for eighteen months. And, significantly, an arms embargo on Libya that had been imposed by Giscard d'Estaing in the wake of Qaddafi's intervention in Chad was lifted, thus permitting the delivery of previously ordered Mirage F-1 fighters, helicopters, and fast patrol boats. The lifting of the embargo cleared the way for renewed oil exploration by the French government-owned company Elf-Aquitaine. No new arms would be sold to Libya, however, until it had withdrawn its troops from Chad and finished restoring the French embassy in Tripoli, badly damaged by a street mob in February 1980. This was one more illustration of the complexities often involved in arms transfer decisions.

Prior to the 1981 election, Mitterrand had criticized the "immoral" sale of weapons to Latin American dictatorships and some other authoritarian Third World nations, and had pledged to "moralize" arms sales. Clearly ethical and humanitarian considerations would be of greater import than under the previous regime. Indeed, French governments had got into the habit of boasting that they attached fewer "strings" or conditions upon arms sales—in effect, none—than did other supplier countries. Some countries, such as South Africa and Chile, which are particularly bad violators of human rights, may be singled out for a firm ban on arms sales. This might be, in part, for the effect of deflecting attention of the critics from the sales which will go through.

Equally clearly, however, France will not cease being one of the major arms suppliers. Any government in Paris will pay due heed to considerations of employment, balance of payments, the unit cost of weapons for France's own armed forces, and the widely held belief in the need to maintain an autonomous defense industry. It will also need to protect the availability of oil supplied by arms-purchasing nations.

The continuation of support for arms sales is all the more likely, given Mitterrand's intention to nationalize important sectors of the arms industry. Due for nationalization are Dassault, the Mirage builder; Thomson, whose speciality is sophisticated electronics; and the arms production part of Matra, the guided missile maker. The validity of the need for state-ownership is uncertain. In part it is motivated by long-held ideological beliefs on the left. The long-term consequence of nationalization, however, may be to shift to the French state responsibility for the difficulties of the defense industry that lie ahead.

96

An Uncertain Future

Mention was made earlier of a possible future economic crisis in the French arms industry; this is not as far-fetched a likelihood as it might seem. There is considerable evidence that the French government has allowed the arms industry to become dangerously overdependent upon exports. Purchases of weapons for France's own armed forces were reduced in the late 1970s because of the spiraling costs of arms and the more general economic pressures on government spending, including that for defense. Moreover, priority has been given to nuclear armaments. An increasingly large portion of the nation's production capacity is aimed at foreign markets. Yet overseas demand for arms is always uncertain because markets can become saturated, especially in the Persian Gulf and Middle East, and there is competition from other arms-supplying nations. One of the most knowledgeable persons on the subject of the French arms industry, Joel le Theule, a minister and former rapporteur of the Finance Commission in the National Assembly, gave voice to his concerns over the future of the arms industry at the time the five-year program for the defense budget for 1977–1982 was being debated. For the next several years, at a minimum, plans for arms production would be greatly dependent upon orders from abroad, while French orders would decline or stagnate. He saw a real danger in this trend, given the risk that overseas purchasers might not remain as willing to buy French arms as in the past.[60]

The existing degree of export dependence can be readily illustrated by a few not widely known, yet striking statistics. For the years 1974–1978, of the 338 Mirage fighters that were ordered, 297 were for export. More than half of the aeronautic industry's production consisted of Mirages, yet more than 85 percent of these were destined for export. Indeed, by 1979 more than three-quarters of Dassault's total business came from the export market. Of the 318 helicopters ordered from SNIAS, only 46 were for the French armed forces. Matra, France's leading manufacturer of guided missiles for aircraft, exports 75 percent of its mil-

97

itary output. As to the anti-tank missiles also made by SNIAS, more than 50 percent were manufactured for export. A comparable situation applied to the AMX-30 tank: 103 were ordered for export in the years 1974–1977 and only 30 for the French army. In contrast, the inability of French naval shipyards to win foreign orders led to a grave crisis in that sector of the industry.

Particularly worrisome, as these data would suggest, is the dependence of the aircraft industry upon orders from abroad. This sector of the arms industry accounts for the largest volume of exports, as much as 19,000 million francs out of the total of 25,200 million francs in arms sales for 1979.[61] Moreover, more than 60 percent of French aircraft production is devoted to military purposes.

The loss of the French F-1 to the American F-16 in the competition for NATO orders was a severe blow, as was the failure to receive more orders for the Concorde. The French aircraft industry has intermittently been in a state of crisis; valuable design teams have been broken up. Aérospatiale has been in the red because of the Concorde. Orders for the new Mirage 2000 and its export version the Mirage 4000 have not been promising, and the future of the Dassault-Breguet company—which alone accounted for almost half of aeronautical orders and a third of total arms export orders in the late 1970s—is uncertain. Similarly, Aérospatiale is dependent on military orders for more than half its business. There is a clear necessity to diversify the aircraft industry in preparation for the lean times that may well be ahead.

The French arms industry is thus in a paradoxical situation. Orders for export have never been higher, and they are one of the brighter spots in a generally stagnant economic situation. National autonomy is being more or less maintained at present. But by becoming so export dependent, the industry is increasingly vulnerable to the fluctuations and uncertainties of demand in the international arms market. And should arms sales begin to decline, either because of saturated markets or increased competition from other suppliers, it will have major consequences for

French foreign and national security policy as it is presently set. Indeed, the autonomy and independence so highly valued could be seriously threatened. France's current success, therefore, may only be serving to mask—and even aggravate—the difficulties ahead.[62]

UNITED KINGDOM

As a West European country of approximately the same population and size as France, and with a comparable, indeed greater, experience and tradition in the production of armaments, Britain has many of the same incentives for selling arms. Britain ranks below France as a supplier, although not so much so that it could not surpass France in any given year. Many of the characteristics of the arms transfer picture in the two countries are similar, as, for example, the economic dimensions of weapons exports. Yet important differences are worth noting. The existence of an autonomous arms-manufacturing capability is not accorded the same degree of political significance as in France. Nor are arms transfers often discussed as important instruments of foreign policy. In commercial terms, British industry has not become as dependent on armament exports as that of France. And, finally, the public debate has a somewhat different character, with greater attention given to the possibilities of converting some of the arms industry to nonmilitary production, as well as to the question of the morality of arms sales to poor and underdeveloped countries. Interestingly, there is a tendency in Britain to view the French as ruthless and indiscriminate arms pushers compared to the British; whether this comparison is deserved remains a moot point.

British arms sales in the 1970s followed the same upward trend as those of the United States and France. Exports, measured by receipts from arms sales, rose from 235 million pounds in 1970–1971 to approximately 901 million pounds in 1979 (current pounds). Given the continuing rise in demand, it was forecast by the minister of defense that annual sales would reach 1,200 million pounds in 1980–1981.[63] Exports now account for 25 to 30

100

percent of Britain's total arms production, and they constitute an estimated 3.5 percent of its external trade.

Beyond these rudimentary facts, there are no details released on British arms sales. The whole subject is clothed in official secrecy. Once a year a single estimated global figure is released in the annual white paper on defense; there is no disaggregation by types and quantities of weapons nor any explanation of what is included or excluded from the total sum announced. Nor is there any indication of the identity of the recipients by region or country. An informed student of this phenomenon notes that the British government's "furtive approach" introduces an air of official embarrassment into the whole issue, as if "selling arms to other nation-states was like selling contraceptives to Ireland."[64]

Arms Sales Rationales

The motivations for transferring arms have altered with the changes in Britain's international role. In the first decade after the Second World War, Britain was the second largest exporter of weapons in the world. The United Kingdom still had a world-wide role, and many countries were looking to it for military equipment. Moreover, the British armaments industry had a long history and was the only one in Europe, apart from Sweden's, to have continued uninterrupted throughout the war. A government white paper in 1955 stated that "the general policy of H.M. Government on the sale of arms is primarily governed by political and strategic considerations: only when these have been satisfied are economic considerations—i.e., the contribution of arms sales to export earnings—taken into account."[65]

The dominance of economic incentives by the 1970s was a reflection of Britain's withdrawal from empire and its altered world position. The same economic arguments are made for weapon exports in Britain as in the two other major Western suppliers: to benefit the balance of payments by increasing foreign exchange earnings; to reduce the unit cost of the production of arms for the nation's armed forces through longer production runs; to recoup some of the research and development expenses;

101

and to maintain employment and technical skills in the defense industry. The last argument became particularly important as Britain reduced its armed forces and defense expenditures.

The political arguments—to win friends and assist allies, to influence the policies of other nations, to help maintain regional balances and international security—are much less frequently made, and certainly far less so than in the United States and, presumably, the Soviet Union. Nor do the British insist as strongly as the French upon the existence of an independent foreign policy underpinned by an autonomous arms industry. It is no accident that Britain decided to purchase Polaris missiles from the United States for its nuclear submarines, while France developed its nuclear force quite independently (and would have essentially done so even if some U.S. atomic assistance had been made available).[66] With Britain's armed forces now almost completely based in Europe, there are very few strategic rationales, such as securing foreign base rights, or the like, for selling arms. There remains a general sense that having an arms industry is an attribute of an important middle-level power, that the ability to manufacture advanced technology is another source of strength, and that the arms industry may somehow enhance Britain's flexibility in foreign and military affairs. But this sentiment has less force than one might expect, and such arguments are rarely used to justify weapons sales. Arms sales, in short, are seen less as an instrument of foreign policy than as a commercial benefit or economic need.

Defense Industry and Export Production

The defense industry has a public and a private sector. The eleven Royal Ordnance factories manufacture mainly tanks, armored fighting vehicles, light arms, and ammunition; they employ some 23,000 people. Most defense manufacturing is thus undertaken by private industry. An estimated 275,000–280,000 people are employed on contracts let by the Ministry of Defence, of whom 70,000–80,000 are working directly on contracts attributable to overseas sales. Roughly an equal number of persons are

102

indirectly employed by spinoffs on these contracts because of purchases made by defense suppliers.[67] Weapons manufacture is limited in its significance for British industry as a whole, but is of critical importance to key sectors of the aeronautics industry, 60 percent of whose work has been done under government defense contract, and to shipbuilding, which undertakes about one-third of its work for the military. The major warship-building companies were nationalized in 1977. In addition, the more diversified electronics sector, which manufactures communications, radar, navigation equipment, and the like, is heavily involved in defense work.[68]

The promotion of British arms exports is undertaken with dead seriousness and receives high priority within the Ministry of Defence. Having watched the success of the American arms sales program instituted by Secretary of Defense Robert McNamara in the early 1960s with considerable fascination and some envy—to which the author can personally attest as he was dealing with defense matters at the U.S. embassy in London at the time—the Labour government that came into office in 1964 asked the managing director of British Leyland, Sir Donald Stokes, to advise on the best way of promoting the export of military equipment. Britain's balance of payments was then in especially bad straits, and this was uppermost in the minds of Harold Wilson and Denis Healey, then minister of defense. This led to the creation in 1966 of the Defence Sales Organization (DSO), a semiautonomous unit within the Ministry of Defence, whose purpose was to stimulate arms exports. "We believe," Healey said, "it is not only our right, but our duty, to ensure that British defence industries have a market which enables them to survive and have a proper share of the international market."[69] The DSO has sought to bring the marketing and promotion techniques of private industry to the government. It has now had three directors, all of whom came from the business world with past records of commercial success, and has a staff of 400, including its own personnel stationed at key embassies abroad. In 1976 a special arms trade fair to which eighty countries sent delegations was organized in Aldershot, and this was repeated in 1978 with the

103

presence for the first time of a delegation from the People's Republic of China. The Aldershot fair, with its elegant display of weapons for sale, is remarkably similar to the French exhibition at Sartory. Earlier in 1977 a Royal Navy ship, *The Lyness*, sailed to foreign ports carrying a floating exhibition of armored vehicles and other items on sale. The head of the DSO travels widely; Sir Lester Suffield, during his years as director in the 1970s paid special attention to Iran, going there almost monthly.

The increase in British arms exports is undoubtedly related to the astute salesmanship of the Defence Sales Organization. The clear disposition is to make sales whenever and wherever possible. The style is aggressive and achievement oriented. A government review by the Central Policy Review Staff of Britain's overseas representation and activities judged the DSO to be a success.[70] The products of the Royal Ordnance factories are sold directly by the DSO, but its more important role is in advising and supporting the private companies' sales efforts abroad by acting as a sort of middleman. The preponderance of British sales are now to Third World countries, most of whose governments prefer to deal with other governments rather than with companies. Another role of the DSO is to advise on what types of weapons would sell well abroad at the time that requirements are being drawn up for Britain's own armed forces.

Not surprisingly, the British military services have shown some resistance to new equipment being designed according to export-related criteria for foreign armies rather than their own requirements, but this has become less of a problem as the purchasing countries ask for more and more sophisticated arms. Yet in the case of the Chieftain tanks sold to Iran, their engine was better—and more expensive—than those being built for the British army; and the Iranian army was due to get the new, revolutionary Chobham armor on its Shir tanks (an export version of the Chieftain especially designed for the Shah) before Britain's own Chieftain. This was also to be the case with the Tracked Rapier surface-to-air missiles. As it turned out, after the new Islamic government in Teheran canceled the remaining orders, it was determined by the Thatcher government in late 1979 that the

104

British army was to receive 200 of the Shir tanks. Altogether, the Shah had ordered 1,200 heavy tanks for the Iranian forces, indeed more than were to be in the service of the British army. The majority of these were delivered before the revolution.

Yet the extent to which arms exports actually lower the cost of weapons for Britain's own armed forces remains a very open question. A parliamentary committee looking into this found evidence to question the conventional wisdom that exports significantly reduce unit costs, thereby coming to a conclusion similar to that of the U.S. Congressional Budget Office with regard to American sales. The report of the Public Accounts Committee revealed that exports from the Royal Ordnance factories often did not yield a profit and frequently failed to contribute to fixed costs, while the recoupment for research and development expenditures coming to the government on private industries' sales of weapons developed at government expense was minimal.[71] A similar conclusion was reached in 1980 by a British scholar: "Those areas which absorb R & D defence funds in Britain do not generate a large share of British arms exports."[72] Overseas sales can, however, maintain production lines and hence employment when there is a drop in domestic orders. This may be of greater significance than the lower unit cost and research and development savings.

Policy and Politics

London's decision-making process on arms sales and the setting of policy are not, however, held within the confines of the Defence Sales Organization. An Arms Working Party, on which sit representatives of various ministries but which is chaired by the Foreign and Commonwealth Office, makes most decisions. The FCO makes the principal recommendations, and if it is opposed to a sale on foreign policy grounds the Ministry of Defence is unlikely to persevere. Occasionally, however, difficult or sensitive cases, or particularly large sales, are referred to a cabinet-level body, the Defence and Overseas Policy Committee, which may be chaired by the prime minister for final decision.

105

At the political level, it is rarely forgotten that arms sales have been known to kick off emotional parliamentary debates which can be awkward for the government.

There is not much evidence of any comprehensive, overall policy on arms sales. Decisions are made on a case-by-case basis, reflecting the essential pragmatism of the British style of government. A memorandum from the Ministry of Defence submitted to the Defence and External Affairs Sub-committee of the House of Commons—a rare occurrence in itself—noted that it was difficult to devise a broad strategy for future arms sales because of the "highly competitive character of the international trade in defence equipment" and the fact that "changes in the situation of countries abroad may occur very quickly."[73] Contrary to the announced intention of the Carter administration, the presumption seems to be to sell arms to a prospective buyer unless there is good reason not to, rather than to sell only when there are sound foreign policy justifications for the transfer.

Because of this pragmatic approach, constraints on arms sales typically occur on a selective basis, usually as a result of a particular political context. Often the constraint reflects a certain sensitivity within British politics. The most notable refusals to sell arms have arisen in emotive and politically charged situations. This was the case, for example, with South Africa, which received most of its arms from Britain until a partial embargo was instituted in 1967. The tension in Britain between the opposition to apartheid, on the one hand, and the close historical and commonwealth relationship with South Africa as well as the need to defend the strategic Cape route, on the other hand, often produced sharp differences over Harold MacMillan's handling of the issue between the Labour and Conservative parties, as even among the Tories. An arms embargo was also placed on Chile after signs of repression came to the fore in Santiago following the military takeover in 1973. There was an undeclared embargo on Uganda during the years of Idi Amin. Sales to the federal government of Nigeria were an issue of dispute during the war over Biafra's secession. Refusals to sell arms in certain cases are handled quietly, so as not to create embarrassment. Libya is believed to have been refused some arms, and Iran at one time was discouraged from seeking nuclear-powered submarines.

Perhaps the most important, though formally powerless and still quite indirect, source of constraint is the Parliament. Westminster has been the scene of heated debates on sales to some of the above-named countries, and acts as an implicit restraint on any truly egregious sales being proposed by a government. Nevertheless, with the exception of particular cases that have captured public and political attention, general arms sales policy does not receive much attention in the House of Commons. There are no debates on the United Kingdom's arms sales policy, and members of Parliament can only raise the question in relation to some other issue. Concerns about arms stability within a region, such as the Persian Gulf or Latin America, are rarely heard. When Julian Critchley, a Tory backbencher well versed in foreign affairs, suggested in the Commons in 1975 that greater attention should be given to the cumulative impact of arms transfers to the Persian Gulf, he found little interest among his colleagues.[74]

Apart from the ebbs and tides of the debate surrounding sales to particular countries—a debate that is often quickly politicized and used as a verbal weapon by the government against the opposition, or vice versa—there is a more continuous discussion on Britain's arms exports chiefly to be found on the left and among members of the Labour Party. Some maintain a moral or ideological opposition to arms sales, which on closer examination is part of a broader opposition to arms and defense expenditures in general. The Campaign Against the Arms Trade, a vocal grouping of church people and pacifists, has sought to have most, if not all, arms sales abolished. This has also been true of many members of the left-wing Tribune group of the Labour Party. But the great majority of the critics of British arms exports simply believe that the economic and human resources used in the arms industry could be more productively—and socially more usefully—employed in the manufacture of civilian goods. This proposition, so attractive at first sight, has placed the Labour Party in a quandary, as a curtailment of arms production without

107

a successful conversion of industry to other products would lead to unemployment. Accordingly, the National Executive Committee of the Labour Party created a Study Group on Defence Expenditure, the Arms Trade and Alternative Employment. In its book-length report, *Sense about Defence*, published in 1977, the Study Group argued that the real reason for the effort to expand military exports was the surplus capacity in the British armaments industry; that the industries that produce both civil and military goods have proved themselves to be more efficient at exporting in the civil sector; and that the consumption of resource and development assets by the military sector was responsible for hindering the development of British industry in general. Hence, "there is a good deal of evidence to show that the expenditure of a given amount of resources in the military sector tends to generate less employment and exports than an equivalent deployment of resources in the civil sector of the same industries."[75]

These are all debatable propositions, but their logical conclusion is that a transition from military to civilian production is desirable. Such a process, which also received attention in the Labour Party study, would be enormously difficult, but some degree of conversion may become inevitable if the overseas demand for British arms does not maintain its present level. In recent years several British companies that manufacture defense equipment have taken steps to diversify their products into the civilian sector in the expectation of reduced expenditures on weapons by the British government and a possible downturn in exports. There has also been a renewed interest in joint production of weapons with other European states. In these ways Britain may be in a better position than France is for accepting some multilateral restraints on arms sales, and may also be better prepared for the longer-term future.

THE RESTRICTORS:
WEST GERMANY,
JAPAN, SWEDEN, AND
SWITZERLAND

Several countries have placed serious restrictions on their arms transfers either for reasons of past history (Japan and West Germany) or to give support to their claim for neutrality (Sweden and Switzerland). All four are technologically advanced countries with a clear ability to export sophisticated arms in considerable quantities. What is strikingly noteworthy is that the self-imposed denials do not appear to have done their economies any real harm, for these are the countries with the most solid currencies in the world and are among those with the most prosperous economies. In each case, as we shall see, there are growing pressures of differing natures to adopt a more permissive approach toward arms sales. But their example does suggest that a relatively unrestricted arms export policy is not a sine qua non for economic growth or a strong balance of payments.

West Germany

To place West Germany among the restrictors may at first seem peculiar, for it is in fact the fifth largest exporter. Unlike the sales of the four largest, however, most of its sales have been to NATO countries, particularly Turkey and Greece, rather than to the Third World. In fact, it has placed strong restraints on sales to the Third World. Bonn's arms sales are still relatively unimportant, representing less than 1 percent of total exports, and its weapons transfers to the Third World are still only a fraction of those of France or Britain. Recent years have, however, seen an increase in German arms exports, and most of that increase has been in sales to Third World countries.[76] The probability of further expansion is quite high.

It was assumed by many after World War II that Germany would never again have an armaments industry. But following the decision to rearm West Germany in 1955, military production, which had been banned since the war, was permitted under the control of the Western European Union. (The ban on atomic, biological, and chemical weapons was not lifted. Other restrictions originally in Protocol III of the Brussels Treaty, on guided or long-range missiles, strategic bombers, and warships, were later mainly, though not completely, rescinded.) German private industry remained for many years reluctant, however, to reenter the arms field because of psychological and political inhibitions, and the Bundeswehr was at first equipped solely with American arms. As these inhibitions disappeared, the industry expanded to the point that today it has an estimated 200,000 employees and accounts for 2 percent of the GNP, a figure still lower than for France or Britain.

In the early years, complete emphasis was given to equipping its own armed forces, but starting in 1961 the Federal Republic—with American encouragement—began sending arms supplies through military assistance programs to selected countries in Africa (Nigeria, Sudan, Kenya, and Tanzania, among others) and under secret agreement to Israel. This military assistance policy was designed to gain international support for the Hallstein Doctrine, under which Bonn claimed to be the sole legitimate German state. Recipients of military assistance were expected to recognize the Federal Republic's claim and to have no contacts with East Germany. These arms dealings, however, became a source of acute embarrassment. The clandestine transfers to Israel, once they became known to the Arabs, angered them and caused ten of the Arab states to break diplomatic relations. Other difficulties were caused by transfers of ninety surplus American F-86 Sabres and twenty-eight Seahawks, which were sold to Iran and Italy but inexplicably and illegally wound up in Pakistan and India. These episodes in 1965-1966 pointed up the political risks involved in military transfers to the Third World. Subsequently, in 1966, the German government adopted restrictions on all arms sales to "areas of tension." (Yet in December 1978 it was revealed that between 1966 and 1969 West German intelligence agencies secretly sent weapons and equipment to South Africa, Rhodesia, and both sides in the Nigerian civil war; there was even discussion of providing uranium to China. These revelations were intended to embarrass Karl Carstens, a senior official in the "grand coalition" government of 1966-1969, who was to be a successful candidate for the federal presidency.)

This history has been sketched in order to make the point that German restrictiveness on arms sales to the developing world is as much the result of these fiascoes in the second half of the 1960s as it is of memories of militarism, the Krupp empire, or the heritage of the Second World War (even if the last did create images that any West German government must remain sensitive to). The Social Democratic Party (SPD) in the 1960s severely criticized the military assistance programs as well as surplus sales to the Third World. (Helmut Schmidt was then one of the most outspoken critics.) In 1971, two years after the SPD and the Free Democrats (FDP) had gained control of the government, Bonn after a careful policy review announced still stricter arms export guidelines designed, in principle, to forbid all sales outside of the NATO alliance. Special exceptions were made, however, for "safe" countries such as Australia, New Zealand, Sweden, Switzerland, and Japan. The hallmark of the new policy was that sales to "areas of tension" *(Spannungsgebiete),* as defined by the Ministry of Foreign Affairs, were specifically prohibited.[77]

During the 1970s these restrictive guidelines came under growing pressure from business organizations and labor groups. They were not basically altered, but they were interpreted in a progressively more permissive manner. Some sales were refused: Spain under Franco was denied 200 Leopard tanks and Iran failed to buy 800 Leopard tanks it wanted after Bonn refused to assure it that spare parts would not be cut off in a time of conflict (the order went to Britain for its Chieftain tanks). The latter self-denial cost Krauss-Maffer, one of Germany's main weapons sup-

111

pliers, a contract worth half a billion dollars at a time when it was short of military business and was having trouble with its civilian products.

On the other hand, Germany's military exports have expanded through various indirect means or loopholes: the export of entire plants and the sale of licenses for manufacture; the supply of components for assembly abroad; and the entry into multinational projects with other countries. These forms of technology transfer in effect bypassed many of the formal restrictions in the 1971 guidelines. Accordingly, small arms and ammunition factories have been built by German industry in such developing countries as Guinea, Nigeria, Sudan, Thailand, and Burma. Ammunition plants in Iran were agreed upon which would reportedly have had a larger output than Germany's own ammunition factories. Foreign assembly of essentially German parts is being undertaken for the Leopard tank, which is having its motor and chassis put together in Italy as the Leopardino for the Italian army but with suitable and interested Third World markets in mind, as well as for the Marten armored carrier which is to be assembled in Belgium for sale to the Middle East. Submarines and frigates have been sold to Latin American states under provisions that call for some form of local construction. The restraints appear to have been especially relaxed for the economically hard-pressed shipbuilding industry, and West Germany has become a significant supplier of naval vessels. Bonn agreed in 1977 to supply Iran with six submarines. When the order was canceled after the Iranian revolution, they were sold— amid some controversy—to Chile.

The most widely used means of circumventing arms export restrictions may come to be the sale of weapons systems co-produced with other countries. Multinational projects within Europe are designed to provide standardization and economies of scale, but they also have the effect of blurring the responsiblity for decisions on export. Perhaps not by accident, West Germany has become involved in a large number of such projects, essentially with France and Britain, both of which have, as we have seen, far less restrictive export policies. Up to 60 percent of the equipment procured by the Federal Republic's armed forces may soon come from such joint projects. The French-German close-support Alpha Jet light-attack aircraft is available to Third World countries through French sales, with Egypt at one time having shown considerable interest. Jointly developed anti-tank missiles, such as Hot and Milan and the Roland ground-to-air anti-aircraft missile, produced by the Euromissile consortium, are for sale; France has sold some of these to Syria. Multinational projects usually require consultations and some form of concurrence on sales to third parties, but it is highly unlikely that a German government would seek to veto a transfer by its partner. Reportedly, Paris demanded, and received, assurances on its full freedom to sell the Alpha Jet. The principles of Germany's national export restraint are not likely to take precedence over the benefits of multinational projects. There are a number of ever-widening gaps, therefore, in Bonn's export restrictions.[78]

In recent years strong arguments have been made for further relaxing West Germany's formal restrictions. Since 1974 the economic recession and the rise of oil prices have substantially altered past circumstances, as has an unemployment rate that has reached the 1 million mark. The German arms industry has lobbied for expanded exports, made confident that there is a demand for German arms by the numerous requests received, which have had to be turned down. The high quality of German technology—especially in arms—is well recognized abroad, and it has been claimed, probably with justification, that the present restrictions are forcing West Germany to forgo much money and many jobs. Labor unions, which in the past were strongly opposed to arm sales to developing countries, have changed their position, and some labor leaders have added their voice to that of industry. The Christian Democratic Party, in opposition, has called for the German arms industry to be used "to its full capacity," and its CSU wing in Bavaria, where there are many defense firms, has been especially vocal. By some estimates the Federal Republic could easily raise employment within the arms industry from the present 200,000 to 400,000 and could export an amount equal to 3 to 5 percent of the nation's total export. This would

113

place it in a league with France and Britain, whose arms sales-men are enviously viewed by some Germans as being extremely active and successful while Bonn's stay at home.

Those who are not persuaded point out the risks of becoming more dependent upon arms exports. A liberalization of the arms export guidelines would in all likelihood lead to an expansion of the productive capacity of the industry, which, once in existence, would have to be constantly fed new orders. This would create the type of export dependence that exists in France today, which is a factor in making the French government an active salesman. There is no equivalent in Bonn to the arms sales promotional organizations of the Délégation Générale pour l'Armement in Paris or the Defence Sales Organization in London. The Schmidt government appears to be very sensitive to this line of reasoning. It does not want Germany to be placed in the same situation as France, with the state forced to promote arms sales to prevent unemployment in the industry, nor does it want economic considerations of this type to become a burden on the nation's foreign policy. It is also argued that expanded arms exports would only marginally improve the balance of trade, since other capital goods purchases from West Germany might be reduced at the same time; nor is it certain that they would help the employment situation that much if skilled workers simply shifted to the arms industry from another industry. As to foreign policy considerations, it is argued that a major expansion in arms transfers could make West Germany vulnerable to involvement in international conflicts. West Germany still feels very sensitive about its overseas role, because of both its past and its exposed position on the border of the Communist nations. Finally, moral considerations do play a role, as evidenced by strong church statements on this subject.

The whole issue was put most severely and dramatically to the test in the spring of 1981 when Saudi Arabia indicated a strong interest in a large order of 300 Leopard-2 tanks, about 1,000 Marder armored personnel carriers, and Gespard anti-aircraft vehicles which would provide some mobile air defense protection. This followed Saudi purchases from France and Britain as

114

part of a policy of diversification. Riyadh was also buying more arms from the United States, but did not want to be excessively dependent on it. Saudi Arabia was West Germany's biggest supplier of oil, providing 27 percent of its consumption, and its largest creditor, with $6.3 billion in outstanding loans. Moreover, German industry hopes to play a major role in Saudi Arabia's development; it has become the third largest exporter to that country, after the United States and Japan, and the Saudis had hinted that deals for arms and civil projects were linked. The German business community urged a change in the ban on exports to areas of tension and appeared to have the support of Helmut Schmidt, who was concerned about the political and economic impact of turning down a country on which the Federal Republic is so dependent.

Yet Schmidt, by deciding, in the context of a trip to Saudi Arabia, that it was not feasible "for the time being" for Bonn to sell arms to any Middle East nation, did in effect reject the Saudi request. The opposition to the sale within his own Social Democratic Party was considerable, although some could be found within the ranks of the Free Democrats and Christian Democrats as well. The public debate on this sale raised in stark relief the moral issue of whether a country that attempted to annihilate the Jewish people during the Second World War should sell weapons that could one day be used against Israel. Also expressed was the concern, felt by some, that this was a first step to a West German military presence in the Persian Gulf (a role that some Americans were urging upon Bonn).

For the moment the national consensus remains that West Germany has more to lose than to gain from relaxing its restriction on arms sales to "areas of tension." The top-level Federal Security Council and the cabinet reexamined the policy in 1976 without making any significant changes. But the policy is certain to undergo further review in the early 1980s as a consequence of the Saudi turndown and it may well be loosened up. This appears to be Chancellor Schmidt's desire for the longer run. The Christian Democrats have spoken of the desirability of some further relaxation of restrictions, but it is by no means certain that a

115

CDU government would change the policy more than marginally. Yet there may be an increased discrepancy between the declared policy and actual practice, as the above-mentioned ways of bypassing it are tolerated and even expanded. Additional prospective recipients may be declared outside "areas of tension," and existing loopholes may be enlarged. Still, and contrary to much speculation, West Germany is likely for a while at least to remain among the ranks of the "restrictors."

Japan

Japan, even more than Germany, has tight restrictions on its arms sales. Arms exports remain for the time being relatively small, on the order of $50 million per year. The legacy of the Second World War serves as a more powerful inhibitor on arm sales in Tokyo than in Bonn, though it no longer acts as a brake on production for Japan's own armed forces. Here too, however, pressures have developed for a more permissive approach and a "great debate" on the entire question of Japanese armaments and defense policy is well under way.

To avoid a return to the militarism that characterized Japan prior to the war, Article 9 of the 1946 constitution stipulated that Japan renounce war as a "sovereign right of the nation and the threat or use of force as a means of settling international disputes." An additional clause stated that "land, sea and air forces, as well as other war potential, will never be maintained." However, after the start of the Korean War these clauses were reinterpreted, with American encouragement, to permit the creation of the Self-Defense Forces. Arms were manufactured for Japan's own forces, and as this occurred, pressures arose to export them in order to reduce unit costs and keep plants running continuously. Some Japanese leaders, expecially in the Socialist Party, felt that all arms exports violated the constitution, but Prime Minister Eisaku Sato declared in 1967 that arms "within the concept of self-defense" could in principle be exported, although the government would not encourage the sale of weapons. Subsequently, Japan established very broad restrictive principles pro-

116

hibiting sales to specified areas—Communist countries, South Africa, Rhodesia—or any country against which United Nations economic sanctions were in force or that was involved or likely to be involved in international disputes. In addition, self-restraint was to be exercised on all weapons exports to other areas, according to the spirit of the constitution. These principles were restated in 1976 by the government of Takeo Miki.

Meanwhile during the 1970s the Japanese armaments industry underwent great expansion. The Japanese defense budget increased sixfold during the decade, from $1.6 billion in 1970 to $10.1 billion in 1979, making it the seventh largest in the world. Today some 300 companies are engaged in defense production. Ninety-five percent of the equipment of the Self-Defense Forces is made in Japan, including surface-to-air and anti-tank missiles, helicopters and light aircraft, destroyers and patrol boats, and tanks and armored personnel carriers. Some more advanced systems are co-produced in Japan under American license, as, for example, the Phantom F-4 fighter-bomber and Hawk anti-aircraft missile. A precedent-breaking agreement was reached in 1978 under which Japan will co-produce over the next decade 100 F-15 fighters (Mitsubishi with McDonnell Douglas) and 45 Orion anti-submarine patrol aircraft (Kawasaki with Lockheed) at a total cost of $4.5 billion. The Japanese arms industry, which began with pistols for police forces in the 1950s, is now well balanced, manufacturing a wide spectrum of weapons. There is relatively little that Japan could not produce, but it has a special expertise in electronic equipment and precision-related technologies. Thus it is particularly well suited for manufacturing missiles and aircraft. The shipbuilding industry is also strong. Japan could become a medium-sized arms exporter almost overnight if Tokyo reached a political decision to follow this path.

Japan's powerful business community has urged the government to lift or ease its ban on exports. The Committee on Defense Production, a group of representatives from eighty Japanese manufacturers associated with the Japanese Federation of Economic Organizations, has called on the government to provide more business to the defense industry, as have such large

117

companies as Mitsubishi, which provides 50 percent of the arms procured by the Japanese Defense Agency. The Japanese Chamber of Commerce and Industry has called for an increase in arms sales abroad. Given Japan's almost total dependence on imported oil, arms sales to the lucrative Middle East market would be a relief to Japan's economy and a welcome antidote to domestic stagflation. In Japan, as elsewhere, the usual arguments about reduced unit costs and savings to the defense budget are to be heard.

More than anything else, the changing international political environment is likely to induce Japan to raise its defense expenditures, which still remain slightly less than 1 percent of GNP (but 1.5 percent if the NATO formula, which includes pensions, is applied). The marked buildup of Soviet military power in the Far East, especially the naval expansion in the Sea of Japan, has caused much concern to the Japanese, as has the unstable political situation on the Korean peninsula. The United States has repeatedly urged the Japanese to expand their defense capabilities; after the invasion of Afghanistan these pleas were made more forcefully and had a greater impact. Within Japan, too, there is a growing agreement on the need to increase the nation's military preparedness, not only because of the more threatening strategic environment, but because of uncertainties about the steadfastness of the United States as an ally, which grew out of the handling of the Vietnam War and the Carter administration's early plan to withdraw ground forces from South Korea. Some Japanese fear that the United States will concentrate its attention on the Middle East and Europe, while turning away from Asia. An important report made to the government in July 1980 by a group of foreign affairs specialists, headed by Masamichi Inoki, indicated a shift in perceptions and attitudes concerning the United States: Japan could no longer depend on the United States alone to defend its political, military, and resource-related interests.[79]

Declining faith in American credibility and growing Soviet power have augmented Japanese interest in their own defense role and capabilities. Defense is no longer a taboo subject, and there is growing concern about national security. A parliamentary committee on defense was established in the Diet for the first time in 1979. The same year the Ministry of Defense issued a five-year plan calling for an 18 percent increase in spending on arms within the first year. Prime Minister Masayoshi Ohira suggested in late 1979 that while the size of the Japanese defense forces (240,000) might not be increased, the nation's arms should be modernized. The successor government of Prime Minister Zenko Suzuki has moved fairly slowly, increasing the budget of the defense agency by only 7.6 percent in 1981 (less than the Americans had hoped would be the case). Nevertheless, within the defense budget, the portion being allocated to procurement for new weapons is rising considerably faster than other categories.[80] The question is not whether Japan will rearm but at what rate and in which manner.

As new perceptions induce Tokyo to expand its forces by building more and better arms, the pressures to export are certain to increase—not only because of the savings on the unit costs of production runs that exports would bring on arms for the Self-Defense Forces, but also because these new arms will require large research and development expenditures which could be partially amortized through sales abroad. Thus the continuing expansion of the defense industry will create a base for exports. Not to be overlooked is the fact that these same new perceptions of the changed strategic environment in Asia are persuading such countries as Singapore, Malaysia, and Thailand that they, too, should expand their armed forces. These Asian countries offer enticing markets for Japanese arms exporters.

The nation's political leaders remain, however, conscious of the political risks attached to becoming a major exporter. Selling arms involves a choice of recipients, and the Japanese, who often prefer not to take sides in a dispute, may want to avoid such decisions. Becoming an exporter on a major scale would probably be tied to a large-scale rearmament program, which could have wide international repercussions. Nor is it clear that it would have the support of public opinion, which remains sensitive to any step that would rekindle the nation's fear of militarism. The

119

disapproval of the opposition Socialist Party is fairly deeply rooted, even if diminishing, and any government that considers dramatically increasing exports will have to weigh the intended economic benefits against the potential political damage abroad and at home in a basically antimilitarist society.

Nevertheless, some increase in weapons exports is quite likely as Japan gradually modernizes its armed forces. This could be accomplished through some reinterpretation of former prohibitions, as has occurred in Germany; for example, seaplanes designed for the self-defense forces have already been made eligible for export on the ground that they are not military weapons and thereby fall outside the scope of the restraint guidelines. If Japan should ever undergo a major change away from restrictiveness toward the active promotion of arms exports, then the world arms trade will be deeply affected, for Japan is likely to provide keen and successful competition to the other suppliers. As the *Economist* has commented, "accommodating a Japanese defense industry could prove to be one of the Western world's more difficult challenges for the rest of the country."[81]

Sweden and Switzerland

Sweden and Switzerland restrict arms sales for quite a different reason—as part of their neutrality policies. Both have adopted restrictions that go beyond the accepted laws of neutrality, as codified in the Hague Convention of 1907, which prohibit neutral states from exporting arms to countries at war. Sweden's formal restrictions also apply to states involved in a dispute that could at some point lead to armed conflict; to unstable states in which armed disturbances could occur (aid to national liberation movements is specifically banned in support of a noninterference principle); or to states that suppress human rights as specified in the United Nations Charter. It describes its policy as nonalignment in peace and neutrality in war.

Both countries, however, maintain a posture of highly armed neutrality. They perceive a need for a strong defense capacity, which in turn has been viewed as requiring a national arms industry so as to possess maximum self-sufficiency. This creates a built-in tension with the restraints on weapons exports. A commercially viable defense industry is extraordinarily difficult to maintain without exports, especially for a small country with rather limited weapons requirements.

Nevertheless, Sweden considers its relatively self-sufficient defense industry to be a cornerstone of its neutrality policy. This is costly, and on a per capita basis Sweden spends more on defense than France, Britain, or West Germany, putting it in a class with the United States, the Soviet Union, and Israel. Its arms industry is highly advanced technologically, and its armed forces are the best equipped among the smaller powers in Western Europe. Yet, its exports have been traditionally small in quantity, and among its principal clients have been two other neutral states, Austria and Finland, which received Saab and Draken aircraft. Swedish arms, such as Bofors anti-aircraft guns and Spica fast patrol boats, are to be found in the Third World, but in limited quantities. Sweden's combination of low amounts of production by an advanced industry is unique in the world.

However, the rising cost of sophisticated technology is making even this expensive defense posture increasingly difficult to maintain. Thus Sweden is being forced, for the first time, to alter its stance. One of its most remarkable achievements to date has been the development of an advanced fighter-interceptor aircraft, the Viggen System 37, for its own specific environment. But because of its high price tag, and the restrictions placed on exports, it has not sold well overseas. Now Sweden is giving serious consideration to a follow-on, and a future replacement aircraft may be purchased from abroad. Stockholm has also found it necessary to dilute the self-sufficiency principle by considering entry into cooperative arrangements with other West European producers for the manufacture of missiles and other expensive weapons. At the same time there has been a reconsideration of the restrictive principles guiding arms exports, for Sweden may be forced by sheer economic and technological pressures to expand its supplier role if it is to maintain its armaments industry. Since 1975 there has been a gradual growth in arms sales. In

121

tomorrow's circumstances, a highly advanced arms base may be incompatible with a restrictive export policy. The Swedes will seek to make their adjustment without compromising their neutrality.[82]

The Swiss are caught in a similar bind. Their defense policy emphasizes preparedness, and they want to maintain a national defense industry so that arms will be available in crisis. Yet they wish to do nothing that will compromise their neutrality or their special position as the site of the U.N. agencies and various international organizations, such as the Red Cross. But because of an even more limited national requirement for weapons than Sweden and an economy heavily dependent on exports in general, the Swiss cannot forgo arms exports completely. There are, therefore, few restrictions on the transfer of machinery for arms manufacture or co-production through export licenses. The result is that Switzerland's largest weapon-producing firm, Oerlikon-Buehrle, was at one time producing more military equipment abroad than at home. When it was discovered in 1968 that this company had also illegally exported $20 million worth of arms to Africa and the Middle East, there was a public uproar, followed by an inquiry into Swiss arms exports by a special commission. The commission considered a total prohibition on arms exports but found that this would raise weapons costs for the Swiss army by up to 65 percent and would make the country still more dependent upon arms purchases from abroad, thereby endangering respect for Swiss neutrality. Tighter controls were placed over exports, but these were relaxed in 1979 after lengthy debate in the Swiss parliament.[83] In Switzerland, as in Sweden, restrictive policies on arms sales abroad are being essentially maintained, but they are also being loosened because of economic pressures.

NEW, THIRD WORLD SUPPLIERS

Apart from the arms-exporting states discussed thus far, there are several with small but well-established arms industries: Belgium, Italy, Canada, and Czechoslovakia. Belgium, which manufactures chiefly light arms, grenades, mines, and machine guns, is noteworthy because it exports 95 percent of its production. Its small arms are to be found throughout the world and are of a type that can easily be smuggled into strife-torn countries, such as Lebanon. Belgium has perhaps the least restrictive policy of all nations, yet, like those of the other countries listed above, its exports remain comparatively small, only 10 percent of those of France.

There are, in addition, a growing number of countries within the Third World that are creating indigenous arms industries. An estimated twenty-four developing countries produce weapons of some type.[84] This is one of the most important aspects of the contemporary proliferation of conventional arms. The development of the larger of these new arms industries, and their impact upon neighboring states and within recipient regions, are discussed more fully on a country-by-country basis in the next part; here we are interested in the trend in the context of its significance for the international trade in arms and the possibilities, at some point, for developing arms restraints among the suppliers.

Almost without exception, the larger of the new indigenous arms industries have been established for essentially political and security reasons rather than for predominantly commercial ones. Nations are motivated by the desire to reduce dependence upon outside suppliers in order to bolster their national security. Some countries perceive a threat to their interests, often to their very existence, and want to augment their self-sufficiency because of the perceived unreliability of outside allies: Israel, Egypt, India,

123

South Korea, Taiwan, and South Africa. Others are motivated less by perceptions of a security threat than by broad political considerations relating to their status within a region: Argentina, Brazil, Venezuela, and Indonesia. Some of the countries giving priority to the creation of domestic arms industries are pariah states which, because of their internal or foreign policies, find themselves in an inhospitable international environment. But although security and political considerations are dominant, the development of military technologies can have important spin-offs through the technical and managerial skills acquired and the general contribution to a country's industrial development. Brazil, for example, thinks of its arms industry as an important part of its national development program. It has chosen to forgo the purchase of first-echelon, advanced weapons from abroad in order to develop its own defense technology at home.

The creation of an indigenous arms industry usually involves an incremental process in which the transfer of knowledge and technology from a willing supplier is a critical element. The first step is often no more than acquiring the ability to service and repair imported weapons; this is followed by the assembly of components purchased abroad; a next critical step may be the production of arms, or parts of a weapons "package," under a licensing agreement. This is now widely practiced because it assures the purchasing nation that a major part of its money will be spent at home and will provide domestic employment. Supplier nations, in their competition with each other, often make their "deal" more attractive by offering to have part or all of the production done abroad. But this is also significant because the recipient acquires technical knowledge and experience through such licensing or co-production arrangements which will subsequently allow it to manufacture on its own. Indeed, in recent years, suppliers have become more reticent about entering into licensing arrangements that may in time have the effect of foreclosing future markets or give recipients sophisticated capabilities. This is one of the reasons the United States has been reluctant to allow Israel to co-produce the F-16. India has produced Soviet aircraft, including the advanced MiG-21, under license,

124

but has used the expertise acquired to design and build the Kiran, its own subsonic jet aircraft. The final step may be pure, indigenous manufacture. Trying to bypass any of these steps may be risky. Egypt sought to develop its own supersonic fighter in the 1960s, without possessing the necessary experience with less sophisticated aircraft, and abandoned the project after having built four prototypes. In subsequent years it turned its attention to seeking to co-produce the Mirage F-1 and the French-German Alpha Jet under licensing arrangements.

The extent to which co-production has taken hold is made evident from the following data. According to the U.S. Arms Control and Disarmament Agency, twenty-three developing countries participate in the licensed production of warships, twenty in military aircraft, ten in missiles, and seven in armored vehicles. Examples include the Indian Vijayanta medium battle tank licensed by the United Kingdom in 1965 and now produced 95 percent indigenously; Brazil's Xavante armed trainer, licensed by Italy in 1970; and Pakistan's anti-tank missiles, licensed by France and Germany and now domestically produced.[85]

Nations may enter the arms business to reduce their political or security vulnerability, but they will find themselves under growing pressure to export to maintain the economic viability of their defense industries. This has been the experience of Israel, which has developed a relatively large indigenous industry. To help finance its industry it aggressively promoted military exports, with considerable success; they rose from under $100 million in 1973 to over $1 billion in 1980. Other nations will seek to transfer arms in order to reduce research and development expenses and the unit costs of production. Another way to reduce costs is to manufacture arms collectively: the Arab Military Industrial Organization was founded by Egypt, Saudi Arabia, Qatar, and the United Arab Emirates for this purpose. It entered into an agreement with France for the creation of its own weapons industry and had ambitious plans to sell to other Arab countries. When, however, Egypt signed the Camp David agreement, Saudi Arabia withdrew its funding, and the organization collapsed.

125

The impact of the new indigenous arms industries upon the international arms trade has received a great deal of attention in recent times, much of which tends to overestimate its true importance.[86] While it is correct that more and more developing countries are producing arms of one kind or another, they are unlikely to be in a position to challenge the major producers and exporters. No developing country has yet become the principal arms supplier of another developing country. Moreover, most of these countries will be unable to achieve their aim of independence in arms. The weapons-producing Third World states are often the very countries that feel a security or political need for a higher arms capability; hence as they move up the ladder of technological sophistication they will want more advanced arms which will only be available from a few suppliers. Alternatively, they may shift their requirements from finished weapons of a simpler nature to technologies to manufacture advanced systems. As Israel has found out, self-sufficiency is illusionary. The growth in its exports has been more than matched by a growth in its imports of sophisticated arms. Thus, it is by no means clear that national arms production automatically reduces dependence.

Weapons of a lower or middle range of sophistication may become more readily available as they come to be manufactured by a growing number of states; this may create a new class of secondary suppliers in the global arms trade. But for advanced arms, nations will remain dependent throughout the 1980s upon the principal suppliers discussed in this part. Manufacturing advanced planes, missiles, and ships involves sophisticated components and subsystems, such as jet engines, guidance systems, and computers. This requires a technological infrastructure and resources that are in short supply in most of the developing world—skilled and experienced labor, engineering and technical know-how, special alloys and electronic components, and capital for large investments.

The claim, often heard, that the growth of indigenous industries will foreclose the opportunities for multilateral restraints on the transfer of arms may therefore be exaggerated. The new producers will make the situation more complex, but they may only change the overall picture marginally. Major and sophisticated weapons systems—the type whose transfer is most likely to lead to a real or perceived political change within a given region—will remain the province of only a few suppliers, especially the traditional Big Four. These countries will continue to lead and dominate the market. Thus the oligopolistic condition, which could in theory make a suppliers' agreement on the transfer of arms possible, exists. The problem, apart from the inhospitable nature of the East-West climate in the early 1980s, is how to make such restraints acceptable to the recipients.

PART THREE

RECIPIENTS

More nations wanting more arms is one striking characteristic of contemporary world politics. Proportionally, the largest increase in conventional weaponry has been in the Third World, which receives most of its arms through imports from the developed countries. The trend toward the increased purchase of advanced arms, which set in during the 1970s, is likely to continue and to be reinforced for the rest of the twentieth century, at a minimum. By one estimate, the value of major weapons imported by Third World countries has been increasing each year since 1974 at a rate of 25 percent (in constant prices).[1] In 1978, the most recent year for which we have data, 81 percent of global arms imports were by developing nations.[2]

The new demand for arms is the result of many factors, the most important one being the breakup of colonial empires following World War II and the multiplication of new and independent states. Between 1945 and 1980 the number of independent countries rose from approximately 60 to 150. The creation of a national military establishment, whether or not necessary for defense, has been a first order of priority for almost all of these nations, because the existence of armed forces under the command of the head of state is generally perceived as an important attribute of sovereignty. The quantity and quality of arms that a state possesses become a symbol of both its strength and its status. Their provision may also become an element in maintaining the loyalty of the armed forces to the political leadership. Indeed, the military system often provides a useful route to political power. Many Third World countries are led by military officers, or have influential military elites, who have a direct interest in the condition of the defense establishment. Most of these new countries, as well as older Third World nations, had a very low level of armaments as recently as the end of the 1960s.

But this should not suggest that the acquisition of weapons is based on narrowly defined interests or frivolity. The Third World has become the area of greatest instability, now that there

131

is mutual deterrence through nuclear weapons between the two superpowers. The arrival of a rough parity in their strategic nuclear capabilities, and relative stability in Europe underpinned by a theater nuclear equation, have served to shift much of the arena for competition and rivalry to the developing world. This has induced the Soviet Union and the United States, and to some extent their allies, to transfer arms as a type of proxy and avoid direct involvement. Many Third World countries are involved in regional conflicts that require arms. Of the more than 120 armed conflicts that occurred between 1955 and early 1979, all but 6 involved developing countries.[3]

Instability characterizes not only the relations among states within Third World regions but also the condition of politics within countries, whether it results from economic and social tensions created by the process of development or from the existence of continuing ethnic and religious conflict. Internal strife, sometimes breaking out in civil war, often leads to a demand for weapons. Finally, the erosion of the postwar bipolar system is resulting in a diffusion of power and the emergence of such important regional actors as India, Nigeria, Brazil, Iran, South Korea, Vietnam, Singapore, and Egypt. The military element is only one aspect of the new strength of these nations, and it is often secondary to their economic role; it is not, however, negligible. These "new influentials," as they have been termed by Zbigniew Brzezinski, have demonstrated their interest in possessing the accouterments of military power, and some have gone as far as to create their own small industries for the production of weapons.

Thus for various reasons—the perception of national security requirements based upon real conflict or perceived threat, the dominance of the armed forces within many countries, the availability of money in some oil-rich nations with which to purchase weapons, the interest of outside powers in arming their allies so as to wage war by proxy, and the general diffusion of power— the Third World is becoming far more heavily armed. The value of the sale of arms to the developing world almost tripled in constant dollars between 1969 and 1978, and this upward trend is

132

TABLE 3
25 LARGEST THIRD WORLD MAJOR-WEAPON
IMPORTING COUNTRIES, 1977–1980
in millions of U.S. constant (1975) dollars

Importing Country	Total Value	Percentage of Third World Total	Largest Exporter per Importer
Iran	3,446	8.7	U.S.
Saudi Arabia	3,133	8.0	U.S.
Jordan	2,558	6.5	U.S.
Syria	2,311	5.9	U.S.S.R.
Iraq	2,172	5.5	U.S.S.R.
Libya	2,107	5.4	U.S.S.R.
South Korea	1,987	5.0	U.S.
India	1,931	4.9	U.S.S.R.
Israel	1,778	4.5	U.S.
Vietnam	1,220	3.1	U.S.S.R.
Morocco	1,121	2.9	France
Ethiopia	1,086	2.7	U.S.S.R.
Peru	995	2.5	U.S.S.R.
South Yemen	964	2.4	U.S.S.R.
South Africa	950	2.4	Italy
Algeria	882	2.2	U.S.S.R.
Taiwan	737	1.9	U.S.
Kuwait	664	1.7	U.S.S.R.
Argentina	642	1.6	F.R. Germany
Brazil	641	1.6	United Kingdom
Egypt	594	1.5	U.S.
Indonesia	522	1.3	U.S.
Pakistan	512	1.3	France
Chile	482	1.2	France
Thailand	412	1.0	U.S.
Others	5,657	14.3	—
TOTAL	39,504	100.0	

SOURCE: SIPRI, *Yearbook of World Armaments and Disarmament, 1981*, p. 198.

continuing.[4] As noted earlier, more than three-quarters of the world arms trade is now to the Third World, whereas prior to the 1970s it was concentrated in transfers within the First and Second worlds.

Some observers have gone so far as to speak of the creation of a New International Military Order as an undesirable side effect of the yet-to-be-established New International Economic Order. They condemn the "militarization" of the Third World as leading to a neglect of basic social and economic needs.[5] Such characterizations are surely premature and misleading, for the developing countries remain far less armed than the advanced industrialized states.

Nevertheless, although the United States, the Soviet Union, and other developed countries account for most of some $500 billion now spent annually for military purposes, the Third World's portion of world military expenditures is increasing. During the 1970s Third World expenditures on defense grew from 16 to 23 percent of the global total. Military expenditures per capita remained level in the developed world, but in the developing countries—at a time of great population expansion— rose by one-third.[6]

The largest accumulation of arms has been in the Middle East, reflecting both the high degree of tension in the area and the history of four wars in recent decades, as well as the availability of oil money. During the 1970s there was a fourfold rise in the value (in constant dollars) of the annual import of arms. By 1980 the Middle East, including the Persian Gulf, was receiving 50 percent of all weapons transferred to the Third World. This led some observers to argue that the arms sales "problem" is solely a Middle East problem—but this is far too simplistic an analysis. Arms sales to Africa increased twentyfold from 1969 to 1978 and to Latin America tripled (again, in constant dollars).[7] Although the totality of their arms remains relatively small compared to the Middle East in absolute terms, the increases are quite significant in the context of the respective regions.

We examine, in this part, the politics of arms sales as viewed from the perspective of the recipient nations on a region-by-region basis. Particular attention is given to the Persian Gulf and Middle East for obvious reasons, but we then turn to other regions in the order of the magnitude of their imports: Asia, Latin America, and Africa. Political rivalries within a region, whether based on threats to a nation's security or on images of status, are often the motivation for the competitive acquisition of weapons and regional arms races.

Another important reason for this region-by-region approach stems from the opportunities for regional cooperation in the development of restraints on transfers into an area. The decision not to introduce certain categories of weapons into a region—nonarmament rather than disarmament—may be one type of restraint that could be agreed upon by the states within some regions or subregions. Another would be the control of levels of armaments. In preceding pages it has been argued that the best hope for international restraints on arms transfers lies with the suppliers. True, yet one principal way of structuring at least some supplier restraints is to limit transfers into a region. As we look at the politics of arms in each region we shall look for such opportunities, bearing in mind that to have any chance of success, controls must be acceptable to the states within a region. We are past the stage where the industrialized states can withhold technologies on a discriminatory basis with impunity. Yet there may well be identifiable incentives for countries not to purchase certain arms or go beyond set levels, especially if their rivals or neighbors agree to follow suit. A regional approach is being attempted in Latin America on a very limited scale by the Andean Pact countries in the Declaration of Ayacucho. In the Middle East, restraints on arms supplies to the confrontation states may be essential to the long-term durability of any future peace settlement.

135

MIDDLE EAST

The importance of the Middle East in world politics does not need elaboration. Four wars within the past three decades, and the continuing danger of the eruption of a new conflict, attest to its volatility. The region also provides more than half of the world's oil supply, giving it a unique economic significance. Oil is the lifeblood of the advanced industrialized states, and their dependence upon petroleum from the Middle East is acute. Western Europe receives over 60 percent of the oil it consumes from the Middle Eastern countries, and the United States has also become increasingly dependent upon them, importing more than 15 percent of its oil from the region. The rise in oil prices since 1973 has led to an enormous transfer of wealth to the oil-producing nations, making the viability of the world economic system dependent upon the OPEC countries and giving them considerable economic power.

More than oil and money is at stake, however. The Middle East has long been considered one of the most important strategic crossroads of the globe. Gateway to Africa and providing access to the Indian Ocean, it is an important North-South axis. The Mediterranean, linking Western Europe with the Balkans and flowing into the Black Sea, is also critical as an East-West axis. Tankers passing through the Straits of Hormuz from the Persian Gulf carry roughly one-third of the oil consumed by the non-Communist world. Iran's 1,250-mile-long border with the Soviet Union and its position adjacent to South Asia give it unusual geographic significance.

For these economic and geographic reasons alone the Middle East is bound to be viewed as a critical area by the United States and the Soviet Union. But it is, of course, the persistence of the Arab-Israeli conflict that gives the region its special salience. The

136

Middle East is considered by most thoughtful observers as the most dangerous area in the world, not only because of the deep religious antagonism that exists there, the mosaic of differences within the Arab world, or the propensity of the disputes to lead to armed conflict, but also because of the risk that a regional conflict will escalate to the global level through the involvement of the Soviet Union and the United States.

The transfer of arms into the Middle East has, in this context, been of extraordinary significance. Arms have been supplied by East and West in order to affect the Arab-Israeli military equation, either to create and maintain a military balance or—depending upon one's perspective—to give an edge to one of the parties in the conflict. Arms have been sent to gain influence and favor with the recipient states. This has been a factor in Soviet transfers to Syria and Iraq, as well as in American transfers to Iran and Saudi Arabia, for example.

And—not without irony—the assurance of the supply of arms has been a major ingredient in achieving political settlements. Thus Secretary of State Kissinger's 1975 promise to Israel of sophisticated weaponry, including the F-15 and the Lance missile, facilitated acceptance of the second Sinai disengagement agreement between Egypt and Israel.[8] By far the largest grant of arms to help make possible a political settlement occurred at the time of the signing of the peace agreement between Israel and Egypt in 1978. The United States held out the promise of military assistance to make agreement along the lines of the Camp David accords more attractive, raising the total amount to be given several times during the negotiations as a form of inducement. In the end, Washington pledged to furnish $4.5 billion in arms and related assistance over the following three years. Israel was to get more than half of this through Washington's undertaking to deliver 800 armored personnel carriers, 200 tanks, artillery weapons, Sidewinder air-launched anti-aircraft missiles, and Maverick anti-tank missiles. Advanced delivery on F-16s, as well as an increase in the total of F-16s from the earlier planned 80 to 130, were also included. Yet of more political significance was the American commitment to Egypt of approximately $1.5 billion in arms. Although this represented less than Sadat asked for—he wanted weapons equal in sophistication to those of Israel and asked for the F-16—it nevertheless marked the beginning, as Secretary of Defense Harold Brown noted, of a new arms supply relationship with Egypt.[9]

That the provision of arms should be so directly linked with the process of reaching a peace settlement struck many observers as an odd and puzzling development. Yet it is readily explainable. The United States is committed to the security of Israel, and the latter, in giving up the Sinai territory it considered a buffer, sought weapons to offset that loss. At the same time the United States wished to augment Egypt's sense of security, and the latter possessed a military establishment badly in need of modernization and upgrading. The Egyptian armed forces had received hardly any new supplies since Russian advisers had been expelled some six years earlier, and most of its aging Soviet equipment was rusty and not maintained. (Even Israeli officers recognized that their Egyptian counterparts had legitimate defense needs which had to be met and muted their objections.) The United States, in turn, had important political objectives in wanting even a limited Middle East settlement, and the parties in the dispute were able to play upon this in their dealings with President Carter. Thus it was that the promised arms supplies became part of the currency in the Egypt-Israel peace negotiations of 1978.

Role of the Superpowers (I):
The Soviet Experience in Egypt and Syria

The Soviet Union has seen the Middle East as an area of vital interest since the early 1950s. The proximity of the region to the U.S.S.R. is an important strategic consideration, as is Soviet reliance upon the Mediterranean for shipping and naval routes. NATO's southern flank is seen as something to be guarded against, as is the presence of American missile-firing nuclear submarines in the Mediterranean, while the Suez canal is important as the point of access to the Indian Ocean. The growing awareness within the Soviet Union of the limits of its own oil and gas reserves cannot help but augment its interest in the area, a concomitant being the unusual dependence of the West upon Middle East oil and the potential opportunity this gives Moscow to create serious difficulties for its opponents. Another factor motivating Soviet behavior in the area has been the ideological competition with the West and the opportunities for developing allies among the more radical states and political forces in the region through support of anti-Western regimes and movements for national liberation, including the Palestine Liberation Organization (PLO). Related to the direct benefits of establishing a presence in the region, therefore, has been the desire to balance, if not reduce, Western influence.

For these reasons the Soviet Union has sought the role of a major power in the area. Close relations were first established with Egypt, Syria, and Yemen in the mid-1950s. As the colonial regimes came to an end, emergent Arab nationalism turned more readily to the East than to the West, making easier the Soviet entrance. In time Moscow acquired naval facilities in Egypt and access to some in South Yemen and Syria, and established strong military links with Baghdad.

The great facilitator in all this was the Soviet willingness to sell arms to the Arabs. A Moscow-supported arms accord between Czechoslovakia and Egypt in 1955 was the first in a long and continuing history of weapons transfers to the Middle East. Following the Six Day War of 1967, Egypt and Syria were quickly resupplied, and the pattern of transfers was maintained during the so-called war of attrition from 1969 to 1970. During the 1973 war a Soviet airlift of arms to Egypt was inaugurated, and contrary to some impressions there was a continuing, though piecemeal, flow of arms for several years thereafter. This was on such a scale as to become economically costly to the Soviet Union, and during the 1970s it increasingly pressed the recipient states to pay for the arms in cash. This was especially the case for Iraq and Libya which had oil and could afford to pay. But it also applied to Syria whose economy was in better condition than Egypt's. Although fully reliable data are not available, by one knowledgeable estimate Soviet military equipment supplied to the Middle East between 1955 and 1970 represented up to 4.4 percent of annual Soviet defense production, and the percentage increased thereafter. Military assistance to Egypt alone accounted for 7.5 percent of the production of Soviet conventional weapons.[10]

The question to be asked is how significant and long-lasting the political influence these arms provided has been. Egypt has been the leading recipient of Soviet arms in the developing world. For a while the Soviet Union's military presence in Egypt was the largest Soviet presence outside a Warsaw Pact country. Between 1969 and 1972 the Soviets had access to six air bases, several ports, and dry dock and other naval facilities in Alexandria and elsewhere, as well as having approximately 20,000 military personnel in the country. This military presence enhanced the U.S.S.R.'s strategic position in the Mediterranean, with some of the air bases being used for naval patrol aircraft. Perhaps even more meaningful, being in the most populous state in the Arab world, it symbolized a Soviet political presence in the region. Egypt became, in effect, the linchpin of Soviet policy in the Middle East.

But we now know that relations between Moscow and Cairo were fraught with tension and hostility. Much of the ill-feeling was in fact generated by the question of arms transfers, as Egyptian officials constantly complained to their Soviet counterparts that they were not receiving all the weapons promised, and that shipments were often long overdue. The fact that the Soviets refused to deliver certain offensively oriented arms the Egyptians requested became another irritant. In addition, the sociological relationship that can develop between supplier and recipient became a source of difficulty. The massive Soviet presence in Egypt included an attempt to penetrate political, police, and military circles, without apparent success but leading to a characterization of the Soviet presence as "imperialist." Egyptians complained that the Soviet military advisers were heavy-handed, made no effort to understand local conditions and the Arab mentality, and were exploiting their assignments in Egypt for their own training purposes.[11] The Russian advisers were scornful of the Egyptian ability to handle weapons and openly displayed a patronizing and often racist attitude. Their expulsion in July

140

1972 and the curtailment and eventual denial of base facilities to Moscow were well received in Cairo, as was Sadat's *coup de grâce* four years later, when he unilaterally abrogated the Soviet-Egyptian Treaty of Friendship and Cooperation, a step that caught the Kremlin by surprise. Given the heavy economic cost of the investment in Egypt and, more important, the large commitment of diplomatic prestige, the benefits that accrued to Moscow were remarkably meager and short-lived. After the 1973 war Cairo began to look to the United States as its principal ally, and in a short time Moscow's influence became negligible.[12] (We turn to the present Western phase of Egypt's arms diplomacy subsequently.)

In Syria, as discussed more fully later on, the situation for the Soviets has been marked by ups and downs. Moscow has been Syria's primary arms supplier. After the 1967 conflict, and again after the 1973 war as its influence with Egypt faded, Moscow sought to cement its ties with Syria by shipping ever more sophisticated arms, including SAM air-defense missiles and MiG-23s. The same pattern could be seen in 1980 as a result of tensions between Iraq and the U.S.S.R. But relations between Damascus and Moscow have been far from smooth. President Assad has indicated annoyance at several Soviet attempts to interfere in Syria's internal affairs and has turned down Moscow's requests for naval and base rights, allowing in only a relatively small contingent of Soviet advisers. He has complained about not receiving all the arms he wanted, even though he was willing to pay cash for a substantial portion, and has asserted Syria's independence by diversifying its arms purchases to include Western suppliers and by keeping open channels with the United States despite Syria's declared position as a "rejectionist" state in the Arab-Israeli negotiations. That Moscow's influence has not been what it would have liked is hinted at in the reported complaint of a Russian ambassador in Damascus that the Syrians take everything from the Soviet Union except its advice.[13]

Thus, after more than twenty-five years of extensive involvement in the Middle East, much of it dependent upon a massive transfer of arms, the Soviet position remains precarious. Seen

141

from Moscow, the deterioration of its position during the second half of the 1970s must have looked especially bad. The U.S.S.R. was effectively excluded from the largest Arab country, a state to which it had made a commitment of resources unequaled in its activities in the Third World. Its influence was essentially restricted to the more radical and maverick actors in the area—Libya, the People's Democratic Republic of Yemen, and the PLO; relations with Syria and Iraq remained problematic. At the same time the Soviet Union became a bystander in the diplomacy of war and peace in the Middle East as the United States took on the role of mediator, first in the Sinai and Golan Heights disengagement agreements and then in the Camp David accords. Although the Carter administration was initially less inclined than its predecessor to seek to exclude the Soviet Union from the Middle East peacemaking process, and went so far as to sign a U.S.-U.S.S.R. declaration in October 1977 calling for a joint approach, the "Geneva route" for a comprehensive political settlement to include all the parties in the dispute simply proved impracticable. It was overtaken by Sadat's trip of November 1977 to Jerusalem and the ensuing diplomacy that led to the Camp David accords. Measured against the intrinsic importance of the region for Soviet interests, including Moscow's desire to make itself a power in the area at least equal in stature and influence to the United States, the record must surely be judged unsatisfactory. Indeed, there have been indications that important military and political leaders in senior Soviet echelons have questioned the wisdom of the large outlay of arms sent to the Middle East, provoking internal debate in the Kremlin on the subject.[14]

Role of the Superpowers (II):
The American Experience in Iran

The American interest in the Middle East stems from four basic considerations. The first is the fundamental commitment to the existence and security of Israel, a role the United States undertook when President Truman supported the creation of the state

142

of Israel. Second, the United States has sought to prevent Arab-Israeli armed conflict, not only to safeguard Israel, but also to avoid a direct confrontation in the area with the Soviet Union, which could have global consequences. Third, the continued flow of oil at stable prices from the Middle East has been a vital interest, which took on greater significance during the 1970s as the West's dependence on oil from the area grew. Fourth, Washington has sought to limit Soviet influence and presence in the region because of the high geopolitical stakes involved. These considerations have led the United States to play a major role in the area through diplomacy, and through economic and military forms of assistance.

The rationale for arms transfers to the states directly involved in the Arab-Israeli confrontation has been well understood: to safeguard the basic security of Israel and to seek to maintain a military balance between the opposing parties. This has led the United States to transfer arms to Arab states as well, not only to buttress their security but also to assist political processes conducive to a peaceful settlement of the dispute. Countering the Soviet arms supplies to its friends in the Middle East has also been a consideration. Thus, Jordan has been a traditional recipient of American arms because of Hussein's pro-Western stance, his moderate policies, and his willingness to deal responsibly with the Palestinian question—recent disagreements with Amman over its refusal to join the post–Camp David negotiations notwithstanding. Similarly, Egypt began receiving arms as it shed the Soviet relationship and entered into political negotiations. Saudi Arabia bought American warplanes as far back as 1957; this was seen as being of symbolic importance in cementing Washington's relationship with the critical oil-producing country. Only with the emerging impact of Saudi Arabia on the Middle East as a whole, and its purchase of sophisticated aircraft such as the F-15, did sales to that country begin to arouse concern.

American arms sales policy toward Iran was cut of different cloth, however. The failure to think through fully the implications and possible costs of the massive transfer of arms to Iran was a principal aspect of the debacle of American policy in that country and may have contributed to the creation of the conditions that led to the overthrow of the Shah. The final outcome of the revolution will not be evident for several years, but it is already clear that Iran has moved from being a close ally of the United States to being either an opponent or at least in a more neutral or "equidistant position" (to use the phrase of former Foreign Minister Ibrahim Yazdi of the Bazargan government) between the United States and the U.S.S.R.

Iran for some years was by far the largest recipient of American arms, and yet there was no carefully formulated U.S. policy on arms sales to Iran or the Persian Gulf states. That no well defined policy existed is more than a personal judgment; it is attested to by the fact that for years the American bureaucracy struggled but was unable to agree upon an authoritative document on the subject. The accepted view was that the United States had a major interest in a pro-Western and strong Iran, because of the strategic location of this populous and resource-rich country upon the periphery of the Soviet Union and between the Near East and South Asia. The flow of oil was seen as vital to the economies of the West. The sale of arms to the government of Iran, it was assumed, would help ensure the friendly relations upon which the supply of oil depended and would be a form of insurance against political instability in the country and the region as a whole. It would also help to recycle the large amounts of petrodollars which were paying for the oil.

Rarely asked, or adequately addressed, at the senior levels of government were questions whose answers might argue against the large-scale sale of arms. With Iran allotting roughly 25 percent of its general budget to military expenditures, what were the social, economic, and political strains being created by the rapid military buildup undertaken with purchased arms? Were the armed forces really able to absorb the highly sophisticated, state-of-the-art weaponry they were being sold? What was the true nature, imminence, and magnitude of the security threat to Iran against which the country had to undertake a massive defense effort? What would be the consequences of the Iranian military buildup upon the other states of the Persian Gulf and

144

upon stability in the area? Could it lead to an arms race or conflict in the region as Iran's oil resources approached depletion? Finally, and hardly asked at all, the simple question: how much is enough?

The Shah of Iran was America's friend in the region, and there was little disposition to question his judgments or long-term intentions. Doubts about the wisdom of arms sales to Iran were voiced in the Congress and in the press, and were known to exist in corners of the U.S. government, but they were not allowed to challenge the existing policy.[15] The suggestion, made by Senator Kennedy in 1975, that there be a moratorium on arms sales to the Persian Gulf until the executive branch provided an explanation of its objectives and policies in the Gulf was never given serious consideration.

We now know the reason for this. The approach of the Nixon and Ford administrations was set in May 1972 when the President and Secretary of State Kissinger told the Shah during their visit to Teheran that the United States would sell him any nonnuclear weapons system he wanted, including the advanced F-14 or F-15. It should be noted that this was before the oil crisis and the onset of the rise in the price of oil. Apparently, the thinking at the time was that with the British withdrawing from the Persian Gulf, Iran was to become its new "protector." This also fit in well with the Nixon Doctrine of placing greater reliance upon regional powers and their military forces. When Iran's oil revenues dramatically increased, beginning a year and a half later and leading to the enormous arms purchases, the policy was not reviewed.

This meant, in effect, that the United States was implicitly accepting Iran's own perception of threats to its security. It also accepted Teheran's assessment of the amount and level of sophistication of the military weapons its forces would require. Until 1977 there was little inclination to suggest restraints on Iran's buying spree, to question specific requests, or to discuss with Iranian officials the nature of their strategic requirements. In his memoirs Henry Kissinger tells us that Nixon ordered that "in the future Iranian requests should not be second-guessed."[16]

145

The presidential decision to supply Iran with all the arms it wanted was made without prior consideration within the government. It had the effect of exempting sales to Iran from the existing review processes within the State and Defense departments, thereby discouraging any incentives for restraints. In mid-1976 a special study, prepared on the scene for the Senate Foreign Relations Committee, concluded that U.S. arms to Iran were "out of control."[17]

When asked about the threat against which the nation was arming, Iranian officials drew a geopolitical map that could best be described as "*tous azimuts.*" A basic premise was that the Persian Gulf, with the world's greatest concentration of petroleum deposits, lying close to the Soviet Union and existing in a strategic vacuum, was highly vulnerable. It was to be expected that the Persian Gulf would become the center of power rivalry in future years, attracting the interest of covetous external states. Linked to this consideration was the "power vacuum" in the Indian Ocean and the consequent need for Iran to establish a naval presence to safeguard the Gulf and to patrol the sea lanes of communication—and the "lifeline" of oil—into the Arabian Sea and through the northwest quadrant of the Indian Ocean (from which the tankers moved on either to Japan and the Far East or around the Cape of Good Hope into the South Atlantic and on to Europe and North America).

The most compelling threat to Iran was perceived to be the Soviet Union. The Shah was especially sensitive to this because of the Russian invasion during World War II, which forced the abdication of his father, Reza Shah, and the Soviet reluctance to leave Azerbaijan after the war. It was recognized that Iran, alone, could not defend itself against a determined Soviet attack, but it could delay the drive and call upon the United States to come to its assistance. The generally pro-Western policy of the Shah was therefore seen as a form of credit with the United States, but it was also recognized by the Iranian foreign ministry to be an irritant to the Soviet Union, raising the level of hostility and in time perhaps tempting it to intervene. It was never to be forgotten that as the Soviet Union exhausted its oil fields, it would covet the petroleum of its neighbors.

To the west, Iran had a longstanding border dispute with Iraq with the real possibility of its turning into armed conflict as, in fact, occurred in 1980. Although tensions were alleviated by the signing in 1975 of a boundary accord on the Shatt al-Arab waterway, and by the decision to terminate support for the Kurdish insurgency in Iraq, Teheran continued to view well-armed Iraq as a potential enemy. It was often pointed out that on a per capita basis, Iraq's Soviet-supplied arms far exceeded those of Iran. To the east, there was cause for worry about a renewed conflict between India and Pakistan because of separatist tendencies in the Baluchistan regions of southeast Iran and Pakistan. Iran supported Pakistan, and provided it with military assistance, believing that a further dismemberment of that country would jeopardize its own security. Afghanistan was also of concern because of Soviet interest in the country and Kabul's support for the Pashu tribes' aspiration for independence from Pakistan, which added to the centrifugal tendencies in the region. Among the littoral states, Iran deployed forces to assist the government of Oman in putting down the rebellion in Dhofar province, and it seized the islands of Abu Musa and Tunbs. Such actions, viewed as necessary peacekeeping by Teheran, were seen by others as indicative of a desire to be the policeman of the Gulf and to treat it as a private lake. It was a reminder of the traditional rivalries and conflicts in the region with their deep roots in ideology, religion, and culture and of the basic differences between the Iranians who are Aryan and Shi'ite Muslims and the Saudis who are Arab and Sunnis.[18]

Of particular importance were the beliefs and perceptions of the Shah, who, far more than most heads of state in the contemporary world, single-handedly set the course of Iran's foreign and defense policy. The Shah thought of himself as a global strategist, and had a highly developed personal sense of Iran's interests and needs. It was necessary, in his view, for the country to follow an independent national policy to the maximum possible extent. Recognizing that Iran could never fully balance the Soviet Union, he nevertheless thought that it was possible to deter its expansionist drive through the acquisition of a strong defense capability. This would, in his words, at least place a "lock on the

147

door" of Iran. In his last years in power, when Iran was accumulating ever larger and more advanced quantities of arms, he came to regard the United States as a less certain ally. America was seen as so consumed by the Vietnam experience as to make it unreliable in the long-haul competition with the U.S.S.R. This criticism and growing pessimism extended at times to the West as a whole, which he characterized as overly permissive, failing to pay adequate attention to law and order, and in retreat. "If things continue on their present track," he told Arnaud de Borchegrave, "the disintegration of Western societies will occur much sooner than you think under the hammer blows of fascism and communism."[19] Closer to home, the Shah set for Iran the role of guardian of the security of the Persian Gulf. Some of Iran's armaments, such as the large fleet of hovercraft, were designed to provide a quick-reaction intervention force in the Gulf. An Iranian-sponsored proposal for a collective security arrangement in the Gulf was never accepted by the other states in the area, which were suspicious of Iran's intentions and the motivations behind its military buildup. With no agreement, Iran intended to be capable of going it alone.

Arms sales to Iran shot up during the 1970s. From 1950 to 1971, American sales were limited to a total of $1.2 billion, but during the next seven years the cumulative total jumped to about $21 billion. For 1977 alone the figure was $5.7 billion.[20] This made the American sales program to Iran the largest in the world. France, Britain, and West Germany also had large increases in their sales to Teheran, but aggregated, they were still far less than American sales. The list of weapons systems sold to Iran was seemingly inexhaustible. In addition to 225 F-4s and 41 F-5s, there were 80 F-14s and 160 F-16s, with 300 the final desired number, the last two being among the most advanced of the latest generation of American fighters. A strong interest in purchasing 250 F-18s, another advanced aircraft whose production was not yet decided upon, was also made clear. The Iranian air force was also to receive 7 AWACS planes—the only ones sold outside of NATO—and new long-range transport aircraft. It purchased an elaborate, modern air defense system using surface-to-air missiles, and over 900 military helicopters. The army had 1,800 ultramodern Chieftain tanks on order from Britain, a larger number and a more advanced model than Britain's own army had, in addition to 250 Scorpion light tanks to augment the 1,360 tanks (mainly American) already in the inventory. As for the navy, it was to receive 4 Spruance-class destroyers, the best in existence and in a model even more advanced than that being produced for the U.S. Navy, a substantial number of French missile-carrying patrol boats, Harpoon missiles, German and American submarines, and the world's largest hovercraft fleet.

By the mid-1980s, when most of these deliveries would have been made, Iran would have had ground forces roughly equivalent to those of West Germany, and a substantially better equipped air force. Plans for a $5 billion expansion of the navy, which were being formulated in early 1978 after those of the other services, included a large naval and air base at Chah Bahar, strategically located on the southeast coast. The buildup of the navy not only would have consolidated Iran's superiority over its Arab neighbors and its control of the Gulf, but would have given it a fleet presence in the Indian Ocean. All this would have made of Iran a regional superpower. It might well have amounted to the most rapid expansion of military power under peacetime conditions of any nation in the history of the world.

Iran's arms purchases, nominally under the control of General Hassan Toufanian, the vice-minister of war, were closely supervised by the Shah, who was a weapons buff and an avid reader of such journals as *Aviation Week and Space Technology*. There was never much doubt in Teheran as to who made the more-than-routine decisions on what to buy. As he told an interviewer, "The arms I choose. All the systems I choose."[21] At the same time, he was rarely discouraged by American officials in Teheran or Washington from buying expensive arms, at least until the Carter administration began applying some partial brakes. Nor were Iranian officials adequately informed by their American counterparts of the full extent of the training, logistics, and maintenance implications of the systems they were being sold, a matter that later led to serious problems. For the arms manufactur-

149

ers, and for their friends in the procurement branches of the U.S. military services who often competed against each other for sales to Iran as a means of lowering unit costs of their own purchases or as a way to recoup part of their research and development investment, it was, in the words of the Senate study, a "bonanza."[22]

The basic premise underlying America's almost unquestioning support for the Shah of Iran was that he was a rock of stability in a highly volatile region of increasing importance to the United States. The sale of arms to Iran in unprecedented amounts was primarily for the purpose of enhancing American influence in that country. It was not, by and large, the result of Washington's careful appraisal of Iran's defense requirements. There was little inclination in Washington to question the solidity of the Shah's position in his country until quite late in his regime, despite the discontent that surfaced from time to time as a result of the strains created by the process of rapid modernization. It was perfectly clear to many observers, moreover, that Iran was being run as a police state and that there were gross violations of human rights and widespread corruption. Despite these disturbing indicators, American policy under several administrations was to deal only with the government and to pay heed to the Shah's insistence that no attention be given to the opposition.

For these reasons the question of what some successor regime might do with the arms being stockpiled was essentially taboo. The failure to address this question was not due to chance oversight but to the willingness of the Washington bureaucracy to defer judgment on issues the political leadership found embarrassing or would rather not face up to. The United States, in failing to examine the possible long-term consequences of its arms sales to Iran, exhibited a degree of irresponsibility or shortsightedness seldom matched in the postwar period.

The assumption that the provision of arms bestowed influence remained unquestioned, or inadequately challenged, despite some contradictory evidence of the highest importance: the price of oil. The Shah took the lead in initiating the increase in the OPEC price in 1973 and subsequently was a "price hawk" in

150

supporting those members of the cartel who wanted to raise the per barrel price. It was perfectly obvious, but frequently overlooked, that he needed higher revenues from oil exports to pay for the expensive arms purchased from the West in the first place.

Did the massive sale of arms lead in a significant way to the Iranian revolution? It obviously would be a mistake to make a single-factor analysis, expecially in a situation as complex as the Iranian revolution. Yet the expenditures on arms contributed to the country's social, economic, and political strains. The Iranian defense budget rose rapidly during the 1970s, from $880 million in 1970 to $9.4 billion in 1977, a more than tenfold increase in current dollars. With 25 percent of the national budget being spent on the defense establishment, the opportunity costs in terms of economic development and infrastructure projects forgone were considerable. Spending on weapons manufactured overseas led to the curtailment of construction at home, which in turn contributed to unemployment. It also led to corruption, which fueled social frustration and public discontent. By 1978 every class of society had its grievances. The military was unpopular, for it clearly had received from the Shah, and was taking full advantage of, a privileged place in Iranian society. The expected benefits of modernization, such as better housing, health services, and education were insufficient and were being very unequally distributed.[23] This helped fan the religious reaction against modernization.

It is noteworthy, also, how little the Shah did to develop public support in Iran for his ambitious defense and foreign policies. There was little encouragement of the sort of debate that would clarify the need for the massive purchase of arms and the large military expenditures. Most of the Shah's pronouncements on the dangers facing the world were for foreign audiences. Thus the identification of his own citizens with his vision and goals was fragile. Indeed, to many the Shah appeared to be following the foreign policy interests of the United States rather than those of Iran. It was not clear why Iran had to be the policeman of the Gulf or why developments in the Horn of Africa were of importance to Iran. Thus when his position at home became threatened, the argument that his regime had to be preserved because of a hostile world had a hollow ring.

It was, in addition, far from clear that Iran was able to absorb the sophisticated weaponry it was being sold. The Shah was attempting to create a modern military establishment in a country that still lacked the technical, industrial, and educational base to provide effectively for such an establishment. This required large numbers of trained personnel capable of operating, maintaining, and servicing highly complex weapons. It also required the extensive logistics systems and support operations that must accompany such arms. Yet less than half of Iran's population was literate, and there were comparatively few persons with experience in handling technology. Because of the difficulties in assimilating the arms and support systems being purchased, it proved necessary to have a substantial number of Americans, both military personnel and civilians under contract, placed in the country.

The presence of up to 40,000 Americans in Iran by 1978, and a smaller number of West Europeans, the majority of whom were there for military-related purposes, served as a constant reminder of the dependence upon outside powers the Shah's policies had led to. As the subsequent Islamic revolution demonstrated, this was resented by many sectors of society, even though the image of sponsorship by outside powers may have been greater than the reality. Starting as early as 1973, there were occasional assassinations of American military officers and of employees of American defense contractors. The Shah's hated intelligence service, SAVAK, was thought by many to have American support, and it was noted that President Carter embraced the Shah in spite of his criticism of human rights violations in other countries. (On the other hand, the Carter administration did undertake some steps to support human rights in Iran, and these were later criticized for helping unleash some of the forces that led to the revolution.) No doubt, the opposition in the country found it convenient to exaggerate the American role in Iran, occasionally going so far as suggesting that the Shah was a puppet who was being kept in power by Washington. Nevertheless, it could not be denied that the United States strongly supported the Shah, that this was increasingly resented by those elements of Iranian society that came to power through the revolution, and that the arms transfer relationship between Teheran and Washington came to symbolize much of this.

Once in power, the revolutionary Iranian government lost little time in making an abrupt break with the arms-purchasing practices of the past. This actually occurred in several stages, for after the revolution began and the Shah was under siege, he indicated his intention to cut back on a part of Iran's existing contracts. An attempt to placate the opposition, these curtailments amounted to an admission that his arms purchases were unpopular. Because of the usually long interval between placement of an order and its delivery, as much as $12 billion of U.S. arms was still in the pipeline. The Bazargan government, following on some earlier moves in this direction by the Bakhtiar government, canceled most of the undelivered arms. This included the $2.5 billion contract with General Dynamics for 160 F-16s and the $1.3 billion order for 7 AWACS aircraft. (The loss of both orders had the effect of raising the price that European nations paid for these planes.) The order for Spruance-class destroyers was also curtailed, along with other sales for military items, although a portion of the orders, mainly for spare parts, was maintained for a time. Only after the seizure of the hostages at the American embassy did Washington stop all military sales to Iran. French and British contracts, including the United Kingdom's large order for tanks, were also canceled. In addition, the new Iranian government asked the United States if it would like to buy back some of the arms already delivered. These included the 80 F-14 Tomcats, which had been purchased for $3 billion and which were proving difficult to service, but nothing ever came of it. At one point the Saudis expressed an interest in buying Iran's F-14s, but the United States used its right of veto on transfers to third parties because the Saudis were already scheduled to receive the F-15.

The risk of what can happen to advanced arms once they are

153

actually transferred to another country was underlined by the F-14s. These planes are among the most advanced combat aircraft in the world. The Phoenix missile, with which the F-14 is equipped, is by far the best of its kind and is used in conjunction with another sophisticated technology, the Hughes weapons control system. Several hundred of these missiles, which cost about $250,000 each, were stockpiled in Iran. The chaotic situation there created deep worries in Washington that important weapons secrets could be compromised through the transfer of an F-14 with Phoenix missiles, or simply through the loss of associated operations and maintenance manuals. Any of these would be highly prized by the Soviet Union, which does not have as advanced air-to-air missiles or command and control systems.

Arms and Influence

The somewhat analogous experiences of the Soviet Union in Egypt and the United States in Iran are instructive with respect to the uncertain benefits of arms sales. One would not want to make too much of the parallels, which are limited. Yet for each of the superpowers these were its largest arms transfer programs up to that point. In each case the arms were sent for what was perceived at the time to be overriding foreign policy reasons, rather than economic ones. And in each case the desired result was ultimately not achieved.

The influence the transfer of arms was intended to provide was uncertain, and finally, transitory. The Soviet Union did not establish a permanent military base in Egypt, nor did it achieve through Cairo a political position in the Middle East. The United States did not make of Iran a military power capable of maintaining the strategic equilibrium in its part of the world. The bilateral relationships with the superpowers, in which arms transfers played an important role, created counterpressures in both Egypt and Iran which made the superpowers far less welcome. Ironically, in both cases, relations between recipient and supplier deteriorated so rapidly that diplomatic relations were broken in one case and became negligible in the other.

154

Still, American arms remain in Iran in large quantities just as Soviet weapons are in Egypt (even if in both cases, they are only partially operational owing to the lack of spare parts and other maintenance difficulties). Technology has outlived the political relationships. Arms may well remain in a country long after the political conditions under which they were provided have dramatically altered. The U.S. arms left in South Vietnam are another example. In transferring weapons the long-term risks and dangers must be weighed as carefully as the shorter-term benefits and gains.

Because of the continuing importance of the military balance in the Arab-Israeli conflict, arms transfers into the region will remain a critical aspect of the Middle East problem. As we have seen, arms sales may not bestow the influence or otherwise totally achieve the purposes the suppliers have in mind. But they are likely to remain closely intertwined with the diplomacy of the region and have a consequential role to play in the process of establishing, and then maintaining, a political settlement.

For this reason, the careful modulation of arms transfers to the Middle East is of great importance. Arms transfers are a useful instrument for promoting and nurturing the peacemaking process. To be sure, arms transfer restraints by themselves will not create a political solution to the complex Middle East problem. Accordingly, progress toward a settlement, whether comprehensive or, as is more likely, only partial, must depend upon political movement toward compromise and accommodation. But restraints may clear the way and facilitate the settlement. And *without* arms restraints to underpin a settlement, it is far less likely that a comprehensive peace will be stable or enduring.

Any type of arms restraint in the Middle East will have to take fully into account the interests of the states in the region. To a large extent this holds true in any region, but it is especially the case in the Middle East because of the high degree of military tension there compared, for example, to Latin America or even Africa. Moreover, although the outside suppliers could in theory agree to impose restraints on sales to the recipients, the long-standing network of political relationships between suppliers and

155

recipients makes the Middle East the least likely region in which such an approach would be feasible if it were opposed by the purchasing nations.

Accordingly, we must look at the perspectives and interests of the recipient states. Before we discuss any arms restraint concepts for regulating the flow of arms into the Middle East, we must examine the security perspectives of the nations in the area. This is done one nation at a time, for each has a unique set of interests, fears, and concerns, as well as a particular history of arms supply relationships.

Israel

Israel is the state in the Middle East with the most to fear in the sense that its very existence has yet to be acknowledged by any Arab state but Egypt. It has a strategically unfavorable location with its back to the sea, a long border, and a narrow land space for its population, which provides little territorial depth for defense. To this must be added the intangibles of historical experience and psychology. The preference some Israeli statesmen have often given to shorter-term, yet secure, solutions to problems over longer-term, more visionary yet inherently more risky, settlements is related to Israel's fundamental insecurities, which have deep roots in the history and experience of its people.

Nevertheless, Israel is militarily by far the strongest country in the Middle East. In its defense planning it aims to avoid a protracted war by putting the emphasis on offensive forces, notably air and armor, which are designed to disrupt and destroy an enemy quickly, and to keep the battle at a distance. The buildup of Israel's armed forces since the 1973 war has been marked. The war caught Israel off balance and demonstrated how advanced Soviet weapons in Arab hands, notably air-defense and anti-tank missiles, could neutralize for a time the previously dominant Israeli air force and armor. In the following years, Israel acquired impressive new capabilities. These included the F-15 aircraft and its own Kfir fighter, various air-to-surface and anti-tank precision-guided munitions, an increase of about 40 percent in the

156

tank force, and an even greater increase in naval forces. An additional though secondary factor was the improved combat readiness of the Israeli army, a response to widespread criticism, after the Yom Kippur War, of its prewar condition. The net result is that by 1978 Israel was already estimated to have combat capabilities about 50 percent above those of 1973. In contrast, Syria had only succeeded in rebuilding to its prewar level and Egypt remained slightly below.

Israel's strength is in substantial measure due to the United States, which, since Israel's creation, has been a major supplier of economic and military assistance. In many ways, America has been Israel's sponsor and protector, even though the latter role has not been embodied in written guarantees. Military assistance from the United States rose from $307.5 million in 1973 to $2.48 billion in 1974 following the Yom Kippur War, and came to $1.5 billion in 1976 and approximately $1 billion in each of the next two years. Most of this money was used to purchase American arms and military equipment. In addition, the United States promised at the time the Israeli-Egyptian peace treaty was signed in 1978 to grant Israel an additional $3 billion for new weapons, the construction of two air bases to replace those abandoned in the Sinai, and the removal of civilian settlements. Economic assistance has been less than military aid but also large. Combined American economic and military aid to Israel was on the order of $2 billion per year in the late 1970s and during the decade totaled approximately $18 billion, more than half in direct grants and the rest in long-term loans.[24]

Despite this close arms relationship, there has been a long-standing difference between American and Israeli defense planners regarding the Arab-Israeli military balance in the Middle East and the scale of the military threat to Israel. Pentagon officials compare Israeli forces with those of Egypt and Syria. They assume that Jordan would deploy only token forces, as in October 1973, because of its vulnerability to an Israeli attack that could easily overrun the country. Similarly, the assumption regarding Iraq and Saudi Arabia is that, at most, only small units would be committed to a conflict with Israel. The Arab forces are seen as

157

having serious deficiencies with regard to training, competent officers and military leadership, effectiveness of equipment, and adequate logistics and support systems. In contrast, Israel is seen as having a highly competent fighting force, well motivated and kept combat ready through effective mobilization plans and well-trained reserves. The peace treaty with Egypt should have the effect of further reducing the Arab threat to Israel.

Israeli officials, on the other hand, have quite another conception of the military balance. Israel, they argue, must be prepared to defend itself by launching rapid offensives into the territories of Jordan and Lebanon as well as Syria (and possibly Egypt). They believe that Iraq could well join forces with Syria, particularly should Egypt stay apart from a conflict. With the sale of F-15s to Saudi Arabia they began to regard it as a "confrontation state" because of the range of the aircraft; the Tabuk base in Saudi Arabia is about 150 miles south from the Israeli port of Eilat. (The proposed sale of AWACS surveillance planes and extra fuel tanks for these F-15s was seen as greatly increasing that threat.) Moreover, since Israel cannot hope to come near the Arab totals in manpower, they argue that it must maintain a qualitative edge in its weaponry.[25]

These differences in conceptions, especially as to what must be included in the total count of Arab forces, have led to different assessments of what arms Israel needs from the United States. Israel set forth its force goals and its request for U.S. arms in 1974 in a plan called Matmon B, which was followed in 1978 by Matmon C. The latter called for $12.5 billion in U.S. arms over the next eight years, leading Secretary of Defense Harold Brown to tell Israeli Defense Minister Ezer Weizman that the United States does not make commitments even for its own armed forces that far ahead. Both plans posited an all-encompassing view of the Arab threat as a base for Israeli armed forces requirements, which the United States did not accept. Accordingly, American planners have developed their own evaluations of the future strength of Arab forces and their threat to Israel in order to reach judgments on Jerusalem's requests for arms. Usually the United States has found itself arguing that the threat has been overesti-

158

mated and deciding that the list of requests could be pared down without harming Israel's ability to win a war. In American eyes, Israel has received over the years sufficient arms to maintain the military balance against any likely combination of Arab forces. A secret Pentagon study in 1979 reportedly concluded that Israel had enough military power to repel any Arab attack between then and 1984, and that any increase in the transfer of American arms to Israel beyond those already authorized would be destabilizing.[26]

The argument is often heard, particularly within the Arab world, that the United States should take advantage of Israel's dependence upon American assistance to exert leverage over its policies. Clearly the Israeli economy is very much dependent upon the infusion of money from abroad, whether in the form of government assistance or the result of the generosity of private supporters. American military assistance and credits cover about half of the defense budget.[27]

Yet the leverage this provides is limited. The tough stance of the Begin government in the protracted negotiations that ultimately led to the 1978 accords, or the subsequent "autonomy" negotiations on the occupied areas, is testimony to this. Any American president, moreover, will be conditioned in his approach toward an Israeli government by the existence of the American Jewish community and domestic political considerations. Over the years, Israel's leaders have given a high priority to cultivating, and maintaining close bonds with, that community as well as with Israel's supporters in general.

The United States has sought on occasion to induce Israeli flexibility in the Middle East peace negotiations through either granting or withholding arms. The Egyptian-Israeli disengagement accord of January 1974 was accompanied by a Memorandum of Understanding by which the United States committed itself to be "fully responsive on a continuing and long-term basis to Israel's military equipment requirements," and during the 1975 negotiations on the second Sinai disengagement agreement the United States promised Israel a $1.5 billion military aid package.[28] Arms may also be withheld to achieve political ends. In the

159

spring of 1978 the Carter administration had a negative attitude toward the Matmon C proposal because it did not wish to give new arms to Israel that could have the effect of complicating the quest for success in the peace negotiations. This, however, is a sensitive matter, and there is a tendency to disavow in public any link between ongoing aid relationships and Israeli political concessions. Thus Vice President Mondale stated in June 1977 that "we do not intend to use our military aid as pressure on Israel. If we have any differences over military aid . . . it will be on military grounds."[29]

Throughout most of the 1970s the accepted wisdom in Washington was that for Israel to feel sufficiently secure and confident to make the territorial concessions necessary for a peace settlement with its Arab neighbors, it must receive large quantities of arms and military aid. This was the rationale used to justify many arms sales.[30] Yet it is not clear that strength through arms has made Israel more flexible or willing to accept some risk in the negotiations. When Israel's leaders felt strong or self-confident, they would resist pressures for changes in the status quo. This dilemma was aptly summarized by Secretary of State Kissinger: "When I ask Rabin to make concessions, he says he can't because Israel is weak. So I give him more arms, and then he says he doesn't need to make concessions because Israel is strong."[31]

For its part, Israel has sought to reduce its dependence on the United States for weapons. This aim has been approached in two ways, through the creation of its own arms-manufacturing industry and by the purchase of arms from the United States so as to maximize its self-sufficiency. Thus, for example, in the Matmon C request of 1978, Jerusalem asked for such a large quantity of ammunitions that it would have been capable of fighting an extensive Middle East war without the need of resupplies from the United States; in the 1973 war Israel could not continue without the large-scale and rapid airlift from America. Israeli officials, especially under the Begin government, sought to reduce their vulnerability to American pressures. The United States, on the other hand, has been reluctant to grant arms on a scale that would give Israel full freedom of action so as to be able, for example, to wage a preemptive or offensive war.

160

*Israeli
Arms
Industry*

The Israelis have built up their own arms industry with the political aim of maximizing independence very much in mind. De Gaulle's arms embargo following the Six Day War in 1967 and the British embargo on spare parts for the Centurion tanks in 1973, as well as the exercise of American pressure on Israel in the latter stages of the Yom Kippur War, are cited as having reinforced awareness of the risks of dependence upon outside suppliers. Such vulnerability to political pressures became increasingly undesirable as Israel entered into protracted political negotiations with its Arab neighbors.

Accordingly, the development and expansion of the Israeli arms industry were matters of priority during the 1970s. By the end of the decade Israel was manufacturing 40 percent of its own weapons, and was self-sufficient in some areas, such as small arms, bombs, and some types of guided missiles. Approximately 20,000 persons are employed by the arms industry; it is divided into the Israeli Aircraft Industry which is owned by the government even though it has an independent board, and the Israeli Military Industry which is run by the Ministry of Defense and produces a wide array of surface battle weapons. The list of Israeli manufactured arms is impressive and includes the Shafrir air-to-air missile, the Gabriel sea-launched missile, the Chariot tank, and most notably the Kfir fighter which is modeled after the French Mirage III.

As the industry has grown so have its sales abroad. With such a relatively small home market, exports become important as a means of reducing the unit costs for weapons given to the Israeli forces. From a total well under $100 million in 1973, exports climbed to over $1 billion in 1980. Most of the exports have been to countries in Latin America and Africa, and a number of sales have been criticized. Weapons have been sold to South Africa and Chile, even though these governments have been subject to Western arms embargoes, as well as to other repressive regimes such as Somoza's in Nicaragua and Videla's in Argentina. The broad cooperation in arms between Israel and South Africa has become a matter of international concern, with occasional talk of a Pretoria-Jerusalem axis between two states that are both pariahs within their own regions. In exchange for gunboats and missiles sent to South Africa, as well as sensitive electronic surveillance systems which could be used along South Africa's borders in dealing with guerrillas, Israel has received raw materials needed by its steel industry and the rough diamonds that have made its cut and polished diamonds industry the world's largest. As many as sixty countries have purchased the famed Uzi submachine gun, including the United States, which uses it for the White House secret service.

Despite these successes, it is most unlikely that Israel will achieve a level of self-sufficiency adequate to its political needs. Relatively unsophisticated weapons can be manufactured cheaply because of labor costs about 40 percent lower than those of the United States and West European suppliers. Such arms have sold well overseas. But the markets for exports may not expand much in the future because of political considerations. Many of the countries that are dependent upon oil from the Arab states are reluctant to purchase arms from Israel, and, of course, no OPEC nation will be a customer. An even greater problem arises from the growing sophistication of modern weaponry. Such arms require high technology components which are very expensive to develop. Israel's response has been to seek to combine Western technology with domestically made components. Thus the Kfir fighter adds a General Electric engine, made for the U.S. Phantom F-4, to an Israeli manufactured airframe. Such co-production arrangements have their disadvantages, as the Israelis found out to their dismay when the Carter administration refused to allow Israel to export 24 Kfir fighters to Ecuador because of arms restraint considerations in Latin America.

American officials have become increasingly concerned in recent years that Israel could acquire knowledge of sophisticated military technologies from the United States and then export Israeli arms containing such technologies, thereby effectively circumventing American restrictions. They have, accordingly, looked askance at some requests for "technical data packages," and Washington has turned down repeated requests for licensing arrangements to co-produce the F-16 in Israel. (Israel will nevertheless receive at least seventy-five F-16s, as agreed upon in the

162

1978 three-nation "plane package." Ironically, the downfall of the Shah sped up delivery to Israel, as it received aircraft originally intended for Iran.)

This has led Israel to examine the possibility of manufacturing its own very advanced fighter for the 1980s, a plane that would be comparable to the F-15 and F-16, or even their successors. The production of the proposed Arieh fighter was recommended in February 1978 by a subcommittee of the Knesset's Defense and Foreign Affairs Committee on the grounds that it was "imperative to take into account situations where supply sources might be cut off for Israel which would deprive her of essential arms for preserving military and political freedom of action."[32] The argument for the Arieh was that it was necessary to increase both the reality and the image of Israel's self-reliance. Yet the economic arguments against the Arieh overpowered its political attractiveness. The research and development costs could have reached well over $1 billion, even though they were estimated at $440 million by its supporters, and were clearly prohibitive. Production runs for the Israeli air force would have had to remain quite restricted in comparison to the normal production runs for American planes, thereby raising unit costs. And the export market would also have been limited, either because of the political consideration involving sensitivity to the reaction of the OPEC countries or because of the inability to compete in price and quality with the major suppliers. Finally, it might still have been impossible wholly to avoid relying upon advanced technology from abroad. In early 1980, plans were unveiled to produce a less advanced fighter, known as the Lavi, as a successor to the Kfir fighter. This was clearly a compromise solution. By developing its "own" aircraft, Israel, it was suggested, would not need to purchase an equivalent American plane, and it would be possible to use the nation's design and development capability. Yet the Lavi will require an American jet engine, the General Electric F404, as well as other high technology items.[33] It is hoped that the Lavi will become a major export item, but its sales will be subject to American restrictions.

Israel's desire to enhance self-reliance through a national arms industry, and the failure to achieve true autonomy by shedding its dependence upon outside supplies, are the counterparts to America's predicament. The United States provides much of the political, military, and economic support that guarantees the survival of Israel and yet has a limited amount of leverage over its policies in the Middle East. Such is the nature of power and influence.

Egypt

Egypt's quest for arms has a long history and is closely related to the shifts in its foreign policy. We have earlier discussed the arms relationship with the Soviet Union, which began in 1955 and lasted for approximately two decades. It should not be forgotten that this turn to the East was preceded by six years of disappointment in seeking arms from the West. Following the Palestine War of 1947–1949, Egypt sought arms from the United States, Britain, and France, a search that was reinforced after Nasser came to power in 1952. Because of British concerns about the future status of the Suez Canal, the policy of the United States to defer to Britain in this domain, and the Western attempt to regulate the supply of weapons going into the area in conformance with the Tripartite Declaration of May 1950 (which is discussed later), Nasser never received the arms he felt he needed for the confrontation with Israel. It was this frustration that led to the arms accords with Moscow.

Sadat's objective became to break the arms relationship with the Soviet Union and to rely instead on the West for arms. Since at least the spring of 1976 he has been actively looking for new arms with which to reequip the 500,000-man Egyptian forces. Because of the Soviet refusal to send needed spare parts, Sadat characterized much of the equipment of the Egyptian armed forces as "nothing but scrap." Although his description was a considerable exaggeration, one well suited to win Western sympathies, it nevertheless underscored the need for new weapons. In April of 1976 Sadat went to Europe to shop for arms. The warmest welcome was received in France, where there was a

164

discussion of purchasing 40 Mirage F-1s and 120 Alpha Jets. In Italy the possibility of buying anti-tank and anti-aircraft missiles as well as communications equipment was explored. West Germany refused to sell any arms directly, in accordance with its policy of not transferring weapons to zones of conflict, but Bonn did not object to the possibility of a French sale of the Alpha Jet which is co-produced with Germany. Earlier, soundings had been made in Britain regarding the availability of some 200 Jaguar strike aircraft, a number of Hawk jet trainers (which can also be used for attacking ground targets), and various missiles. Perhaps most interesting was the visit to Yugoslavia, which had over 100 MiG-21s and had started a plant to produce spare parts for that plane's engine. The Egyptian air force's MiG-21s and 23s, no longer benefiting from the maintenance of the Russian technicians who had been withdrawn, were in deplorable condition, with many actually grounded. An attempt to purchase spare engine parts from India, where the MiG-21 was being produced under license, failed to gain the approval of Moscow, which threatened New Delhi with the loss of its licensing arrangement—hence, Sadat's visit to Tito, who was not seen as being as susceptible to Soviet pressure as the Indian government.

Sadat's European trip did not lead to much in the way of concrete results but it illustrates the attempt to diversify Egypt's arms purchases. Until the "plane package" of 1978, in which Egypt was sold fifty F-5s with the understanding that Israel and Saudi Arabia were also to receive aircraft, by far more advanced, Cairo received very little from the United States. American administrations were reluctant to begin a true arms relationship with Egypt, even after the Soviet ties were cut, because of the view that Congress, always sensitive to Israeli concerns, would not permit it. Hence, despite Sadat's repeated requests, only insignificant "nonlethal" arms were approved by Washington, with the largest sale being for six C-130 Hercules transport aircraft. (This total was later augmented to twenty early in the Carter administration.) Egypt did, however, receive jet fighters from China—which illustrates some interesting dimensions of the global arms trade. Beijing wanted to examine a Soviet

MiG-23, with the apparent aim of manufacturing a Chinese version. Sadat made it available, as a "small gesture of Arab hospitality," and in exchange was given forty Shenyang F-6s, a Chinese version of the MiG-19.[34] China has also made available technicians to assist in the maintenance of Egypt's MiG-21s.

Between 1976 and 1979, West European countries were the largest suppliers of arms. Far more sales were announced than were actually consummated—a persistent pattern in the European-Egyptian arms relationship—but contracts were signed for several weapons systems. Britain was to supply Westland Aircraft's Lynx helicopters and British Aircraft Corporation's Swingfire anti-tank guided missiles, and Vosper-Thorneycroft was to overhaul the Egyptian navy's Russian-built missile boats. Rolls Royce was to help refurbish the MiG-21 engines. Britain was the leader, but France was not far behind. An accord was signed by the Egyptian minister of defense, General Abdel-Gany Gamassy, in Paris in 1978 for a range of French arms, including the Gazelle helicopters and the Alpha Jet. That few European weapons were in Egyptian hands at the end of the decade was a reflection of the economic and political uncertainties that surrounded most of these deals, but an important exception was the forty-six Mirage III fighters which had been transferred to Egypt by Saudi Arabia and Libya at the time of the 1973 war.

Yet it was American arms that Sadat really wanted. His reasons were not merely that they might be technologically superior in some cases, or that they might be given or sold on more favorable terms. More important was their political symbolism. Sadat took a major gamble in evicting the Soviets and placing all his eggs in the American basket, a gamble whose seriousness and risk were magnified when he signed the Camp David agreement against the wishes of most of the other Arab states, thereby isolating himself. American arms would be a visible proof that the United States had become Egypt's "partner," as he was asking it to be, in the Middle East.

Part of the motivation for seeking American arms was therefore related to Sadat's political concerns at home. Many influential Egyptians, even though they were no friends of either

Moscow or Baghdad, thought it a mistake to break with the Soviets and to alienate a good part of the Arab world. Some of these critics were in the military hierarchy. Sadat needed new arms not only because the Soviet weapons were aging and rusty, but to keep his professional officers loyal and content. The military establishment in Egypt, as elsewhere in the Middle East, can be a potent political force. (It should not be forgotten that Sadat himself was the beneficiary of a military coup that brought Nasser to power.) The receipt of American arms would be a demonstration that Sadat's policy of working with Washington could produce direct and concrete dividends.

Another motivation, of a strategic character and yet quite separate from the need to have armed forces ready for any conflict with Israel, was not well understood in the West. Sadat had a vision, or dread, of Egypt being encircled by hostile forces. A heavily armed, Soviet-supplied Libya under the radical regime of Colonel Qaddafi was a worry. An even greater source of concern was the perceived Soviet inclination to stir up regional turmoil in such places as Ethiopia and South Yemen; this could then lead to problems elsewhere in Africa, especially in Sudan on Egypt's doorstep. After the fall of the Shah, Sadat was worried about the spread of a revolutionary ideology. Adequate arms were therefore needed to provide a hedge against radical or Marxist forces to the south or west in a volatile region.

Finally, following the revolution in Iran, Sadat suggested that Egypt might logically replace Iran as America's surrogate in the Middle East. Secretary of Defense Harold Brown, on a visit to Cairo, was told that Egypt, having the largest army in the region, would promote stability and help police the region in exchange for an infusion of American arms. Such a rationale had to remain problematic, however, as long as Egypt remained an isolated state within the Arab world.

Sadat was not shy about asking for American arms, especially after his path-breaking trip to Jerusalem and the warm response his initiative received in the United States. In a speech before the Egyptian parliament following the breaking off of the Egyptian-Israeli-U.S. political negotiations in Jerusalem in January 1978,

167

he declared that Israel was able to take a tough stand on the retention of the Israeli settlements in the Sinai because of its large stockpile of American arms. Sadat indicated that he would ask the United States for "every armament" that it had transferred to Israel. They would not be used to attack Israel, but to give Egypt "equivalent bargaining power." When Sadat subsequently went to Washington, he said that he wanted F-15s and F-16s, not just the F-5s, which he described as "tenth rate." Israel, he said, should not be allowed to "monopolize" close arms relations with the United States.[35]

What may have appeared as bravado in 1978 looked more like reality by 1980. After the signing of the Camp David accords, Egypt became an ever increasing beneficiary of American arms. In time, the scale of U.S. arms assistance could come to equal the Soviet commitment of a decade earlier. As part of the Camp David package, Egypt received $1.5 billion in military credits. This was used to purchase 35 Phantom F-4s with Sidewinder and Sparrow air-combat missiles, 500 Maverick air-to-surface missiles, Hawk air defense systems, 800 armored personnel carriers, and other weapons. The displeasure of the Saudis with Camp David led them to withdraw their earlier offer to finance F-5Es for Egypt, made at the time Saudi Arabia was promised the F-15s, but this loss was more than compensated for by the offer of the more advanced Phantom F-4s. In early 1980 the Carter administration presented the Congress with Project Peace Vector, under which Egypt was to receive an additional $1.1 billion in military credits in the following two fiscal years. By far the most significant element of this, however, was the announced intention to allow Cairo to purchase both the F-15 and the F-16 in the future. This would "open the door," in the words of the Egyptian minister of defense, Lieutenant General Kamal Hassan Ali, to what was estimated as a needed $5 billion to $10 billion arms-modernization program, as the United States reportedly would no longer restrict the types of weapons that Egypt could choose.

Egypt has thus achieved symbolic equality with Israel and Saudi Arabia. Only those two countries have the F-15, and Saudi

Arabia has not been allowed to add the F-16 to its F-15s. As of 1980, Cairo only planned to purchase, with U.S. credit, forty of the F-16s, having been told that the simultaneous sale of both planes would arouse strong congressional and Israeli opposition, but it will retain the F-15 option. Thus, Sadat has succeeded in using cooperation with the United States in the Camp David process to achieve equal rights in the American arms market. At a military parade in 1979 marking the last Arab-Israeli war, the first American arms, including some F-4 Phantoms, were put on display. The minister of defense spoke of the new military cooperation with the United States as a great achievement which would show its effect in subsequent years, noting that "we have succeeded in confronting the challenge imposed upon us by the Soviet Union's refusal to supply arms after the 1973 war."[36] As supersonic jets streaked across the sky there was a parade of border guards astride camels.

A far-reaching defense relationship appeared to be in the making. The United States, concerned by developments in the Persian Gulf and Southwest Asia, began looking for bases in the Middle East that could be used to project its military power. Egypt offered the use of naval facilities at Ras Banas on the Red Sea and an air base at Cairo West, to which U.S. Air Force units were deployed on a rotational basis. In the summer of 1980 a U.S. Air Force squadron of F-4s spent three months with Egyptian pilots training on the same plane in joint exercises involving simulated combat missions—these were the same pilots who formerly flew Soviet MiG-21s—and U.S.A.F. Chief of Staff General Lew Allen announced that future deployments might include F-15s and B-52 strategic bombers. Aircraft used in the American hostage rescue attempt in Iran flew out of Cairo West, as may have American AWACS. For their part, the Egyptians appeared to be pleased to be the ally of the United States in helping support Western strategic interests in the Middle East. Their military leaders also spoke of the need for $5 billion in U.S. weapons to reequip their armed forces. The Reagan administration shortly after coming into office agreed to explore the development of a five-year plan for upgrading Egypt's armed forces. When Sadat

169

came to Washington in August 1981, he asked for 100 to 150 more F-16 fighters.

The question that all this raised, however, was whether some day the United States could find itself in a situation comparable to its experience in Iran. (There is one big difference—this time the United States is paying for the arms!) The American involvement in Egypt has become increasingly open-ended. Yet Egypt does not have a clearly established method of transferring power from one leader to another. No one can foretell the turn of Egyptian politics or foreign policy after Sadat. And there is absolutely no way of knowing how the arms will be used once Anwar Sadat is no longer on the scene, a fact that cannot help but make the Israelis nervous.

At the same time that Egypt sought to diversify its source of arms, it also wished to reduce its dependence upon overseas suppliers. This was the aim behind the ambitious plan to establish the Arab Military Industrial Organization, later renamed the Arab Organization for Industrialization (AOI), for the indigenous manufacture of arms. The creation in Israel of an arms industry was perceived by many Arab leaders as potentially leading to an important structural change in the Middle East conflict, reducing Israeli dependence upon the United States in a manner dangerous for them. Through its experience with the Soviet Union, Egypt had learned many lessons regarding the dangers of dependency. Along with its ardent search for arms from the West, Egypt also wished to achieve the maximum degree of autonomy.

The AOI was established in May 1975 by the governments of Egypt, Saudi Arabia, Qatar, and the United Arab Emirates. Under the direction of Ashraf Marwan, the dynamic son-in-law of former President Gamal Nasser, its board consisted of the defense ministers of the sponsoring countries, and its headquarters were located in Cairo. Most of the factories were to be located in Egypt, although in 1978 plans were made to build plants for missiles and electronics in what was to be a specially created city in Saudi Arabia. About 17,000 Egyptians were employed in factories outside Cairo, but all the money came from Saudi Arabia and the United Arab Emirates. An initial capitalization of $1 billion was later increased by 40 percent, and there was discussion of a $4 billion to $5 billion industry.

From its inception, the AOI was both an Egyptian weapons industry and something wider, designed to serve other Arab states. It was the first major attempt in the Arab world to build weapons. The development of an Arab arms industry, according to Sheik Khalifa Bin Zayed, commander of the armed forces of the United Arab Emirates, "was a vital necessity for the peoples of the Arab nation to promote their own forces and break the weapons monopoly of the advanced countries."[37]

There were two difficulties with this vision, however. The AOI never reached out to include the more radical Arab states such as Syria, Iraq, or Libya, all of which were oriented principally toward the Soviet Union for their weapons purchases. This was to be expected. Far less predictable was the severity of the break between Saudi Arabia and Egypt following the signing of the Camp David agreements. In May 1979 Saudi Arabian Defense Minister Prince Bin Abdul Aziz angrily announced the withdrawal of his government, Qatar, and the United Arab Emirates from the AOI, thereby effectively making the organization moribund.

Second, it proved to be quite difficult to create in Egypt the capability to produce weapons of a middle-level technology even with the assistance of willing Europeans. Paris and London newspapers were full of announcements of plans that never came to fruition. Thus, highly touted intentions to co-produce 200 Mirage F-1s in Egypt were abandoned in favor of a future assembly of the Alpha Jet and the eventual co-production of the Mirage 2000. The engines of the British Lynx helicopter were to be installed at plants in Egypt. The Swingfire anti-tank missile of the United Kingdom was also to be co-produced. None of these weapons was actually produced in Egypt by the time the four-nation consortium dissolved in 1979. The single exception was the beginning of the production of jeeps through an assembly arrangement with the American Motors Corporation.

The experience of Egypt—the most technologically advanced and populous Arab state—indicates some of the problems in set-

171

ting up an indigenous arms industry. The slow progress of the
AOI after its initial organization was partially owing to the lack
of both trained personnel and an adequate technological base. In
addition, when the organization was put under strain the
required political consensus proved to be lacking. Although
Egypt alone, or a revived consortium, may some day succeed in
manufacturing arms, the Middle East countries will continue to
be highly dependent upon military assistance from suppliers outside the region, whether in the form of aid in the assembly or
construction of weapons or through the outright sale of the more
sophisticated arms.

Jordan

Perhaps no country better illustrates the fragility of a Middle
Eastern state totally dependent upon the outside supply of arms
than Jordan. Since the end of the British mandate in 1946, the
existence of Jordan has rested on the twin pillars of the Hashemite monarchy and the military establishment. The relative stability of the kingdom, as represented by Hussein's reign of more
than a quarter-century, is the result of the harmonious balance
between these two institutions. The 70,000-man Jordanian army
is the successor to the famed Arab Legion formed by the British
in 1923 under General Sir John Bagot Glubb, the legendary
Glubb Pasha. British traditions and customs are still very much
in evidence. Although as much as half of Jordan's 3 million population is made up of Palestinians, either residents or refugees,
the army is essentially composed of soldiers of Bedouin origin
who have been loyal to the Hashemite monarchy.

Jordan is a small and highly vulnerable state, susceptible to
inner subversion from the large Palestinian element and outer
subjugation by a far stronger Israel as well as an occasionally hostile Syria. Under Hussein the armed forces have become the most
important political institution in the country. The king himself
is a soldier, a graduate of the Royal Military Academy at Sand-
hurst in the United Kingdom, with an avid personal interest in
strategic matters. He has a special interest in aircraft, and it is

said that he will not allow any type of plane to be bought until he has had the opportunity to test it himself.

Hussein has not tried to hide his intention of taking "good care" of the armed forces, in part to assure their fidelity, which has not been taken for granted. Under Hussein the army has grown in size and prestige, yet its armaments remain far more modest than those of many Middle East countries. In contemporary Jordan's first decade, Britain was the primary source of arms; but after 1957 as the British influence in the Middle East decreased, the United States began to take up this role, first through financing London's arms transfers and then by direct U.S. grants or credit sales. In the late 1950s the Eisenhower administration concluded that it was critically important to maintain Hussein's regime in power and that this would require direct economic and military aid.[38] After then, successive American administrations supplied arms on that assumption, while Hussein became dependent upon Washington's support. For many years Hussein has been viewed as one of the more moderate Arab leaders in the Middle East struggle.

Accordingly, Jordan has been supplied with three squadrons of F-5s and one squadron of the earlier F-104s as well as helicopters. The army has about 550 tanks, 200 of which are British Centurions, the rest being M-47s, M-48s, and M-60s of American origin. Jordan's vulnerability was amply demonstrated in the 1967 war, when it not only lost the West Bank but had its entire air force wiped out in the first day of combat. After being forced, in effect, to sit out the 1973 war Jordan put priority upon the acquisition of an air defense system. The U.S. Congress was reluctant to make this available because of the opposition of Israel. But Hussein had the support of the Saudis who were prepared to pay for the anti-aircraft missiles. For the first time he turned to the Soviet Union, visiting Moscow in June of 1976 to discuss the purchase of an air defense. The gambit paid off, for neither Israel nor the Congress was willing to facilitate a Soviet inroad into such a strategically situated country, and the transfer to Jordan of fourteen batteries of Hawk anti-aircraft missiles was thereupon approved.

In persisting in the quest for air defense, even though it could

173

be overwhelmed by the Israeli air force, Hussein was responding to pressure from the armed forces to provide them with modern arms like those with which other Arab governments had equipped their forces. The Jordanian military leadership was humiliated by the loss of the West Bank and the defeat of the nation's forces in 1967 as well as by its inability to participate in the 1973 war. It watched the resupply of Syria by the U.S.S.R. and of Israel by the United States with some envy. For his part, Hussein became ever more dependent upon the army's support when he was seriously challenged by Syrian-supported Fedayeen guerrillas in 1970–1971. In what amounted to a civil war, Hussein relied upon the Royal Army to defeat the Palestinians in a bloody intra-Arab conflict which threatened to overturn the Hashemite kingdom. The army's fierce personal loyalty to the king was considered a key factor in its willingness to take on the Palestinians in defiance of much of the Arab world.

Jordan illustrates in microcosm some aspects of the contemporary politics of arms sales. Even though it has historically been dependent on the United States for military and economic assistance, it was unwilling to join the Middle East peace negotiations, either at Camp David or in the subsequent negotiations on Palestinian autonomy. The Carter administration made repeated attempts to bring King Hussein into the process, all to no avail. Jordan's objections were based upon the king's view that the framework was too limited for the negotiations to succeed and that they must include Syria, the PLO, the Soviet Union, and other interested parties; he believed that the negotiations had to be moved to a wider arena, perhaps the United Nations; and he was deeply skeptical about Prime Minister Begin's willingness to return the Arab section of Jerusalem or the West Bank of the Jordan River which were captured from Jordan in the 1967 war. Hussein's refusal to enter the negotiations underscored the limits of the influence the United States had obtained with its arms deliveries.

At the same time, Amman needs new arms. Accordingly, it has sought to diversify its source of supply. Thirty-six Mirage F-1s were ordered from France in 1979. When a more modern

174

tank was needed as a replacement for 300 M-48s, Amman began a complicated minuet. The United States was willing to sell M-60 tanks but only under the condition that Jordan scrap an equal number of M-48s, to conform with the U.S. estimate of the regional balance with Israel. It was also unwilling to provide sophisticated equipment for the tanks, such as laser range finders and night vision equipment. In addition it wanted a delay of three years to assuage Israel. Hussein then turned to the Soviet Union, sending his chief of staff of the armed forces for preliminary talks, and to the United Kingdom. The possibility that Jordan might begin an arms relationship with Moscow, first raised four years earlier with respect to air defense systems, became real. The British were delighted to have an opportunity to sell some of the Chieftain tanks that had been intended for Iran and imposed no restrictions on the associated equipment. These events, in turn, led the United States to relax in part its own earlier restrictions, and the deal was finally closed when Hussein visited Washington in June 1980. Jordan is to receive at least 100 of the tanks it had wanted all along, but despite President Carter's renewed entreaties it still continued its refusal to join the Egyptian-Israeli peace talks. United States officials hoped that the M-60 sale would improve strained relations between Amman and Washington and help persuade Jordan to engage itself in the negotiations at some future time.

Saudi Arabia and North Yemen

Saudi defense officials do not plan the composition of their armed forces in terms of a single threat. Rather, a mosaic of concerns and fears, some of which are more dominant at one time or another, has impelled the Saudis to pay greater attention to their defense requirements. The oil fields are the nation's greatest physical asset. They are a tempting target for takeover, and may become more of one in the future as the Soviet Union faces an energy shortage; they also remain quite vulnerable to destruction. Saudi concern about the Soviet Union's ambitions and unpredictability increased measurably after the invasion of

175

Afghanistan, the onset of revolution and chaos in Iran, and Soviet involvement in South Yemen and Ethiopia. Another concern, of greater importance to the Saudis than is generally appreciated in the West, is their responsibility as the guardians of Islam's holy places, Mecca and Medina. This role enhances their claim to being the leading Muslim state—some 2 million pilgrims from eighty countries now make the *hadj* to Mecca each year—and this is a matter of great significance to the more conservative among the Saudis.

Israel has not been viewed by the Saudis as a major threat, although the latter continue to seek the return to Muslim control of Jerusalem's holy Islamic sites, which are within a very short distance of both the Wailing Wall and the Church of the Holy Sepulcher. As Saudi Arabia plays a larger role in the politics of the Middle East, however, it may find itself increasingly drawn into more direct participation in the Arab-Israeli confrontation, perhaps, for example, providing arms to Arab allies. Saudi Arabia with its oil fields will, however, remain hostage to Israeli air attack even after the Saudis gain possession of the F-15s they are scheduled to receive in 1982. (This would be less true, however, if Saudi Arabia receives the AWACS it seeks to purchase.) Israeli concerns that the F-15s could be stationed at the Tabuk air base in the northwest of Saudi Arabia, close to the border of Israel, were met with a Saudi assurance to the United States that this will not occur. For their part, however, the Saudis have been concerned about Israeli reconnaissance flights into their country and see the Tabuk base as a way of discouraging this.

The military buildup in Iran was watched by the Saudis with considerable unease. The contention sometimes made that the West, and the United States in particular, was abetting an arms race between Iran and Saudi Arabia through the sale of arms to both countries was not easy to prove, for there has been little direct evidence of such a causal relationship. Yet the Saudis were never comfortable with the dominant position that Iran under the Shah was creating for itself in the Persian Gulf. They were sensitive to the fact that they would have oil reserves long after those of Iran ran out, and that Teheran would continue to

176

require oil revenues to finance its long-term aspirations for industrialization. Thus, thoughtful Saudis understood that Iran could
become a threat to their security in coming years and were therefore anxious about the panoply of sophisticated and long-range
arms that Iran was purchasing, against which Saudi Arabia was
relatively defenseless. The revolution in Iran fostered a new set
of fears that Islamic fanaticism would spread to the faith's birthplace, which would have implications for the continued authority and rule of the Saudi family. These fears were intensified by
the seizure of the Grand Mosque in Mecca and the disturbances
among the Shi'ia population in the Eastern Provinces in November 1979.

It is their radical Arab neighbors, Iraq and the People's Democratic Republic of Yemen, that have been in the past the greatest worry to many Saudis. They still remember their inability to
respond to Egyptian-supported South Yemen incursions across
their borders in the 1960s. The Iraqis have one of the most
impressive military forces in the Middle East (they were not fully
used in the war with Iran), and their MiG-23s and tanks could be
a threat to the oil fields around Dhahran. But what has been most
troublesome is the radical orientation of these two states and the
possibility that the Soviet Union could stir up conflict in the
region using them as proxies. The Saudis are, if anything,
strongly anti-Communist and have a deep skepticism about long-
run Soviet intentions in the area. They believe that the Soviet
Union might attempt to close shipping lanes in the Persian Gulf
and Red Sea through bases in Iraq and South Yemen, where
there are many Soviet and East European advisers. Saudi relations with Baghdad improved with the onset of the Iraq-Iran
conflict, but the underlying suspicions remain.

The Saudi interest in augmenting their defense capabilities
can also be seen as part of a desire to increase the nation's political credibility. Here the intended audience is less the West,
which is already duly impressed by the nation's oil power, than
the Arab world, which has the latent capability of undermining
the Saudi leadership structure. Having watched the weapons
acquisition of such other Arab countries as Iraq, Syria, Jordan,

and Egypt, at a tempo that in the past outpaced their own, the Saudis in the late 1970s did not wish to have the image of being left behind.

Within Saudi Arabia there is deep concern about a radicalization of more of the Arab world and its further polarization. This could isolate the country and ultimately undermine the control of the royal family. For this reason the Saudis have sought to contain the Palestinian problem by supporting the creation of a Palestinian state and calling for Israel's return to the 1967 boundaries. Riyadh has also expanded its regional role through its support for moderate regimes, as well as for less moderate ones such as Syria, tempering their behavior through economic assistance and offers to pay for the purchase of weapons. Funds have been distributed from the Saudi treasury with increasing largess. In 1977 Egypt was the largest recipient, with $2.5 billion in economic and military aid (although it was later cut off following the Camp David accords); Syria received $1 billion to help pay for its military forces in Lebanon; Jordan, $500 million; and North Yemen, $150 million; undisclosed amounts went to the PLO. In addition, the Saudis have funded arms for Sudan and for Eritrean troops fighting the Soviet-backed Ethiopians. The Saudis have used their "money weapon" to fight Soviet expansionism and Arab radicalism, which individually or together are seen as major threats to their regime.

For a variety of reasons, therefore, Saudi Arabia began during the mid-1970s to give greater attention to its national security. Its growing importance as the largest holder of oil reserves in the West made it more conscious of its potential enemies. Its increased oil revenues made the equipment of its armed forces with sophisticated arms possible. The country's military establishment is divided into two quite separate forces, with different training, logistics, and chains of command. The regular armed forces are the largest, although totaling only approximately 50,000 men; they have the usual division into three services, and report to the minister of defense, Prince Sultan. Alongside is the National Guard, also known as the White Army, which has about

25,000 men and is under the control of the deputy premier, Prince Abdullah. The National Guard is tribally based and primarily comprised of Bedouins from the Nedj Province in central Arabia, the birthplace of the Saud family. The National Guard is considered intensely loyal to the royal family and a formidable obstacle to would-be usurpers. (Nevertheless, the king's personal protection is in the hands of yet another separate unit, the Royal Guard, a battalion of hand-picked, fanatically loyal Bedouins.) Responsibility for the protection of the oil fields has been entrusted directly to the National Guard, indicating a full appreciation of the comparative importance of this unique asset.

Since 1974 Saudi Arabia has been using the increased oil wealth made possible by the rise in OPEC oil prices to finance major improvements in its military establishment. Indeed, by 1980 Saudi Arabia ranked sixth in the world in annual military expenditures at $20.7 billion after only the United States, Soviet Union, China, Britain, and West Germany, and was first in expenditures per person. It has tried to some degree to diversify its sources of supply. The French have been asked to train four mechanized armored brigades and have supplied 300 AMX tanks and various artillery at a cost of well over $1 billion. A long-term, $3.4 billion contract was signed with Paris in 1980 to equip the Saudi navy. Similarly, Britain has supplied 250 Scorpion light tanks, well suited for desert warfare, and other arms for at least an equivalent amount. West Germany was sounded out about selling Leopard-2 tanks, as noted earlier. Other purchases have been made from Italy, West Germany, Belgium, Taiwan, and South Korea. The United States, however, has been given most of the market. Purchases from the United States through 1980 came to $34.9 billion, 97 percent of which were made since 1973.[39]

In addition, there are ambitious plans for creating at Al Kharj, once a small village sixty miles southeast of Riyadh, the King Khalid "military city" of 100,000 which will have a complex of weapons-producing facilities for missiles and ammunition. Originally intended to be part of the now defunct four-nation Arab

Organization for Industrialization, it is not clear at what pace this project will proceed, but a master plan has already been drawn up while publicity has been kept to a minimum.

The United States has been accorded a special role in safeguarding the security of Saudi Arabia for over a quarter-century. Implicitly, it has been the nation's protector. This was initially the natural concomitant of the arrangement with the Arabian American Oil Company, made in 1938, for developing the country's oil production. To assist the Saudi government, a U.S. military training mission was established in 1953. The next year the U.S. Army Corps of Engineers completed construction of a military airfield at Dhahran. Since then the Corps of Engineers has been deeply involved in supervising construction activities in Saudi Arabia with the purpose of creating a military infrastructure for the nation. This has included airfields, naval port facilities, radar and communications systems, supply depots and related logistical support, and training programs for personnel to maintain the military facilities. The Corps of Engineers has even built a mosque for the headquarters of the Ministry of Defense and Aviation![40]

For these reasons a large part of what is classified by the American government as its foreign military sales to Saudi Arabia, approximately 60 percent, is actually in the form of construction, logistical facilities, and training. The modernization of the National Guard, for example, has been entrusted to the Vinnell Corporation of California and a group of about seventy-five U.S. officers.

At the same time, the United States has also been the largest supplier of weapons, which, apart from fighter aircraft, have included an array of advanced missiles such as the TOW antitank, Sidewinder air-to-air for the F-5E fighter, Dragon, Maverick, and Redeye missiles; armored personnel carriers; and light naval craft. In the case of the Sidewinder and Maverick missiles, the Senate Foreign Relations Committee questioned the need for 850 and 650, respectively (pared down from the original Saudi request of 2,000 and 1,500) because of both the magnitude of the sales and the possibility that the fighter-borne missiles might be used against Israel at some point. Only after an urgent appeal by Secretary of State Kissinger (and vague warnings of a possible oil embargo) did the full Senate agree to the sale.[41] In the wake of the Iranian revolution Secretary of Defense Harold Brown made a trip to Saudi Arabia in 1979 after which the United States agreed to sell additional missiles and to construct a $1.5 billion system of shelters for aircraft. And on its last day in office, the Carter administration approved another arms deal of $2 billion in assorted military equipment and services. By the end of the 1970s, Saudi Arabia had far surpassed Iran as the largest peacetime recipient of American arms (in sales rather than deliveries).

By far the most important and controversial American sale to Saudi Arabia (prior to the Reagan administration's proposed sale of AWACS) was that of the sixty F-15 Eagle fighters, which were part of the Middle East "plane package" of 1978. This sale acquired tremendous symbolic significance. In Saudi minds, the recommendation of the sale by the executive branch and its approval by the Congress (or more correctly, the unwillingness of the Congress to exercise its right of veto) became the litmus test for the existence of what many perceived to be a "special relationship."[42] For this reason (and because it is integral to the proposed follow-up sale of extra fuel tanks and bomb racks for the F-15) it merits closer examination.

In 1968 Great Britain announced the end of its protective role in the Persian Gulf, and in 1971 it withdrew its troops. As the British withdrew, several of the Persian Gulf states began to expand and modernize their armed forces so as to be able to better protect their individual interests. This coincided, roughly, with the Nixon Doctrine's stated preference for building up the power of friendly states in important regions so as to permit a more selective American worldwide engagement. In this context, the Saudi government in 1970 asked the United States to evaluate its national security situation and defense programs. A Pentagon team under the direction of Major General O. A. Leahy recommended that a five-year defense plan be developed, that the air force be placed on an equal level with the army, and that the aging F-86 American-built fighters be replaced. This led to the

Peace Hawk program through which the Saudis purchased over 100 F-5s and a training program by the U.S. Air Force to make the Saudi air force self-sufficient. Another survey was requested in 1973 to be based on a five- to ten-year projection of Saudi requirements. A forty-five-man survey team included in its recommendations the replacement of British-made Lightning fighters with advanced fighters at the level of the F-14, F-15, F-16, or F-18.

From this time the Saudis believed that they had at least an implicit commitment from the United States to sell them one of these state-of-the-art aircraft. In fact, no official commitment was made at the time, and at the middle level of the U.S. government there were misgivings. An attempt was made, unsuccessfully, to delay the trip to the United States of a Saudi military team which was to seek additional data on the various aircraft, on the grounds that the issue needed further examination. But in the course of their visit in March 1976, Saudi pilots were invited by Grumman and McDonnell Douglas, with Department of Defense concurrence, to test fly both the F-14 and the F-15. The Saudi officers expressed a strong preference for the F-15.

In Washington there was a variety of views. Deputy Secretary of Defense William Clements, Jr., sought to persuade the Saudis that the F-15 was too sophisticated for their needs and would be difficult for them to absorb. He suggested that they build their air defense around the latest E generation of the F-5, which they were already scheduled to receive. This was resisted by Riyadh, which then began perceiving the issue in political rather than technical terms. The Saudi view received strong support from Secretary of State Kissinger in the fall of 1976, who reportedly argued that the sale of the F-15, like other transfers of advanced weapons to the Persian Gulf, would help create a web of interdependence that would allow the United States to maintain leverage over these countries. President Ford accepted this judgment, and the government of Saudi Arabia was informed by Secretary Kissinger and Deputy Secretary Clements during trips to the region that the executive branch would support a request for the fighter *of their choice*, including the F-15.

182

Accordingly, the Carter administration came into office with its options substantially circumscribed by the pledge made to the Saudis. Although the pledge's fulfillment would contradict, at least in spirit, President Carter's new arms transfer policy, the administration concluded after much internal debate that the increasingly important Saudi-American relationship could not stand a policy reversal on the F-15 and that such a step would adversely affect the administration's emerging policy with respect to the crucial Arab-Israeli peace negotiations. Crown Prince Fahd was told by the president on a visit to Washington in May 1977 that the administration would agree to the sale. Nevertheless, the Arms Control and Disarmament Agency opposed the sale on the grounds that it would lead other countries in the Middle East to seek comparable aircraft, thus contributing to an accelerated arms competition in the region. The Bureaus of Politico-Military Affairs and Congressional Affairs in the State Department continued to argue that, in addition to damaging the credibility of the new arms transfer restraint policy, the sale would face major opposition in the Congress. Reacting to these concerns within his administration, the president approved a suggestion that the Saudis be urged to accept the single-engine F-16 instead of the F-15. But this was rejected by Riyadh, as was also a further request for delay until progress was made in the peace negotiations. On a visit to Saudi Arabia in January 1978, the president promised King Khalid that he would personally involve himself in persuading the Congress on the merits of the sale.

A special staff report to the Senate Foreign Relations Committee, made in preparation for the hearings on the "plane package," came to the conclusion that three factors dominated the history of the sale of the F-15 to Saudi Arabia. The first was the Department of Defense survey which established for Saudi Arabia the need for an advanced fighter and in the Saudi view created an implied U.S. commitment to sell such an aircraft. The second was Secretary Kissinger's desire to use arms sales as an active foreign policy tool. And the third was the political pressure the Saudis put on the United States whenever doubts were raised about the sale.[43] To this must be added two significant considerations. One is that the prior sale to Israel of the F-15, in the context of the Sinai disengagement agreement of 1975, set an important precedent. Once Israel acquired this fighter, which is thought to be in many ways the best in existence, and the United States thereby first sold it abroad, it was almost inevitable that the Saudis would ask for it too. The new wealth of their country and a changed sociocultural pattern encouraged the Saudis to simply buy the "best" in existence, without a careful appraisal of the need. (This was occurring with some civilian technologies in Saudi Arabia, as in the case of the fully computerized King Faisal Hospital.) The Saudis could not understand why they should not be sold the same type of arms as the Israelis. The other factor was the Carter administration's tactical decision to link the sale of the F-15 to Saudi Arabia with additional sales of the same aircraft plus F-16s to Israel as well as F-5Es to Egypt, declaring that it must be all or nothing. Although this strategy was resented in the Congress, it enabled the president to argue that the package would not upset the military balance in the region.

(A new controversy came to the fore in 1981 over the Reagan administration's intention to sell the Saudis extra fuel tanks, advanced air-to-air Sidewinder missiles, and possibly bomb racks for the F-15 fighters, in addition to five AWACS electronic surveillance planes and some aerial tanker aircraft. The Congress had been assured by the Carter administration in 1978 that the range and firepower of the F-15s sold to Saudi Arabia would not be enhanced in the future. But President Reagan concluded that this was now necessary because of the increased Soviet threat to the oil fields of the Persian Gulf. Strong pressure for the sale was being exerted by Riyadh. Critics of the sale were primarily concerned by the additional threat this would present to the security of Israel, with the F-15s, assisted by the tankers, becoming capable of deep strikes into the country and with the AWACS able to monitor all Israeli air activity from Saudi skies. The AWACS planes, moreover, could provide a command platform in the air to guide attacks against Israel. They also pointed out that Saudi Arabia was not making any political concessions in return, such as cooperation in the post-Camp David peace process or assurances regarding the supply of oil. But those in favor of the sale underscored its desirability for paving the way for eventually placing American military forces—or, short of that, stockpiles of U.S. equipment—in Saudi Arabia to be used in case of an emergency. They also noted the implicit guarantee regarding the employment of the AWACS in the fact that they could not be operated without American technicians and would remain dependent upon U.S. spare parts and maintenance. As a "sweetener," Israel was promised fifteen additional F-15s and was told that past restrictions on the exports of its Kfir fighter, containing American parts, would be dropped.)

The "special relationship" between Saudi Arabia and the United States is, of course, composed of multiple strands which far transcend the military dimension. But when an arms sale such as the F-15 (or AWACS) comes to be viewed by the Saudis as a test of that relationship, as it certainly did in this case, all the other strands make their effects felt.

Oil is the single most important one. America has become increasingly dependent upon Saudi oil, which accounts for more than 25 percent of its oil imports, and still larger amounts from the Arabian peninsula may be needed in the future. Saudi Arabia will remain the most critical country in determining world oil production and price levels. Related to this is Saudi Arabia's place in international finance and its important dollar holdings. In 1978 at the time of the F-15 sale, the Saudis had invested over $10 billion of their surplus funds in American industry and a large, secret amount on the order of $30 billion in U.S. Treasury bonds and other government securities. A switch by the Saudis from dollar holdings to other currencies could have grave consequences for the U.S. economy.

Arms and oil have rarely been explicitly linked—it is not necessary, it is understood. An exception occurred during the week of the Senate hearings on the "plane package," when Sheik Ahmed Zaki Yamani, the urbane and internationally known Saudi oil minister, warned that a refusal to sell the F-15 would have an adverse effect on his country's oil production policy and its support for the dollar. Given that the Saudis were being asked

185

to pump more oil than their revenues required, his comments that Saudi friendship and willingness to help the United States were at stake were not to be disregarded.[44] On another occasion, an announcement by Saudi Arabia in July 1979 that it would increase its oil production by a million barrels a day was quickly followed by an American approval of a $1.2 billion additional arms request for the Saudi National Guard. A link between the two was widely perceived, despite official denials.[45]

As to the Arab-Israeli conflict, the Saudis and the United States have not usually been seriously at odds. Saudi Arabia has been seen by Washington as having a generally moderate policy, counseling caution within the Arab world, and being opposed to Soviet encroachments in the region. Thus, Saudi Arabia has not normally been thought of as a confrontation state even though its growing political involvement within the region may make it more difficult for Riyadh to stay apart in any future war. Sadat's trip to Jerusalem in 1977 displeased the Saudis because it led to a split in the Arab world. Prior to Camp David, they nevertheless supported the general peacemaking diplomacy of the United States, if not all the specifics, often stressing the overriding need to resolve the conflict. Latent in the Saudi position was the fear that divisions within the Arab world on the Palestinian problem and on how to deal with Israel could create instability and pressures that would have a subversive impact at home. The Camp David accords did, however, deepen the fissures considerably. At the Baghdad conference that followed, the Saudis joined in the censure of Egypt and withdrew most of their large-scale financial support for Cairo. This inaugurated a period of coolness in their ties with the United States.

Another cause of the strain in Saudi-American relations that developed in 1979 came as a consequence of the Iranian revolution. The fall of the Shah created political and psychological ripples on the Arabian peninsula. Saudi relations with the Shah had never been especially warm. But the American failure to come to the effective defense of such a close ally was interpreted, rightly or wrongly, by some Saudis as having fairly clear implications for their own regime. America no longer seemed as invincible to those in the immediate region as it once had. The Khomeini regime's espousal of neutralism exposed Saudi Arabia's uncomfortable isolation in the Persian Gulf. And the dispatch of twelve unarmed American F-15s for a brief stay in the country, together with the indecision about deploying a U.S. naval contingent in the Persian Gulf, did little to limit the Saudis' loss of confidence in the United States.

Finally, the Saudis were critical of the lack of effective American action in dealing with Soviet and Marxist influence in Africa and South Yemen. Riyadh was concerned about the thousands of Cuban troops just across the Red Sea in Ethiopia and the strong Soviet-Cuban presence in South Yemen. In the wake of Angola and the strife in Zaire, Saudi Arabia gave financial assistance to pro-Western governments, and it supported Somalia through large purchases of arms to be used against Ethiopia after President Mohammed Siad Barre, with Saudi approval, cut his ties with the Soviet Union. Washington's failure to send arms to Somalia was seen as showing a lack of American resolve; it was thought the United States was perhaps unduly reacting to pressures from some of the black African states opposed to such a step.

In response to such criticisms and the growing Saudi sense of encirclement, Washington quickly agreed to airlift $390 million in arms to North Yemen (Yemen Arab Republic) in March 1979, shortly after that country had been attacked by troops from the People's Democratic Republic of Yemen (South Yemen) using Soviet arms. In recent years the Soviet Union has acquired naval facilities at Aden and is thought to have stockpiled arms there. A twenty-year friendship treaty has been signed, and several thousand Soviet, Cuban, and East German military advisers are present. Riyadh has a strong interest in the two Yemens on its southern border, with an estimated one million workers from North Yemen forming part of the Saudi work force. This arms transfer was to be a cooperative venture between the United States and Saudi Arabia, which agreed to pay for the weapons

187

and which asked that they be sent to Saudi Arabia first for assembly by Saudi and American military technicians before being sent on to North Yemen. Among the arms were twelve F-5E fighters (which were to be flown by pilots from Taiwan who could speak neither Arabic nor English!), sixty-four M-60 tanks, and fifty armored personnel carriers. The North Yemen army was to be instructed in their use and maintenance by Jordanian instructors. This was the first time that an American president had invoked the special waiver provision in the Arms Export Control Act of 1976 which permits bypassing the thirty-day delay during which Congress can object to an arms sale when there is a presidential determination that the situation is an emergency.

What actually followed had comic overtones. The day before President Carter signed the waiver, a truce promoted by Syria and Iraq was agreed upon, and a few days later the Arab League began to supervise the withdrawal of South Yemen forces from North Yemen. But the arms were shipped anyway, and the government in Sana (North Yemen) made clear that it still expected to receive the weapons. Meanwhile unification talks between the two Yemens began. But this worried the Saudis who are as concerned about the possibility of a unified Yemen, which might later turn Marxist, as they are about the People's Republic in the south. Because of this ambivalent attitude, Riyadh held up the forwarding of the American military supplies, much to the frustration of Washington, which discovered that by allowing the Saudis to act as middlemen it had lost control. The North Yemen government then turned to the Soviet Union, which many years earlier had helped equip its armed forces. Moscow quickly sent arms shipments far in excess of what Washington had promised, including ten MiG-21s and Polish T-54 tanks. The end result was that North Yemen eventually acquired arms from both rival superpowers. Some of its units are equipped equally with Soviet and American tanks, and Soviet and American personnel have reportedly run simultaneous instructions for North Yemenis on the same parade ground![46]

Syria and Iraq

Of the Middle Eastern countries, Syria and Iraq are generally considered to be most within the Soviet orbit (apart from South Yemen). Both have a long history of purchasing arms from the Soviet Union and of admitting Russian military advisers. Both have taken a hard line against Israel, have generally failed to support American diplomacy in the Arab-Israeli dispute, and were "rejectionist" states in their attitude toward the peace negotiations of the late 1970s. These are the countries, along with Qaddafi's Libya, that are least reconciled to the existence of Israel and its acceptance within the region.

The Syrian government can best be described as socialist and military. After the country received independence from France in 1946, it underwent two decades of political upheavals in which the lineup of factions within the military was often the controlling element. Nasser's appeal for Arab nationalism had support in Syria and led to the union with Egypt under the banner of the United Arab Republic. A military coup led to Syria's secession from the union, and eighteen months later, in March 1963, leftist officers within the Syrian army took over the country in another coup. This second coup was carried out by officers who were members of the Ba'ath Party, a previously clandestine political movement that had been active since the 1940s. (A month earlier a similar Ba'ath coup had taken over the government in Iraq.) President Assad came to power in 1971, after a career in the Syrian air force, and has tried to widen the base of political support by the creation of a National Progressive Front, which is nevertheless led by the ruling Ba'athist party. The fact that the Ba'ath leadership is made up of Alawite Muslims who represent only 15 percent of the Muslim population, the rest of whom are Sunnis, helps account for the strict control under which the population is kept and for some of the political insecurity that manifests itself in the government's policies. At home, the regime has on occasion been quite repressive and the middle class has simply ceased participating in political life. Abroad,

189

President Assad has championed the cause of Arab unity and the rights of the Palestinians.

An important portion of Syria's budget is spent on military expenditures, ranging in the 1970s from 23 percent to 45 percent. This reflects the privileged position of the military, the continuing conflict with Israel, and, since 1975, some of the cost of maintaining part of the Syrian army in Lebanon. The territorial losses to Israel suffered in the 1967 Six Day War were only partially recovered through the Golan Heights disengagement agreement following the 1973 conflict. For this reason, among others, Syria remains on a war footing.

The military relationship with the Soviet Union goes back to the mid-1950s when Syria was considering joining the Central Treaty Organization (CENTO), even though the anti-Soviet organization was considered a distraction from the more important problem of Israel. Moscow successfully discouraged Damascus from joining CENTO by offering economic and military aid. This led to an arms deal with Czechoslovakia in 1956 which initiated what has been a long flow of Soviet arms. Syria for a number of years ranked next to Egypt as the second largest recipient of Soviet arms in the Third World.[47]

The Six Day War of 1967 was a severe setback for Syria not only because of the loss of territory to the Israelis but because of the destruction of the armed forces' military equipment, including two-thirds of its aircraft. Moreover, the nation's vulnerability was exposed as Israeli forces rolled across the Syrian fortifications on the Golan Heights to within twenty-four miles of Damascus, with a demonstrated ability to capture the capital. With Syrian resistance on the point of collapse, the Soviet Union threatened to intervene militarily, a threat that had its effect in part because of simultaneous American urgings on Israel to call a halt, but which also was embarrassing for Damascus. Within a year Soviet resupply, which included late-model MiG-21s and SU-7 fighters as well as 400 tanks, had more than replaced the losses. At the same time the construction of naval support facilities under Soviet supervision began in the ports of Lataqia and Tartus.

190

These later became useful ports of call for the Soviet Mediterranean fleet. As many as 1,000 additional Soviet advisory personnel arrived in Syria after the war, reportedly a precondition for the arms assistance, and Russian officers were assigned to help train the Syrian forces.

The experience in the 1973 war was only marginally different. This time Syria and Egypt had the benefit of surprise on their side, but Syrian forces were again badly mauled even though Russian advisers were present at command posts during the conflict and supervised the firing of recently installed surface-to-air missiles. Indeed, the overall Syrian losses would have appeared even greater were it not for the emergency resupply effort by air and sea during the war, which allowed the Syrians to continue fighting for a longer period. As earlier, Syrian losses after the 1973 war were made good with a remarkably high level of arms transfers in 1974, including the delivery of MiG-21 and MiG-25 aircraft.

Yet despite what may appear as a highly one-sided, dependent relationship, neither Damascus or Moscow has fulfilled all the wishes of the other, and relations between the two countries have been fraught with tension. Until the start of the Iran-Iraq war in the fall of 1980 the Syrians repeatedly refused to sign a broad-ranging Treaty of Friendship and Cooperation, of the type once accepted by Iraq and Egypt, which the Soviets had sought since 1972. They consistently offered the Russians less than they wanted in the way of military facilities, such as permanent home-port facilities at Lataqia and Tartus and airfields for their reconnaissance aircraft. Although about 2,600 Soviet military advisers were in Syria, Moscow was rebuffed in its request for its own bases. Assad's decision to send 30,000 troops to Lebanon as part of the Arab Deterrent Force to stop the fighting between the Muslims and the Christians was an embarrassment to the Soviet Union in its relations with the PLO and led to a curtailment of the transfer of Soviet arms in 1976. The size of weapons sales was somewhat increased again starting in late 1977 as Moscow sought to encourage Damascus in its rejection of American peacemaking efforts in the Middle East. Nevertheless, Assad has displayed considerable astuteness in maintaining independence in his foreign policy dealings.

Probably with the aim of enhancing Syria's leverage, Assad began in 1975 to develop some alternative sources of supply for arms. In the first arms purchase of note from a Western country in over a decade Syria bought Super Frelon helicopters from France; a subsequent order for Milan and Hot anti-tank missiles created some concern in Bonn, for these missiles sold by the French are co-produced with Germany, but it went through. Diplomatic relations between Damascus and Washington were severed by the Syrians in June 1967 but were restored in 1974 on the occasion of President Nixon's visit to Damascus. Since then Syria has received very small amounts of economic assistance from Washington.

For their part, the Soviets have not given Syria all the arms it has sought. This is all the more noteworthy because of Syria's ability to pay for some of the arms in cash with earnings from recent oil discoveries. Syrian reluctance to accept a Soviet-American proposed cease-fire on the Golan Heights during the 1973 war apparently made the Soviets more aware of the risk of losing control in a situation of conflict in the Middle East. Following the Egyptian-Israeli peace treaty, Assad asked for more Soviet arms, contending that Syria was now the principal Arab country confronting Israel; he was only partially successful although Damascus did for the first time receive sixty-five T-72 tanks, the most advanced produced by the Soviet Union. The Syrian armed forces have been adequately armed to be a viable military force, but Moscow has not given them the capability to vanquish Israel. Clearly the Soviets are conscious of the danger of a war in the Middle East leading to a confrontation between the Soviet Union and the United States.

Nevertheless, whatever the frustrations involved, the Soviets are not likely to give up their weapons supply relationship. This became very clear when a twenty-year Treaty of Friendship and Cooperation was finally signed in October 1980. This occurred after Moscow's relations with Baghdad had cooled because of the

192

Iraq-Iran war and at a time when Assad's political position at home had become more shaky than usual. There was a new influx of Soviet arms and advisers, and the two countries pledged close cooperation in the military field. Arms to Syria and Iraq provide for the Soviets their best point of entry into the politics of the Middle East. The loss of their previous position in Egypt makes these two countries all the more significant for them. And with the relative successes of American diplomacy in the disengagement agreements and the Camp David accords, overall Soviet influence in the region has been relatively reduced. Thus the supply of arms is important as the best means of access.

We turn now to Iraq, which ranks after Egypt and Syria as a major recipient of Soviet arms. The close and longstanding Soviet-Iraq arms supply relationship began in 1958 after the coup of General Abdul Karim Kassem, who changed Iraq's foreign policy to one of nonalignment. Kassem severed military ties with the West and approached the Soviet Union for military assistance. Moscow responded to the opening with alacrity, delivering a squadron of MiG-15s in the same year and sending a military training mission. Since then Iraq has been armed predominantly, but not exclusively, with Soviet weaponry. Unlike Syria, which refused to sign a similar treaty until 1980, Iraq signed a fifteen-year Treaty of Friendship and Cooperation with Moscow in 1972, thus serving Moscow's interest in reinforcing part of its position in the Middle East at a time its relations with Egypt were deteriorating.[48] An unprecedented accord for the transfer of $1 billion in arms was signed at the time of Premier Kosygin's visit to Baghdad in 1976, under which Iraqi forces received large numbers of MiG-21s and MiG-23s, Scud missiles, T-62 tanks, and other high-quality weapons.[49] Altogether, Iraq's military establishment of 220,000 men, well equipped and trained, was considered to be one of the Middle East's most powerful defense establishments prior to the Iran-Iraq war of 1980.

Baghdad's ability to pay for much of these arms with hard currency made available through oil exports was no doubt attractive to the Soviet Union. During the 1960s oil was exchanged for arms in barter deals. Yet economic considerations played a sec-

193

ondary role to the political aim of guaranteeing the Soviet presence in the Middle East. Nevertheless, the arms accords were beneficial to Moscow in that they were accompanied by extensive construction projects paid for by the Iraqis for developing irrigation and water management systems as well as oil refineries and petroleum pipelines. East European countries have also been heavily involved in these projects, many of which are likely to have a direct benefit, through oil resources, for the COMECON states.

Iraq's relations with the Soviets have not been trouble free. The Ba'athist political leadership moved ruthlessly against the country's Communist party in 1978, executing twenty-one middle-grade officers for attempting to organize Communist cells in the armed forces. A major source of difficulty has been the differences in perspectives regarding Kurdish separatism. The rebellious Kurd tribesmen in northern Iraq posed a challenge to the Baghdad regime, but Moscow viewed the Kurdish minority in Iraq as a potential base from which to foster similar separatist tendencies within the larger Kurdish population in neighboring Iran. Accordingly, the Soviets counseled against the use of arms that they had supplied in opposing Kurdish dissidents, some of whose leaders had Communist party affiliations. When an anti-Kurdish offensive in 1975 stalled and Baghdad asked for more Soviet artillery and infantry weapons, Moscow's unwillingness to make them available made the Iraqis reconsider the desirability of being so dependent upon a single supplier of arms.

Thus in the mid-1970s, after a decade and a half of nearly exclusive reliance on the Soviet Union, Iraq took steps to diversify gradually its source of arms supplies. The most far-reaching deals were discussed with France, although Britain, Italy, and West Germany also agreed to relatively minor sales. After Saudi Arabia, Iraq ranks as France's largest supplier of oil from the Middle East. Prime Minister Jacques Chirac traveled to Baghdad and initiated negotiations on the sale of both Mirage F-1 fighters and a nuclear reactor; and Iraq agreed to buy French tanks, missiles, naval vessels, and 100 Mirage F-1s, for a value of approximately $1.5 billion, in exchange for guaranteed oil supplies. The nuclear reactor transfer, which caused considerable concern that Iraq was intending to produce its own atom bomb, was delayed by a mysterious act of sabotage in 1979 although the French government assured Baghdad that it would be replaced. Subsequently in 1981 the nuclear reactor was bombed by Israel, using American-built aircraft.

This movement away from relying exclusively upon the Soviets for arms is part of a wider and growing interest in acquiring Western technology. The discovery of major new oil deposits, and the nationalization of the Iraqi Petroleum Company in 1973, have given the country a new ability to import European and American industrial goods. Iraq remains one of the more radical of the Arab states and is one of the countries least friendly to Israel. Although diplomatic links with the United States were severed after the 1967 war and, unlike Syria's, have not been resumed, the Baghdad regime is emerging out of its somewhat xenophobic isolation.[50]

The revolution in neighboring Iran and the Soviet intervention in Afghanistan had a significant impact upon the Iraqis. Baghdad condemned the Soviet invasion at the United Nations and at the conference of Muslim states in Islamabad. Ayatollah Khomeini's vow to spread his Shi'ite Islamic fervor to the more secular Iraq made President Saddam Hussein see a Soviet-influenced Iran as a potential major threat. This led him to loosen further the relationship with Moscow and build closer ties within the Persian Gulf; relations with Saudi Arabia, once a favorite target of Baghdad, were improved. Even before the war with Iran, Iraq had let it be known that as it distanced itself somewhat from the Soviet Union it would like closer ties with the West. In the process arms-purchase missions were sent to London, Rome, and Paris.

The war between Iraq and Iran in 1980–1981 pitted Russian and French arms in the hands of the Iraqis against American and British arms in the hands of the Iranians. Teheran was able to use its American arms to better advantage than expected. It managed initially to place about half of its F-4s and F-5s in the air, using them for sorties against Iraq, although most of the F-14s stayed grounded because of inadequate maintenance. The very

195

few that were airborne were used only for their radar capabilities to help guide other planes to target. Because of poor maintenance, British Chieftain tanks were hardly used. The Khomeini regime's desperate need for spare parts for its American aircraft at one time became a factor in the intricate negotiations for the release of the hostages at the American embassy. As for Iraq, it chose to make only a limited use of its Soviet-built fighters, sending many of them to safe havens in other countries in the Gulf region even though it was considered to possess the superior air force. The hesitant pace of Iraqi tactics surprised most analysts although it did not diminish Israeli concerns about Baghdad's war potential.

Moscow's neutral stance toward the war and its unwillingness to resupply Iraq quickly despite several requests by high-level Iraqi missions sent there turned Baghdad more to the West. Most of Moscow's friends in the Middle East (Syria, Libya, and South Yemen) supported Iran, whereas friends of the West (Jordan and Saudi Arabia) supported Iraq. An additional factor in the war was the willingness of the French to continue their arms flow. Paris quickly turned over four Mirage F-1s as a token of its intent to supply as soon as possible the fighters ordered earlier. The French made clear that they would honor the commitments made in previous years to supply a large quantity of tanks, armored vehicles, and helicopters, and there was talk of a large Iraqi order of Mirage 2000 and Mirage 4000 jets and warships. About 20 percent of France's oil is imported from Iraq, France being Iraq's largest oil customer. At no time, however, did the French government appear to use its close ties with Iraq to restrain the evolving conflict.

The Iran-Iraq war provided some further ironies illustrating the global politics of arms sales. American M-60 tanks captured by Iraq from Iran were given to Jordan in exchange for King Hussein's allowing Iraq to use the port of Aqaba. This delighted the Jordanian army which has never received as many tanks from the United States as it wants because of Washington's concern about the military balance with Israel. Other captured American arms, such as TOW anti-tank missiles and 155 mm.

artillery, as well as M-60 tanks, were turned against Iranian forces. It is perhaps the best example to date of the supplier's loss of control over how weapons are used, or where they may end up, once they are transferred.

The war underscored the limited ability of many Third World countries to absorb sophisticated arms. The conflict also had a highly irrational pattern that troubled many Western observers. This conflict between two Muslim neighbors, unlike the Arab-Israeli wars, did not conform to the unwritten rule of avoiding population centers. Both sides struck at each other's cities and oil facilities. Moreover, outside powers were not able to influence the war by withholding or granting arms supplies, as has usually been the case in the Middle East. The unpredictable nature of the conflict may prove to be characteristic of future Third World military engagements between countries armed by the major suppliers and stands as a warning of the dangers of equipping countries in unstable regions with sophisticated arms.

Libya

No survey of arms purchases in the Middle East can omit discussion of Libya. Measured against the needs for the country's security, or even its ability to absorb the weapons, the scale of Libya's purchases is truly staggering. The nation's oil resources have permitted its leader, Colonel Muammar Qaddafi, to spend on arms lavishly. An initial $1 billion deal was made with the Soviet Union in 1974 under which Tripoli received MiG-23s, TU-22 medium bombers, surface-to-air and Scud missile systems, and an array of modern equipment. More recently, MiG-25s, new T-72 tanks, and missiles have been bought from Moscow. Altogether more than $2 billion has been spent on Soviet arms. France has sold the air force much equipment, including Mirage III and F-1 fighters. In 1981 Libya had over 100 MiG-23s, 40 MiG-25s, 20 MiG-21s, about 50 Mirages and additional planes in storage. Libya has bought over 2,000 tanks and several submarines. It has even purchased 400 Rattlesnake armored personnel carriers from Brazil.[51]

197

The rapid growth in Libya's inventory of arms has not been matched, however, by an equivalent increase in the size of the armed forces or the ability to service and maintain the weapons. The armed forces total 42,000 men, and the air force has only 4,000, far too few to fly and service its numerous combat aircraft as well as handle its missiles, helicopters, and the like.[52] Moreover, the educational and technological level of the military remains quite low. It has been necessary to bring in Syrian pilots to fly the new MiG-25s, and Pakistani, North Korean, and Palestinian pilots have been used on other fighters. A not insignificant portion of Libya's weapons, including some of its Mirage fighters, are thought to remain at a depot near Tubruq in their unopened crates. The deterioration of the equipment under tough desert conditions is likely to be considerable. Indeed, well-serviced and therefore usable weapons may be a relatively small percentage of the nation's stockpile of weapons—by some estimates only one-third of its aircraft.

For the Soviet Union, the principal attraction of Libya as an arms recipient is its ability to pay prices reportedly higher than those charged less affluent countries, because of its oil income. In addition, Qaddafi is opposed to Sadat and American peacemaking initiatives in the Middle East. But Moscow has substantially less influence in Tripoli than it has had in Baghdad or Damascus, and it has not been able to use its role as an arms supplier to influence the nation's policies. It is sometimes suggested that Libya is being used as a base for prepositioning Soviet arms, should Moscow some day need to have them on hand to go to war itself in the Middle East. One cannot totally discount this possibility, but it is remote. There are 1,750 Soviet and East European military technicians in Libya, but the Soviet assistance mission has not been permitted to expand, and when further aid is needed, Libya prefers to turn to Cuba.[53] Soviet interest in acquiring naval bases or refueling facilities has not met with any positive response. After the 1969 revolution, Qaddafi moved quickly to expel American and British forces and close their bases, and it is not likely that he will want to replace them with Russians. Qaddafi, although an Arab radical, does not follow the

Moscow line. He never carried out his 1978 threat to join the Warsaw Pact! In economic terms the country leans toward the West. Oil is sold to the United States and Western Europe in exchange for Western technology. Libyan students are trained in Western universities.

Why Libya has bought such large quantities of arms remains something of a puzzle. One element is the personal interest of its highly unpredictable leader and the fact that he heads a military regime. A primary incentive, however, is the apparent desire to give Tripoli the capacity to be a prominent reexporter of arms. Arms from Libya have been sent to such diverse parties and countries as the Moro National Liberation Front in the southern Philippines; Basque, Corsican, and other separatists throughout Europe; Eritrean nationalists; factions in Mozambique and Angola; Somalia and later Ethiopia; left-wing Muslims in Lebanon; insurgent forces in Western Sahara; and Idi Amin's Uganda. Qaddafi is drawn to national liberation movements and some terrorist groups; he assisted the Palestinian terrorists who attacked the Israeli team at the Munich Olympics in 1972 and has offered arms to the Irish Republican Army. In most, if not all, of these cases the motivation has been personal and political, rather than commercial, for the weapons have probably been given away. For Qaddafi, arms are a way to support a messianic drive to spread revolution far beyond Libya's desert frontiers.

Arms Restraint in the Middle East

Given the diversity of motivations for acquiring arms to be found in the Middle East, agreement on some form of restraints will be no easy task. Yet an enduring political settlement of the Arab-Israeli conflict is unlikely to be achieved without some form of multilateral restraints on arms transfers, either tacitly agreed upon or negotiated. One reason is that an overall political "settlement" would not eliminate the long history of distrust. Both Israelis and Arabs would for many years remain armed, if only to ensure against a breakdown of the settlement. In such an atmosphere, a large infusion of arms by one side or the other

199

would immediately threaten to undermine the political settlement. Thus without some arms control dimension, a political
accord would be vulnerable and uncertain.

The relationship between negotiating a political settlement
and multilateral arms restraints in the Middle East needs new
analysis and thought. It has long been the conventional view that
political agreement must precede restraints on arms. It is, of
course, perfectly true that the roots of the Arab-Israeli dispute
are religious and political, rather than military. (Even so an
imbalance in the military equation can have dire political consequences.) Nevertheless, a complete political accord need not be
a prerequisite for some degree of arms control. Regulating arms
transfers into the Middle East could facilitate the process of
reaching a political settlement. It could be part of the negotiating
process. And it could play a critical role in maintaining the integrity of the political settlement by preventing a military deterioration which could then undermine hard-won political gains.

As we have seen, as a practical matter the supply of arms is
interwoven with political negotiations. This was the case with the
two Sinai disengagement agreements and the Camp David
accords. Conversely, arms have been withheld at certain times
by both the United States and the Soviet Union in order either to
create pressures for flexibility in negotiations or to prevent either
side from aquiring a "war option" that would guarantee its vic-
tory at acceptable costs, thereby risking an inducement to conflict. With the achievement of an important political accord in
the Egyptian-Israeli treaty of 1979, greater attention might now
be given to the possible role of arms control measures as part of
the future negotiating process.

Hypothetically, an arms control framework for regulating the
transfer of arms could take three forms: agreement could be
reached exclusively among the suppliers; the recipient states
within the region could take the initiative and come to an agreement among themselves to limit weapons imports; or there could
be an understanding between the suppliers and the recipients.

Realistically, only the third alternative is likely to be politically
feasible. With respect to the first, the Big Four of the world's

arms suppliers—the United States, the Soviet Union, France, and Britain—also transfer the large bulk of the arms sent to the Middle East. And since many of these weapons are of a degree of sophistication matched by no other suppliers', the Big Four could theoretically control among themselves the flow of arms. But these states are quite vulnerable to pressures from the recipients, either because of their desire to retain political influence with the receiving state or because of their dependence upon its oil. In as politically volatile and dangerous an arena as the Arab-Israeli confrontation, one with considerable domestic political overtones for the democratic states, no outside state that has established an arms supply relationship will want to be charged with changing the ground rules unilaterally in a form of *diktat*.

The second alternative, an agreement on restricting arms purchases made by the parties within the region, would involve even more insurmountable problems. It will be some time before the political climate of the states in the Arab-Israeli confrontation will allow this possibility. The necessary degree of common purpose—and confidence—does not exist for such an arms control initiative to be developed and implemented solely by the states within the region.

This leaves the most promising possibility—one that is still enormously difficult to achieve—of an agreement that includes both the suppliers and the recipients. Such an accord would have to be built upon the common assumption that no party is likely to make gains worth the costs in a future conflict. It would have to be seen as stabilizing a military balance. And it would have to be part of a more comprehensive approach toward an overall political settlement than has been the case thus far.

Something along these lines was proposed by President Giscard d'Estaing.[54] Its attraction to Paris stems from the perception that although France no longer has the diplomatic weight to play a significant role in negotiating a peace settlement, it could well play an important role in establishing guarantees through limits on arms sales. During the negotiations leading to the Camp David accords, Egypt proposed limits on conventional arms as part of the peace treaty. This was not acceptable to Israel on the

201

stated grounds that it had to have a free hand to deal with the other Arab states. Nevertheless, Sadat's proposal, not well known, had much merit and would be highly desirable if it became possible to include all the states in the confrontation.

We need not address in detail here the various types of quantitative and qualitative restraints that could be applied on transfers into the Middle East. Many of these restraints could also be applied to other regions of the world, and they are summarized in Part Four. Because of the existing trend toward sending ever more sophisticated military technologies into the area, limits of a qualitative nature would seem to be especially important. A rough quantitative balance already exists, an objective to which the outside suppliers have paid some attention in the past, and one that would merely have to be carefully maintained. An additional reason for giving priority to restraints of a qualitative nature arises from the geographical proximity of the cities of the opposing parties. The introduction of highly accurate, surface-to-surface cruise missiles and long-range precision-guided munitions could threaten population centers and have a very destabilizing impact upon the region. A good deal could be done to limit such weapons systems in the Middle East, even if some of them have already made an entry in small numbers. Arms control measures of another type, it should be noted, have already been accepted in the Middle East as part of the several accords reached in the 1970s. These include the creation of demilitarized buffer zones, limits on the deployment of manpower and weapons systems in areas contiguous to the buffer zones, and the creation of early warning systems.[55]

The initiative for an accord that includes both the suppliers and the recipients would have to come from the former. Ultimately it is the arms producers who have the power to withhold the weapons. To reach a common understanding on desirable restraints, it would first be necessary for the suppliers to discuss their perceptions of the requirements for stability—or at a minimum, the avoidance of war—in the region. This would in all likelihood necessitate a relatively complete exchange of views on the defense needs of the individual states and ways of maintaining the military balance.

202

Accordingly, what would be desirable is the creation of a continuing forum for discussion and of informal, perhaps even tacit, agreements, rather than anything resembling the formal negotiation of an accord or treaty. What would be sought is the *coordination* of policies so as to *regulate* the flow of arms into the Arab-Israeli confrontation area in such a way as to avoid creating instability. It would be essential, however, to include the recipients at a second, but nevertheless early, stage. If the agreed restraints were perceived by them to be adversely affecting their fundamental security interests, it is doubtful that the limitations could be made lasting. The security perspectives of the recipient states must therefore be adequately taken into account. But it should not be assumed that they will oppose all restraints, for, having fought four bitter and costly wars, these countries have a desire for peace and a common interest in achieving it.[56]

A very limited step in this direction was undertaken in 1950 following the signing of the Tripartite Declaration by the United States, France, and Great Britain. Concerned that an arms race was developing in the Palestine area after the war of 1947–1949, these three countries undertook to regulate the flow of arms to the Middle East which, at the time, they monopolized. This was done through the establishment of the Near East Arms Coordinating Committee, which was quite effective in controlling the transfer of arms until 1955 when the Soviet Union negotiated the Czech arms deal with Egypt. Although Israel and the Arab states at one time or another voiced their discontent, they also saw some advantages in the arrangement. The nationalization of the Suez Canal and Nasser's turn toward the Soviet Union for arms led to dramatically altered circumstances, and the restraints broke down.[57] The clear lesson of this attempt at arms control, which was relatively successful until the Soviet Union stepped in, is the necessity of including all the potential major suppliers. The competitive nature of the arms race in the Middle East, and the high stakes involved for the outside powers, make a comprehensive approach that includes all the principal arms exporters essential for success.

Given more recent circumstances, what are the chances for eliciting the participation of the Soviet Union? Moscow's experience in the Middle East during the 1970s was not a happy one, so that some of the traditional Soviet objectives in the Middle East, discussed earlier in this chapter, are now subject to revision.

An Israeli specialist on Soviet behavior in the Middle East, Amnon Sella, has come to the conclusion, shared by some other Israeli experts, that for several reasons the U.S.S.R. is not prepared to pay as high a price for its position in the region as in the past. The high level of economic and military assistance given by Soviet Union has not been translated into a commensurate level of political and ideological support for Soviet interests in the Middle East. Thus a number of the Arab countries have proved to be unreliable from a Soviet point of view. The October 1973 war, which led the U.S. and the U.S.S.R. to place their military forces on the alert, was a sobering signal that a regional conflict runs the risk of escalating into a global confrontation. Because of the plan to replace the U.S. Polaris submarines with the longer-range missile-carrying Trident submarines, thereby permitting American submarines to operate at a greater distance from the U.S.S.R., the Soviet navy's strategic interests are moving from the eastern Mediterranean to the periphery of the Middle East, that is, to North Africa, the Persian Gulf, and the Indian Ocean.[58] Although Moscow was clearly not pleased by the relative success of American diplomacy in dealing with the Arab-Israeli question during the 1970s, and felt embarrassingly excluded, this did not lead it to maximize its potential role as a spoiler. Nor did it allow the Arab-Israeli issue to interfere with the development of Soviet-American relations. Thus the Soviet leadership has appeared to some to share, at least partially, the Western perspective on the critical importance of peace and stability in the area. Ironically, a contributing factor is the shift in Soviet attention toward areas of greater instability, such as Southwest Asia and the Horn of Africa, each of which may provide greater opportunities than the neighbors of Israel for gaining important political and economic advantages.

In the past the Soviets have, in fact, imposed restraints on their arms sales to Middle East countries when it suited their purposes.

The best-known example is, of course, the restrictions on transfers to Egypt. But even sales to Syria and Iraq have been moderated. In early 1974 Moscow limited arms to Damascus in order to put pressure on Syria to adopt a more flexible approach toward the prospect of a disengagement agreement with Israel.[59] More recently, the Soviets have feared that the Syrians might challenge Israeli incursions into Lebanon or even start a war of attrition with Israel. Their overriding "nightmare," according to a close observer, is of a Syrian military collapse that would necessitate a direct Soviet involvement to save an ally and that could thereby risk a confrontation with the Western supporters of Israel. Accordingly, arms to Syria have been rationed in such a manner as to limit the "war option" available to Syria's leadership—this in spite of the fact that the Syrians are able to pay for some of the arms in hard currency. Repeated requests from Damascus for larger quantities of more advanced arms have been trimmed down by Moscow, leading to friction in the bilateral relationship. Soviet restraint in selling arms to Syria indicates that Moscow is capable of closely calculating the benefits and costs of its transfers.[60] Similarly, the Soviets have been careful not to give Iraq too strong a capability against Israel.[61]

Instability in the Middle East does provide the Soviet Union with opportunities in its political and strategic competition with the West. Nonetheless, the Soviet leadership is well aware of the risks the Arab-Israeli conflict presents to it, principally the danger that it could lead to a direct confrontation with the United States. As noted, the possible advantages of a more concrete military presence in the area, in geostrategic terms, may be decreasing. Thus there exist some incentives for Soviet participation in a multilateral approach to restraints on transfers into the Middle East, *provided* the restraints are part of an overall settlement that clearly acknowledges Moscow's role. Perhaps more than anything else, the Soviet Union wishes to be recognized as a major partner in the peace process—hence its interest in a Geneva settlement and its willingness to sign the joint declaration of 1977 with the United States. As long as the Soviet leadership values détente with the West it will have an interest in avoiding serious instability in the Middle East, but its price for participating in restraints on arms transfers into the region is likely to be a recognition of its status as a co-guarantor of the peace.[62]

As for the United States, there can be little doubt that it would be to its advantage to participate in some multilateral restraints if they could be instituted. Washington has always kept an eye on the military balance in the Middle East as it sent weapons to Israel. But as a consequence of its new arms relationship with Egypt and its greatly expanded one with Saudi Arabia, it finds itself in the anomalous position of being a major supplier to both sides in the Arab-Israeli conflict. Moreover, in sponsoring the Egyptian-Israeli peace treaty it has undertaken costly obligations, which in a period of five years may exceed $10 billion in military and economic assistance. The United States has an interest in limiting the armaments of both sides in a balanced manner; during the negotiations leading to the Camp David accords it proposed a provision, which ultimately was not accepted, under which Israel and Egypt would agree to begin discussions on reducing their armaments. For a long time the United States justified to the Arabs the special arms supplier relationship with Israel as being necessary to make Jerusalem more secure, and thereby more flexible, in political negotiations. This argument is unlikely to be acceptable in the future, but a direct commitment to guarantee Israel's security through some type of mutual defense agreement could accompany an overall peace settlement. The Carter administration would have been willing to discuss such an agreement with Israel in 1978 if the Israelis had wanted one.

The incentives to Israel for placing a cap on military purchases by the Middle East states are often overlooked. The cost of arming the country has escalated with each successive war, to the point that military expenditures now put an enormous drain on the nation's increasingly shaky economy. Over 35 percent of Israel's gross national product is absorbed by defense needs (compared to less than 4 percent for Germany or France, and 5 percent for the United States). This figure is by far the highest in the world. If one adds repayment on debts which are mostly defense

206

related, the figure rises to an astounding 59 percent. (Before the 1967 war, only 10 percent of the GNP was devoted to defense; defense outlays increased annually by more than 20 percent between 1967 and 1979.) By 1978 the military budget came to about $1,000 per capita, compared to an average of about $100 per capita in Egypt, Jordan, and Syria. In short, the economic burden of Israel's defense requirements is huge.[63] The manpower toll is also great. Of a Jewish population of 3 million, close to 600,000 men and women have active or reserve status—again the highest proportion in the world. The psychological drain of constant military preparedness is unmeasurable, but very real; it is underlined by the growing rate of emigration. Moreover, the high rate of inflation which is attributable to defense outlays has forced reductions in social welfare and education programs.

To this must be added the consideration that Israel no longer has the degree of monopoly on America's interests in the Middle East it once enjoyed. Saudi Arabia and, increasingly, Egypt have become central to the economic and geopolitical interests of the United States. Whereas Israel could in the past successfully object to proposed American arms sales to Arab countries, and through actively lobbying against them in the Congress, see them curtailed if not canceled, the situation has changed dramatically. This was illustrated by its inability to have the sale of F-15s to Saudi Arabia canceled in 1978; it was noteworthy that two years later Israeli spokesmen did not even publicly object to the sale of F-16s and many other arms to Egypt or to renewed sales of anti-aircraft missiles to Saudi Arabia. (The pending sale of AWACS and F-15 components to Saudi Arabia led, however, to new objections.) Rather, the Israeli government contented itself with asking for delays in the weapons deliveries to the Arab states and requested an increase in military and economic aid for itself. It is not so much that Israel has lost influence with the United States but that because of such events as the Camp David accords, developments in the Horn of Africa, the collapse of Iran and instability in the Persian Gulf, and the Soviet invasion of Afghanistan, other states in the region have gained in influence.

In the long run, Israel's security can best be guaranteed through a negotiated peace settlement. Despite the impressive nature of its defense industry, its armed forces will remain dependent upon advanced arms from abroad. Economic prosperity cannot be achieved as long as the nation remains on a war footing. The demographic growth of the Arab states continues; Israel's population is declining. The oil-rich states are becoming ever richer and more able to afford military arms, or to endure a war of attrition. The revival of Islamic fervor and the pull of ideological forces in the Arab world are creating pressures toward a political radicalization which is likely to make added difficulties for Israel. An arms control framework that imposes restraints on transfers into the region should therefore be in its interest.

Economic conditions in the Arab countries bordering Israel also argue for reduced spending on arms. This was clearly one of Sadat's motivations as he went to Jerusalem and pursued the negotiations. The withdrawal of Saudi Arabia's economic assistance to Egypt put still greater strains on the sinking Egyptian economy. Although the peace agreement with Israel may permit a slight reduction in the overall size of Egyptian forces, the continuing tensions in the region have made the modernization of the armed forces with higher-quality weapons from abroad seem necessary. Jordan is also caught between the desire to modernize its armed forces and economic dependency; while Syria, though better able to afford arms, cannot ensure either its political stability or its economic prosperity without peace.

Viewed realistically, the establishment of restraints upon arms transfers into the Middle East confrontation area is a most difficult, sensitive, and complex task. Nevertheless, there may be sufficient common interests among the states that would be involved to make the task worth pursuing. To succeed, an accord on transfers into the region would have to involve the four major suppliers and also be acceptable to the recipients. The basic initiative would have to come from the suppliers. Initially it might involve little more than an agreement to consult on the consequences of the intended transfer of certain weapons. But even this could be

208

highly significant as a way of ensuring or creating a military balance between the opposing parties. Multilateral arms restraint cannot of itself prevent a conflict, but it could reduce the risk and help build confidence among the states in the region. Accordingly, arms restraint might be sought in parallel to the negotiations for an Arab-Israeli political settlement. Such restraints should be an important dimension of a comprehensive Middle East settlement, and should help to underpin it. Indeed, arms and politics have become so intertwined in the Middle East that a lasting settlement may well depend upon restraints on arms sales.

ASIA

The second largest arms recipient region in the developing world is Asia, comprising both East Asia from Japan to Indonesia and South Asia from Bangladesh to Afghanistan. This region accumulated far more arms from outside suppliers during the past two decades than either Latin America or sub-Saharan Africa even if we exclude the large transfers into the Indochinese states because of the Vietnam War. According to ACDA statistics, arms transfers to Asia between 1969 and 1978 came to $34.4 billion, of which $18.2 billion went to the two Vietnams, Cambodia, Laos, and Thailand.[64] The geographical spread of nations in Asia is so great, and their political nature and security concerns are so diverse, that it is impossible to conceive of any regime for arms restraint except for one or two subregional groupings, such as the Korean peninsula or South Asia. There are, however, very important arms sales issues in the region: the impact of sales to the People's Republic of China and Taiwan on Soviet-American and Sino-American relations; the maintenance of the military balance between the two Koreas; and the prevention of escalation in the India-Pakistan arms race.

South Korea

South Korea has been the largest recipient of arms, with the exception of the two Vietnams, and has relied almost exclusively for its more advanced weapons upon the United States (with relatively insignificant purchases from France). From the beginning of the Korean War to 1978 the United States provided more than $7.8 billion in military assistance in the form of grant aid, excess defense articles, foreign military sales credits, and military edu-

210

cation and training. By the end of 1978, the South Korean armed forces had sent 34,225 officers and men to the United States for training. In addition, Seoul has benefited from American technological assistance in the establishment of an indigenous arms-manufacturing industry.

Despite the close ties inherent in this security relationship, South Korea's relations with the United States have been far from trouble free. The authoritarian nature of President Park Chung Hee's government and its alleged violation of human rights and suppression of the opposition, as well as the Korean Central Intelligence Agency's attempt to bribe American congressmen, deeply troubled many Americans. Conversely, South Koreans could not understand or accept the early decision of the Carter administration to withdraw American ground combat forces from the country, arguing that it was underestimating the magnitude of the military threat from the north. As a consequence of the American intelligence community's upward revision of its estimate of the strength of North Korean armed forces, concern expressed by other Asian nations about the withdrawal, and the lack of domestic support for the withdrawal plans, President Carter decided in 1979 to suspend indefinitely the pullout of the remaining 31,000 American troops, about 4,000 having already gone home. Subsequently, President Reagan promised that American forces would remain indefinitely.

Nevertheless, as a result of the withdrawal initiative the United States committed itself to a vast program of arms sales. To preserve the military balance on the Korean peninsula, the United States agreed in 1977 to modernize and strengthen Republic of Korea forces with $2 billion in equipment. As part of the "compensatory measures" for the U.S. withdrawals, Seoul was promised military sales credits over a five-year period for the purchase of aircraft, Nike-Hercules surface-to-air missiles, anti-tank missiles, and other weapons. In addition, stockpiles of equipment with U.S. forces in Korea were to be turned over to the Korean armed forces. We have here an instance of a recipient country, long dependent upon an outside supplier, that had substantially improved its security and its economic condition—yet, ironically, the "price" of that progress was a still greater sale of arms to facilitate a partial American withdrawal.

The development of South Korea's own defense industry has been motivated by a desire to increase its self-sufficiency and reduce dependence upon the United States. The nation's dynamic economic growth in the 1970s and its export-oriented industrial policy have contributed to a growing sense of national strength and independence. Seoul now manufactures a wide assortment of unsophisticated military equipment from helmets to howitzers, mortars, and ammunition. Increasingly it is moving toward the production of more advanced items, such as M-48 tanks, rocket launchers and missiles, and high-speed patrol boats; some of these are already made under licensing arrangements with American companies. As its defense industry expands, it is expected that South Korea will become an exporter of arms to other countries in the region. It is already exporting its version of the M-16 rifle, and light vessels have been sold to the Indonesian navy. Washington has given its general support to the development of a defense industry by permitting some co-production agreements. These are designed to increase Seoul's self-confidence.

The United States must, however, carefully calibrate its arms sales to Seoul so as to maintain the regional balance and not allow North Korea to feel threatened by the possibility of South Korea launching an offensive. If the South Koreans were to become overarmed, it might give Pyongyang leverage over Moscow sufficient to induce Moscow to resolve their differences and resume large-scale arms shipments, this time of highly advanced arms. A competitive arms race on the peninsula would not be in the interests of the United States, South Korea, or China. Thus, co-production of aircraft and missiles, which Seoul wants, should be approached with caution. For this reason, also, the United States has been unwilling, thus far, to sell South Korea a highly sophisticated longer-range fighter aircraft which could easily outperform those of the North Koreans. In the fall of 1978, President Carter sided with the State Department and ACDA in deferring a Pentagon request for permission to sell sixty F-16s to South

Korea, with associated co-production rights.[65] The aircraft's long-range penetration capability was seen as needlessly provocative to the North. The result of such a sale, it was judged, would have been the escalation of the arms competition on the peninsula with pressures from Pyongyang on Moscow to make available the MiG-23. Up to then Moscow had only transferred MiG-21s, although the more advanced MiG-23s had been supplied to other countries such as Iraq, Syria, and Libya. The proposed $1.2 billion sale of F-16s would also have violated the Carter administration's policy against introducing into a region of conflict advanced weapons systems that would create a significantly higher combat capability. On the other hand, Washington has given approval to the assembly in South Korea of the more limited-range F-5E fighter. The Reagan administration, however, has viewed the situation differently. (Already in the last year of the Carter administration attitudes were changing.) In March 1981 it decided to sell 36 F-16s to South Korea, along with related equipment, for $900 million. The actual impact upon the North awaited to be seen.

North Korea

North Korea has received about 90 percent of its major arms from the Soviet Union, with the remainder coming from China. It, too, is developing a light-arms manufacturing capability and has received assistance from Moscow in developing co-production and assembly plants for weapons, especially artillery pieces. But even more than the South, it will continue to rely upon outside suppliers for more advanced arms. And the Soviet Union has been cautious in what arms it has shipped, so as to help maintain some balance and restrict Pyongyang's freedom of action against South Korea. This suggests that were the United States and the Soviet Union someday to undertake discussions on arms transfer restraints to specific countries or regions, the two Koreas could usefully become the subject of such talks. Similarly, any negotiations between South Korea and North Korea on steps toward eventual reunification, the possibility of which has been raised

213

from time to time, or alternatively diplomatic steps toward a full recognition of two separate states, could well have an arms control component. The political conditions that would be needed for such types of restraints remain, for the moment, very distant.

Taiwan

The next largest arms recipient in Asia is Taiwan. Although its population is only about 2 percent the size of mainland China's, Taiwan is economically prosperous and militarily well equipped. Ostensibly, Taiwan's strategic goal is to attack the mainland and recover lost territory. Realistically, its armed forces need only be adequate to deter, or defend against, an invasion of Taiwan and the smaller islands of Quemoy and Matsu. For this task there are 475,000 men in arms, an additional 100,000 in the militia, and over 1.1 million in the reserves. Taiwan's armed forces have for many years been generously equipped by the United States, with $5.2 billion in grants or sales from 1950 to the end of 1979. American planners have carefully restricted assistance to defensive arms, with emphasis on naval and air weapons defenses, in quantities more than sufficient to prevent an invasion or air attack from the mainland. Thus Taiwan has a wide array of destroyers, frigates, artillery, and combat aircraft such as the F-5E, of which it has 200, and the aging F-104, as well as a considerable quantity of tanks and ground equipment. Short-range missiles have been purchased from Israel and several submarines were ordered from the Netherlands in 1981, much to Beijing's dismay and anger.

The People's Republic, on the other hand, has not developed a significant capability for transporting troops across the sea to Taiwan, nor does it have the necessary forces to protect an invasion fleet through command of the sea and air. One PRC airborne division has been situated on the coast opposite Taiwan, but the vast portion of its armed forces is deployed along the border with the Soviet Union. Nationalist Chinese on Taiwan like to point out their apparent vulnerability, as suggested by their small numbers in comparison to the People's Republic, but the natural barrier created by the sea, the adequacy of the weapons they have received, and Beijing's concentration of its military forces in another direction, have actually made them quite secure.

The normalization of relations between Beijing and Washington at the end of 1978 created a new political situation for Taiwan. To a noteworthy extent, the question of American arms sales to Taiwan was an important dimension of both the process of normalization and its consequences. Beijing had long insisted upon three conditions for normalization: a shift in formal diplomatic relations with China from Taipei to Beijing, the withdrawal of all U.S. forces from Taiwan, and the abrogation of the 1954 Mutual Defense Treaty between the United States and Taiwan. After the signing of the Shanghai communiqué in 1972, American forces on the island were gradually reduced from 10,000 to a nominal 750, who were performing noncombat functions. The Carter administration was prepared not only to shift recognition from Taipei to Beijing but also to withdraw the remaining U.S. military personnel and end the treaty. The latter was done after normalization by giving one year's notice, as provided in the treaty itself, rather than through abrogation. But an impasse remained since the United States insisted it would continue the sale of arms to Taiwan. This was essential to avoid both the appearance and the reality of abandoning the island. The breakthrough that ultimately made normalization possible was the concession by Beijing to proceed even though it recognized that the United States intended to continue to supply defensive arms to Taiwan in the face of PRC objections. Actually, in an intricate duet the two countries implicitly agreed to disagree. Beijing denounced the American sale of weapons to Taiwan while the United States, it subsequently was revealed, agreed not to make any fresh commitments for arms sales for one year, until termination of the treaty. Meanwhile, however, the supplies in the pipeline, which came to about $800 million, would continue to flow, and Washington made clear that new sales would be made again, starting in 1980 at the end of the moratorium.[66]

The ending of the defense treaty may, in fact, lead to greater

215

sales than would have been the case otherwise. The U.S. Congress in the Taiwan Relations Act of 1979 went on record in support of future weapons sales to Taiwan; and in January 1980, in the first week after the moratorium ended, the United States announced the resumption of arms sales with $280 million credits for anti-aircraft missiles and other defensive weapons. Sales that year came to about $1 billion. For several years Taiwan has been asking for a more advanced fighter aircraft. Although it co-produces the F-5E on the island, and was offered forty-eight more of them in 1978, it wanted to obtain the F-4 Phantom. Because of the plane's 1,000-mile range and a concern about giving Taiwan an offensive capability that would upset the military balance in the Taiwan Strait region and be politically provocative to the PRC, the Carter administration refused to approve the sale. Some administration officials favored suggesting as an alternative that Taiwan consider the shorter-range Israeli Kfir. Although a Nationalist delegation visited Israel to inspect the Kfir, and reportedly left very impressed, it was decided not to purchase it because of concerns about relations with the Arab world. Taiwan receives oil from Saudi Arabia, as well as credits for the purchase of oil. Moreover, the Nationalists have long attached special importance to the receipt of arms from the United States, as a measure of support for them, and this factor became of still greater import with the end of formal relations.

For the Reagan administration, finding a way to satisfy Taiwan's desire for an aircraft to replace the F-5 has turned out to be a major dilemma. It has complicated the development of expanded political and military relations with Beijing. The natural replacement would be the FX, in either the Northrop F-5G version or the General Dynamics F-16/79. Given the close support which Taipei has received from the conservative wing of the Republican Party and Ronald Reagan's oft-repeated pledges of sympathy, it had reason to believe it would receive the FX. But Beijing made it crystal clear, especially on the occasion of Secretary of State Alexander Haig's trip to China in June 1981, that this would be seen as a very unfriendly act, making the further development of relations impossible. So as to underline its concern, China's leaders let it be known that they would prefer a situation in which they would forego U.S. arms, with Taiwan not receiving the FX, to one in which the FX was sold to Taiwan and Beijing received the same or a commensurate weapons system. To complicate the issue further, most defense analysts in the Pentagon agree that there is no military necessity for Taiwan to receive the FX. It is superior to anything Beijing has, and the argument made by the Nationalists that it is necessary for the defense of the Taiwan straits is rejected. Yet the FX acquired great symbolic importance—for the Nationalists as confirmation of U.S. support, for many Americans as not abandoning an old friend, and for the Chinese on the mainland as a litmus test for future Sino-American relations.

The management of the arms sales relationship between the United States and Taiwan has been, and will continue to be, closely linked to the evolution of America's relations with Beijing. Washington's concern is that Taiwan not receive offensive weapons capable of being used against the mainland, yet possess adequate arms to ensure its security. Taiwan's interests, on the other hand, are likely to lead it toward reducing its hitherto almost complete dependence upon the United States for arms. A start toward developing a diversity of supply occurred in 1977 with the purchase of Gabriel surface-to-surface and Shafrir air-to-air missiles from Israel. Discussions have also taken place with South African defense officials regarding weapons cooperation. The choice of these nations is not accidental, for like Taiwan they are pariah states in the international community, having in common their diplomatic isolation and anxieties about their long-term security.[67] In addition, Taiwan can be expected to give greater priority to the development of its indigenous weapons industry. A good base for such a capability already exists through the experience acquired with the co-production of such American arms as the F-5E, Bell helicopters, and the Sidewinder missile, as well as the creation of weapons research laboratories. After the normalization of relations, Taiwan's Premier Y.S. Sun

217

announced that the defense budget would be increased to strengthen the capacity to make weapons and establish a self-sustaining defense industry.

Japan

Japan has been discussed in the previous part on suppliers. Its indigenous arms industry is well developed, if not well noticed, and Japan produces approximately 95 percent of the equipment used by its Self Defense Forces. Some of the higher technology items are co-produced with American assistance, as notably will be the F-15 during the 1980s. The critical question about Japan is not whether it will become a major recipient of arms, but the extent to which it will become a significant exporter. There has already been pressure for this from industrial and other defense-oriented quarters, which thus far has been resisted. Japan's growing role in Asia, changing perceptions of the regional balance between China, the Soviet Union, the United States, and Japan, and an evolution in its attitudes toward its own defense activities may, however, push it in that direction.

Southeast Asia

Turning to Southeast Asia we find a mixed picture. The ASEAN (Association of Southeast Asian Nations) states have shown a growing interest in acquiring arms from the West. In the Indochinese states, particularly Vietnam, there are stockpiles of both Soviet and Chinese arms as well as weapons left by the United States at the end of the Vietnam War. It has been suggested that a regional arms limitation scheme, as well as some form of weapons standardization, might be instituted among the ASEAN countries, but their highly distinct security concerns would make this very difficult.[68]

The five ASEAN states—Thailand, Indonesia, Singapore, Malaysia, and the Philippines—are in a period of unprecedented though uneven economic prosperity. At the same time they do not have a high level of armaments, either in quantity or sophis-

218

tication. Three of them—Malaysia, Thailand, and the Philippines—have internal insurgency movements to deal with. These countries exist in an uncertain environment, in which the future involvement of outside powers such as Vietnam, China, and the United States is unpredictable. This combination of factors accentuates their desire to modernize their forces.

Thailand has had a long history of receiving American arms. Because of the conflict in Indochina, there have also been close defense ties: as many as 48,000 American troops operated from ninety-three installations in the country during the height of the Vietnam War. By the end of 1976, however, all American forces had been withdrawn, and the Thai government had turned its attention to strengthening its own defense capabilities. Among its concerns were the Communist guerrilla activities in the country. The Vietnamese invasion of Cambodia and the fighting against the Chinese-supplied troops of Pol Pot increased Thailand's security concerns. When Prime Minister Kriangsak Chamanand visited Washington in February 1979, he was promised an increase in U.S. military sales to $30 million, still a modest amount. Once again, when the Vietnamese made incursions into Thailand from Cambodia in June 1980, the United States responded with a rapid airlift of artillery pieces and ammunition, with tanks to follow by sea.

Indonesia, by contrast, received most of its current weapons from the Soviet Union prior to the abortive coup and suppression of the Communist party in 1965. While Sukarno was in friendly contact with Moscow, Indonesia acquired a modern military capability with 200 jet fighters, 12 submarines, and a large amount of Soviet and Czechoslovakian armor and artillery. Today these forces are described as decrepit, and the Indonesians are embarked on an urgent replacement program. Arms are being purchased from a wide variety of sources, including France, Belgium, West Germany, South Korea, and the United States, which has sold them 16 F-5Es.

Singapore acquired substantial amounts of weapons from Britain as it withdrew from east of Suez, shortly after Singapore became an independent state in 1965. Later it purchased more

British arms from a line of credit offered by the United Kingdom to cushion the impact of the departure. After the fall of Saigon, Prime Minister Lee Kuan Yew, who saw the American departure from South Vietnam as sharply altering the balance of power, placed a new emphasis on building up the nation's small armed forces, which his economically prosperous country is well able to afford. In 1977 Singapore purchased twenty-one F-5E fighters from the United States.

With a historical background similar to Singapore's, *Malaysia* initially purchased British arms. Subsequently, France and the United States became its principal suppliers, but Washington exercised caution in order not to exacerbate Malaysia's dispute with the Philippines over Sabah (North Borneo). In 1976 Malaysia announced plans to double its armed forces of about 40,000 men over the next four years.

Finally, in the case of the *Philippines*, the principal motivation for the increased arms purchases in the latter half of the 1970s was not any external threat, which is practically nonexistent, but the Muslim insurgency in the south. As the rights for the American bases at Subic Bay and Clark Field came up for renegotiation, the government of President Marcos initially asked for $1 billion in aid, half of it in military assistance. Although this demand was cut in half, the United States is making available substantial defense equipment, which, in effect, is a form of rental for the bases. This is viewed by some Americans as a source of embarrassment because of the repressive nature of the Marcos regime and its regrettable record on human rights.

The non-Communist countries of Southeast Asia are not likely to want a dramatic increase in the quantity or quality of their arms, although each nation will have its set of reasons for improving its defense capabilities. There is no reason this cannot be accomplished without increasing the neighboring states' perceptions of threat; a gradual improvement in the still modest military capabilities should enhance feelings of security and confidence. Such nations might be considered by Washington as potential candidates for a new medium-capability FX fighter, or for more F-5Es, rather than becoming recipients of advanced

aircraft such as the F-16 or F-15. The growing political cooperation among the ASEAN nations and their economic prosperity
are among the brighter spots on the international political land-
scape. The big question will remain the future direction of
Vietnam.

Vietnam is by far the strongest state militarily in Southeast
Asia although it is not as powerful as it appears on paper. Its
armed forces have more manpower than those of the five
ASEAN states combined, and they are battle hardened. There is
a surplus of weapons. During the war the North received most
of its arms from the Soviet Union, and it still possesses squadrons
of MiG-19s and MiG-21s, as well as batteries of SAM missiles,
Russian tanks, and more. In addition, it captured large quantities
of American weapons from the South Vietnamese army and took
possession of weapons left by the departing U.S. forces. These last
include 75 F-5 fighters and another 900 aircraft, 600 tanks, 1,200
armored personnel carriers, and much more. By the end of the
1970s, however, many of these arms were no longer usable.
Without careful servicing and the replacement of parts that were
unavailable to the Vietnamese, they could not be kept in fighting
shape. Nevertheless, Vietnam has sufficient weapons in relation
to its needs so that it is not likely to be a purchaser of arms for
some time.

India and Pakistan

One subregion where there has been a veritable arms race is
South Asia. Prior to the conflict between India and Pakistan in
1965, Pakistan received most of its arms from the United States.
As a member of both SEATO and CENTO, it was seen as a bul-
wark of anticommunism. India, in keeping with its policy of nonalignment with the two superpowers, bought the largest portion
of its arms from Britain and a far lesser amount from France. At
the time of the 1965 war, when to some extent American and
British arms were being used against each other, Washington and
London decided to impose an arms embargo on both participants. This embargo lasted until 1975, during which time India

221

turned to the Soviet Union. The U.S.S.R. seized the opportunity to gain influence in what was considered by many at the time the most significant of developing countries—as went India, it was said, so went the Third World. Moscow extended very favorable terms for an array of weapons purchases, with long-term credit payable in rupees, and it allowed the co-production of the MiG-21 in India. All three of the Indian military services were basically equipped with Soviet arms.[69] Pakistan, on the other hand, turned to China, the rival of India and the Soviet Union, for military aid.

Following the lifting of the embargo in 1975, both nations sought to diversify their arms purchases. India continued to depend upon the Soviet Union as its principal supplier, but it also bought arms from France and Britain. Included in the weapons from Europe were the Harrier STOL plane for India's only aircraft carrier and the Anglo-French Jaguar fighter as well as tanks. In addition, New Delhi sought to reduce its dependence by further developing its own arms-manufacturing industry. The defense industry now employs 250,000, is capable of producing all but quite advanced arms with the aid in some cases of co-production arrangements, and includes an aircraft company making India's own Marut jet fighter. Pakistan has also succeeded in developing an arms industry even though it is on a far more modest scale than New Delhi's. It asked the United States for an intermediate level jet fighter, the A-7, but its requests were turned down by the Carter administration on the ground that the A-7 would provide too great an offensive capability against India. Washington was, however, receptive to supplying a shorter-range aircraft, such as the F-5E. After 1976, the Symington Amendment to the Foreign Assistance Act, which forbids military and economic assistance credit to countries believed to be developing a nuclear weapons capability, was also a limiting factor. Instead, Pakistan bought from France Mirage III fighters, Alouette helicopters, Crotale missiles, and other arms. China has also come to Pakistan's aid by giving substantial technical support to help establish an aeronautical complex for the overhaul of older aircraft.

Shortly after the Soviet invasion of Afghanistan the Carter administration, perceiving the Russian troops on the border of Pakistan as a new threat to the region, urgently sought to provide assistance to Pakistan. Setting aside some of the administration's former non-proliferation concerns as well as reservations about the repressive nature and the human rights record of the Zia regime, it offered to provide Islamabad with $400 million in military and economic assistance, with more to come according to NSC Assistant to the President Zbigniew Brzezinski. The Congress was to be asked to make a special "exception" to the Symington Amendment to permit the United States to furnish aid on an open-ended basis as long as the new situation lasted. This turned out to be unnecessary, however, as General Zia ul-Haq turned down the American offer as "peanuts," compared to the estimated need of $2 billion. Zia apparently calculated that acceptance of a limited American offer was not worth the price he might have to pay in terms of relations with the Soviet Union; he may also have had doubts about the constancy of American support.

A new page was turned, however, after the Reagan administration came into office. Whereas the Carter administration had limited its military assistance offer to "defensive" arms—anti-tank weapons, radars, and other equipment usable on the frontier—Pakistan was now offered a large five-year package worth $3 billion that included the F-16, a sale that had previously been refused. Even the U.S. Air Force had reservations about the F-16, making a recommendation that the F-5G, one of the two prototypes for the FX, would be sufficient as a counter to the MiG-23s that India was receiving. Political considerations appear to have been paramount, however, as the Reagan administration gave priority to countering the Soviet threat emanating from the Hindu Kush and the Indus Valley in Afghanistan. It insisted, moreover, that dealing with Pakistan's insecurities by selling conventional weapons and reestablishing a relationship of confidence was the best way in the long run to restrain Islamabad's nuclear ambitions.

Yet in New Delhi the willingness of the United States to come to Islamabad's support was viewed with deep misgivings. The Indians assume that Pakistan's arms are intended for use against them, rather than for the defense of the northern frontiers. They contend that Pakistan uses American concern about the Soviet Union to obtain arms that would not be used against Russia but against India. The Pakistanis make a mirror-image appraisal of India's motivations. President Carter sought to reassure the Indians by sending a special emissary, Clark Clifford, to New Delhi to stress that any new American arms for Pakistan would not be used against them and by offering to provide sophisticated electronic gear for guidance systems for aircraft, missiles, and so-called smart bombs that Washington had earlier refused to sell to India. This did not, however, prevent India from signing a major new arms deal with the Soviet Union in May 1980 providing for $1.63 billion in arms to modernize the Indian armed forces over five years. In this accord, Moscow reverted to its former practice of offering extraordinarily favorable terms; in this instance, India has seventeen years to pay for the arms at a 2.5 percent annual rate of interest. The deal enabled India to build under license arrangements two major weapons systems: the MiG-23 (as a successor to its MiG-21s) and the T-72 tank. Reportedly, the MiG-25 is also to be sold to India. For the Soviet Union this was an opportunity to cement ties with the new government of Indira Gandhi, recently returned to power, and to counter a negative impression following its actions in Afghanistan. During a trip to New Delhi in December 1980, Brezhnev offered a wide array of military and economic joint projects designed to restore close relations with the U.S.S.R.

The underlying tensions between Pakistan and India are likely to continue. With all the major suppliers involved in selling arms to the antagonists, it is essential that they weigh carefully the risk of a new war breaking out in South Asia. The dangers are especially critical because of the nuclear aspirations and growing capabilities of both parties. Pakistan at the beginning of the 1980s was making great efforts to become a nuclear power through the clandestine construction of a nuclear fuel-reprocessing plant; its motivation and drive were so strong that any new provision of conventional arms, by itself, was not likely to induce it to abandon the nuclear option. If Pakistan detonates a nuclear device, India is likely to resume its testing and military nuclear program. The uneasy India-Pakistan military balance should be high on the priority list for consultations among the Western suppliers. Britain and France have been, and are likely to continue to be, major suppliers in the region, while West Germany and Japan have given economic assistance. As long as Soviet troops are in Afghanistan along the Pakistan border, the challenge will be to satisfy Islamabad's legitimate defense requirements without supplying arms that could be used to undermine India's security. Over the longer run, the Soviet interest in not having to deal with a conflict in the subcontinent might be drawn upon for some type of multilateral consultations. Both the powers outside the region, and those within it, have a stake in the stability of South Asia.

People's Republic of China

The question of whether to sell arms to the People's Republic of China has become a major issue for the Western suppliers in the past few years.[70] Given the deep tensions between the Soviet Union and China, would the transfer of arms to Beijing be viewed by the Soviets as so provocative and hostile an act as to lead to a major reassessment in the Kremlin and a further serious deterioration in relations with the West? Would the sale of arms by such countries as France and Britain be less likely to offend the Soviets than sales by the United States? What are China's legitimate military needs? Are they principally to defend itself against the Soviet Union? And how can one be certain that the arms would not be used against Taiwan, or even in Korea, should war break out on the peninsula again?

Almost all of China's military equipment, except for the nuclear force, is badly out of date. Most of the conventional arms now in the hands of the armed forces either were given by the Soviet Union prior to the termination of military assistance in the years 1958–1960 or are Chinese-built copies of early designs.

225

China's air force consists in large measure of the early-generation MiG-17s and 19s, and the Shenyang F-7 fighter modeled on the MiG-21 obtained before 1960; the army's 10,000 tanks are mostly copies of Soviet models from the 1950s; and the navy is essentially limited to coastal defense. Equally important, China's forces almost completely lack the technology that is now commonly found in the armed forces of the major powers, such as anti-tank weapons, surface-to-air and air-to-air missiles, precision-guided munitions, and advanced communications equipment of all kinds. The consequences of this lack of modern equipment were seen in the difficulties that the Chinese army had in dealing with the better equipped Vietnamese during the incursion into Vietnam in early 1979. With an armaments base that is essentially obsolete, China's basic problem is not one of quantity but of quality.

Only recently have the Chinese come to accept the need for more advanced conventional arms. During Mao's tenure, Chinese defense planning was based on two extremes, nuclear deterrence and the "People's War." A land invasion would be defeated through mass mobilization of the population. Under Mao's strategic concepts, men were far more important than weapons. The emphasis was upon self-reliance and ideological purity. The post-Mao leadership put forth in 1978 its goals for the economic and political development of the country during the rest of the century in its plan for the "Four Modernizations," the last of which was defense. The People's Liberation Army was probably a key factor in the accession to power of Hua Guofeng and the reappointment of Deng Xiaoping to major positions, including for a time chief of the PLA General Staff. With its newly acquired influence, the military has, not surprisingly, been interested in more modern weapons and has expressed the need to be able to engage in a more limited conflict in the wide zone between nuclear war and a mass People's War. In contrast to the time of the Cultural Revolution, when there was a tendency to deemphasize technology and modern warfare, there now appears to be a consensus on the need to modernize China's armed forces as part of the broader modernization of the country.

Beijing is not likely, however, to begin a massive arms-purchasing program. Its capacity to absorb and finance high technology weapons from abroad is very limited. Defense has the lowest priority among the Four Modernizations, ranking after agriculture, industry, and science and technology. The government's objectives in the modernization of the armed forces appear to be moderate and defensive in character. Moreover, the Chinese will want to develop their own capability for producing arms. This requires an industrial base and production capacity that are still lacking. During 1977–1978, Chinese military missions toured Western Europe visiting arms fairs with weapons displays and factories manufacturing weapons. To the dismay of their hosts, they often left after having asked many questions but having purchased virtually nothing. These appear to have been exercises in self-education, for the Chinese interest in possessing arms is not balanced by an ability to pay. Foreign exchange is scarce and there appears to be a reluctance to go into debt. What the Chinese are most interested in is manufacturing know-how and technology transfers which will enable them to build themselves or to co-produce arms under licensing arrangements. Clearly, the China market for arms will not create a bonanza for salesmen similar to the Persian Gulf trade during the 1970s.

Nevertheless, Beijing may be prepared to make substantial purchases at some point. Negotiations have taken place with France for an arms package of $350 million to include the Hot and the Milan anti-tank missiles and anti-aircraft weapons such as the Crotale and Roland missiles, some of which would be manufactured in China under license. To the surprise of the French, the Chinese have also expressed interest in purchasing a large quantity of the supersonic Mirage 2000 once it becomes available. After considerable uncertainty, Britain in 1979 agreed in principle to sell eighty Harrier vertical takeoff and landing strike fighters, as part of a wider $1.2 billion trade deal. As of 1980, however, the Chinese had still not fully committed themselves to any of these sales, perhaps because of foreign exchange shortages. Earlier, London sold Rolls Royce Spey engines to be fitted to MiG fighters or to a new Chinese interceptor, the F-12, expected to be operational in the early 1980s. And following the normalization

227

of relations with the United States, Beijing let it be known quietly that it hoped the refusal of the United States to sell arms would be reassessed. American aviation industry officials who visited China in 1979 were told of the Chinese interest in buying Lockheed C-130 military transport and P-3C anti-submarine patrol planes. These aircraft may well have been chosen at the time because of their less objectionable nature, and as a way of promoting a less restrictive American policy. After the Soviet invasion of Afghanistan, however, Chinese officials expressed interest in eventually acquiring F-16s or F-15s.

The sale of arms to China raises difficult and complex issues for the Western countries. The Soviet leadership harbors a deep distrust of China bordering on paranoia, for it goes far beyond any real danger Beijing could pose to the U.S.S.R. in even the medium-term future. The possibility of Western sales of arms or weapons-related technology to China strikes a particularly sensitive nerve in the Soviet body politic. Brezhnev, in bilateral communications with the supplier countries, has repeatedly warned that such sales would further damage détente and relations with Moscow. Although the Western countries show few signs of being intimidated, they must view any sales decisions in the overall context of what goals they wish to achieve in their other dealings with the U.S.S.R. and in East-West relations. As Lawrence Freedman has written, the "concern is not so much with Soviet retaliation but with the danger of feeding Soviet neuroses."[71] This concern, it should be noted, is not restricted to Washington. The French stepped back from a very lucrative sale of Mirage fighters because of the potential Soviet reaction. Related to this is the concern that a Chinese military buildup could greatly aggravate the confrontation between China and the Soviet Union and increase the likelihood of further hostilities. In addition, one must weigh the risk that the arms could one day be used against Taiwan, South Korea, or other Western-supported states.

Yet good reasons do exist for selling arms to China on a careful and selective basis. China is at present militarily very weak and vulnerable. It is desirable that it be able to defend itself better against Soviet threats. This might also be of strategic value to the

228

West by tying down large Soviet forces on the U.S.S.R.'s eastern borders and complicating Soviet military planning, rather than having these forces near Europe; in this sense a better armed China could also act as a counterweight and inhibit Soviet actions in Asia. A less unequal balance in the military strength of the two powers might serve to increase the stability of their relationship and lessen the Soviet temptation to make a "surgical" strike against China, as has been discussed from time to time. The creation of some limited military ties between China and the West through arms sales would give sustenance to the ongoing process of normalizing and deepening relations and might thereby diminish the risk of a Sino-Soviet rapprochement. To turn Beijing down would be to discourage its opening to the West. Finally, arms sales to China may at some point be a concrete incentive for Moscow to cooperate with the West on managing arms transfers on a global basis.

The Carter administration, after two years of internal debate on the question, decided in 1979 not to sell arms to China but not to object to sales by its West European allies either. It officially maintained an "evenhanded" policy of not selling arms to either Moscow or Beijing. This middle course made sense, for it left the United States, as the leading power of the West, free of the onus of what would be strongly perceived by the Soviets as a hostile act, while allowing Beijing to receive some of the arms it wants. The assumption, probably correct, was that the Soviets would be less disturbed by European than by American sales. Moreover, it was the intention of the European powers to sell only "defensive" arms, weapons such as anti-tank or anti-aircraft missiles, or short-range aircraft that could be used for the defense of China but would not be effective in an attack upon either the Soviet Union or Taiwan.

Symbolism has been of great importance in the matter of arms sales to China. The Chinese would prefer American to European arms in part because of what this would say about an American commitment. The United States, at least in the past, preferred to let the Europeans take the lead because for Washington to sell arms would be symbolically inciting to the Soviets. (Actually to change the Sino-Soviet military balance would require an enormous transfusion of weaponry.) Following the Soviet invasion of Afghanistan it was decided to modify U.S. policy so as to make it less restrictive; this was intended as a signal to Moscow. Secretary of Defense Harold Brown, on a trip to Beijing in early 1980, told the Chinese that the United States was prepared to sell "nonlethal" military equipment such as radar, communications and training equipment, trucks, transport aircraft like the Lockheed C-130, helicopters, and some "dual-use" technologies (items primarily of civilian use but with possible military applications), such as computers—but still no actual weapons. The Reagan administration went a major step further on the occasion of Secretary of State Alexander Haig's trip to Beijing in June 1981. At that time the United States agreed in principle to sell "lethal" weapons on a case-by-case basis. No specific sales were agreed to, however, and initial sales are likely to be limited to "defensive" weapons.

Influencing Soviet behavior on a global scale has been a key consideration in the evolving American policy on arms sales to China under both the Carter and the Reagan administrations. As concern about a Soviet invasion of Poland grew, American officials indicated that such a step would lead to a further willingness to arm China. Secretary of State Cyrus Vance remained, however, highly sensitive to Russian reactions and fears of encirclement. Secretary Haig, on the other hand, was more inclined to "play the China card," to see in a developing military relationship with China an opportunity for creating a strategic Chinese-American consensus that could lead to coordinated policies on such issues as Afghanistan and Cambodia. The danger was that once the card was on the table, it would no longer provide leverage for constraining Soviet actions.

In the future it would be desirable to coordinate carefully the policies of the Western supplier states on selling arms to China, and to discuss individual sales of significance. To what point should the West assist the Chinese in modernizing their armed forces? What are the risks of allowing the co-production of advanced arms in China if one then loses control over the

230

amounts manufactured? What are the dangers of transferring certain technologies through sales, or co-production arrangements, if the same technologies can be used on more sophisticated weapons? Where does one draw the line between "defensive" and "offensive" arms? Thus far COCOM, the consultative group set up in 1949 for controlling strategic exports to Communist countries, which includes the NATO countries (except Iceland) and Japan, has not been very effective in dealing with sales to China (this is discussed further in the next part). Neither has NATO itself succeeded in developing any guidelines on sales to Beijing, despite an attempt in 1978. The result is that although there is some exchange of information, there is no systematic coordination of arms sales. Between France and the other Europeans, for example, competition is the rule. Some multilateral coordination is clearly both desirable and necessary.

LATIN AMERICA

In contrast with the Middle East or Asia, Latin America is not a region purchasing huge amounts of arms. Only 6 percent of the arms imported by developing countries between 1969 and 1978 are accounted for by Latin America.[72] Most countries of the region spend less than 2 percent of their gross national product on military expenditures, with the notable exception in recent years of Peru and Chile, which have spent more than 5 percent, and Cuba, which by one estimate spends 8 percent.[73] The sophistication of the weapons to be found in the armed forces is several notches below that of some other regions, where armed conflict is more likely to occur.

Still, Latin America is of special interest in examining the global politics of arms sales. The diversity of suppliers is greater than in any other region, with the United States no longer dominating the market as it did prior to the mid-1960s. Political factors in the supplier-recipient relationship are less significant than elsewhere, so that commercial considerations play a greater role. The Soviet Union has entered the open market in one country, Peru, with aspirations for penetrating other markets. It is Cuba's sole provider. The insecurities states feel and their perceptions of the threat against which they must have a defense capability lie in the main outside the East-West axis or the Communist versus Free World dichotomy found in the politics of most other parts of the world. Yet there are very real or perceived sources of insecurity based on local geopolitical factors that drive these countries to acquire armaments. The fact that many countries have come under the control of military and authoritarian regimes adds to the incentive to arm. It also creates policy dilemmas for the supplier countries, especially the United States, when human rights considerations are a factor in arms sales decisions. Finally, there has been more interest in Latin America than in any other area in developing regional restraints on armaments, as demonstrated by the Declaration of Ayacucho of 1974. Because of the diversity of suppliers, and the still relatively low level of arms, Latin America has been suggested as a test case or model for creating regional arms control.

There are several identifiable trends in Latin American arms purchases. One is their steady progression, with the total amount of weapons imports increasing by 300 percent (in constant dollars) between 1969 and 1978. The largest recipients of arms have been Argentina, Brazil, Chile, Cuba, Peru, and Venezuela, which together bought 80 percent of the weapons received by twenty-five countries over the decade. Another trend is the increase in diversification of suppliers. As elsewhere, the Big Four lead the suppliers, but West Germany and Canada are not far behind, and other countries such as Israel and Italy have sold well in Latin America's relatively open market. The American share of the market has been decreasing since the mid-1960s, with the West Europeans combined now selling twice as much as the United States.[74] By one set of data, France was the largest supplier of arms to Latin America during the 1970s.[75] For Britain, Latin America at the end of the decade became the largest arms purchasers after the Middle East. In addition, indigenous arms industries are emerging, principally in Brazil and Argentina, but on a smaller scale also in Chile and Venezuela. Altogether, Latin America is the most competitive market, in commercial rather than political terms, in the world.

Particular note should be made of what led to the opening of the Latin American market. After World War II the United States supplied most of Latin America's arms, mainly through grants of equipment from surplus stocks. Hemispheric security was the essential concern. In the early 1960s the emphasis shifted to counterinsurgency in response to Cuban support of insurgent activities. But within a few years some Latin American countries wanted more sophisticated and expensive weapons. This was opposed by many American officials committed, under the principles of the Alliance for Progress initiated by the Kennedy administration, to giving priority to economic development. Advanced arms were not only seen as wasteful and a diversion of scarce development resources but were judged as unnecessary for counterinsurgency purposes. Several countries wanted the new F-5 aircraft, a barely supersonic aircraft, regarded as a low technology item a decade later. But U.S. officials informed Latin American governments in 1967 that they would not permit sales that would cross the supersonic threshold on the continent for at least two years. Washington offered to sell Peru, among other countries, more of the subsonic F-86s, despite repeated Peruvian expressions of interest in the F-5. At this point France, without consulting the United States, filled the breach by offering to sell the supersonic and more expensive Mirage 5. The deal was quickly made, and subsequently the Latin American countries turned to the European suppliers who rapidly expanded their arms exports to the continent. While the United States unilaterally maintained restrictions on sales and credits for several years, the West Europeans sold $1.3 billion of arms between 1968 and 1972. This represented 84 percent of Latin American arms purchases (excluding Cuba).[76]

Security Concerns and the Military

For several reasons there has been an increase in tensions within Latin America in recent years and a growth in concerns about national security. Writings on strategy and geopolitics have come into vogue, especially in the more authoritarian southern cone countries of South America. Most observers of the world's trouble spots think of Latin America as a peaceful continent and tend to ignore, or be ignorant of, its latent conflicts. Within the region, however, the national military establishments take seriously the possibility of war erupting over any one of a series of disputes. These conflict contingencies are a major, though not exclusive, source of pressure for increasing expenditures on the armed forces.

There are a surprisingly large number of border disputes and territorial claims within Latin America which lead to local rivalries and revanchist attitudes: (1) One of the sharpest conflicts is between Peru and Chile over land conquered by Chile during the War of the Pacific in 1879; Bolivia lost its access to the sea at the same time and wishes to regain it. In the several years just prior to the centennial of the war, there was much talk in Lima of preparing to redeem the national honor and there was a military buildup along the Tacna-Arica frontier. (2) Argentina and Chile have been priming for war over islands in the Beagle Channel, to the point of practice air alerts being held in Buenos Aires to prepare for a Chilean bombardment. The underlying sources of this dispute, which has been the subject of international mediation, relate to mineral and fishing rights, off-shore oil, and portions of the Antarctica. It led both countries to spend over $1 billion each for new ships and weapons in the late 1970s and to deploy forces along their long border. (3) Venezuela and Colombia are in conflict over territorial waters that are likely to have oil reserves. (4) Ecuador arms itself to be able to reconquer land in the Amazon lost to Peru in 1941; border clashes occurred between the two countries forty years later. (5) Guatemala has periodically threatened a military solution to enforce its claims to the disputed territory of Belize. (6) Honduras and El Salvador have disagreed over boundaries and fought briefly in 1969. Other disputes could be cited, as well as the longstanding rivalry between Argentina and Brazil. Although in the latter case there is little chance of armed conflict, the factor of national pride still exists. If Brazil were to join the nuclear club, the pressures within Argentina to follow suit would be strong.

That there has been a rise in intraregional tensions during the past decade is indisputable. Whether this is matched by a greater likelihood of actual military conflict breaking out, however, is questionable. Why then the increased concern about national security and military preparedness? The answer appears to be the coming into power of military-dominated, authoritarian governments in the large majority of states of South America. In

1963 all the major countries of South America had civilian governments; by 1976 only Venezuela and Colombia had civilian governments that could be described as democratic or representative.[77] Of the six largest purchasers of weapons in Latin America, five had military governments and the one civilian government, Venezuela, was the smallest buyer among them.

Military governments are likely, of course, to be attentive to the needs of their defense establishments, but one should not draw an overly simple conclusion. In some cases military juntas came into power in Latin America after a long and difficult period during which the civilian government was not able to maintain order against guerrilla and illegal movements of opposition. These governments assumed that they had a mandate to develop counterinsurgency capabilities, and some of the spending for arms has been for this type of weapons. In most cases these governments also had a mandate to straighten out economic chaos, a task in which they have been less successful. To some extent, therefore, emphasizing subversive threats and drumming up nationalist fervor have been convenient ways to take attention away from domestic economic realities. And, of course, the traditional interest of the military in weapons has not been overlooked, especially on a continent where the prestige of the armed forces tends to be relatively high because of the lack of a large middle class. The possession of modern arms adds to the institutional dignity of the military, and under the previous civilian governments there had been less support for up-to-date weaponry. The urge to modernize the armed forces has been coupled with a respect for arms as an attribute of sovereignty. The motivation to create national arms-producing industries in Latin America (even though they are necessarily modest in scale) has been as much political as economic. Finally—and perhaps most important—the military profession is by training and inclination highly sensitive to external threats and the requirements of national security. The territorial and border disputes to be found in Latin America may seem relatively unimportant on the world scale, but they are taken quite seriously by the military governments of the region.

Brazil

Brazil has the largest armed forces in Latin America with 281,-000 men in arms and a defense budget of over $2 billion. It has also been the biggest recipient of arms, buying weapons from Western Europe and the United States. This may change as it proceeds with the rapid development of its own arms industry.

The size of the military is not related to any security problem; indeed there is little of a security threat to Brazil even in Latin American terms. Rather, it is a reflection of Brazil's emergence as the premier power of South America and, many believe, one of the most important middle-level powers in the globe's pecking order. Brazil has one of the world's ten largest economies and a population of over 120 million people; it is a territorial giant sharing borders with ten other nations. Since 1964 it has been ruled by a military-dominated government with authoritarian tendencies, most recently led by General João Baptista Figueiredo, the former chief of internal security. Although the leadership in Brasília, somewhat isolated from the mainstream of the country, is dependent upon the cooperation of the business and technocratic elite in São Paulo and Rio de Janeiro in running the country, defense and aspects of foreign policy remain very much under the control of the military.

The leaders of the armed forces are highly nationalistic and have great-power aspirations for the country. They speak, unrealistically, of Brazil in the year 2000 reaching the technological and economic level of the United States a quarter-century earlier. They have sought a more independent stance in foreign policy, with more distant relations with the United States, especially after deep tensions arose over the Carter administration's policies on human rights and nuclear non-proliferation. The professional military class has been much influenced by geopolitical concepts that see the nation's destiny in the development of Brazil's vast interior, and that stress the importance of providing for the security of the South Atlantic and assuming a leadership role within the Third World.[78]

This outlook has heavily influenced the development of Brazil's own arms-manufacturing industry. Although there was very limited weapons production before the generals came to power, in 1965 the new military government set up the Industria de Material Belico do Brasil to oversee and expand the industry. Its aim has been to make Brazil as self-sufficient as possible in arms. This has had the interesting result of giving preference to second-echelon but Brazilian-made weapons over more advanced arms that could be purchased from abroad. The air force has been less than happy with the policy, as it in effect rules out sophisticated aircraft, but within the defense establishment it is the army that rules. The arms industry is seen as an important aspect of the nation's industrial and technological development. Accordingly, when purchases from abroad are necessary, co-production with other nations is sought so as to obtain the transfer of technology and permit local production. Joint ventures have been established with France, Germany, and Italy. Roland missiles are assembled in Brazil with a French-German consortium, and the West German Cobra anti-tank missile has been locally produced under license. The air force has Mirage III fighters and two squadrons of F-5Es, with important components such as tail units and underwing pylons made in Brazil. But a major effort is underway to expand the aircraft industry, and a majority of the nation's military aircraft are now manufactured in Brazil. The Empresa Brasileira de Aeronautica has become one of the largest aircraft companies in the developing world, making a range of planes including the Xavante jet fighter-trainer and the Bandeirante light transport. Nonetheless, with these two aircraft as with others, the industry remains critically dependent upon foreign know-how and technology.

In recent times the Brazilian arms industry has progressed to the point that it is becoming an exporter in world markets. Four hundred Cascavel armored personnel carriers were sold to Libya in 1977, and other ground arms have been sold to Abu Dhabi and other Arab states, while aircraft have been sold to Chile and Togo. Here again, however, the novelty of the situation should not be allowed to overshadow the limits of its significance, for total Brazilian arms exports in the decade prior to 1979 only came to $227 million.[79]

Peru

Peru is of interest as an arms recipient not only because of its relatively large purchases, which it cannot rationally afford, but because of its willingness to buy arms from both the West and the Soviet Union, thereby also accepting the presence of some Soviet and Cuban advisers on its soil. The military came into power in Lima in 1968 as the result of a leftist revolution, ostensibly dedicated to reform and to eradicating the enormous disparity in the nation between the few very rich and the vast population living at a low Third World poverty level. The average Peruvian has an annual income of $350, cannot read or write, lives in miserable housing, and has a one in three chance of being unemployed. The foreign debt of the country is staggering, and it is dependent upon loans from abroad. Nevertheless, the government has spent large sums on defense, in some years between 3 to 5 percent of the GNP, and accounting for a third of the national budget at the expense of badly needed social and development programs. This may be a classic case of defense spending diverting scarce economic resources.

The explanation for this state of affairs is related to what may be called the Andean arms race. Peruvian military officers have had misgivings about Chile ever since they lost their southern territories and underwent a four-year occupation of Lima in the War of the Pacific a century ago. They still speak about the need to avenge the past of a hundred years. Because their conscripts are essentially Inca Indians and illiterate, and the Chileans are more educated, the Peruvian army leadership works on the assumption that it would require five of its soldiers to match one Chilean. Since this is not possible, it argues that it must offset its inferiority in skilled manpower by superiority in weapons.

After taking control of the government the military establishment embarked on a modernization of its forces, purchasing

Mirage fighters, Alouette helicopters, and AMX tanks from France; Canberra bombers, Hunter fighters, and destroyers from Britain; and other arms from the Netherlands and elsewhere. This very substantial buildup alarmed the Chileans, who consequently sought new weapons for themselves and succeeded in receiving from the United States eighteen F-5s just before Allende came into office. After Pinochet came to power, Chile continued and expanded its buildup, receiving arms from South Africa and Israel, thereby resuming the Andean arms race. The Peruvian military buildup also alarmed the Ecuadorians, who suspect Peru of having designs upon their valuable oil fields and who in turn have a territorial claim against Lima stemming from a brief war in 1941. Accordingly, Ecuador began strengthening its own armed forces, purchasing some weapons in Europe. From France it bought the Mirage F-1 fighter after the United States would not allow Israel to sell it the Kfir fighter on the grounds that it would have a destabilizing impact upon the region.

Lima's decision also to turn to the Soviet Union for arms is the most interesting aspect of the Andean arms race. In addition to purchasing 250 Soviet tanks, as well as artillery and helicopters, Peru acquired 32 SU-22 fighter-bombers, known in the West as the Fitter C and used by East European air forces. Another two squadrons of SU-22 were bought in March 1980 just two months before the national election, which ended twelve years of military rule. A dozen MiG-21s are also "on loan" from Cuba.

It is often assumed that the links with Moscow came into existence as a result of the leftist, allegedly pro-Communist orientation of the military junta first led by General Juan Velasco Alvarado, who nationalized many of the multinational corporations that had thrived in the country under the previous regime, and subsequently led by the more moderate General Francisco Morales Bermudez. But this is in error, for there is little evidence that the Peruvians had an initial preference for Russian weapons. Peru actually turned first to the United States, using the argument that the coming acquisition of the F-5s by Chile had to be offset and voicing deep concern about the rearmament program instituted there after General Pinochet came to power. As discussed earlier, Washington refused to sell Peru the F-5 aircraft. Several reasons were given, the principal one being that there was no military need for such a plane. The United States measured Peru's requirements by balancing them with Chile's capabilities, and Lima already had American F-86s and some very early-generation French Mirages. Peru, on the other hand, calculated its requirements by the need to balance both Chile and Ecuador. An unstated factor, however, was President Nixon's dislike of the populist and leftist military regime which had expropriated American-owned companies.

Seizing the opportunity, the Soviet Union offered a wide range of arms at very low cost and with most generous credits and low interest rates. The establishment of the arms supply relationship with the Soviet Union led some Western observers to fear that it would give Moscow an important political presence in the heart of Latin America, but this has not proved to be the case. Soviet military advisers, who were sent, along with some Cubans, to train Peruvians to use Soviet arms, have been kept isolated from the society. Moscow does not appear to have enhanced its leverage or influence through the provision of arms. Some observers believe that the Soviets see the possibility of a favorable market situation for the purchase of their arms in Latin America, under more advantageous commercial terms for Moscow than they gave Peru, and that they are therefore anxious to be seen as being on good behavior. Be that the case or not, Peru has become one of the Soviet Union's ten largest recipients of arms. Meanwhile, it has bought other arms from Western suppliers such as Italy and West Germany, which is providing it with submarines. It is a rare example, in the global politics of arms sales, of a recipient state buying weapons from both East and West fairly openly and without a resulting political impact of realignment.

Argentina and Chile

As a result of their authoritarian regimes and the condemnation of their violations of human rights, Argentina and Chile have been forced to alter the pattern of their arms purchases. In an

241

earlier period Chile was seen as a paragon of democracy in the southern hemisphere, and its military establishment was perhaps the best equipped on the continent, mainly with American arms. Argentina, also, had little difficulty in procuring American or West European arms even after Perón returned to power in 1973. After Salvador Allende came into office in Santiago, the modest flow of Western arms slowed considerably, but it did continue. The Soviet Union is said to have offered arms to Allende, but the Chilean armed forces reportedly did not want them. The repressive nature of the junta led by General Pinochet, however, led to demands for a cutoff on the sale of weapons to Chile on the assumption that these arms could be used against the population. The Kennedy Amendment to the Foreign Assistance Act in 1974 went a long way toward banning U.S. military assistance and weapons sales to Chile, and some remaining loopholes were filled with restrictions in the International Security and Arms Export Control Act of 1976. A similar though less severe curtailment was undertaken by Britain; it was rescinded by Margaret Thatcher in 1980. As to Argentina, the Carter administration's criticism of the regime of General Jorge Rafael Videla in its human rights report to the Congress of 1977, and the subsequent cut in military assistance credits, had the effect of stopping all American weapons sales. A formal ban on arms sales to Argentina was passed by the U.S. Congress in 1978. The Reagan administration urged the Congress to lift the ban in 1981 on the grounds that there had been a reduction in human rights abuses and that the cooperation of Argentina was essential for the collective defense of the hemisphere.

These embargoes have had different impacts in the two countries. In Chile the junta has not been slowed down in its drive to expand the armed forces. Although such data are not made publicly available, it is believed that the armed forces under Pinochet have been considerably enlarged and that the defense budget accounts for more than 20 percent of the national budget and 6.5 percent of the GNP. The ratio of soldiers to civilians is said to be high, in Latin America second only to Cuba. Chile has acquired arms from Israel, South Africa, Brazil, and possibly elsewhere; to a large extent its weapons purchases have been kept secret but are estimated to have reached a half-billion dollars between 1973 and 1979. Nevertheless, the Chilean military is angered and deeply resents the Western embargoes. Rather than turn to the Communist countries it has sought with considerable success to get arms from fellow pariah states—Israel has been a major supplier—often surreptitiously.

Argentina has been less adamant about seeking conventional arms from abroad, perhaps in part because of the positive psychological impact at home of its nuclear program, which has far outdistanced that of Chile and is perceived as a rival to Brazil's. Another factor has been its own arms industry, the Dirección General de Fabricaciones Militares, which dates back to the Second World War. With twelve arms-producing plants scattered around the country, it is the only home-grown arms industry in Latin America to rival that of Brazil. Some of its early technicians were German émigrés. Argentina produces the Pucara, a twin-turboprop aircraft designed to be particularly effective for counterinsurgency purposes, and the TAM (Tanpue Argentina Mediano) tank, which was designed with West German assistance. The TAM, claimed to be comparable to the French AMX-30 or the German Leopard I, is available for export, although Argentinian officials refuse to identify existing or potential customers. Other arms are produced in its small but diversified arms industry. It is significant that, contrary to some predictions, the Videla government did not choose to expand greatly the production capabilities of its arms industry after the American curtailment of sales, preferring to wait for the change in Washington's policy it expected at the end of the Carter administration. In the first months of the Reagan presidency, Argentina expressed an interest in receiving U.S. reconnaissance aircraft and anti-submarine weapons for the modernization of its navy. At the same time, some arms have been purchased from abroad, and, most notably, West Germany has contracted for the production of six submarines and six destroyers to be assembled in Argentinian naval yards. The prime limitation on new acquisitions has been the cost for an economically hard-pressed government. West

European suppliers, including Britain and France as well as West Germany, have been far less reticent in selling arms to Buenos Aires than to Santiago, even though the reasons for objecting to the sales are quite similar.

Cuba

Cuba is in an anomalous situation. Castro has relied exclusively upon the Soviet Union for arms since his revolution, and received at least $900 million worth in the decade prior to 1979, all free of charge. Additional weapons have been sent by Moscow for use in Latin America and Africa. The small island of Cuba is heavily stocked with quite advanced Russian arms, including about 185 MiG aircraft. The level of its armaments is comparable to that of some East European countries. When Havana received more than a dozen of the nuclear-capable MiG-23s in 1978, questions were raised in Washington as to whether this was a violation of the 1962 post–Cuban missile crisis understanding reached with Moscow prohibiting the employment of "offensive" forces in Cuba. The Carter administration subsequently announced that it had been assured by the Soviet Union that no "offensive" weapons had been introduced, presumably meaning that the MiG-23s were not configured to carry nuclear bombs. In addition to its MiGs and other planes, Cuba has a vast array of tanks, artillery, and naval vessels from the Soviet Union. Some of these have quietly been used for training pilots and other military personnel from some African and Middle Eastern countries.

During the 1960s when Castro supported revolutionary movements in Latin America, arms were supplied to guerrilla forces in Peru, Colombia, Venezuela, and Brazil. His attempt to export the Cuban revolution to Latin American countries produced strains in relations with the Soviet Union and came to an end with Ché Guevara's ill-fated venture in Bolivia. By 1975, Castro was again involved in sending Soviet arms abroad as Cuban troops (16,000) and large numbers of weapons were dispatched to Angola to assist the MPLA. Cuban military advisers were to

244

be found elsewhere in Africa; over 1,000 were sent to Ethiopia (in addition to 17,000 Cuban combat soldiers) to train personnel in the use of Soviet weapons as the arms poured into that country in 1977. As mentioned earlier, Cuban MiG-21s and training officers have been sent to Peru. More recently, Cuba has been used to channel Soviet and East European arms to insurgents in Central America. Weapons advisers have also been sent to South Yemen, Libya, Guinea, and elsewhere. There is little doubt that the Soviet-Cuban arms relationship is very close and that Havana is willing to serve as Moscow's proxy, although it may prefer to give its support in those situations in which it itself believes in the revolutionary cause.

Venezuela

Venezuela, the smallest of the six largest Latin American arms recipients, sought a maximum diversification of suppliers in its purchases in the 1970s and has intentionally moved away from its previous dependence on U.S. arms. Among its acquisitions have been Mirage III fighters and tanks from France, frigates from Italy, submarines from West Germany, machine guns from Belgium, and aircraft from Britain. Some of Venezuela's arms purchases are motivated by its rivalry and border dispute with Colombia; when the latter bought Mirage fighters the Venezuelan air force successfully demanded of the political leadership that it be allowed to follow suit. During the 1960s the armed forces were deeply involved in fighting guerrilla groups, but since then they have had no overriding mission. The vulnerability of the oil fields is some cause of concern, but there is less of a perceived military threat in Venezuela than in the other Latin American countries discussed here.

Unlike the major arms-purchasing countries to its south, Venezuela is a civilian democracy in which the military role is circumscribed. But the political class, mindful of past military dictatorships which lasted until 1959 and the intermittent attempted coups thereafter, takes pains to keep the military services con-

245

tent. Hence, the armed forces, though relatively small, are well equipped and well paid, which is not overly difficult, given the availability of oil revenues. The defense budget was increased during a time of major arms purchases in the 1970s even while the portion of the national budget spent on defense was substantially reduced. In addition, the military has been given a new mission. The creation of a national arms industry has been seen as a way of further integrating the armed forces into a civilian-run society. This nascent industry, which is initially concentrating on small arms and shipbuilding, is almost entirely military run. Venezuela emerged in the seventies as an important regional power on the basis of its oil, economy, and international diplomacy, but there has been no equivalent military role. The management of an arms industry by the military establishment, some Venezuelans are convinced, could have political as well as economic benefits.

The sale of the F-16 to Venezuela, as first proposed by the Reagan administration in the summer of 1981, would set an important and unfortunate precedent for all of Latin America. Up to then none of the supplier countries had sold their most advanced, supersonic fighters to nations in the southern hemisphere. Venezuela's request was viewed with sympathy because the government of Luis Herrera Campins was moderate and generally supported U.S. policy in Latin America and the Caribbean, including its approach to El Salvador which was not especially popular elsewhere. In addition, the United States imports some Venezuelan oil. Nevertheless, Venezuela has no serious security problem which would justify the F-16. Testifying before the Senate Foreign Relations Committee, Under Secretary of State James Buckley cited the threat to Venezuela from Cuba, but this was a highly questionable justification. Selling the F-16 to Caracas would break the tacit threshold on sophisticated weapons in Latin America and would be a matter of real concern to at least one neighbor, Colombia. It would, moreover, make it more difficult for Washington to turn down other nations which requested the F-16, or the F-15, without legitimate security needs.

Central America

Central America has always had a very modest level of armaments, being poor and of relatively little significance on the world stage. In recent times, however, internal political tensions and violence within several countries have attracted international attention. In Nicaragua the Sandinista Liberation Front's successful overthrowing of the dictatorship of Anastasio Somoza in 1979 was aided by Cuban support and Israeli arms. Indeed, Israeli arms were used by both sides, as they had also been bought by the Somoza regime. Arms from Israel were sold in the late 1970s to Honduras, El Salvador, and Guatemala, and Israeli infantry weapons were used by both antagonists in the 1976 border conflict between Honduras and El Salvador.

The Reagan administration in its first weeks claimed in a special White Paper that a massive supply of arms was being shipped to Marxist guerrillas in El Salvador seeking to overthrow the Duarte government. These weapons, supplied by the Soviet Union, East European countries, Vietnam, and Ethiopia, were being shipped via Cuba to Nicaragua for delivery to El Salvador. The United States countered with a modest level of military ($35 million) and economic ($100 million) aid, including helicopters and light arms for the Salvadoran armed forces, and fifty military advisors to provide training in their use. In its statements the Reagan administration gave the conflict international significance by declaring that it should be seen as a "litmus test" of Soviet intentions and behavior in the Third World. Many Americans, and most of the European governments which were asked to cooperate, were not persuaded. The White Paper, which purported to document the allegations of a steady large flow of Communist arms to Salvadoran rebels, was subsequently revealed to be inaccurate in many of its details, thereby increasing the credibility problem.

Guatemala ceased to receive American military assistance in 1977 when it rejected such aid rather than comply with human rights standards set by the U.S. Congress. In May 1981 General Vernon D. Walters on a visit to Guatemala announced the new administration's intention to help its government resist terrorism and guerrilla warfare allegedly fomented by Fidel Castro. As it was certain there would be difficulties and tough questions in the Congress, the Reagan administration chose to circumvent the legislation by having large military trucks and jeeps taken off the "crime control" list. Under U.S. law, items on that list cannot be sold to governments "engaged in a consistent pattern of gross violations of internationally recognized human rights." Subsequently, President Reagan quietly approved the sale of $3.2 million of vehicles, and it was suggested that the next items would include spare parts for Huey helicopters used by the armed forces in counterinsurgency operations.

Mexico

Finally, mention should be made of Mexico because of its very recent decision to modernize its military establishment. Long a poor country, Mexico has spent very little on arms. The small air force is still equipped with planes of 1950s vintage, and the twenty-three cavalry regiments have 14,000 horses. Growing oil-based wealth is now augmenting the nation's economic power and political clout, and the argument is being made that these should be backed by a more impressive military presence. The defense budget was increased by 54 percent in 1981, and plans were made public to purchase armored vehicles from France, amphibious craft from Spain, and at least a dozen F-5 fighters from the United States. The military rationale for needing more advanced arms is not clear. The main role of the Mexican army up to now has been to keep internal order. Defense of the new oil fields could not be undertaken except by a force many times the size of the envisaged one, and the potential uses for the F-5s are few. For this reason the Carter administration for several years discouraged a request for the F-5s. But the politics of maintaining good relations with an important oil producer and neighbor eventually persuaded Washington. And the other arms suppliers, the Brazilians and Israelis as well as the West Europeans, became active in Mexico City seeking orders. Mexico's incentives seem to be dominated by national pride, the quest for a more assertive foreign policy, and a desire to consolidate the nation's prestige and influence as a regional power.

American Arms Sales Policy and Human Rights

A new concern has made itself felt on questions involving arms sales to Latin America in recent years—human rights. "At no time in the recent history of the hemisphere," Richard R. Fagen tells us, "has the incidence of military rule been so high, the gross violations of political and individual rights so widespread, and the use of officially sponsored assassination, torture and brutality so systematic."[80] Among the states most culpable of the above practices are some that traditionally are the largest purchasers of weapons—Chile, Argentina, and, to a lesser extent, Brazil. The objection to selling arms to these countries is based on several assumptions: that the arms could be used to suppress liberalizing forces and in police actions against popularly based political movements; that the provision of arms may therefore help sustain unpopular governments; that the condemnation implicit in the refusal to sell arms can help curtail repressive measures; and that the identification of the supplier with a regime violating human rights is unfortunate and could even be construed as indicating approval.

Under the Carter administration, human rights were the prime consideration in U.S. decisions on arms sales to Latin America, and this accounts for the low level of transfers. A number of restrictions, initiated by liberal Democrats, were mandated by the Congress prior to the Carter administration, in reaction to the previous administration's continuing close ties with some of the most repressive regimes in South America. But it was President Carter who brought the human rights issue to the fore, here as elsewhere. The response was predictable. A State Department report in the spring of 1977 critical of human rights in Brazil led that country to suspend a longstanding military assistance agreement and reject $50 million in credits for arms (due to be canceled in any case), with accompanying criticisms

249

about American moralizing and interference in domestic affairs. Similar responses came from Argentina, Chile, Uruguay, El Salvador, and Guatemala. Under existing legislation, as forcefully interpreted by the Carter administration, these countries were no longer eligible to receive American arms. Very specific prohibitions were also enacted by the Congress with regard to Argentina and Chile.[81]

What judgment is one to make of the human rights standard as applied in American arms sales to Latin America? We shall not review here the arguments advanced on behalf of the political benefits of arms transfers, already discussed in the opening part, except to note that in Latin America it has been the development of influence and good relations with the country, rather than security concerns, that has been the traditional justification. Military assistance programs have been seen as an effective way of maintaining professional contacts and access to important elites.[82]

The new American policy obviously angered and alienated the targeted countries. It was seen by many conservative governments not only as an act of foreign interference in their internal affairs but also as an affront to their nation's dignity. This was especially true of the military leaders, who consider themselves natural friends of the United States, often having attended the Inter-American Defense College in Washington or other American military schools, and who have been educated to believe that their common purpose with their American colleagues is to fight communism. And more than one American ambassador in the field privately bemoaned the loss of arms sales as an instrument of influence and leverage.

When Washington decided to impose a ban on grain sales to the Soviet Union following the invasion of Afghanistan, it sent a respected senior military officer, Lieutenant General Andrew J. Goodpaster, superintendent of the U.S. Military Academy and former supreme allied commander in Europe, to speak with General Videla and ask that Argentina join the United States in the sanctions. Although the Argentinian military leaders are no friends of the Soviet Union, Goodpaster was flatly turned down. Videla pointedly asked when the United States would restore military equipment sales and stop denouncing human rights violations. Thereafter, Buenos Aires signed a five-year agreement with the Soviet Union to provide grain. The United States has been equally ineffective in persuading Argentina to follow its nuclear non-proliferation policy. Gerard Smith, ambassador for non-proliferation matters, also traveled to Buenos Aires in 1980 to ask that a proliferation-prone heavy water plant not be constructed with German and Swiss assistance, but to no avail. Completing a three-year stay in Argentina, American Ambassador Raoul H. Castro complained that "we keep asking Argentina to do things for us, but we don't offer anything in return."[83]

Washington can also be faulted for inconsistency in applying the human rights standard. Latin American countries have been deprived of the opportunity to purchase arms, but other countries with regrettable practices, such as South Korea, Iran under the Shah, and the Philippines, have not had similar difficulties. This may well be perfectly justifiable, given the broader political, economic, and security considerations that affect American policy toward those countries, but it is nonetheless true that Latin America thereby tends to become the repository for ideals that cannot be carried out elsewhere. The "big stick" approach on human rights has been applied far more to Latin America than to any other region, thus creating understandable resentment.

A key question must be whether the restrictions on arms sales have been effective in altering the human rights practices of the would-be purchasers. There is little evidence that the curtailments, of themselves, have had the desired impact. In Argentina the government, if anything, stiffened its resistance to American pressures for the release of political prisoners and a halt to assassinations; by 1980, however, there was a slow evolution toward a less repressive system. Chile has seen very gradual lifting of repressive measures, but this is more the result of internal differences within the ruling junta than of anything else, and the basic nature of the Pinochet regime remains unchanged. Similarly in

251

Brazil, the trend toward liberalization is a consequence of social and economic factors, and the play of political forces within the country, rather than external opprobrium.

Moreover, with respect to avoiding the use of American arms for repressive actions, most of the arms employed in police actions against civilian populations are of a very simple nature, ranging from riot control equipment and armored cars to leg irons and thumbscrews. These are not the type of militarily significant weapons whose transfer has been curtailed. Indeed, many items of this type are not on the Munitions List of the State Department at all, and, being legally exportable to any country, have found their way to the regimes where they are most likely to be used! As to regular military weapons, we have seen that these countries have been able to satisfy much of their needs by turning to more willing suppliers or producing the arms themselves.

To conclude that denying arms sales has not been an effective instrument for improving human rights is not, however, tantamount to rejecting the human rights policy as a whole. This is an important distinction. In general, the Carter administration's policy was credited in Latin America with having a restraining effect on authoritarian tendencies. It helped set constraints on how far a Videla or Pinochet felt he could go without incurring further international condemnation. It was popular with the great majority within the countries who were not directly committed to the regimes. And it did a great deal to restore a badly tarnished image of the United States in the hemisphere, after decades in which America had been associated with "exploitative" multinational corporations, "hegemony," and other sinister forces. Whatever the limits of its effectiveness, the Carter policy was symbolically important.

We have here a paradox: to refuse to sell arms to repressive regimes may not do much to restore human rights, but to sell arms may suggest approbation and negate a more general policy intended to enhance human rights. The path out of this policy dilemma may be to formulate a more selective approach, using the opportunity for specific arms sales as an inducement to

252

improvement in human rights conditions, rather than the inflex-
ible restrictions and admonitions of the past which have often
turned out to be counterproductive.

The Reagan administration as it came into office approached
Latin America from a very different perspective. The primary
concern was hemispheric security and the competition for influence with the Soviet Union rather than human rights or economic development. A new strategic importance was given to
the Atlantic coast of South America, especially Argentina and
Brazil, because of the tankers that bring Persian Gulf oil around
the tip of Africa to Europe and the east coast of the United States.
This would require closer cooperation with the military of those
two countries to strengthen naval and air control of the South
Atlantic sea lanes. Another perceived threat which was given
great weight was Soviet- and Cuban-supported expansionist and
subversive activities in Central America and the Caribbean.

Given these priorities, the approach toward arms sales and
contacts with Latin American military regimes was considerably
different than that in the Carter years. Washington now sought
to improve relations with those regimes. High-level military
emissaries were sent to re-establish or improve contacts which
had become very frayed, and senior military officers were invited
to the United States; joint naval exercises (with Argentina and
Chile) and other forms of military cooperation were suggested;
and the renewal of arms sales was actively discussed. The Reagan
administration asked the Congress to lift the embargoes which
had been applied to a number of Latin American nations, including Argentina, Chile, and Guatemala. As officials turned to the
need for hemispheric defense planning, the past restrictions in
weapons transfers seemed like an anachronism.

It was not clear, however, that the new American perspective
would be accepted by more than a few nations. Poverty and in
some cases political repression at home, rather than Communist
agitation from the outside, were seen as the primary problem by
many in Latin America. Economic development rather than
security was likely to have priority. Many countries would resist
moves toward a tighter hemispheric and ideological alliance.

This was the case even where there was a welcomed and renewed friendship, as in Argentina and Brazil. Buenos Aires was likely to continue its contacts with the Soviet Union, and both countries valued highly their independence in foreign policy. The Americas were characterized by such economic and political diversity that it was unlikely a focus on the Cuban challenge or the Soviet influence in the area could be a unifying concept.

The opportunities for regional arms restraint in Latin America are discussed more fully in Part Four. There is already a history of initiatives within the region for developing multilateral controls. Eight Andean nations signed the Declaration of Ayacucho in 1974, which pledged that they would limit the acquisition of arms for offensive purposes.[84] Although the practical effect of Ayacucho has been very modest, there has been a continuing interest in such restraints. Venezuela initiated a new round of regional arms limitation discussions in 1978, designed to reaffirm Ayacucho, and Mexico subsequently proposed the creation of a consultative mechanism and the exchange of information on arms purchases.

The potential for conflict within Latin America appears to have increased in recent years, underscoring the significance of and need for such steps. The rising cost of arms and of efforts to modernize the armed forces provides another incentive. Moreover, the establishment of some qualitative ceilings on the type of arms that might be introduced into the region may be feasible, given the still relatively low level of military technology in the inventories. Latin America would also be an especially appropriate region for consultation among the suppliers. No nation has a dominant share of the arms market that it would be asked to give up. The essentially commercial competition that exists at present among the suppliers could therefore be regulated so as to ensure that political objectives, such as regional stability, are best met. And the fact that much of Latin America remains basically apart from the East-West competition, and that most of the nations in the region want to keep it that way, suggests that the prospects for multilateral regulation encompassing suppliers and recipients may be somewhat better here than elsewhere.

SUB-SAHARAN AFRICA

In the late 1970s the increase in the flow of arms into sub-Saharan Africa was greater than in any other region of the Third World. Africa remains the least heavily armed region of the world, as measured by such indices as military expenditures per capita and the number of soldiers per civilians. It still has the smallest quantities of weapons, especially of the more advanced ones. Yet the trend is clearly in the direction of rapidly escalating expenditures on arms, with African nations as a whole already spending more of their GNP on defense than Latin America. The value of arms imports was twenty-one times higher, in constant dollars, in 1978 than a decade earlier.[85]

The reason is the increasing potential for armed conflict, reflecting the trend toward violence which was evident in the 1970s. The future is likely to bring several types of conflicts: civil wars and jockeying for power, particularly among ethnic groups; military coups as a way of transferring power—the plethora of military governments in Africa suggests that this is likely; ethnic irredentism resulting in pressures for altering borders in such states as Ghana, Chad, and Zaire; regional clashes, as between Kenya and Uganda, or Ethiopia and Somalia; ideological differences leading to conflict, as between Zaire and the Congo; and finally, of course, the possibility of racial conflict involving the future governance of South Africa. In many of these types of potential conflicts, the availability of arms from outside suppliers can in itself spur the growth of mutual fears and encourage a military response.[86] In addition, arms will be sought for ostensibly nonbellicose reasons involving the modernization of the armed forces. And some states will seek to build up their military strength in order to project an image of power or of leadership within Africa. As late as the beginning of the 1970s, sub-Saharan

Africa was a relatively unarmed region. Today the African demand for arms is growing rapidly, and there is little reason to believe that it will soon abate.

Closely related to the rapid rise in arms sales of recent years is the shifting pattern of suppliers to sub-Saharan Africa. Until the mid-1970s, transfers were relatively small, with most of the arms coming from France and Britain. This reflected the continuing economic and sometimes military ties between the West European states and francophone or anglophone black Africa. Since 1975, however, transfers from the superpowers, especially the U.S.S.R., have increased substantially. The Soviet Union is now by far the largest supplier of weapons to sub-Saharan Africa, followed by France, the United States, West Germany, and Britain in that order. Soviet transfers at the end of the decade were approximately four times those of America.[87]

Soviet and Cuban Designs

Increased arms transfers reflect the extent to which sub-Saharan Africa has been transformed into an arena for East-West competition. Credit for this must go to the Soviet Union, which has been attracted to military involvement on the continent. Much debate has focused on the issue of whether the Soviets have been motivated by some grand, geopolitical design, or by pragmatic opportunism. Are Moscow's ultimate intentions to seize a commanding position on the rim of the crucial oil-shipping routes and to gain bases for direct access to the Indian Ocean? Or is it merely taking advantage of opportunities for extending its influence in Africa as they arise? We need not resolve this question to agree that Africa has provided Moscow with the possibility of championing movements of national liberation and guerrilla forces supporting Marxist aims or black rule. This has been undertaken with the expectation of political rewards, not least in the continuing ideological struggle with China for Communist leadership in the Third World, while simultaneously reducing Western influence. It has also been facilitated by an American reluctance, spawned by the Vietnam experience, to match the

Soviets in their degree of military involvement in each instance, particularly with regard to arms sales. In this sense the new Soviet role in Africa has been a relatively low-risk operation, with only a remote chance of its leading to a direct confrontation with the United States.

An additional factor, too often overlooked, is the extent to which the Soviet Union acquired only in the 1970s the capacity to transport large quantities of men and materiel over long distances. The inability to project power far from its borders had weakened its claim for equal status with the United States in world politics. What Angola and, later, Ethiopia demonstrated was a new capability not only to provide large quantities of arms at short notice, but to dispatch them with speed. In Angola, the Soviets rapidly sent by sea and air over the period of a few months in 1975 some $200 million in weapons to ensure the victory of the MPLA and airlifted 16,000 troops from Cuba. Similarly in the Horn of Africa, a massive sea and airlift in 1977–1978 of over $1 billion in arms and 17,000 Cuban troops, in addition to 1,200 Soviet advisers, helped Mengistu's Marxist group which seized power in Ethiopia to rout Somali-led insurgents in the Ogaden and counter Eritrean secessionists in the north. Over 200 aircraft were involved, some even carrying MiG-21s in crates, in this impressive display of long-range transport capability.

The Soviet Union and its East European allies Czechoslovakia, Poland, and East Germany, plus Cuba, have supplied weapons and advisers to as many as twenty-two countries in sub-Saharan Africa. They have been the predominant suppliers to Angola, Equatorial Guinea, Ethiopia, Guinea, Guinea-Bissau, Mali, Mozambique, Sudan, and Uganda. Most of these countries have had at least a rhetorical leftward orientation, creating some political affinities with the U.S.S.R. Some of them have granted Moscow access to military facilities and overflight rights. But another important motivating factor has been the inability or disinclination of the Soviet Union to use other instruments of diplomacy to establish political ties. Economic aid to Africa has been kept to a bare minimum, and there is nothing in their cultural rela-

257

tionship that brings Russians and black Africans together; many Africans consider the Russians to be racists. This explains the fact that the actual number of Soviet military advisers has been kept limited, and even in the special cases of Angola and Ethiopia, they only numbered 500 and 1,200 respectively. For the Soviets, the sale of arms is the most easily available instrument of diplomacy and one in which they feel they can successfully compete with the West.

As for the Cubans, their role in Africa is far more complex than that of a recent surrogate or pawn of the U.S.S.R. It is, it should be noted, of long standing; Ché Guevara was in the Congo (Brazzaville) in the early 1960s, and Castro's contacts with the MPLA in Angola go back to 1965. Cuba had early ties with anticolonial liberation movements in the Portuguese and Spanish territories of Africa. True, the involvement of the Cubans permits Havana to pay Moscow back for billions of dollars in aid received since 1961. But another motivation has been Castro's image of Cuba as a source of revolutionary inspiration and as a model for other Third World countries, which has found its fulfillment in Africa. Indeed, Castro has been able to play a revolutionary role in Africa with a success that eluded him in Latin America. This helps explain the astonishingly large Cuban presence in Africa, which numbered 56,000 men and women in a dozen nations in 1978.[88]

The second half of the 1970s brought a surge in Soviet diplomacy-through-arms in sub-Saharan Africa. Whereas in 1975 this region received only 5 percent of Soviet arms sales to the Third World, in 1978 it received almost half.[89] But the final results are not yet in, and it is too early to judge whether the benefits reaped by Moscow will be commensurate with the efforts undertaken. It is well to remember that some of the Soviet Union's biggest "gains" have turned out to be its biggest losses, as in Egypt, Sudan, and Somalia. In the last case the Soviets had a fourteen-year record of military assistance to Mogadishu and had trained and equipped the army, in return for which it had obtained important communications and naval facilities at Berbera. But when Moscow developed closer ties with Ethiopia, with the intention of organizing a new federation of the Horn of Africa states with both Addis Ababa and Mogadishu as members, relations with Somalia quickly deteriorated. Within months Soviet advisers were leading an Ethiopian offensive against Soviet-armed and Soviet-trained Somali forces.[90] It is possible that Moscow will have lost more in Somalia than it gained in Ethiopia. Meanwhile, as the world's attention was focused on the Horn, Sékou Touré, one of Moscow's first and closest friends in Africa, was in 1977 quietly reducing Guinea's ties with the Soviet Union and developing stronger ones with the United States, while mending his fences with his pro-Western neighbors, the Ivory Coast and Senegal.

The record of the Soviets in Africa over the past two decades has been a very mixed one, with its share of failures as well as successes. There is little reason to assume that the apparent successes in Angola and Ethiopia are the wave of the future. The political environment of Africa is too unpredictable for that, as are the constant shifts in the internal politics of so many of its states. The ideological appeal of the U.S.S.R. to Africans remains very limited. The Soviets have little to offer that is attractive other than arms, whereas the West is able to offer economic assistance and technology to aid the development of Africa. As a Nigerian once commented on Soviet aid, "You can't eat bullets."

Changing American Perspectives

The Carter administration from the outset sought to avoid reliance on arms sales as an instrument of diplomacy in sub-Saharan Africa, preferring to stress economic cooperation and an activist approach in negotiating settlements to the continent's pressing conflicts. The United States would recognize the force of African nationalism and align itself more closely with the principle of black majority rule; there should be "African solutions to African problems." This approach implicitly downgraded the significance of East-West competition and global strategic factors in Africa while putting the accent on "local realities." It was thought to stand in contrast to the policy of Secretary of State Kissinger, who sought to counter the Soviet actions in Angola with covert military assistance to pro-Western factions. His policy led the Congress to enact the Clark Amendment in 1976 banning covert activities and U.S. military aid to internal factions in Angola.

International realities—or the perceptions Americans held of them—forced the Carter administration, however, to recognize the importance of dealing more directly with Soviet advances in Africa. The large-scale Soviet and Cuban intervention in the Horn of Africa, in particular, led to warnings regarding the impact that the breaking of the "code of conduct" of détente, to use Zbigniew Brzezinski's phrase, could have upon Soviet-American relations in general. Secretary of State Vance announced that the United States would look sympathetically upon requests for assistance from states that were threatened by a buildup of foreign military equipment and advisers on their borders in the Horn or elsewhere in Africa. Recognizing the risk that supplying arms to Africa might run counter to the administration's broad arms transfer policy, he emphasized that transfers to Africa would only be made as an exceptional tool of policy and only after the most careful consideration. Subsequently, Washington agreed to supply Sudan, which borders on Ethiopia and Libya and which had expelled Soviet military advisers in mid-1976, with aircraft, including twelve F-5s (to be financed by Saudi Arabia) and other arms. Kenya was provided with foreign military sales credits to modernize its forces and cover the purchase of helicopters and F-5s. Aid was also offered to Chad, which had part of its northern territory occupied by Libyan forces.

Of particular interest was the case of Somalia. After Somalia expelled the Soviets, the United States, at the urgent request of President Mohammed Siad Barre, agreed to supply it with "defensive" arms to protect itself against an incursion by Ethiopia. But Washington changed its mind and declined to send arms when it became clear that the weapons might be used by Mogadishu to buttress the insurgents in Ethiopia's Ogaden region or to support irredentist designs against Kenya and Djibouti. A new situation, however, developed after the Soviet invasion of Afghanistan, with Washington desiring to expand its presence in the Indian Ocean and Arabian Sea by acquiring air and naval facilities in Oman, Kenya, and Somalia. Small military and economic aid packages were promised to Oman and Kenya in exchange for the use of facilities. But Somalia, at first, pressed for $2 billion in arms and economic aid in exchange for the use of the Berbera base (with its Russian-built 15,000-foot airfield, which can be used for long-range transport aircraft and bombers), raising concern that the United States could become party to an expansion of the Ogaden war. After protracted negotiations, Washington agreed to a far smaller sum, and Mogadishu promised not to intervene directly in the Ogaden.

Such American steps were designed to counter the Soviet challenge in Africa, to respond to charges of inactivity or passivity by some at home and abroad, and in the last case to improve the U.S. strategic position near the Persian Gulf. They were selective and quite modest steps, calibrated to satisfy requests for arms sales based upon reasonable defense needs without fueling local conflicts or arms races.

Yet they had to be seen as a part of an upward trend. The United States had already provided small quantities of arms to Zaire and Nigeria and could be expected to be called upon to increase them. After the Soviets began sending large quantities of weapons to Angola, the Ford administration in 1976 raised its military assistance to Zaire from $2 to $11 million, and President Carter followed in 1977 with $13 million in "nonlethal" military aid (transport aircraft and spare parts) to help President Mobutu resist an invasion of Shaba province by Katangan exiles in Angola. During the second invasion of Shaba, in 1978, the United States ferried French and Belgian troops to the conflict and gave additional assistance worth $17.5 million. It is quite possible that Zaire, one of Africa's largest and most populous countries and critical to the West because of its minerals, will call for a continuing flow of arms and military training to ensure its security from externally launched incursions. It will probably ask for substantially larger quantities than have yet been provided by either

West European countries (France has been the principal supplier) or the United States.

Nigeria has received even less from the United States up to now while spreading its purchases among the Soviet Union, Britain, and France. In the past the Soviet Union has been its principal supplier, equipping it with fairly advanced arms, including MiG-21s, but by 1979 there were signs that Lagos wished to scale down the military relationship with Moscow and considerably expand its purchases of weapons from the United States. A new five-year national development plan adopted in early 1981 called for a significant increase in defense spending. Nigeria with 90 million has the biggest population of any black African nation and the largest armed forces south of the Sahara, more than three times the size of South Africa's, yet much of its defense equipment is badly out of date. As it is also the second largest exporter of oil to the United States, it would be able to pay for weapons in cash. For these reasons, and given the political and economic importance of Nigeria within Africa, as well as the significance of the role it would play in the coming dénouement in southern Africa, the case for increasing Western arms sales to Lagos will be powerful.

In the future, therefore, the United States may be impelled to increase its arms sales to countries in sub-Saharan Africa. At the end of the 1970s weapons transfers to Africa accounted for less than 1 percent of the U.S. worldwide total, but this percentage is likely to rise. As we have seen, there may be a number of countries with compelling claims for American arms. A more active and involved American diplomacy on the continent, even if it gives priority to economic development, may not be able to avoid expanded weapons sales. Local upheavals and conflicts will create situations that will place the superpowers in competitive positions, and they are likely to be drawn into a military supply relationship, in part to avoid a more direct form of intervention. The declining role of Western Europe, except perhaps for France, in helping maintain stability in Africa, may also place greater responsibilities upon the United States.

French, British, and Chinese Roles

The trend in arms transfers to sub-Saharan Africa is toward larger transfers by the superpowers and less from the other suppliers—France, Britain, and China. As is to be expected, the pattern of past transfers has reflected the former colonial relationship. Thus France has been the traditional supplier of the Ivory Coast, Togo, Senegal, and other former colonies. (It also sold arms to Ethiopia and Sudan.) Selling to these black African countries did not prevent it, however, from having South Africa as by far its largest client in sub-Saharan Africa during the 1970s. French aspirations have been as much economic as related to a concept of its *"mission civilatrice."* It obtains valuable raw materials from the continent, including uranium ore. France has also kept a surprisingly large military presence on the continent with approximately 14,000 men in twenty-three countries, with the largest contingents in Djibouti, Chad, and Réunion. Paris has been prepared to intervene effectively when it is deemed necessary.[91]

Britain has sold most of its arms in Africa to Nigeria, Kenya, and Ghana, in that order. In recent years it has limited its activities to military training and economic assistance, with only quite small arms sales.

The Chinese case is by far the most interesting. The proliferation of new states in Africa in the early sixties provided Beijing with opportunities for gaining diplomatic recognition. Also provided were circumstances for political competition with the Soviet Union, as Beijing demonstrated its support for People's Wars and national liberation movements. Although China had few valid geostrategic interests on the continent, it sent important amounts of economic and military assistance to Africa, which after China's immediate neighbors in Asia (North Vietnam, North Korea, and Pakistan) received almost all the remaining foreign assistance. In contrast to the Soviet Union, China gave more economic assistance than arms. Although the size of its total aid was overshadowed by that of the U.S.S.R., it reaped political benefits by selecting its recipients carefully. Most favored by far was Tanzania, because of its socialist orientation and commitment to support liberation movements in southern Africa. In addition, in competition with the Soviets for ideological leadership, arms were also supplied to the Congo, Guinea, and Sudan, all of which received weapons from Moscow as well. In Angola, Beijing supported the National Front for the Liberation of Angola (FNLA) against the Soviet-supported MPLA, even though the former was conservatively oriented; and in Rhodesia it backed Robert Mugabe's wing of the Patriotic Front, while the Soviets gave their assistance to Joshua Nkomo.

Nevertheless, China's role in Africa was in decline as the 1970s drew to a close. It had clearly been surpassed by the Soviet involvement in Angola and the Horn. Presented with a choice between Beijing and Moscow, left-leaning African governments or movements of a radical persuasion are more likely to turn to the U.S.S.R. for arms and military support in the future. Some nations, such as Equatorial Guinea and Mozambique, have Chinese military advisers, while others, such as Zambia and Somalia, have Chinese economic development technicians in the thousands; but they are only part of a general Communist presence in those countries which often includes Soviets and East Europeans. Perhaps, also, the venue of the continuing struggle with the U.S.S.R. is shifting back to a concentration on Asia and the new Sino-American-Soviet triangular relationship. In the 1980s China may only be a marginal actor in sub-Saharan Africa, and its arms transfers are likely to be modest in scale.

South Africa

Black Africa's acquisition of arms must be seen in the context of the possible use of the weapons in a war with the white government of South Africa. In any such conflict, whether it originated in black insurgencies within South Africa or in an attack from the neighboring states opposed to apartheid, Pretoria would be heavily outnumbered. For this reason South Africa has given the highest priority to equipping its armed forces, especially during the 1970s as it found itself increasingly isolated and condemned in the global arena. By 1978, Pretoria was spending $2.6 billion a year on defense, a sum equal to 19 percent of its national budget. South Africa has been developing a siege mentality—and an awesome war machine to go with it.

The history of South Africa's arms purchases has reflected the changes in world politics. Britain had been its traditional supplier, not only because of the Commonwealth links, which led to close cooperation between the military services of the two countries, but because of the importance that was attached in the United Kingdom's defense planning to South Africa's role as the guardian of the route to the Indian Ocean. South Africa fought alongside the Western powers in both world wars and sent a symbolic contingent to Korea, so that during the fifties it had no difficulty in receiving weapons from the United States and Canada as well as Britain. The creation of a score of independent states throughout Africa in the early 1960s had two effects. The United Nations imposed its first embargo—albeit a voluntary one—on the sale of arms to South Africa in 1963. Thereafter, the British weapons flow was gradually reduced to a trickle. Second, Pretoria began a major buildup of its defense capabilities, which continues to this day. Although France joined the embargo on a proforma basis, it proceeded to take full advantage of the loopholes. Thus France became South Africa's largest supplier, providing $365 million worth of arms between 1967 and 1976, as compared to $10 million worth from Britain and $30 million from the United States. The latter two sold electronic equipment and other items that were only indirectly of military character. During this period Pretoria received more arms than any other country in sub-Saharan Africa.

A proposal for a *mandatory* embargo on arms to South Africa was vetoed by the Western members of the U.N. Security Council in 1976, but the next year, following a violent South African crackdown against black dissidents, the Carter administration threw its support behind the proposal. Backed by France and Britain, as well as the United States, the United Nations imposed a mandatory embargo under Chapter Seven of the Charter.

(Under pressure from francophone black African states, France had already for several years been turning off the tap; in 1975 it stopped sales of weapons such as machine guns and aircraft that could be used against guerrillas, and in early 1977 it banned the sale of spare parts for military equipment already supplied. Thus the only immediate impact of the new prohibition was to prevent the transfer of two submarines and two patrol boats that were already ordered and under construction.)

Yet by the time the mandatory embargo was agreed upon its effect could be little more than symbolic. For fourteen years—since the time of the first voluntary embargo—South Africa had been assiduously developing its own arms industry. Self-reliance has become a major aim, as Pretoria's security options have narrowed and as the nation has moved toward what one close observer describes as a "fortress Southern Africa" mentality.[92] Self-sufficiency has been sought through a vast program of licensing arrangements providing for the co-production of weapons in South Africa, thereby circumventing the ban on direct arms sales. Through this technique, Pretoria has also made certain that it was acquiring the full technology and know-how, should it one day be forced to continue the production runs entirely on its own. In 1968 the Armaments Development and Production Corporation was set up to direct South Africa's arms production. Light infantry arms, artillery, and ammunitions are now made under exclusive national control. But in addition, with French assistance it has manufactured 1,400 Eland armored cars which are a version of the Panhard AML, Cactus surface-to-air missiles which are copies of the French Crotale, and Mirage III and F-1 fighters. Unlike some co-produced weapons which are unlimited, the number of F-1s is in principle to be limited to 100; this nevertheless represents a major achievement. The South African air force had 46 Mirage F-1s and 22 of the less advanced Mirage IIIs in its inventory in 1980. Machine guns and rifles have been made with Belgian assistance, and Italy has helped with light aircraft.

In the second half of the 1970s, as unfavorable Third World opinion led France to curtail its assistance, Israel—another pariah state—emerged as an important arms ally. Much of the Jerusalem-Pretoria arms relationship has been kept secret, but it is known that Israel's Gabriel missiles have been placed on South African frigates and that its Reshef missile patrol boats have been manufactured locally. The respected Uzi submachine gun is also produced under license. There have been rumors of other forms of assistance, ranging from electronic fences for counterguerrilla warfare to military nuclear technology, and there can be little doubt that the defense ties with Israel are deep and of growing importance. More modest arms links have been established with Taiwan, another pariah state. Apart from co-producing arms at home, South Africa has also over the years purchased many items abroad, despite the embargoes. This was done by "laundering" the transfers through third parties or by clandestine routings. Such weapons ranged from 150 British Centurion tanks which it acquired from Jordan in 1974, to a large fleet of French Alouette and Super Frelon helicopters, to light Soviet and East European arms purchased mysteriously.

The net result is that South Africa has by far the most advanced, balanced, and powerful military capability on the African continent. As the political pressures on the Pretoria regime increase, with majority rule in Zimbabwe and Namibia, its security situation may only be marginally affected. More than half of the white men between 18 and 45 serve in the active armed forces or in reserve units. They are well trained for guerrilla conflict. Ample armaments are available to fight such a conflict, or even wage a conventional war, while keeping the black population at bay. The international embargoes have resulted in South Africa making itself virtually self-sufficient in arms. (In its one continuing form of dependence, on the local co-production of weapons, even the mandatory embargo has been ineffective, for it did not lead France and others to cut off licensing arrangements or withdraw their technicians.) And in reserve looms the probability of a nuclear capability as an instrument of last resort. South Africa, some experts believe, has more effective striking power than all of black Africa combined. This conclusion will be highly relevant over the next decade or two to various possible contingencies for conflict localized within Africa. Intervention by the Soviet Union or the United States would, of course, create an entirely different situation.

East-West Competition and Arms Restraint

This brings us back to the trend toward an increasing military involvement by the superpowers in sub-Saharan Africa and the risks that it presents. If one thing is certain, it is that Africa is and will remain for some time an unsettled continent, in which there will be conflict, violence, and political upheaval. This will present many opportunities and temptations for indirect intervention by the outside powers through the transfer of arms. Even if an out-side power is strongly adverse to becoming involved in an Afri-can dispute, it may find that it is unable to stand aside because of the broader ramifications that its absence or seeming passivity would have upon the global stage. Yet there is the real danger that East-West competition in Africa could get out of hand, and place enormous strains upon Soviet-American relations. We have already seen evidence of this in 1978–1979 when the Soviet involvement in the conflict in the Horn of Africa became linked, in Western discussions and perceptions, with the wisdom of rat-ifying SALT II and pursuing further arms control negotiations. Much more far-reaching difficulties would arise in South Africa if the Soviet Union were to supply arms to national liberation movements that were fighting the Pretoria regime (not to men-tion the dilemmas this would create for the Western nations which are no friends of apartheid, yet are reluctant to arm guer-rilla forces).

For these reasons there is much to be said, in principle, for opening a dialogue with the Soviet Union that could lead to restraint on arms sales to sub-Saharan Africa. The basic concept of the multilateral regulation of arms sales to the Third World is discussed in the next part. In Africa the need would seem to be especially acute, and the chances for a miscalculation by one side or the other especially great, given the unpredictable nature of many of the conflicts there.

One must, of course, consider that there may be few, if any, incentives for the U.S.S.R. to adopt restraints on arms supplies to Africa. For Moscow there may be no more favorable terrain available in the Third World for competition with the capitalist societies than sub-Saharan Africa. In the struggle for majority rule it is in a better position than is the West to give its unqualified support to black nations. The language of criticism of neo-colonialism and support for national liberation movements can be put to extensive use. And the West may be restrained by far more self-inhibitions than the East.

Yet there are reasons why the Soviet leadership could someday be attracted to some degree of moderation or regulation of the competition in Africa. By now, the transitory nature of the influence that the provision of weapons gives must be perfectly evident. Despite years of military assistance and support for Somalia, for example, Moscow was unable to prevent it from invading Ethiopia at a time when the Soviet Union was trying to develop close relations with Addis Ababa. There is, in fact, the possibility that extensive involvements, as in Angola and the Horn of Africa, could develop into quagmires, increasingly costly and politically complicated, from which it would become difficult for the Soviet Union to extricate itself. The course of ethnic rivalries, growing nationalism, and shifting political alignments and leadership is no more predictable to the Soviets than to anyone else. There is some evidence that the Cubans began by the end of the seventies seeing their African intervention as a quagmire. Havana's manpower commitment on the continent was greater, in proportion to the country's 10 million population, than the American involvement in Vietnam at the height of the war; the casualties and related costs of the conflict were making themselves felt at home.

Moscow must also consider the risks that the United States would "rise to the challenge" of a cold war competition in Africa. This could, indeed, become the policy of the Reagan administration, which has lobbied for the repeal of the Clark Amendment so as to be able to assist the anti-Marxist faction in Angola. Under such circumstances, the United States would be perfectly capable of pouring vast amounts of arms—and if need be, men—into

Africa. The call for a far more activist Western response to the Soviet interventions in Angola and the Horn in the late 1970s is indicative of what could become a loud and compelling chorus in the 1980s. This underscores the dangers that a continued competition in Africa could create for the maintenance of stable Soviet-American relations, in which the stakes of the U.S.S.R. are as great as those of the West.

Any dialogue with the Soviet Union on restraints on arms sales, if it were ever undertaken, should include the West Europeans, at an early if not the opening stage. Even if their role as suppliers to African nations is diminishing in relation to that of the United States, it remains quite significant, and their political ties with their former colonies in most cases are sounder and deeper. Moreover, it may be desirable to encourage the West Europeans to take the clear lead once again in future sales to sub-Saharan Africa. This could partially mute the confrontational or competitive dimension of the transfers in East-West terms.

Involving the West Europeans points up, in turn, the necessity for close transatlantic consultation and cooperation on policy toward Africa in general and the arms sales aspect of it in particular. The French-British-American coordination of policy on Somalia in 1977, which led to the joint decision not to send arms to Mogadishu on the grounds that it would amount to supporting a country that was seeking to change national boundaries by force, was a step in this direction. So were the French-Belgian-British-American-Moroccan consultations on Zaire in 1978 which led to a concerted Western effort to assist President Mobutu in dealing with the invasion of Shaba province. These were constructive precedents which might be followed in the future. But they could be supplemented by a more broad-ranging discussion that goes far beyond the question of military assistance and deals with Western policy toward sub-Saharan Africa as a whole. This might lead to the acceptance of an approach based upon coordinated spheres of influence or division of responsibility.

Finally, the Africans themselves could become more involved in conflict management and peace-keeping on their continent. This would create regional incentives for restraints on arms trans-

270

fers. The Organization of African Unity could play a role, as its accepted principles provide for the maintenance of the territorial integrity of the member states and nonintervention by outside powers. At the annual summit meeting of the OAU in Khartoum in 1978, a new concern was expressed about the dangers of foreign intervention and of Africa's becoming entangled in international rivalries for influence. This was coupled with an awareness that responsibility for what was happening lay with Africans themselves, because of their reliance on external support to deal with internal African disputes. The most desirable solution to African problems would be their peaceful political settlement by the African states acting on their own. But when this is not feasible, and outside powers are called on for assistance, particularly of a military nature, this should be done in such a way as to maximize the African consensus on what needs to be done and minimize the risk that the effects will spill over into great-power relations.

PART FOUR

RESTRAINTS

A *rms sales are a barometer of politics among nations.* The conclusion to be drawn from the preceding analysis is that the prime significance of most arms sales lies neither in their military impact nor in their economic consequences, as is often assumed, but in their political dimension. Whenever arms are transferred, they affect the political relationship between the supplier and the recipient. There is also likely to be an important impact upon other states within the region of the recipient country. And the transfer may well have consequences for the relations among the principal suppliers.

NEW SIGNIFICANCE OF ARMS SALES

Arms sales are now firmly ingrained in international politics. Although there is nothing novel about arms sales, during the past decade they have acquired a new significance in world affairs. Three fundamental reasons account for this. The first is, of course, the sheer increase in the quantity and quality of the weapons being transferred, a trend that became particularly marked in the mid-1970s. Furthermore, the number of states acquiring major arms from abroad has risen.

A second, and more consequential reason, is the decline of other, more traditional instruments of reassurance and diplomacy, such as alliances, the stationing of forces abroad by an ally, and the credibility of the threat of direct intervention. In a world in which the major powers are less likely to intervene with their own armed forces to protect their interests, they are more prone to shore up friendly states through the provision of arms or to play out their competition through the arming of their proxies. As the risk of a direct nuclear confrontation between the great powers forces them to shift their competition to presumably safer ground, developments in the Third World are of ever greater import. Yet as regional tensions and political rivalries in such

275

areas as the Middle East or the Korean peninsula persist, or heat up, the outside powers must seek to reassure friends and stabilize situations to prevent an escalation that could have damaging consequences for them. In this quest to maintain stability or avoid war, weapons transfers, ironically, now have a major role. *Arms sales are instruments of diplomacy as well as of security.*

The third explanation for the new prominence of arms sales is the heightened demand for weapons as a corollary, and contributor, to the global diffusion of power. The redistribution of the elements of power in the world has many well known causes, previously discussed. As new nations have been created in the Third World, and as older ones have developed further, they have sought to acquire the modern arms possessed by the advanced, industrialized states. In some cases, as with the oil-rich countries, they have been relatively able to afford the weapons. But even when the weapons have been less affordable, new nations have sought arms anyway, either because of political or bureaucratic incentives or because of real or perceived security needs. The past quarter-century has seen the breakup of historical empires and the erosion of the cold-war alliances. Accompanying this have been the emergence of regional powers, and the expectation of an expanding role for the "new influentials" in world politics. But none of this change has resulted in greater stability in the Third World, the diminution of conflict, or the damping of regional political rivalries. The trend has clearly been in the opposite direction, and this has had important consequences for the expanding arms trade.

It is sometimes suggested that the "arms boom" of the 1970s was a unique episode which will be followed by a period of reduced demand for arms in the Third World. According to this view, the saturation point of the recipient countries has been or is about to be reached.[1] It may be that arms sales to the Middle East will taper off after the rapid upsurge of the past years, although even this is uncertain. While Iran has practically brought its arms imports to a halt, Saudi Arabia, Syria, Iraq, and Israel show no signs of having declared "enough," and other countries such as Egypt and Jordan are actively seeking to modernize their forces. Moreover, as the discussion in preceding pages indicates, the demand for arms is growing *throughout* the developing world. In Africa, Asia, and even Latin America, there is an increasing interest in acquiring weapons. Although the incentives for each country are distinct, the developing world in general is deeply affected by the systemic factors mentioned above. The potential for conflict within regions appears to be on the rise. Thus it is unlikely that the arms boom is over.

Indeed, arms sales can be expected to have an increased role in the international politics of the 1980s, for an additional three reasons.

First, the transfer of weapons will be a key element of the continuing East-West competition in the Third World. The capability of the Soviet Union to project its military influence to distant places expanded greatly during the 1970s, and Moscow shows no reluctance to use arms transfers to support its political aims. This was amply demonstrated by the Soviet arms sent to Angola, Ethiopia, and Cuba. At the same time, the United States, and perhaps to a slightly lesser extent its European allies, will be constrained from direct intervention in the developing world. In place of its own soldiers the West will prefer to send military supplies.

Second, the rise of regional powers will be accompanied by large arms purchases. History has taught us that states rarely achieve a significant political or economic rank without seeking commensurate military power. Such power will give the regional powers the capacity to intervene and could increase the incidence of regional conflict. Even when actual conflict is avoided, the potential for it will lead other states within the region to upgrade their defenses through their own arms purchases. The maintenance of balances within regions, especially to the extent that the direct involvement of the superpowers recedes, will depend upon the careful calibration of the size, quality, and rate of receipt of weapons from outside suppliers.

Finally, nuclear proliferation will create a more fragmented world in which local military power, in general, will be of greater importance within the Third World. Although the rate and degree of proliferation cannot be accurately predicted, it is safe to assume that with time and the spread of knowledge of the technology, the number of nuclear powers will grow. This is likely to increase, rather than reduce as some expect, the incentives for acquiring conventional arms. In a more multipolar, fragmented world, nations will be less willing to base their national security upon alliances and the increasingly uncertain prospect of direct military support from friends. They will want to assure their safety with their own capabilities, to the maximum extent feasible. The ability of the present nuclear powers to extend their deterrence so as to cover their allies (what is known as "extended deterrence" in strategic parlance) in a credible manner, will be reduced. Thus nations will want conventional arms to increase their safety, and suppliers will make them available, in part to forestall or delay the nuclear urge.

THE NEED FOR INTERNATIONAL MANAGEMENT

The conditions outlined above are likely to lead to a less stable and secure environment in the Third World, with a propensity for armed conflict. Hence, there would be much to be gained by the development of some international restraints on arms sales. It is important to bear in mind, however, that arms sales are neither "bad" or "good" in themselves. Arms sales may or may not be destabilizing, and even "stability" may not be an acceptable aim in all instances. All depends on the particular case and how it is perceived. Certainly it is not inevitable that the transfer of arms will lead to conflict. Nor should it be automatically assumed that all use of force is to be avoided or is undesirable. The dilemmas in making judgments about arms sales are manifold, as we have observed in Part One. Nevertheless, there are important reasons for regulating and moderating in some way the transfer of weapons to the Third World.

At present there are no "rules of the game" worked out by the Soviet Union and the United States to maintain the lid on their competition in the developing world. Yet such unbridled competition could easily spill over and affect the central East-West balance. The two superpowers need to discuss regional security problems and instabilities in the Third World. A major component of such an approach could be an attempt to elicit some restraints on the competitive transfer of arms.

At present there is no system for regular consultation between the United States and its European allies on arms sales to the Third World. This global problem is not discussed in NATO because it is believed to be outside of its charter. Yet uncoordinated arms sales to certain areas can undermine regional balances; they can also conflict with the diplomacy of other Western suppliers in such a way as to prevent a political evolution desired by all of them. Moreover, competition among the Western suppliers for sales to the Third World has negative effects on defense collaboration within the Atlantic Alliance and has inhibited progress on the necessary standardization of weapons within NATO. There is a need for the Western allies to consult about important prospective sales and to develop joint approaches toward arms transfers to the Third World.

At present no fully adequate mechanism exists among the Western powers for discussing arms sales to China. COCOM, the consultative committee set up in 1949 for controlling strategic arms exports to Communist nations, which includes all the NATO countries (except Iceland) and now Japan, is essentially oriented toward sales to Warsaw Pact countries and has not been effective in dealing with sales to China. It operates on the basis of a master list of sensitive "strategic" technologies, such as computers whose transfer would be militarily undesirable, but it has not dealt very much with actual weapons. Observance of COCOM rulings is voluntary rather than mandatory, with no enforcement mechanism, and most sales are discussed after the details have already been agreed upon with the buyer, thereby limiting its utility for setting broad foreign policy criteria. NATO in 1978 considered and rejected a plan to develop "NATO guidelines" on arms sales to China. Each member of the Alliance has been free to adopt its own policy, and France (unlike Britain) has made a point of not consulting with other Western supplier countries before announcing its sales to Beijing. Nor has the sensitive question of sales to China been the subject of discussions with the Soviet Union. Yet few problems are likely to be as delicate in the Western-Soviet-Chinese triangular relationship of the 1980s. If not handled judiciously, the transfer of Western arms to China could lead to a serious further deterioration of East-West relations, could exacerbate the already very tense situation between Moscow and Beijing and possibly lead to undesirable armed conflict, and could even boomerang if the issue were to become a source of basic disagreement between China and the West. On this critical issue, in particular, there is a need for dialogue and policy coordination at least within the West.

The principal question, therefore, is whether and how to create some international management of arms sales. What forms of multilateral restraints are desirable, and what types are likely to be feasible and acceptable? To help provide some conclusions, a number of subsidiary questions must be addressed.

If the major initiative is to come from the suppliers of arms rather than the recipients, as suggested in this book, what priority should be assigned to cooperation on restraints among the Western suppliers compared to East-West efforts at regulation? What are the incentives for the Western allies and the Soviet Union to cooperate, and what are the real limitations upon such incentives? How does one reconcile the possible contradictory aims of weapons standardization within the Atlantic Alliance and multilateral restraints on arms sales to the Third World?

As for the recipients, given the sensitivity of developing countries to outside interference or great-power paternalistic attitudes, under what conditions might international restraints be acceptable to them? What are the new and evolving perspectives of Third World nations upon the arms trade? What would be the impact of new arms industries within the Third World upon attempts to regulate arms transfers?

As to the actual restraints, should they be global or regional in character? What types of controls are most needed, or achievable? Should restraints be negotiated as arms control agreements, or informally agreed upon as the result of consultations, or unilaterally and tacitly implemented?

280

These questions are addressed in the remainder of this book. But first it is necessary, and instructive, to take a brief backward look at earlier approaches—both proposed and actual—to the problem of restraining international arms transfers.

PAST APPROACHES TO INTERNATIONAL RESTRAINTS

The record is, to be generous, a very mixed one marked by a number of unproductive approaches. As far back as the Middle Ages, nations were reaching informal agreements on the selling of arms, such as the understanding among the Christian nations of Europe not to transfer weapons to the "infidel" Turks. There were cries of anguish when these agreements were periodically broken. Provisions in the General Act for the Repression of the African Slave Trade, known as the Brussels Act of 1890, prohibited the introduction of all arms and ammunition other than flintlock guns and gunpowder, except under effective guarantees, into a vast zone of Africa.[2]

In modern times, an enduring favorite has been the proposal that a register of arms transfers be undertaken by the United Nations and that greater publicity be given to the arms trade in general. Such a register would follow upon the precedent of the League of Nations, which from 1925 until 1938 published a statistical yearbook on the trade in arms and ammunitions. In 1965 Malta made such a proposal at the United Nations, followed by Denmark two years later. After the idea of an arms register failed to gain approval in 1970 at the Geneva Committee on Disarmament, Sweden and the United Kingdom suggested more modestly that greater public attention be drawn to the arms trade. The most serious approach of this type occurred in 1976 at the thirty-first U.N. General Assembly when thirteen countries, led by Japan, sponsored a resolution calling upon the secretary-general to make a "factual study" of the international transfer of conventional arms and asking that member states communicate their views and suggestions on the matter to him.[3] Private groups in the United States have also endorsed the establishment of a United Nations mechanism to keep track of the global arms trade.[4] None of these proposals was adopted by the United Nations, however, because of the many countries that felt that the publication of information relating to their existing military capabilities might in some way be prejudicial to their national security. Opposition to the Japanese resolution was led by India. In addition, some Third World countries have viewed the whole idea with suspicion as politically divisive for the non-aligned group. It was also seen as discriminatory in that it appeared to focus more on the responsibilities of the recipients than on those of the suppliers.

The fundamental flaw with the arms registry approach is that it is based on the assumption that arms sales are bad in themselves, and that greater publicity will somehow lead to their curtailment. Although placing the spotlight on arms sales may have such an effect in cases in which a nation is excessively acquiring arms while still remaining sensitive to international opinion or to groups within its own society that oppose the policy, in the majority of cases a public airing of arms acquisitions is unlikely to lead to opprobrium. Indeed, in some instances it might have the opposite result, especially when the nation's citizenry feels a military threat from abroad. Be that as it may, a substantial (even if disparate and incomplete) amount of information is already available through the annual publications of the U.S. Arms Control and Disarmament Agency, the International Institute for Strategic Studies, and the Stockholm International Peace Research Institute. None of this publicity appears to have discouraged arms sales.

Another approach to international restraints has been to place the burden of responsibility for their creation upon the recipient states. Indeed this has been, not surprisingly, the traditional approach of the principal supplier countries whenever the global arms trade has come up for discussion in disarmament talks. At the Geneva Conference on Disarmament, American and British representatives have ritualistically talked of the need to reduce the conventional arms trade through the limitation of purchases. "This would be much the most satisfactory way," Minister of State for Foreign and Commonwealth Affairs, Lord Goronwy-

Roberts told the conference in 1976. "If the demand is not there, the suppliers will not be able to export." Once the initiative was taken by the recipients and an arms control regime was established, the outside powers would "respect" the regional arrangements.[5] A similar approach was adopted by Secretary of State Kissinger in a 1976 unclassified Department of State paper sent to members of Congress who had expressed interest in steps to curtail arms sales. Agreement among the suppliers to regulate weapons sales, it was argued, would amount to a "cartelization" of the world arms trade; cartels had historically worked effectively when suppliers shared some interests; there were no common interests among the larger producers of arms. The paper concluded that the most promising multilateral restraint proposals "will be those that derive from initiatives taken by leaders in the regions concerned."[6]

Yet this is a formula that is almost guaranteed to lead to no progress. As the discussion in this book has shown, many of the regions that might be involved remain somewhat inchoate and ill-defined. At times they only become "regions" when they are treated as such by external powers, for the level of commonality and intraregional cooperation is often quite limited. Thus, shifting the burden of responsibility for creating arms transfer restraints to the recipients is unlikely to lead to constructive results. One of the principal themes of this book has been that although the recipient states must be brought into a regime of restraints—on the basis of their self-interests and in a cooperative manner rather than having curbs imposed upon them—the primary initiatives must be made by some combination of suppliers.

To date Latin America is the only region in which recipient states have made a relatively serious attempt to develop some multilateral restraints. In the Declaration of Ayacucho of 1974, eight Andean countries committed themselves to "create conditions which permit effective limitations of armaments and put an end to their acquisition for offensive warlike purposes in order to dedicate all possible resources to economic and social development."[7] Concerned by deteriorating economic conditions, attributable to some degree to high expenditures on armaments, the

Peruvian government of General Juan Velasco Alvarado, which came to power in 1968, initiated this declaration in the hope that it would curb Chile's arms race with Peru. Discussions among the signatory states, designed to freeze existing ratios of weapons-to-manpower and levels of military expenditures in relation to gross national product, ensued, but they broke down within two years. Subsequent negotiations restricted to Peru, Chile, and Bolivia made a little more headway but also bogged down. Nevertheless, there were discussions between the chiefs of staffs of the several military services of the countries regarding their respective national security concerns and their weapons requirements. Monitoring weapons inventories, establishing demilitarized zones, and thinning out border units were among the items on the agenda. In June 1978 President Carlos Perez of Venezuela took the lead in reactivating the Ayacucho Declaration, and organized a meeting of the foreign ministers of the signatory states as a side activity of the United Nations Special Session on Disarmament. Subsequently the foreign minister of Mexico proposed to the Organization of American States that there be created a regional body comprising all the nations of Latin America and the Caribbean which would set, and periodically revise, limits on the acquisition and transfer of conventional arms. At a meeting in Mexico City in August 1978, twenty of these states, including Cuba, agreed to exchange information on weapons purchases and work toward a regime of restraints on arms transfers.

Clearly, Latin America is still a long way from having effective regional restraints. The Ayacucho Declaration did not succeed in preventing further sizable arms purchases by such states as Chile, Ecuador, and Peru. Nevertheless, an important start has been made. The lessons to be learned from the experience thus far are clear. The failure to bring Brazil into the Ayacucho framework greatly limited its possible effectiveness. This is an excellent example of the principle that all the important and relevant states in a region must be brought into an arms control regime if it is to achieve its aims. Second, recipient initiatives must be complemented by restraints among the possible suppliers. After 1974 the Soviet Union sold advanced fighters to Peru, and France sent Mirage fighters to Ecuador. To succeed in their purpose, restraints organized by recipients need to be respected by the suppliers, and should, if at all possible, be coordinated with them.

Over the long run, only multilateral restraints on arms sales implemented by the suppliers, in some cases with the assistance of the recipients within a region, will be truly effective. Yet this has barely been attempted. Some steps in this direction have been taken, but they have remained quite rudimentary. As has been noted, the Near East Arms Coordinating Committee, consisting of Britain, France, and the United States, regulated with considerable success the flow of arms into the Middle East from 1950 to 1955, but this effort collapsed with the beginning of Soviet and Czechoslovakian transfers to Egypt following Nasser's takeover and the nationalization of the Suez Canal. Embargoes have been declared on the transfer of arms at various times. The United States and Britain blocked sales to India and Pakistan following the outbreak of the 1965 war, and South Africa has been the subject of both voluntary and mandatory embargoes declared by the United Nations. But embargoes are by their nature crude instruments, usually designed to punish through a total blockade on transfers. They offer little precedent for establishing multilateral mechanisms intended to maintain regional balances in a cooperative manner.

The Conventional Arms Transfer Talks
with the Soviet Union

The most interesting attempt to develop suppliers' restraints was that of the Carter administration, although there were no results for reasons to be examined. From the outset, as the new administration set forth its guidelines for American policy on arms transfers, it was understood that the other major suppliers would be approached. America's laissez-faire practice on arms sales required reform under any circumstances, it was thought, but it was also recognized that no unilateral policy of restraint could long succeed without some restraint on the part of the other suppliers. Shortly after the inauguration, Vice President Mondale left for major European capitals and broached the subject of cooperative restraints on arms sales. Low-key soundings of the allies were made in the following weeks. The responses ranged from expressions of interest and support, if not enthusiasm, to considerable skepticism. The latter was especially manifest in parts of the French bureaucracy even though the Elysée was more inclined to give it a try. A consistent theme in the responses of the West Europeans was the need to involve the Soviet Union. Thereupon the administration quickly focused its entire energies on approaching Moscow and persuading it of the need to participate in a multilateral approach. The net result was to let the Europeans off the hook, and to this day they have not been forced to face the issue squarely.

In the United States it had been the conventional wisdom for many years that the Soviets would never be interested in discussions on arms transfer restraints, and a few in the incoming Carter administration, as well as many in the bureaucracy, shared this view. Yet following President Carter's election, Leonid Brezhnev in addressing the sixteenth Congress of Trade Unions noted that the "problem of the international arms trade seems to merit an exchange of views." When Secretary of State Vance made his first official visit to Moscow in March 1977, his proposals on SALT II were rejected, but agreement was reached on setting up bilateral working groups on a few key subjects, of which arms transfers was one.

American and Soviet delegations met four times between December 1977 and the de facto collapse of the Conventional Arms Transfer (CAT) talks a year later. A brief review of the meetings is instructive. At the first, the Soviets essentially listened as the Americans, headed by Leslie Gelb, director of the Bureau of Politico-Military Affairs in the Department of State, explained the administration's policy on American transfers and its views concerning the desirability of a multilateral approach. At this stage the Soviets limited themselves to asking questions about the administration's policy, especially the new annual ceiling on arms sales.

At the second meeting held in Helsinki in May 1978, the Soviets, led by Ambassador Lev I. Mendelevich, a responsible and constructive diplomat, agreed that unrestrained arms transfers were a serious problem requiring attention and that the two countries should hold regular meetings on this question. In addition, the Soviets presented some legal and political principles or criteria, which might have global applicability, defining when arms transfers may or may not be permissible. The United States suggested some guidelines that reflected its own unilateral policies, such as no introduction into a region of advanced weapons systems that would create a new or significantly higher combat capability, and limitations on re-transfers to third parties. By the end of the second round it was clear that substantive progress was possible. But American officials also felt that if the talks were to have concrete results, it would be desirable to discuss transfers to specific regions of the world as soon as possible. This reflected the State Department view that CAT should be seen as a foreign policy negotiation and as a way of regulating Soviet behavior in the Third World. ACDA, which preferred a classical and more technical arms control approach, initially argued for concentrating on global restrictions on certain weapons without entering into discussions of regions.

Two months later at the third meeting a framework was agreed upon for subjecting weapons transfers to both regional and arms control restraints. General principles of mutual restraint of a political-legal and a military-technical nature would be drawn up. The latter would include prohibitions on the export of certain types of weapons such as long-range surface-to-surface missiles, naval mines, or arms of particular use to terrorists. In addition there would be frank exchange of views on arms sales on a region-by-region basis, which might eventually lead to some joint understandings, or "harmonized guidelines," for restraints on transfers into a region. Initially reluctant to discuss

287

regions, the Soviets were persuaded of its necessity by the Americans. By the end of the third round it was even more evident that the Soviets were earnest in their approach to this undertaking and that the CAT talks were progressing better than many in Washington had first expected.

In preparing for the fourth round in Mexico City in December 1978, the Department of State, building upon discussions at the previous round, proposed through diplomatic channels that the discussions begin with two regions: Latin America, where neither country sold large amounts of arms, and sub-Saharan Africa, which also received comparatively few arms although the U.S.S.R. had been substantially increasing its shipments there over the previous three years. The Soviet Union accepted these two regions for discussion as the "American-proposed regions" while making its own suggestion that West Asia and East Asia be discussed. Although the "Soviet-proposed regions" were never officially defined, the former was thought to include Iran and the latter to include China and South Korea. Moscow appeared to be most concerned about arms sales to China. In earlier CAT rounds the Soviets had suggested that among the principles that should be adopted would be one prohibiting transfers to states bordering one of the suppliers and another banning transfers to states that refused to participate in disarmament discussions; these two principles were clearly directed at Beijing and were rejected by the United States.

But at a National Security Council meeting prior to the Mexico City round, deep differences emerged over the purpose of the CAT talks and the very desirability of discussing with the Soviet Union arms transfers to sensitive states or regions. In a "savage bureaucratic struggle," Zbigniew Brzezinski opened the meeting with a strong attack on the CAT talks; he particularly objected to any discussion of West Asia or East Asia. Leslie Gelb, replacing Cyrus Vance who had been unexpectedly called out of town to tend to some pressing negotiations on Namibia at the United Nations, pointed out that it would do no harm to listen to what the Soviets had to say, but he did not win his case. Prior to the

288

third round the president had agreed to discussions of regions, but he now reversed himself, siding with Brzezinski and Secretary of Defense Harold Brown. Among the factors that could have influenced Carter's decision were the pending normalization of relations with China (which was not known to everyone at the NSC meeting) and the unstable situation in Iran. Some later felt that Brzezinski opposed the entire concept of talking to the Soviets about Third World regions as giving them a *droit de regard* that would not otherwise exist, but did not bring his weight to bear on this issue until this late stage. Moreover, by then there had been a change of attitude in the Carter administration on relations with the Soviet Union. After much debate the American delegation was instructed to refuse to listen and to walk out if the Soviets brought up arms transfer restraints to West Asia and East Asia. Such a refusal may have been unprecedented in the annals of American diplomacy. (The dispute continued in the cable traffic between Brzezinski and Gelb in Mexico City as messages "dripping with venom" were exchanged. At one point Gelb was ordered by the White House to leave the delegation and return to Washington, but the order was subsequently rescinded.)[8]

In Mexico City the Soviets were incredulous and angry at the American unwillingness to hear what they had to say about the regions of concern to them. Not surprisingly, they refused to limit the agenda to the "American-proposed regions" of Latin America and sub-Saharan Africa. As a result the fourth-round discussions led nowhere and cast serious doubt on the future of the entire CAT enterprise. The deterioration of détente in 1979 foreclosed the revival of CAT, and the Soviet invasion of Afghanistan surely drove the nails into its coffin.

What conclusions are to be drawn from this unhappy experience? Some observers saw the internal American wrangle over the Mexico City talks as a personal feud or a clash of personalities, and the subsequent announcement that Leslie Gelb was to leave the government lent credence to this. Yet the disarray within the Carter administration that became evident reflected

289

a more fundamental lack of consensus regarding the purposes and limitations of the Conventional Arms Transfer talks and even the role of arms transfers in foreign policy. And this in turn was related to the longstanding differences in conceptions within the administration regarding policy toward the Soviet Union, especially with respect to the East-West competition in the Third World.

We can now see that it was a mistake to concentrate so heavily upon bilateral talks with the Soviet Union, without a greater involvement on the part of the West European suppliers. If intra-Alliance consultations had been far more extensive they might have given a resulting Western position greater solidity, making it less vulnerable to internal Washington bureaucratic struggles. At a minimum they would have forced the United States to think through its approach before the negotiations had reached a sub-stantive stage.

The basic lesson is that more thought and attention need to be given to the role that multilateral restraints on arms transfers can play in East-West competition in the developing world. This would entail a realistic assessment of the limitations on what can be achieved—given the fundamental ideological differences and the tendency to exploit them—as well as the benefits that might result from some forms of moderation or regulation. Greater clarity of purpose would also help in assessing the link between what will surely be an ongoing competition in the Third World and the overall East-West relationship.

Despite the collapse of the CAT talks, the experience thus far suggests the feasibility of discussions among the suppliers. Initially there was widespread skepticism about the Soviet Union's willingness to take part, and yet Moscow found it in its interest to do so and in a relatively constructive manner. At a minimum the importance of the undertaking was recognized. Sufficient progress was achieved to encourage the idea that sustained atten-tion be given, at some point in the future when there is a more auspicious international climate, to the creation of multilateral restraints on arms sales.

Forms of Multilateral Regulation

Cooperative, multilateral regulation of arms sales must be seen in a long-term perspective. The goal is not impossible, but if it is ever to be achieved, time will be necessary. There must first be a greater recognition of the new importance of arms transfers in world politics, and the bad as well as the good that can come from this. There must also be greater clarity regarding the desirability of creating some management, if not restraint, of the global politics of arms sales. The initial aims should remain modest. As arms transfers are part of foreign policy for both the supplying and the receiving countries, *care should be taken to ensure that any arms control approach is not artificially separated from the reality of foreign policy.*

Before outlining a politically realistic strategy for achieving multilateral regulation, it is instructive to examine the issue in a somewhat hypothetical framework so as to have the various possibilities in mind. Multilateral regulation could take several forms. Initially, agreement should be reached among the principal suppliers, but it would be preferable that the regulation be of a type that has the greatest degree of possible support among the recipients.[9]

1. *Mutual Example:* Policies of restraint adopted unilaterally, but undertaken with the expectation that other countries would reciprocate, would be the easiest to adopt. Unilateral restraints could be intentionally signaled to other suppliers, along with an indication of what is expected or desired from them. The drawbacks to such an approach are, however, fairly evident. Countries such as Sweden or Switzerland may announce that they will not export to "areas of conflict or tension," but greater differentiation is required on the part of the principal suppliers, all of which have direct political interests in most, if not all, areas of actual or potential conflict. An additional complication, if qualitative limitations on transfers were sought, would be the difficulty of identifying comparable weapons systems, or arms below a certain technological threshold; this would entail direct contacts among

291

suppliers, which would go beyond an approach based upon expectations of reciprocal restraints. Finally, the approach by mutual example lends itself too readily to misunderstandings and misperceptions. Exposed to the pressure of competitive arms sales, it could prove vulnerable and in time collapse. Nevertheless, we should not totally dismiss the benefits of unilateral actions adopted in parallel by separate countries. In the absence of something more organized, if the principal suppliers were to adopt roughly similar national policies and controls, a great deal could be achieved.

2. *Formal Agreement:* Theoretically, it should be possible to set specific limits, or prohibitions, on transfers of certain weapons or on sales to identified regions. However, this also is unlikely to commend itself as an approach. The first question that would have to be addressed is whether verification is necessary, and if so, how verification is to be achieved. But even if verification were not required, negotiations leading to a formal agreement would face immense difficulties in dealing with continuously changing conditions of two sorts. Weapons technology is in constant evolution; reaching set agreements on such technologies would not only be difficult, but possibly self-defeating, since perceptions of the transfer of certain technologies are likely to shift over time. Second, except in cases in which one might want a worldwide prohibition, restraints are likely to have a geographical focus. Political balances and conditions in a region also shift over time. Nations will not want to lock themselves into prohibitions through formal agreements when regional political conditions are subject to change. Finally, the mind boggles at the thought of a truly comprehensive agreement on arms transfers given the variety of arms that could be involved. Negotiating such an agreement would make SALT look like child's play.

3. *Informal Negotiations:* Such an approach might be the most suitable in that it would permit the close, continuing contact that would not exist under "mutual example" and would also provide the flexibility that would be lacking in the legalism of a "formal agreement."

A possibility worth consideration would be a forum for informal negotiations on Conventional Arms Transfer Restraints (CATR) at which the principal suppliers would discuss qualitative, quantitative, and regional limitations to which they might agree on an informal basis. ° At first limited to the Big Four suppliers, CATR might in time be expanded to include secondary suppliers. CATR would seek to establish *criteria* by which to *regulate* transfers. In doing this it might create guidelines that lead toward a certain specialization of sales. Some guidelines might be geographical, while others might be qualitative. For example, country A might be given the dominant role in transfers to country Y, or perhaps more broadly to the region in which Y is located; or country A might be given a free rein in selling a certain type of weapons system, leaving other arms to other suppliers. We have here the makings of a market-sharing approach, which might not only restrain a competitive arms sales race, but have a direct benefit in promoting a more rational international arms-production pattern based upon specialization of labor.

CATR would be most useful, and successful, not as a one-time international conference but as a continuing forum, meeting as required, for purposes of discussion and for reaching informal agreements on the regulation of arms transfers. It would be analogous, in some ways, to the nuclear suppliers' meetings which deal with the export of nuclear technology.

In developing criteria for the sale of arms, CATR would seek to regulate exports so as to avoid transfers that would have a destabilizing influence within a region. Among sales that would be subject to restraints are those that could:

- create an imbalance that upsets an existing balance,
- start or exacerbate a local arms race,
- foster instability because of the sudden acquisition of new arms,

° I have retained the CATR acronym, which I discussed in a paper circulated within the U.S. government well prior to the CAT talks with the Soviet Union. Note, however, that my concept of CATR is substantially different from what CAT turned out to be. CATR would be a continuing, multilateral forum in which a number of countries would participate.

- provide incentives for a surprise attack,
- provide incentives for a preemptive action,
- quicken the pace and scale of escalation,
- introduce starkly inhumane weapons into a region,
- provide weapons that might be used internally in a civil war, police action, or violation of human rights.

A more difficult and delicate task would be to regulate the flow of arms according to the judgment of the CATR nations as to whether the recipient needs the arms for its national security, or whether such arms are the optimal way to use financial resources that might be better employed otherwise. Most nations are reluctant to form judgments, at least openly, that impinge upon the decisions of other states. Yet there is no obligation to sell arms. Accordingly, the CATR countries might decide not to sell certain arms for reasons relating to the domestic politics or economy of the recipient. This is, in fact, already widely done on an individual basis.

Restraints might be qualitative, quantitative, or geographical. In practice they would be combined. Although some qualitative restraints might be worldwide, many of the qualitative and perhaps all the quantitative restraints would be regional or national.

Qualitative restraints might cover such weapons as:

- surface-to-surface cruise missiles over a certain range,
- dual purpose weapons that could deliver nuclear as well as nonnuclear warheads,
- arms that can be used by terrorists, such as the shoulder-fired Redeye,
- some types of precision-guided munitions and other new technologies whose introduction into a region of conflict could be destabilizing,
- particularly inhumane weapons such as concussion bombs, lethal chemical arms, and napalm,
- weapons that could inflict large-scale damage on population centers,
- certain arms such as aircraft carriers, attack submarines,

294

attack aircraft whose performance exceeded specified parameters of range, speed, and payload.

Quantitative restraints might include:

- overall arms ceilings within a region,
- the maintenance of a prescribed ratio of arms among states within a region,
- limits on the arms possessed by a country,
- permissible rates of replacement.

Transfers would be made with great selectivity according to the criteria agreed upon by the CATR members. An important consideration would be to avoid the rapid infusion of arms into an area, involving a major leap in inventories, in such a manner as to create instability either in military terms or through drastically altered political perceptions. The criteria might favor arms of a defensive, nonprovocative nature, although deciding when the criteria are met is not always easy. The CATR states might also agree to discuss among themselves all sales over a certain amount. Most important, the member states might agree on a fundamental principle: all transfers to which one of the nations participating in CATR has grounds for objection, or regarding which it seeks consultations, will be discussed multilaterally in the CATR forum before they are approved.

To regulate arms transfers effectively it would also be necessary for the CATR participants to deal with co-production programs. Agreements might be reached among the supplier governments on the types of assistance extended to countries that want to achieve indigenous weapons-manufacturing capabilities. Licensing arrangements could be limited to assistance within certain categories of arms.

Finally, the CATR participants might agree on controls over the end use of arms and their re-transfer. Such controls would be intended to forestall the unwanted transfer of arms to third parties. They might apply to relatively new arms provided by a recipient nation to its allies during a time of war or increased tensions, or to the transfer of used and surplus equipment. The

295

relevance of such controls to the Middle East, where unauthorized re-transfers have taken place, is evident. The CATR states could, for example, agree among themselves that none will provide additional weapons to any government that has violated an agreement on re-transfer or end use.

PRIORITY TO THE EUROPEAN-AMERICAN DIMENSION

In the future, if an attempt is made to develop some pattern of cooperative, multilateral regulation among the principal suppliers of arms, we should initially seek arrangements between the United States and the West Europeans rather than place priority upon the development of Soviet-American accords. This would reverse the order pursued by the Carter administration. A serious effort to engage the West Europeans was never made, according to Barry Blechman, a former assistant director of the Arms Control and Disarmament Agency, in part because of a lack of policy coordination among the Departments of State, Defense, and the ACDA.[10]

There are important reasons for embarking on such a new approach. The acceptance by the Soviet Union of some restraints on its transfers to the Third World is a goal that should be maintained, but it should be seen as a very long-term aim that will be extremely difficult to achieve. For the Soviets, political competition with the West in the developing world has strong ideological roots, and they will not be quick to curtail voluntarily what may be their most valuable instrument in that contest. On the other hand, the very nature of the East-West struggle in the Third World creates a pressing need for greater cooperation within the West. Whereas for most of the post–World War II period the greatest danger to the West has been seen as a war beginning in Europe, in the coming decades the greatest likelihood of danger may come from Third World regional conflicts and instability that threaten Western economic and security interests.

296

A coordinated approach on arms transfers should become a central element of a more common Western approach toward such unstable regions as the Persian Gulf and Middle East. The present pattern of competitive, uncoordinated sales is contrary to Western political interests. The Soviet invasion of Afghanistan and its troubling potential consequences for the region, as well as the great difficulties in developing a unified after-the-fact Western response in an atmosphere of crisis, demonstrated the necessity of closer intra-West consultations on policies toward regions outside the formal NATO area of responsibility.

A first step would be for the principal Western arms suppliers to begin foreign policy consultations on political and security developments within regions and specific countries. This would include discussion of the policies that would best serve Western interests. Although differences in assessments of situations, and the policies to be followed, would surely surface in many circumstances, such consultations would on the whole be beneficial. Foreign policy consultations among the Western powers would also provide an important base for making arms transfer decisions in a coordinated manner. Such an approach would place the question of multilateral regulation of arms sales in a wider and more politically significant framework than that of the half-hearted proposals for arms transfer restraints made to the West Europeans in the early days of the Carter administration.

It is remarkable, in fact, that systematic foreign policy consultations among the major Western powers on developments in the Third World do not already take place, given the importance to the First World countries of what happens in some of the more volatile parts of the world. Because the North Atlantic Treaty Organization at the time of its founding was restricted to responsibilities in a fixed geographic area, it has never developed a continuing system of consultations on regions outside of what is known as the NATO "guidelines area." The annual seven-nation "economic summits" of recent years among the leaders of the advanced industrialized countries are too infrequent and diffuse, and occur at too high a level, to provide an adequate forum for what is envisaged here. What is needed, among the Allies, is a continuing process of joint assessments of trends and developments in the Third World, followed by some degree of contingency planning so as to deal constructively with evolving situations. This would require regular meetings at the the foreign minister or deputy foreign minister level several times a year, supported by more frequent lower-echelon consultations. Although this could be undertaken within the context of NATO, the absence of Japan and other considerations relating to not hindering the regular activities of the military alliance, or distracting attention from its main purpose of defending Europe, argue for a separate framework. Yet there is no need to create a new international organization; such consultations could take place without a new secretariat, as is already the case with the annual economic summits.[11]

The next step would be to adopt a market-sharing approach towards Western arms sales to the Third World. This could be organized along geographical lines, by segments of military technology, or by some combination of the two. Certain countries might be encouraged to take the lead in arms sales to some regions; an obvious candidate would be France in francophone black Africa or in Syria, where it has historical ties. The United States might be given the dominant position in Latin America or South Korea. Alternatively, there might be a far greater specialization by country than exists today in categories of weapons systems. Advanced fighter aircraft might be left, in large measure, to the United States which has a stronger technological base in this area while the Europeans would be encouraged to take the lead in other categories, such as armored vehicles and helicopters, or perhaps naval vessels.

Such a division of labor could have considerable economic consequences, especially for the Europeans, and it would be absolutely essential to its adoption that it be seen as equitable. Each of the major arms producers must be assured a fair share of the total market. The continued viability of their defense industries would be an important consideration for them. This might entail some methods of compensation for restrictions that are voluntarily undertaken. The United States, as the largest weapons producer and exporter of arms in the West, might be called upon to reduce its share of the world market in a fair division of labor. This might create difficulties for particular American corporations, but it is unlikely to lead to much hardship for the American defense industry as a whole, because that industry is not so export-dependent as to be seriously affected. Such a division of labor, if carefully done, need not be inimical to European economic interests. Looked at from a wider perspective, a greater degree of specialization in arms manufacture would permit larger production runs and thereby lead to more substantial economies of scale. The economic "need" to export arms might be considerably reduced.

Skepticism is often expressed regarding European willingness to regulate arms sales, and it is usually based on economic considerations.[12] The first point to be made is that to regulate is not necessarily to reduce. Multilateral cooperation on arms exports need not automatically lead to their curtailment. Indeed, it could result in an agreed plan for increasing sales so as to meet a foreign policy objective. Thus a market-sharing approach or the specialization of labor could well result in economic benefits to the supplier countries. But beyond these considerations lies the fact that the economic benefits of arms sales are not as great as is generally assumed. One overall conclusion that emerges from our detailed country-by-country analysis in Part Two is that none of the arms suppliers is really heavily dependent upon arms sales as a part of its foreign trade (3 to 5 percent of exports), as a source of employment, as a means of reducing the unit costs of production, as a means of recouping research and development expenses, or for balance-of-payment purposes. Economic considerations are not of sufficient importance that they should be allowed to override major foreign policy aims.

There are, moreover, some positive economic incentives for seeking international cooperation. Sectors of the French arms industry are becoming dangerously overdependent upon exports and need to be rationalized through international arrangements; the British could gain from greater weapons cooperation with the continental Europeans; and the West Germans could use consultations with the other suppliers as a way of sorting out their paradoxical situation of having a declared policy of restraint while indirectly increasing their export of arms through co-production arrangements.

An additional advantage to the establishment of European-American cooperation would be that it could help realize the NATO goal of achieving greater standardization of weapons systems within the Alliance. Specialization of labor and markets in Third World sales would be a form of guarantee to national defense industries that would reduce the incentives for attempting to keep every sector of their industries viable. Accordingly, it should be possible to accept a greater rationalization of the weapons-manfacturing industries within the Alliance, whose products are now often duplicated. This might be assisted by a system of "offsets," whereby some of the sales to the Third World given up by West European suppliers are compensated for by increased sales to the United States. The lack of cooperation among the Western suppliers on Third World sales has inhibited collaboration within the Atlantic Alliance.

Conversely, the past dominance of the NATO market by the United States has led to added pressures in Europe to export. A more equal sharing of the Atlantic market through the achievement of a better "two-way" street in arms purchases would reduce such pressures by making exports less economically necessary. The twin goals of regulating arms sales multilaterally and of achieving arms standardization in the Alliance are not contradictory, as is often suggested, but could be complementary if adroitly pursued.

But it is the political benefits that would be paramount. The adoption by the Western producers of a suppliers' "code of conduct" could help ensure that arms sales are kept within the confines of foreign policy goals that are in the overall interest of the non-Communist world. Too often in the past, unbridled economic competition for arms sales has resulted in politically undesirable weapons transfers.

EAST-WEST "RULES OF THE GAME"

After the Western suppliers have developed among themselves some pattern of multilateral regulation of arms sales, they should turn their attention to the East. We need to find some way to damp or keep within acceptable boundaries the East-West rivalry and competition in the Third World. Otherwise local conflicts and disputes are likely to escalate, draw in the superpowers, and get out of hand. Third World conflicts may well be the most likely source of war in the 1980s. In recent years Moscow has shown an increasing ability and a decreasing reluctance to become involved through arms and advisers in conflicts in the Third World. This is likely to continue, for the Soviet leadership sees the quest for influence and allegiance in the developing countries, and the support of "progressive" forces, as central to its ideological principles. It has been, moreover, supported by a new capability to project military power into distant areas. These long-range intervention capabilities are likely to be further strengthened in the 1980s through the modernization and improvement of sea and airlift forces.

The international atmosphere at the beginning of the 1980s is not propitious, yet we need to develop some rules of the game for managing East-West competition in the Third World. Even such a skeptical appraiser of Soviet intentions as Secretary of State Alexander Haig, Jr., spoke of the necessity for an "international code of conduct." A first step, once political conditions improve, might be to engage the Soviets in discussions of regional security problems. Such discussions, while recognizing the global interests of the two superpowers, should also seek a better understanding of local situations and circumstances. Some insulation of local conflicts from the superpower rivalry would be desirable, and the chances of its achievement would be enhanced through a continuing exchange of views on the specific situation at hand. When interests sharply conflict, as they inevitably will at times, the need for crisis management may arise. Maintaining contact can reduce some real misunderstandings and facilitate much-needed predictability in a period of tension and crisis.[13]

Part of this process should be to seek to moderate the flow of arms into regions of instability. It is unrealistic to expect the Soviets to call a halt to using arms sales as an instrument of policy, probably the most effective tool at their disposal, and there would be reluctance to follow such a course of self-denial even in the West. But we should seek some rules of the game that introduce a pattern of restraint. The understandings worked out after the 1962 Cuban missile crisis regarding the nontransfer of "offensive" weapons to the island may provide one type of precedent.

Can the Soviet Union be engaged in some multilateral regulation of arms transfers? The experience of the Conventional Arms Transfer talks suggests that the task is far from hopeless. Indeed, the blame for the collapse of the CAT talks is more properly placed in Washington than in Moscow. Although the Soviets were quite naturally making proposals that suited their own interests, they approached the negotiations on arms transfer restraints with seriousness of purpose.

The Soviet motivations for engaging in the multilateral regulation of arms transfers would undoubtedly be mixed. Such a process would provide an opportunity to create difficulties between the United States and its allies. It would be one way of seeking to place a lid on Western transfers, given that in the long run the West has a greater capacity to increase arms sales than has the Soviet Union. It might be a way of avoiding arms transfers that Moscow does not really want to make, grounds for a "diplomatic excuse" to would-be recipients. The Soviet experience as a supplier has not been altogether satisfactory, as, for example, in Indonesia, Egypt, and Somalia. Moscow's military exports have not always been a reliable means of cementing political relationships. But beyond such considerations, some

302

Soviets are also conscious of the dangers that an unrestrained arms transfer competition could pose for regional stability. Avoidance of an unbridled weapons race with the West may be seen as desirable in areas of high tension such as the Middle East, in areas of incipient conflict such as southern Africa, or in areas of regional confrontation such as the two Koreas. In addition, the Soviets clearly are fearful of Western arms sales to China and could see regulation as potentially an important means of restraining such sales. Finally, if and when East-West relations improve considerably, the Soviets may find that unrestrained competition in arms transfers could quickly undermine a renewed détente relationship.

Developing rules of the game with the Soviets and engaging them in arms sale restraints should be perceived as a long-term task. The CAT experience must be seen as a first attempt rather than a dead end. The incentives for progress on this matter exist. But we should now shift gears and approach the West Europeans more intensively before raising the issue again in the still more sensitive East-West context. This reversal of priorities from that pursued by the Carter administration in the late 1970s is particularly appropriate in the wake of the chill in Soviet-American relations stemming from the invasion of Afghanistan.

THIRD WORLD ARMS INDUSTRIES— A LIMITED ROLE AS SUPPLIERS

When considering possible restraints on arms sales by the suppliers, attention must be paid to the substantial number of countries that are creating their own armament industries. Many of these are located in the Third World, as we have noted. They will want to export arms, as some already do, to reduce their unit production costs and earn foreign exchange as well as to gain other economic and political benefits. Will this not enormously complicate, or even make impossible, the achievement of any coordinated suppliers' restraint? A 1979 Senate Foreign Relations

Committee report, commenting on the Conventional Arms Transfer negotiations, suggested that the emerging new producers might soon "need to become part of any suppliers' effort to reduce the worldwide arms traffic."[14]

Discussion in the previous parts leads to the conclusion that the new weapons-producing countries are not about to become large-scale exporters of arms. This is especially the case for advanced systems, which would be likely to have a political impact within a region. Manufacturing sophisticated weapons requires skilled labor, a resource that is in short supply in the developing world. Moreover, such weapons also require engineering and technical knowledge which often cannot be readily found at home. Some Third World countries, such as Brazil, South Korea, and Taiwan, are indeed making impressive strides in producing low technology items, such as hand-held weapons, armored personnel vehicles, and relatively simple ships and aircraft, on their own. But only Israel, India, and South Africa are manufacturing medium-level technology items independently, according to a recent survey of the International Institute for Strategic Studies. Even in these countries most of the research and development has been undertaken elsewhere and been made available through licensing arrangements.[15]

There is some irony here, for almost all of the countries that have embarked upon creating an arms-manufacturing industry have basically done this for political and security reasons. They wish to become more independent by becoming self-sufficient. Yet as they develop and equip their military establishment, they feel the necessity for more up-to-date arms—often their opponent is doing the same—and this introduces requirements for still more advanced weaponry, which can only be made available from abroad. Israel is the classic example. It has the most advanced weapons industry (after the major suppliers), producing a range of relatively sophisticated aircraft, missiles, and patrol boats (albeit often using some foreign technology or components). But under the pressure of the competition with its opponents, who also rely upon imported arms, it continues to need the United States for such very advanced weapons as the F-15 and the F-16.

There are several impediments to many more countries becoming major exporters of arms. Some of the principal Third World manufacturers are pariah states. Israel has probably reached the limits of its ability to export, because most of its potential new customers are dependent upon Middle East oil and do not want to offend the Arab states. South Africa is ostracized by most of the world community. Taiwan is limited as to where it can export. Often, purchasing countries prefer to receive arms from one of the major suppliers because of the political relationship involved. And finally, American, West European, and Soviet weapons are usually the best technologically, are often cheaper, and carry the greatest "prestige."

The major suppliers have become more sensitive in recent years to the risks involved in too freely granting licensing arrangements or permitting the co-production of weapons. Such steps could come back to haunt the suppliers if they lead to the emergence of regional powers whose military actions do not coincide with the suppliers' interests, or if arms are manufactured and sold in a manner contrary to the wishes of the original provider of the technology. A U.S. congressional report warned in 1977 that the transfer of technology through co-production and foreign licensing agreements could imply American support for a nation's military buildup; such assistance might also increase independence from the supplier.[16] Accordingly, the major suppliers have begun examining requests more critically and are becoming less supportive of the ambitions of some Third World nations to develop their own weapons capabilities.

Clearly the emergence of new suppliers will make the question of developing international restraints on arms sales somewhat more complex. But these new suppliers, mainly in the Third World, are not in a position to challenge the traditional exporters. Although the number of countries producing arms is gradually growing, only 4 percent of global arms exports in 1978 came from within the developing world.[17] Contrary to some expectations, therefore, the global arms trade is only being altered at the margins, with the new producers not creating insuperable impediments to restraint. The market for major weapons remains essentially oligopolistic, and would be amenable to restraints if they were politically acceptable for both suppliers and recipients.

RECIPIENT PERSPECTIVES AND REGIONAL APPROACHES

The attitude of the recipient states toward any form of arms restraint would, of course, be critical. Ideally, states within a region might initiate restraints on transfers into their area by agreements among themselves to curtail purchases. This is what has been attempted with limited, but not insignificant, success in the Declaration of Ayacucho among the Andean nations. The comparatively small volume of transfers to most parts of sub-Saharan black Africa provides another good opportunity for genuine, regionally inspired restraint. Regional (or subregional) arms control arrangements, such as zones of limited armaments, might involve quantitative ceilings on the purchase of certain types of weapons. Such limitations would recognize legitimate defense needs but, within a regional plan, seek to avoid an excessive transfer of arms which could be destabilizing. Limitations might restrict the importation of certain types of military technology, such as cruise missiles; this might be especially feasible if such weaponry had not been previously introduced into the area.

Realistically, though, the suppliers would have to be directly involved in most plans for regional restraints. The best would be a form of restraints on arms flows that involved both the purchasers and the producers. If a plan is initiated by recipients, the suppliers should be prepared to be responsive. In the more likely case of a supplier-initiated plan, it would be essential to its success that it be worked out in a carefully coordinated manner with the states in the region. What is required, at root, is a symbiotic relationship. A regionally developed recipient's approach which

306

was complementary to a supplier plan would legitimate the efforts of the suppliers and forestall charges of discrimination.

The political and psychological dimensions of the problem of regional restraints are important. Politically, any attempt to restrain arms sales should be linked with diplomatic efforts to resolve disputes within the region. Psychologically, such restraints must be seen as justified and not as an attempt to deprive states of their sovereignty or their legitimate security needs.

Until the growth of concern about arms sales in recent years, Third World countries had a tendency to view any restraints upon transfers as inherently discriminatory. Worse still, proposals for restraint were denounced as arrogant manifestations of paternalistic attitudes. The perspectives of the recipient states were strongly influenced by the political and economic tensions between South and North. Any measures that would curtail the transfer of technology to the developing countries were seen as running counter to the needed redistribution of the world's resources and knowledge. Moreover, there was a suspicion that arms sales restraints were a stratagem designed to perpetuate the military inferiority of Third World countries. The major powers were not succeeding with arms control among themselves, yet they presumed to tell the developing countries what their true security requirements were. Many rationales for resentment were available.[18]

A very different Third World perspective began gradually to emerge in the late 1970s. The arms-supplying countries were seen as pushing their wares upon the less developed nations with great zest and fervor. The purchase of arms was increasingly viewed by some as diverting scarce resources from urgent social and developmental needs. Addressing the United Nations General Assembly, S. Rajaratnam, Singapore's foreign minister, concluded that "the massive flow of arms to the Third World confronts it with a new danger. It is first of all a drain on their economies. But even more important, is the fact that it creates a new form of dependence on the Great Powers who can exploit the Third World's dependence on them for arms, to manipulate them, to engineer conflicts between them, and to use them as their proxies in their competition for influence and dominance."[19]

Interestingly, the notion that developing nations are nefariously made dependent upon the industrialized countries through arms purchases has helped spawn a whole new school of analysis, dependency theory. Mary Kaldor has written that "the acquisition of armaments is one mechanism whereby Third World countries are drawn into the global confrontation between the superpowers and are incorporated into a world division of labor which limits their full potential for development ... military dependence induced by the acquisition of modern armaments may actually reduce political power."[20] And a German university study group on armaments and underdevelopment has argued that the importation of arms is a form of penetration by industrialized countries into societies in the underdeveloped world; instead of assisting the establishment of political and military independence, it creates new forms of dominance and dependence.[21]

Neither the paternalistic-discriminatory nor the manipulative-dependency view of restraints on arms sales is likely to be the prevalent one in the Third World in the decades ahead. These nations will want to assure themselves of adequate armaments. But they may also, in some cases, be sensitive to the risks of regional arms races and the tensions that competitive arms purchases can induce. Many are concerned about the introduction of very sophisticated weapons into unstable regions. Thus they may well perceive some value in carefully designed, multilateral, supplier-recipient, restraints on arms sales. In a region of conflict like the Middle East, nations may support an arms restraint understanding, worked out in the context of a comprehensive Arab-Israeli political accord, that seeks to maintain a political and military balance.

That recipient country perspectives were evolving became clear at the 1978 U.N. Special Session on Disarmament. The non-aligned group dropped its previous objections to dealing with conventional arms transfers and supported a statement in the Final Document that "consultations should be carried out among major arms supplier and recipient countries on the limitation of all types of international transfer of conventional weapons, based in particular on the principle of undiminished security of the parties with a view to promoting or enhancing stability at a lower military level."[22] Among the ideas that have been discussed, though not yet adopted, at the United Nations is the creation of regional working groups under the Security Council or under the aegis of the Committee on Disarmament in Geneva to examine various aspects of the arms transfer problem on a region-by-region basis.

A regional approach is likely to be the most successful. A global approach, whatever its conceptual attractiveness, is likely to be found wanting when the attempt is made to apply it in all circumstances. This was one of the difficulties that the Carter administration ran into as it sought to implement the universalistic guidelines of its arms transfer policy in actual situations. One might conceive of a set of guidelines whereby each major supplier keeps its total world sales within a given annual ceiling, but it is not clear that this would necessarily serve a useful purpose. The perceived need for arms, the requirements of stability, and the level of sophistication of weapons vary enormously from region to region and over time. Each region is unique and offers a different mix of problems and opportunities.

Regional arms control has, to be sure, its own difficulties. One is that the geographic boundaries of a region are not always self-evident. Would restraints on arms sales to the front-line states in the Arab-Israeli dispute (Egypt, Syria, Jordan, and Israel) make sense if Saudi Arabia and perhaps Libya were not also included? Yet any restraints on sales to Saudi Arabia would also have to take into account the balance of power in the Persian Gulf, particularly as it involves Iraq and Iran. A subregional approach, not only in the Middle East but also in Latin America and Africa, might well be the best way to proceed. Subregions would involve more manageable units and provide a greater degree of homogeneity and common interests. In contrast to a globalist approach, a regional or subregional one would allow closer calculation of the military and political factors that must be taken into account in achieving, or maintaining, a balance.

The merits of a regional approach have been understood by the French. Addressing the U.N. Special Session on Disarmament in 1978, President Giscard D'Estaing noted that with the diversity that exists in the world, to seek universal principles would be inefficient and contrary to political realities. He suggested as the "most realistic" way to achieve a limitation on arms transfers a meeting that brought together the countries within a region that purchase arms and all the supplier countries. If this were to be done, he added, France would be prepared to facilitate the implementation of agreements by adjusting its policy on the sale of military equipment.[23]

At some point in the future it might also be possible to use regional institutions as a means to regulate the balance of armaments. The Organization of American States (OAS), the Organization of African Unity (OAU), the Andean group that sponsored the Declaration of Ayacucho, and the Association of South East Asian Nations (ASEAN), for example, could play constructive roles if they were further strengthened and given new responsibilities for arms control. The diffusion of power, of which the transfer of arms is a major dimension, is leading to a more pluralistic and regionally oriented world.

The best approach, in conclusion, would be a supplier-initiated, regionally oriented framework for managing the process of arms sales to the Third World. Consultations among the suppliers should encompass broad foreign policy considerations, possible conflicts within the region and any external threats to it, and the suppliers' evaluation of the local balance of military forces. Initiatives from within a region should be welcomed, but it is likely that it would take the prompting of supplier states to get the process started. A collaborative approach should seek to fully involve the regional recipients in making decisions so as to avoid a sense of discrimination or paternalism. There should be intensive discussions between the producers and the potential recipients concerning the purchasers' security problems and defense requirements. The suppliers should respect any regionally developed plans and be responsive when they seem in the interest of maintaining international security. But in the final analysis it is the suppliers who have the right to say "no sale!" And they must be prepared to exercise it collectively or individually when necessary. Any process of this nature, intended to manage the flow of arms and calibrate restraints must remain flexible and mutable so as to be able to adjust to changing needs and international conditions.

Anthony Sampson, the noted British journalist, has characterized today's arms sales as the "blind spot of a generation." Every generation, he suggests, has its own blind spot which is incomprehensible to future generations—the slave traders of the mid-eighteenth century and the employers of the childworkers of the nineteenth century. Sampson implies that like the other evils, this too shall pass.[24]

This book is not so sanguine about the transiency of our generation's blind spot. We have viewed arms sales as not only a normal and permanent aspect of international politics but one of rapidly growing scale and significance. The continuing diffusion of power, resulting from fundamental systemic causes, will increase the demand for arms. Regional military balances will be of enhanced importance. This will constantly raise new policy issues and dilemmas for governments, whose officials will be forced to give ever more attention to arms sales. The sale of weapons is neither esoteric nor trivial, but central to foreign policy concerns. Arms sales have become the common coin of contemporary diplomacy, and their role in world politics will become increasingly salient.

311

NOTES

PART ONE: DILEMMAS

1. *World Military and Social Expenditures, 1980,* comp. Ruth Sivard (Leesburg, Va.: W.M.S.E. Publications), p. 20.
Accurate and reliable data on arms transfers are an elusive commodity. Most governments do not release figures on their sales or purchases. The United States is the only major supplier that annually publishes data in some detail. Occasionally, official figures are cited by some other countries in parliamentary debates and hearings or given in releases to the press, and these have been culled and used where appropriate. The two principal worldwide surveys of arms transfers are prepared annually by the Stockholm International Peace Research Institute (SIPRI) and by the U.S. Arms Control and Disarmament Agency (ACDA). The variations in the methodology used by the two, as well as their tendency to report different types of statistics, make comparisons difficult and possibly misleading. The SIPRI *Yearbook of World Armaments and Disarmament* records sales when announced, whereas ACDA in its *World Military Expenditures and Arms Transfers* waits for evidence that the arms have actually been delivered. SIPRI only includes in its compilations major items of equipment such as warships, aircraft, missiles, and tanks, while ACDA includes all weapons transfers. Yet because ACDA, in the case of most countries, excludes the crucial items of training, construction, and technical services, which are often an important part of an arms transaction, its figures are often considerably lower than those of SIPRI. The Swedish institute has a tendency to place a high monetary value on weapons transferred, with an implicit assumption in its accompanying analysis that arms sales are bad in themselves. This is not the case with ACDA, whose statistics are based upon information provided by the U.S. intelligence community. On the other hand, these not only appear to be on the low side, but the data are two or three years old, thereby preventing analysis of recent trends. *(continued)*

Additional sources are the compilation of major arms agreements published annually in *The Military Balance* by the International Institute for Strategic Studies (London); *World Military and Social Expenditures*, compiled by Ruth Leger Sivard, a former ACDA official, for a group of eight private sponsoring organizations, including the Rockefeller Foundation and the Arms Control Association; and American data in the annual U.S. Department of Defense's *Foreign Military Sales and Military Assistance Facts*. The Pentagon figures, cited in the last publication, unlike those of ACDA, include the value of training, services, and some nonweapons equipment. There is an additional problem with the Pentagon figures: they are retroactively revised with each annual issue, so that there is considerable lack of consistency in the annual publications for sales during any given past year. Retroactive revision creates problems with the use of ACDA data also.

In accordance with growing usage, arms sales and arms transfers have been used interchangeably, even though the latter, strictly defined, include grants as well as sales. Since the early 1970s, direct grants have been reduced to a trickle, and most transactions are sales even when credits have been extended. This is another source of confusion in the sources listed above. Nevertheless, even with the disparities in the data and the paucity of high-quality information, enough is known to establish important trends and political relationships associated with arms. Major weapons deals, moreover, are usually highly visible; indeed, the sending of a "message" is often an important aspect of such a deal. For the broad purpose of examining the global politics of arms sales, therefore, the available information, when used with circumspection, is adequate.

2. ACDA, *World Military Expenditures and Arms Transfers 1969–1978*, p. 117.

3. U.S. Department of Defense, *Foreign Military Sales and Military Assistance Facts*, December 1979, p. 1. This is a retroactive figure; the 1975 total was $10.1 billion according to comparable 1976 data in ibid., December 1976, p. 13.

4. SIPRI *Yearbook, 1976*, pp. 18–19; ACDA, *World Military Expenditures and Arms Transfers 1968–1977*, p. 16.

5. ACDA, *World Military Expenditures and Arms Transfers 1969–1978*, p. 117.

6. SIPRI *Yearbook, 1980*, p. 65. ACDA figures are based upon shares of the total world arms sales market, rather than transfers to the developing world: United States (39.2 percent), Soviet Union (29.5 percent),

France (7.4 percent), United Kingdom (4.7 percent), and West Germany (4.5 percent) for 1977. ACDA, *World Military Expenditures and Arms Transfers 1968-1977*, p. 18.

7. ACDA, *World Military Expenditures and Arms Transfers 1969-1978*, p. 21. According to SIPRI, Third World suppliers account for 3 percent of arms exports to Third World countries. SIPRI *Yearbook, 1980*, p. 62.

8. SIPRI *Yearbook, 1979*, p. 173. ACDA, for the same year (1978), gives NATO 53 percent of arms exports globally (not just Third World) and the Soviet Union 34 percent. *World Military Expenditures and Arms Transfers 1969-1978*, p. 9.

9. U.S., Congress, Senate, Committee on Foreign Relations, *U.S. Military Sales to Iran*, A Staff Report to the Subcommittee on Foreign Assistance, 94th Cong., 2d sess., July 1976, p. xi.

10. Andrew J. Pierre, "Beyond the 'Plane Package': Arms and Politics in the Middle East," *International Security* (Summer 1978), pp. 148-161.

11. For an excellent further analysis of the military benefits and costs of arms transfers see Geoffrey Kemp with Steven E. Miller, "The Arms Transfer Phenomenon," in Andrew J. Pierre, ed., *Arms Transfers and American Foreign Policy* (New York: New York University Press, 1979), pp. 50-59.

12. ACDA, *World Military Expenditures and Arms Transfers 1969-1978*, pp. 132, 155.

13. Congressional Research Service, Library of Congress, *Implications of President Carter's Conventional Arms Transfer Policy*, September 22, 1977, p. 67.

14. Anne Hessing Cahn, Joseph J. Druzel, Peter M. Dawkins, and Jacques Huntzinger, *Controlling Future Arms Trade* (New York: McGraw Hill Book Co., 1977), p. 66. These figures are based upon compilations from several sources.

15. U.S., Department of Labor, Bureau of Labor Statistics, *Foreign Defense Sales and Grants, Fiscal Years 1973-1975: Labor and Material Requirements*, July 1977, p. 17.

16. U.S., Congress, Congressional Budget Office, *Budgetary Cost Savings to the Department of Defense Resulting from Foreign Military Sales*, Staff Working Paper, May 24, 1976, p. ix.

17. U.S., Congress, Senate, Committee on Foreign Relations, *Arms Transfer Policy*, 95th Cong., 1st sess., July 1977, Appendix 3, p. 94.

18. According to Minister of State for Defence William Rodgers, in

the Commons. Great Britain, *Parliamentary Debates* (Commons), July 8, 1975, col. 416.

19. Section 502B, Public Law 940329, 94th Congress. This act also established the coordinator for human rights, at the assistant secretary level, in the Department of State.

20. U.S., Department of Defense, *Foreign Military Sales and Military Assistance Facts*, December 1978, p. 1.

21. For a good discussion of the dilemmas in applying human rights criteria in foreign policy, see Sandra Vogelgesang, *American Dream/Global Nightmare: The Dilemma of U.S. Human Rights Policy* (New York: W. W. Norton, 1980).

22. U.S., Congress, House, Committee on International Relations, *NATO Standardization: Political, Economic and Military Issues for Congress*, Report by the Foreign Affairs and National Defense Division, Congressional Research Service, Library of Congress, 95th Cong., 1st sess., March 29, 1977, p. 13.

23. Thomas A. Callaghan, Jr., *U.S.-European Economic Cooperation in Military and Civil Technology* (Washington, D.C.: Center for Strategic and International Studies, Georgetown University, 1975).

24. For an exception, see the official record of the European Armaments Policy Symposium, Assembly of Western European Union, Committee on Defense Questions and Armaments, Paris, March 3–4, 1977.

25. Brandt Commission, *North-South: A Program for Survival* (Cambridge, Mass.: M.I.T. Press, 1980), pp. 120–122.

26. These points are discussed by Stephanie G. Neuman in "Arms Transfers and Economic Development: Some Research and Policy Issues," in Robert E. Harkavy and Stephanie G. Neuman, eds., *Arms Transfers in the Modern World* (New York: Praeger Special Studies, 1979), pp. 219–246. See also Emile Benoit, *Defense and Economic Growth in the Developing Countries* (Lexington, Mass.: D. C. Heath, 1974); and John J. Johnson, ed., *The Role of the Military in Underdeveloped Societies* (Princeton: Princeton University Press, 1962).

PART TWO: SUPPLIERS

1. U.S., Department of Defense, *Foreign Military Sales and Military Assistance Facts*, December 1979, pp. 1, 17.

2. ACDA, *World Military Expenditures and Arms Transfers 1968–1977*, pp. 151, 155.

3. This is discussed in some detail in Duncan L. Clarke, *The Politics of Arms Control: The Role and Effectiveness of the U.S. Arms Control and Disarmament Agency* (New York: Free Press, 1979), pp. 89–94.

4. U.S., Congress, Senate, Committee on Foreign Relations, *U.S. Military Sales to Iran*, A Staff Report to the Subcommittee on Foreign Assistance, 94th Cong., 2d sess., July 1978, p. vii. See also U.S., Congress, Senate, Committee on Foreign Relations, *U.S. Arms Sales Policy*, Hearings before the Committee on Foreign Relations and Subcommittee on Foreign Assistance, 94th Cong., 2d sess., September 16–24, 1976.

5. Andrew Hamilton, "Uncle Sam, Arms Dealer," *Washington Post*, August 11, 1974.

6. The practices used in selling arms are outside the purview of this book, but have had a significant part in shaping public attitudes toward the arms trade. See Anthony Sampson's *The Arms Bazaar: The Companies, the Dealers, the Bribes: From Vickers to Lockheed* (London: Hodder & Stoughton, 1977), which is mainly concerned with this question; also Tad Szulc, "Kickback—Corrupting U.S. Arms Sales," *New Republic*, April 17, 1976; and Joseph P. Albright, "How to Get a New Plane (and Its Maker) off the Ground," *New York Times Magazine*, February 8, 1976.

7. Letter released by the office of Senator John C. Culver, November 3, 1975.

8. "State Department Doubts Arms Limit Success," *Aviation Week and Space Technology*, October 4, 1976, p. 16.

9. For their subsequent publications see Andrew J. Pierre, ed., *Arms Transfers and American Foreign Policy* (New York: New York University Press, 1979); and UNA/USA, *Controlling the Conventional Arms Race* (New York: United Nations Association of the U.S.A., 1976).

10. Message from the President of the United States returning without approval S.2662, Senate document 94-185, 94th Cong., 2d sess., May 7, 1976.

11. U.S., Congress, Senate, Committee on Foreign Relations, *International Security Assistance and Arms Export Control Act of 1976*, Report on S.3439, 94th Cong., 2d sess., May 14, 1976, p. 10.

12. Philip J. Farley, "The Control of United States Arms Sales," in Alan Platt and L. D. Weiler, eds., *Congress and Arms Control* (Boulder: Frederick A. Praeger, 1978), pp. 111–133. See also Richard M.

317

Moose with Daniel L. Spiegel, "Congress and Arms Sales," in Pierre, *Arms Transfers and American Foreign Policy*, pp. 228–261.

13. *Conventional Arms Transfer Policy*, Statement by the President, May 19, 1977, Office of the White House Press Secretary. And as amended or paraphrased subsequently by the under secretary of state for security assistance, science and technology, the senior official responsible for the policy, see Lucy Wilson Benson, "Controlling Arms Transfers: An Instrument of U.S. Foreign Policy," *Department of State Bulletin*, no. 1988, August 1, 1977; Benson, "Turning the Supertanker: Arms Transfer Restraint," *International Security* (Spring 1979), pp. 3–17; and Matthew Nimetz, "Review of Arms Transfer Policy," *Current Policy*, no. 145, Department of State, March 6, 1980.

14. See Andrew J. Pierre, "Beyond the 'Plane Package': Arms and Politics in the Middle East," *International Security* (Summer 1978), pp. 148–161.

15. *Aviation Week and Space Technology*, October 29, 1979, p. 20.

16. See "U.S. Weapons Exports: Can We Cut the Arms Connection?," *Defense Monitor* (February 1979), published by the Center for Defense Information, Washington, D.C.; Nicole Ball and Milton Leitenberg, "The Foreign Arms Sales of the Carter Administration," *Bulletin of Atomic Scientists* (February 1979); Michael Klare, "How We Practice Arms Sales Restraint," *Nation*, September 24, 1977; and Max Holland, "The Myth of Arms Restraint," *International Policy Report*, May 1979.

17. See the views of Seymour Weiss, a former senior Department of State official, with experience in this area, *President Carter's Arms Transfer Policy: A Critical Assessment*, Special Report of the Advanced International Studies Institute, University of Miami, 1978; Herbert Y. Schandler of the American League for International Security Assistance, "Foreign Military Sales and U.S. Policy," paper presented at the Center for Strategic and International Studies, Georgetown University, September 19, 1978. An early and critical assessment is to be found in Congressional Research Service, Library of Congress, *Implications of President Carter's Conventional Arms Transfer Policy*, September 22, 1977. The most sophisticated and balanced analysis by a skeptic is Richard Betts, "The Tragicomedy of Arms Trade Control," *International Security* (Summer 1980), pp. 80–110.

18. Jo L. Husbands, "The Arms Connection: Jimmy Carter and the Politics of Military Exports," in Cindy Cannizzo, ed., *The Gun Merchants* (New York: Pergamon Press, 1980), pp. 18–49.

19. *Aviation Week and Space Technology,* March 24, 1980, p. 8. See also "Conventional Arms Sales in the Carter Administration: An Interview with Leslie Gelb," *Arms Control Today* (September 1980).

20. James L. Buckley, "Arms Transfers and the National Interest," *Current Policy,* no. 279, Department of State, May 21, 1981.

21. *Conventional Arms Transfer Policy,* The White House, July 9, 1981.

22. *Aviation Week and Space Technology,* June 29, 1981, p. 29.

23. "Arming America's Friends," *Newsweek,* March 23, 1981, p. 33.

24. "L' 'Assistance à la Sécurité' Joue un Role Central dans la Diplomatie Americaine," *Le Monde,* July 2, 1981, p. 5.

25. Michael R. Gordon, "Competition with the Soviet Union Drives Reagan's Arms Sales Policy," *National Journal,* May 16, 1981, p. 873.

26. General F. Michael Rogers, "The Impact of Foreign Military Sales on the National Industrial Base," *Strategic Review* 5 (Spring 1977), p. 18.

27. U.S., Congress, Senate, Committee on Foreign Relations, "Study of the Economic Effects of Restraints in Arms Transfers," *Arms Transfer Policy,* Annex 2, 95th Cong., 1st sess., July 1977.

28. U.S., Congress, Congressional Budget Office, *Foreign Military Sales and U.S. Weapons Cost,* Staff Working Paper, May 5, 1976.

29. Figures, based on U.S. Defense Security Assistance Agency, cited in "U.S. Arms Sales Abroad: A Policy of Restraint?," *American Enterprise Institute Defense Review* 2 (1978), p. 10. "Northrop's Strategy: Simplify," *New York Times,* February 4, 1980.

30. Surveys are cited in U.S., Congress, House, Committee on Foreign Affairs, *Foreign Assistance Legislation for Fiscal Years 1980–81* (Part 2), Hearings before the Subcommittee on International Security and Scientific Affairs, 96th Cong., 1st sess., February–March 1979, p. 127; NBC News Survey, no. 27a, March 1, 1978; Roper Reports, no. 78-4, March 1978 and Harris Organization Survey May 1, 1978, as cited in ACDA, *World Military Expenditures and Arms Transfers 1968–1977,* p. 16.

31. Foreign Policy Association, *Outreacher,* June 1977.

32. *Time,* June 1, 1981, p. 13. Report on poll taken by Yankelovich, Skelly and White, Inc., during May 12-14, 1981.

33. Seweryn Bialer, *Stalin's Successors: Leadership, Stability and Change in the Soviet Union* (New York: Cambridge University Press, 1980), p. 264.

34. Central Intelligence Agency, *Communist Aid to Less Devel-*

319

oped Countries of the Free World, 1977, ER78-10478U, November 1978; Central Intelligence Agency, *Communist Aid to the Less Developed Countries of the Free World, 1976,* ER77-10296U, August 1977; and Central Intelligence Agency, *Communist Aid Activities in Non-Communist Less Developed Countries 1978,* ER79-10412U, September 1979.

35. ACDA, *World Military Expenditures and Arms Transfers 1968-1977,* p. 11. In 1978 the Central Intelligence Agency released a study that purported to show that between 1974 and 1977 the Soviet Union's weapons deliveries were actually larger than those of the United States. However the CIA used a controversial costing system for Soviet deliveries based on comparable production costs in the United States; this raised the dollar value by about one-fourth. The study also excluded nonweapon military items, which are usually included in U.S. totals. Department of State and ACDA officials in congressional testimony insisted that in overall terms the United States remained the number-one supplier. Central Intelligence Agency, *Arms Flows to LDCs: U.S.-Soviet Comparisons, 1974-77,* ER78-10494U, November 1978. For the testimony see U.S., Congress, House, Committee on International Relations, *Review of President's Conventional Arms Transfer Policy,* Hearings before the Subcommittee on International Security and Scientific Affairs, 95th Cong., 2d sess., February 1-2, 1978, pp. 26-27.

36. Central Intelligence Agency, *Communist Aid Activities in Non-Communist Less Developed Countries 1978*; ACDA, *World Military Expenditures and Arms Transfers 1969-1978.*

37. Central Intelligence Agency, *Communist Aid Activities in Non-Communist Less Developed Countries 1978.*

38. Central Intelligence Agency, *Arms Flows to LDCs: U.S.-Soviet Comparisons, 1974-77,* p. ii.

39. Eberhard Einbeck, "Moscow's Military Aid to the Third World," *Aussenpolitik* 22 (1971), pp. 460-474.

40. Eugene Kozicharow, "Hard Currency Problems Spur Soviet Export Push," *Aviation Week and Space Technology,* April 11, 1977.

41. Roger F. Pajak, "Soviet Arms Transfer Policy: How Effective an Instrument?," paper prepared for the conference on the Soviet Union in the Third World: Success and Failure, Strategic Studies Institute, U.S. Army War College, September 1979.

42. It is noteworthy that the best and most detailed analysis of Soviet defense procurement makes no mention of arms sales to the Third

World as a factor in weapons acquisition decisions. See Arthur J. Alexander, *Decision-Making in Soviet Weapons Procurement*, Adelphi Papers nos. 147–148 (London: International Institute for Strategic Studies, 1979).

43. U.S., Congress, House, Committee on International Relations, *The Soviet Union and the Third World: A Watershed in Great Power Policy?* Report by the Senior Specialist Division, Congressional Research Service, Library of Congress, 95th Cong., 1st sess., May 8, 1977, p. 69.

44. A rare and valuable discussion of the theoretical underpinnings of attitudes toward arms transfers based upon Soviet literature is to be found in Franklyn J. C. Griffiths, "De la Justification des Transferts d'Armes par l'Union Soviétique," *Etudes Internationales* 8 (December 1977), pp. 600–617.

45. Data on French arms sales are notoriously difficult to obtain. *Le Monde* occasionally publishes some figures, and the author has been authoritatively told by a government official that they are reliable, as *Le Monde* is used as a conduit for statistics that the government wishes to release. The figures cited by ACDA, SIPRI, and French sources vary considerably. See the discussion of this problem in Edward A. Kolodziej, "Measuring French Arms Transfers: A Problem of Sources and Some Sources of Problems with ACDA Data," *Journal of Conflict Resolution* 23 (June 1979), pp. 195–225. This book uses French sources (press, parliamentary debates, and parliamentary commissions) as well as Kolodziej. See especially "Les Exportations d'Armes de la France ont Progressé en Dix Ans Deux Fois Plus Rapidement que l'Ensemble de son Commerce Exterieur," *Le Monde*, October 4, 1979.

46. Edward A. Kolodziej, "France and the Arms Trade," *International Affairs*, London (January 1980), pp. 62–63.

47. "Notre Objectif est de Maintenir une Industrie Nationale de l'Armement Independante," *Le Monde*, June 9, 1973. See also the article by Michel D'Aillières, deputy and rapporteur of the Commission of National Defense in the National Assembly, "Les Ventes d'Armes: Une Necessité Nationale Non Nationaliste," *Le Monde*, October 11, 1974; and Jacques Vernant, "Armements et Independance," *Revue de la Défense Nationale* (December 1975), pp. 123–128.

48. These points are ably discussed by Jean Klein in "Commerce des Armes et Politiques: Le Cas Français," *Politique Etrangère*, 6 (1976).

49. They are the Office Français d'Exportation de Matériels Aéronautiques and the Office Général de l'Air, both of which support the

aeronautic industry, the Société Française de Matériels d'Armements for army equipment, and the Société Française d'Exportation des Armements Navals which sells naval equipment.

50. For further details on the structure of the defense industry and related promotional activities, see Jean-François Dubos, *Ventes d'Armes: Une Politique* (Paris: Editions Gallimard, 1974), chapters 4 and 5; Eric Gerdan, *Dossier A . . . Comme Armes* (Paris: Editions Alain Moreau, 1975), pp. 43–61; for economic aspects of arms exports see Jean-Bernard Pinatel, *l'Economie de Forces*, 5, (Paris: Fondation pour les Etudes de Défense Nationale, 1976).

51. "Un Rapport de l'Inspection des Finances sur l'Industrie d'Armement: l'Etat ne Devrait pas Etre en Première Ligne," *Le Monde*, September 29, 1976; "Les Effets Pervers de l'Exportation des Armes," *Le Monde*, November 9, 1976; "Report Finds Waste, Payoffs in France's Arms Purchases," *International Herald Tribune*, October 8, 1976.

52. The process has been described by a former participant, who does not stop short of proposing some improvements, in Claude Lachaux, "La Réglementation des Exportations de Matériels de Guerre," *Revue de la Défense Nationale* (December 1977), pp. 35–41.

53. General d'Armée G. Mery, "Une Armée Pour Quoi Faire et Comment?," *Revue de la Défense Nationale* (June 1976), p. 30. Klein, "Commerce des Armes," pp. 578–580, usefully brings together a collection of statements on arms transfer policy.

54. Especially striking was the statement in defense of French arms sales published in *Le Monde* during the week between the two rounds of the 1978 election under the pseudonym of Frevent but written by a "group of high functionaries," entitled, "Les Marchands d'Illusions," March 16, 1978. For a reply see Roger Godement, "Le Triomphe des Thanatocrates," *Le Monde*, April 12, 1978.

55. See "Mouvement Pax Christi," in *Journal de la Paix*, April 1970; Conseil Permanent de l'Episcopat Français, *Note de Réflexion sur le Commerce des Armes* (Paris: Editions du Centurion, 1973); and *Des Eglises d'Occident Face aux Exportations d'Armes* (Paris: Editions l'Harmattan, 1979).

56. François Mitterrand, "Une Strategie pour le Désarmement: Deux Façons d'Avancer," *Le Monde*, December 15, 1977.

57. "L'Assemblée Nationale Accorde sa Confiance au Premier Ministre," *Le Monde*, July 11, 1981, p. 6.

58. "Un Entretien Avec M. Charles Hernu," *Le Monde*, July 11, 1981.

59. "Cheysson Defines French Arms Sales Policy," *International Herald Tribune*, July 16, 1981.

60. "La France a Reçu en 1975 pour 20 Milliards de Francs de Commandes Etrangères d'Armements," *Le Monde*, May 16–17, 1976; see also *Assemblée Nationale, annexe au procès-verbal* to the session of October 10, 1975, and *Assemblée Nationale*, no. 2525, October 5, 1976.

61. *Assemblée Nationale*, no. 1979, October 9, 1980.

62. In an interview in *Revue de la Défense Nationale* (June 1975), former Délégué Ministériel pour l'Armement Jean-Laurens Delpech spoke candidly about some of these dangers.

63. Great Britain, *Statement on the Defence Estimate 1980* (HMSO), p. 82.

64. Lawrence Freedman, "The Arms Trade: A Review," *International Affairs*, London (July 1979), p. 435. Secrecy and the lack of public accountability are highlighted in Martin Edmonds, "The Domestic and International Dimensions of British Arms Sales, 1966–1978," in Cannizzo ed., *The Gun Merchants*, pp. 68–100.

65. Great Britain, *Export of Surplus War Material* cnd. 9676 (HMSO, 1955).

66. For an account of the British nuclear program see Andrew J. Pierre, *Nuclear Politics: The British Experience with an Independent Strategic Force 1939-1970* (London: Oxford University Press, 1972).

67. Great Britain, *Statement on the Defence Estimate 1979*, (HMSO), p. 42.

68. Lawrence Freedman, *Arms Production in the United Kingdom: Problems and Prospects* (London: Royal Institute of International Affairs, 1978), pp. 1–2.

69. Great Britain, *Parliamentary Debates* (Commons), May 11, 1966, col. 404.

70. Great Britain, Central Policy Review Staff, *Review of Overseas Representatives* (HMSO, August 1977), p. 137.

71. *Fourth Report from the Committee of Public Accounts*, Session of 1976–77, as cited in Freedman, *Arms Production*, pp. 29–30.

72. Trevor Taylor, "Research Note: British Arms Exports and R & D Costs," *Survival* 22 (November–December 1980).

73. Great Britain, Defence and External Affairs Sub-committee, *Second Report from the Expenditure Committee*, Commons (1975–1976), p. 190.

74. Great Britain, *Parliamentary Debates* (Commons), July 8, 1975, cols. 406–411.

75. Labour Party Defence Study Group, *Sense about Defence* (London: Quartet Books, 1977), pp. 40, 103.

76. SIPRI, *Yearbook of World Armaments and Disarmament, 1979*, pp. 173, 181. According to a German official, in 1977 as much as 86 percent of arms exports went to NATO countries. *Zwischenbericht der Arbeitsgruppe Waffenexporte* (Bonn: Federal Republic of Germany, 1978).

77. Federal Republic of Germany, *White Book on Defense, 1971–72*, p. 149.

78. For more extensive discussion of West German arms production and overseas transfers, see Walter Schütze, "La République Fédérale d'Allemagne et le Marché International des Armements," *Revue des Questions Allemandes*, Paris (1976); Hans Rattinger, "West Germany's Arms Transfers to the Non-Industrial World," in Uri Ra'anan, Robert Pfaltzgraff, and Geoffrey Kemp, eds., *Arms Transfers to the Third World: The Military Build Up in the Less Industrial Countries* (Boulder: Westview Press, 1978) pp. 229–256; Mike Dillon, "Arms Transfers and the Federal Republic of Germany," in Cannizzo, *The Gun Merchants*, pp. 101–126; and Helga Haftendorn, *Militärhilfe und Rüstungsexporte der BRD* (Dusseldorf: Bertelsmann, 1971).

79. Gerald L. Curtis, "Japanese Security Policies and the United States," *Foreign Affairs* (Spring 1981), p. 852; see also Isaac Shapiro, "The Risen Sun: Japanese Gaullism?," *Foreign Policy* 41 (Winter 1980–1981).

80. Henry Scott-Stokes, "It's All Right to Talk Defense Again in Japan," *New York Times Magazine*, February 11, 1979; Scott-Stokes, "Japanese Say Groundwork Is Laid for Military Buildup," *New York Times*, January 14, 1981.

81. "A New Sun Rising," *Economist*, July 29, 1978.

82. Nils Andren, "Sweden's Security Policy," in Johan Holst, ed., *Five Roads to Nordic Security* (Oslo: Universitetsforlaget, 1973), pp. 127–152; SIPRI, *The Arms Trade with the Third World* (Stockholm: Almquist and Wiksell, 1971), pp. 328–346; Bjorn Hagelin, "Armament and Armament Cooperation—The Case of Sweden" (unpublished paper); SIPRI, *Yearbook, 1980*, pp. 82–84.

83. "Rüstungprogramm und Kriegsmaterialausfuhr," *Neue Zürcher Zeitung*, September 20,1979; and "Für weniger restriktive Praxis bei der Kriegsmaterialausfuhr," *Neue Zürcher Zeitung*, September 22, 1979.

84. International Institute for Strategic Studies, *The Military Balance 1979–1980*, pp. 101–103.

85. ACDA, *World Military Expenditures and Arms Transfers 1968-1977*, p. 18.

86. Michael Moodie, *Sovereignty, Security and Arms*, The Washington Papers, no. 67, Center for Strategic and International Studies (Beverly Hills, Cal.: Sage Publications, 1969); Peter Lock and Herbert Wulf, *Register of Arms Production in Developing Countries*, Study Group on Armaments and Underdevelopment, Hamburg, Germany, 1977. An excellent analysis is to be found in Steven E. Miller, *Arms and the Third World: Indigenous Weapons Production*, Graduate Institute of International Studies, Occasional Paper no. 3, (Geneva, 1980); and Donald J. Goldstein, *Third World Arms Industries: Their Own Swords and Slings*, CIA unpublished paper presented at International Studies Association Conference (Pittsburgh, 1979).

PART THREE: RECIPIENTS

1. SIPRI, *Yearbook of World Armaments and Disarmament, 1979*, pp. 2, 170–171.

2. ACDA, *World Military Expenditures and Arms Transfers 1969–1978*, p. 117.

3. *World Military and Social Expenditures, 1979*, comp. Ruth Sivard, (Leesburg, Va.: W.M.S.E. Publications), p. 8.

4. ACDA, *World Military Expenditures and Arms Transfers 1969–1978*, p. 117.

5. Mary Kaldor, "International Military Order," *New Statesman*, May 25, 1979; André Gunder Frantz, "Arms Economy and Warfare in the Third World," *Third World Quarterly* 2 (April 7, 1980), pp. 228–250.

6. ACDA, *World Military Expenditures and Arms Transfers 1969–1978*, pp. 33, 75.

7. Ibid., pp. 117–119.

8. See Edward R. Sheehan, *The Arabs, Israelis, and Kissinger: A Secret History of American Diplomacy* (New York: Reader's Digest Press, 1976).

9. "Requests by Israel for Arms Approved," *New York Times*, March 21, 1979; "On Eve of Treaty, Guns Pour into the Mideast," *New York Times*, March 25, 1979. Actually the ice was broken on the new, more even-handed American policy of arms transfers with the previous year's "plane package" of aircraft to Saudi Arabia and Egypt as well as Israel. See Andrew J. Pierre, "Beyond the 'Plane Package'; Arms and

Politics in the Middle East," *International Security* (Summer 1978), pp. 148–161.

10. Gur Ofer, "The Economic Burden of Soviet Involvement in the Middle East," *Soviet Studies* (January 1973), pp. 335–337. Some estimates are higher. According to a congressional study cited in "Industry Observer," *Aviation Week and Space Technology*, November 8, 1976, p. 11, 9 percent of Soviet conventional weapons production over the previous twenty years went to the Middle East, an amount equal to 2 percent of the total defense budget.

11. See the comments of Mohamed Heikal in *The Road to Ramadan* (New York: Quadrangle/New York Times Book Co., 1975), pp. 179–180.

12. For more details on the Soviet-Egyptian relationship, there are several good studies: Alvin Z. Rubinstein, *Red Star on the Nile: Soviet-Egyptian Influence Relationship since the June War* (Princeton: Princeton University Press, 1977); Galia Golan, *Yom Kippur and After: The Soviet Union and The Middle East Crisis* (Cambridge: Cambridge University Press, 1977); and Jon D. Glassman, *Arms for the Arabs: The Soviet Union and the War in the Middle East* (Baltimore: The Johns Hopkins University Press, 1975). See also, Roger F. Pajak, "Soviet Arms and Egypt," *Survival* (July–August 1975), pp. 165–173.

13. Peter Mangold, *Superpower Intervention in the Middle East* (New York: St. Martin's Press, 1978), p. 115.

14. See Golan, *Yom Kippur and After*, p. 12.

15. See, for example, Senator Edward M. Kennedy, "The Persian Gulf: Arms Race or Arms Control?" *Foreign Affairs* (October 1975); U.S., Congress, House, Committee on International Relations, *United States Arms Sales to the Persian Gulf*, Report of a Study Mission to Iran, Kuwait, and Saudi Arabia, 94th Cong., 1st sess., December 19, 1975; Dale R. Tahtinen, *Arms in the Persian Gulf* (Washington, D.C.: American Enterprise Institute, 1974).

16. Henry Kissinger, *White House Years* (Boston: Little, Brown and Co., 1979), p. 1264.

17. U.S., Congress, Senate, Committee on Foreign Relations, *U.S. Military Sales to Iran*, A Staff Report to the Subcommittee on Foreign Assistance, 94th Cong., 2d sess., July 1976, pp. xii–xiii.

18. For a sophisticated discussion of Iranian perceptions of their security environment at the time, see the writings of Shahram Chubin, especially "Iran's Security in the 1980s," The California Seminar on

Arms Control and Foreign Policy, Discussion Paper 73, September 1977; and Chubin, "The International Politics of the Persian Gulf," *British Journal of International Studies* (October 1976), pp. 216–230. See also Abbas Amirie, ed., *The Persian Gulf and Indian Ocean in International Politics*, (Teheran: Institute for International Political and Economic Studies, 1975).

19. "Shah Links Iran Defense Effort to Uncertainty on Commitment by U.S.," *International Herald Tribune*, July 11, 1977.

20. U.S., Department of Defense, *Foreign Military Sales and Military Assistance Facts*, December 1978.

21. "Iran's Vast Purchases of Weaponry Strain Ability of Country to Absorb It All," *New York Times*, January 5, 1977.

22. Senate Committee on Foreign Relations, *U.S. Arms Sales to Iran*, p. ix.

23. See Theodore H. Moran, "Iranian Defense Expenditures and the Social Crisis," *International Security* (Winter 1978–1979), pp. 178–192. For a more benign view, which stresses the beneficial spinoffs of Iran's defense spending upon its economic development, see Stephanie G. Neuman, "Security, Military Expenditures and Socioeconomic Development: Reflections on Iran," *Orbis* (Fall 1978), pp. 569–594.

24. Paul Rivlin, "The Burden of Israel's Defense," *Survival* 20 (July–August 1978), p. 148. The figures in the text have been adjusted to cover the entire decade.

25. See Anthony H. Cordesman, "The Arab-Israeli Balance: How Much Is Too Much?," *Armed Forces Journal International* (October 1977).

26. "U.S. Confident on Israeli Arms," *New York Times*, November 18, 1979.

27. See Ann Crittenden, "Israel's Economic Plight," *Foreign Affairs* (Summer 1979), pp. 1005–1016.

28. See Sheehan, *The Arabs, Israelis, and Kissinger*, pp. 245–257.

29. "Excerpts from Mondale Talk on Mideast," *New York Times*, June 18, 1977. For an interesting discussion of the leverage issue, which concludes that inducement is more productive than coercion as a means of leverage, see Thomas R. Wheelock, "Arms for Israel: The Limits of Leverage," *International Security* (Fall 1978), pp. 123–137.

30. See William B. Quandt, *Decade of Decisions* (Berkeley: University of California Press, 1977).

31. See Sheehan, *The Arabs, Israelis, and Kissinger*, p. 199.

32. *Ha'aretz*, February 2, 1978.

NOTES TO PAGES 163-188

33. *Aviation Week and Space Technology*, March 10, 1980, p. 12; "Israelis Plan to Build Own Fighter," *New York Times*, March 1, 1980.

34. "China Is Reported Delivering MiG-19 Jets to Egypt," *New York Times*, June 23, 1979.

35. "Sadat Asks House for U.S. Arms," *International Herald Tribune*, February 8, 1978; "U.S. Officials Weighing Sales of Fighter Planes to Egypt," *International Herald Tribune*, January 24, 1978.

36. "Egypt Marks 1973 War and Parades New U.S. Arms," *New York Times*, October 7, 1979.

37. "Arab Weapons Consortium Believed Nearing Production," *Washington Post*, September 9, 1978.

38. See Stephen S. Kaplan, "United States Aid and Regime Maintenance in Jordan, 1957–1973," *Public Policy* 23 (Spring 1975), pp. 189–217.

39. U.S., Department of Defense, *Foreign Military Sales and Military Assistance Facts*, December 1980, p. 2.

40. See *Perspectives on Military Sales to Saudi Arabia*, Report to the Congress by Comptroller General of the United States, October 26, 1977; and U.S., Congress, House, Committee on International Relations, *United States Arms Sales Policy and Recent Sales to Europe and the Middle East*, Hearings before the Subcommittee on Europe and the Middle East, 95th Cong., 2d sess., October 5, 1978.

41. See U.S., Congress, Senate, Committee on Foreign Relations, *U.S. Arms Sales Policy*, Hearings before the Committee on Foreign Relations and Subcommittee on Foreign Assistance, 94th Cong., 2d sess., September 21, 1976.

42. See Pierre, "Beyond the 'Plane Package.'"

43. U.S., Congress, Senate, Committee on Foreign Relations, *Middle East Arms Sales Proposals*, Hearings, 95th Cong., 2d sess., May 3–8, 1978, p. 239.

44. "Yamani Warns Oil Policy Is Linked to Sale of F-15s," *Washington Post*, May 3, 1978.

45. "U.S. to Sell Saudis $1.2 Billion in Arms," *New York Times*, July 14, 1979; "Oil Guns Get a Bigger Bang for the Barrel," *New York Times*, July 15, 1979.

46. *Aviation Week and Space Technology*, May 26, 1980, p. 79; "Yemen Seeks U.S. Aid on Border Force," *New York Times*, June 12, 1979; "Saudis Said to Delay Weapons for Yemen," *New York Times*, December 19, 1979; "In Yemen, the East and West Do Meet," *New York Times*, May 7, 1980; *New Yorker*, June 16, 1980, pp. 69–72.

47. See Peter Mangold, "The Soviet-Syrian Military Relationship 1955–77," *Journal of the Royal United Services Institute* (September 1977), pp. 27–33.

48. See Roger F. Pajak, "Soviet Military Aid to Iraq and Syria," *Strategic Review* (Winter 1976), pp. 51–59.

49. See Central Intelligence Agency, *Communist Aid to the Less Developed Countries of the Free World, 1976,* ER 77-10296U, August 1977.

50. For a good discussion of Iraq's evolving outlook, see Claudia Wright, "Iraq—New Power in the Middle East," *Foreign Affairs* (Winter 1979–1980).

51. "Libya's Identity Blurred by Ties with East, West and Terrorism," *New York Times,* October 14, 1979.

52. International Institute for Strategic Studies, *The Military Balance 1979–1980,* p. 42.

53. Central Intelligence Agency, *Communist Aid Activities in Non-Communist Less Developed Countries 1978,* ER79-10412U, September 1979.

54. "Giscard to Propose to Carter Arms Sales Curb in the Mideast," *International Herald Tribune,* January 3, 1978.

55. Yair Evron, an Israeli scholar, has done some excellent writing on this. See his *The Role of Arms Control in the Middle East,* Adelphi Paper no. 138 (London: International Institute for Strategic Studies, 1977); and *Arms Control in the Middle East: Some Proposals and Their Confidence Building Roles* in *The Future of Arms Control:* Part III, *Confidence Building Measures,* Adelphi Paper no. 149 (London: International Institute for Strategic Studies, 1979).

56. An ambitious proposal for a permanent standing arms control committee is elaborated upon in David Astor and Valerie Yorke's *Peace in the Middle East* (London: Corgi Press, 1978), chapter 6.

57. A history and analysis of this experience are to be found in Fuad Jabber, "The Politics of Arms Transfer and Control: The United States and Egypt's Quest for Arms, 1950–1955," Southern California Arms Control and Foreign Policy Seminar, July 1972. A broader, and excellent, discussion of arms control in the Middle East, which was published too late to be taken into account in this book, can be found in the same author's *Not By War Alone: Security and Arms Control in the Middle East* (Berkeley: University of California Press, 1981).

58. Amnon Sella, "Changes in Soviet Political-Military Policy in the Middle East after 1973," Research Paper no. 25, The Soviet and East

European Research Center, Hebrew University of Jerusalem, July 1977. See also Golan, *Yom Kippur and After;* and Mangold, *Superpower Intervention.*

59. Mangold, "The Soviet-Syrian Military Relationship, 1955–77," p. 31.

60. Karen Dawisha, "The Soviet Union and the Middle East: Strategy at the Crossroads?," *World Today* (March 1979).

61. Wright, "Iraq," p. 262.

62. Galia Golan concludes that "Soviet objectives could be served by a settlement of the Arab-Israeli conflict, as long as the Soviet Union herself were a party to the settlement," in "Soviet Power and Policies in the Third World: The Middle East," *Prospects of Soviet Power in the 1980s*, Adelphi Paper no. 152 (London: International Institute for Strategic Studies, 1979), p. 51.

63. See Rivlin, "The Burden of Israel's Defense"; and Crittenden, "Israel's Economic Plight."

64. ACDA, *World Military Expenditures and Arms Transfers 1969–1978*, pp. 117–158.

65. "Pentagon Rebuffed on Korea F-16 Deal," *International Herald Tribune*, November 24, 1978.

66. "Peking Concession on Arms to Taipei Led to U.S. Accord," *New York Times*, December 17, 1978; "U.S. Concedes It Promised Peking Not to Sell Taiwan Arms This Year," *New York Times*, January 13, 1979; Stanley Karnow, "East Asia in 1978: The Great Transformation," *America and the World—1978*, special issue of *Foreign Affairs*, pp. 589–612.

67. See Robert E. Harkavy, "The Pariah State Syndrome," *Orbis* (Fall 1977).

68. Ron Huisken, *Limitation of Armaments in South East Asia: A Proposal*, Canberra Papers on Strategy and Defense no. 16, The Australian National University, 1977.

69. See P. R. Chari, "Indo-Soviet Military Cooperation: A Review," reprinted from *Asian Survey*, March 1979, in *Strategic Digest* (New Delhi: Institute for Defense Studies and Analyses, May 1979), pp. 294–306.

70. See Michael P. Pillsbury, "U.S.-Chinese Military Ties?," *Foreign Policy* 20 (Fall 1975); Pillsbury, "Future Sino-American Security Ties: The View from Tokyo, Moscow and Peking," *International Security* (Spring 1977); A. Doak Barnett, "Military-Security Relations between China and the United States," *Foreign Affairs* (April 1977); Lawrence

Freedman, *The West and the Modernization of China*, Chatham House Papers no. 1 (London: The Royal Institute of International Affairs, 1979); "Chinese Defense Industries" in *Strategic Survey, 1979* (London: International Institute for Strategic Studies, 1980); Leslie H. Gelb, "U.S. Defense Policy, Technology Transfers and Asian Security," in Richard H. Solomon, ed., *Asian Security in the 1980s: Problems and Policies for a Time of Transition*, Report prepared for the Assistant Secretary of Defense, International Security Affairs, RAND R-2492-ISA, November 1979.

71. Freedman, *The West and the Modernization of China*, p. 35.

72. ACDA, *World Military Expenditures and Arms Transfers 1969-1978*, pp. 117-119.

73. International Institute for Strategic Studies, *The Military Balance 1979-1980*. For a rare, perhaps unique, examination from Latin America of military expenditures in South America, and their economic and developmental impact, see Centro de Investigaciones Economicas y Sociales de la Universidad de Lima, *Gastos Militares y Desarrollo en America del Sur* (Lima: Universidad de Lima, 1980).

74. ACDA, *World Military Expenditures and Arms Transfers 1969-1978*, p. 162.

75. SIPRI, *Yearbook, 1980*, p. 115.

76. Philip J. Farley, Stephen S. Kaplan, and William H. Lewis, *Arms Across the Sea* (Washington, D.C.: The Brookings Institution, 1978), p. 80; Luigi Einaudi, Hans Heymann, Jr., David Ronfeldt, and Cesar Sereseres, *Arms Transfers to Latin America: Towards a Policy of Mutual Respect*, R-1173, Rand Corporation, 1973.

77. The participation of the military in Latin American politics is the subject of a vast literature. For an informed review essay see Abraham F. Lowenthal, "Armies and Politics in Latin America," *World Politics* 27 (October 1974). The impact of military governments is also well discussed in Gregory Treverton's *Latin America in World Politics: The Next Decade*, Adelphi Paper no. 137 (London: International Institute for Strategic Studies, 1977).

78. See the classic work by General Goldbery do Coute e Silva, *A Geopolitica do Brasil* (Rio de Janeiro: Livraria Jose Olympio, 1967); and General Carlos de Meira Mattos, *Brasil: Geopolitica e Destino* (Rio de Janeiro: Jose Olympio, 1975).

79. See "Armourer to the Third World," *Financial Times*, April 19, 1977; "Brazil Enters the Arms Deal Business," *Sunday Times*, July 16, 1978; and David Ronfeldt and Caesar Sereseres, "U.S. Arms Transfers,

Diplomacy and Security in Latin America," in Andrew J. Pierre, ed., *Arms Transfers and American Foreign Policy* (New York: New York University Press, 1979), pp. 121–192.

80. "The Carter Administration and Latin America: Business as Usual?," *America and the World—1978, Foreign Affairs*, p. 658.

81. U.S., Congress, House, Committee on International Relations, *Arms Trade in the Western Hemisphere*, Hearings before the Subcommittee on Inter-American Affairs, 95th Cong., 2d sess., June-August 1978, pp. 3–4.

82. See John Samuel Fitch, "The Political Impact of U.S. Military Aid to Latin America," *Armed Forces and Society* 5 (Spring 1979), pp. 360–386; Stephen Kaplan, "U.S. Arms Transfers to Latin America 1945–1974: Rationale, Strategy, Bureaucratic Politics, and Executive Parameters," *International Studies Quarterly* (December 1976), pp. 399–431.

83. "Soviet-Argentine Grain Deal: How Did It Happen?," *New York Times*, July 17, 1980.

84. Argentina, Bolivia, Chile, Colombia, Ecuador, Panama, Peru, and Venezuela. At Ayacucho in 1824 the forces of Simon Bolivar defeated the Spanish colonial rulers, ending the Spanish presence in South America.

85. ACDA, *World Military Expenditures and Arms Transfers 1969–1978*, p. 117.

86. This typology is drawn from Jennifer Seymour Whitaker, *Africa and the United States: Vital Interests* (New York: New York University Press), p. 225.

87. This conclusion is based on a compilation of data which remains inadequate because of a tendency to group North Africa, including Egypt, with sub-Saharan Africa. See ACDA, *World Military Expenditures and Arms Transfers 1969–1978*; SIPRI, *World Armaments and Disarmament Yearbook, 1980;* Central Intelligence Agency, *Communist Aid to Less Developed Countries of the Free World, 1977*, ER79-10478U, November 1978; U.S., Congress, Senate, Committee on Foreign Relations, *Prospects for Multilateral Arms Export Restraint, 1979*, 96th Cong., 1st sess., April 1979; U.S., General Accounting Office, *Military Sales—An Increasing U.S. Role in Africa*, April 4, 1978.

88. U.S., Department of State, *Communism in Africa*, Statement of Under Secretary of State for Political Affairs David D. Newsom, Sub-

committee on Africa of House Committee on Foreign Affairs, October 18, 1979, Current Policy Series, no. 99.

89. Central Intelligence Agency, *Communist Aid Activities in Non-Communist Less Developed Countries 1978*, ER79-10412U, September 1979, p. 21.

90. Dimitri K. Simes, "Soviet Involvement in the Horn of Africa," *Washington Review of Strategic and International Studies* (May 1978).

91. Pierre Lellouche and Dominique Moisi, "French Policy in Africa: A Lonely Battle against Destabilization," *International Security* (Spring 1979), pp. 108–133.

92. Robert S. Jaster, *South Africa's Narrowing Security Options*, Adelphi Paper no. 159 (London: International Institute for Strategic Studies, 1980).

PART FOUR: RESTRAINTS

1. See, for example, "The Arms Boom Is Over," *Economist*, August 13, 1977; also U.S., Senate, Committee on Foreign Relations, *Report to the Congress on Arms Transfer Policy*, 95th Cong., 1st sess., July 1977, p. 11.

2. For accounts of early attempts at international regulation see Robert E. Harkavy, *The Arms Trade and International Systems* (Cambridge, Mass.: Ballinger, 1975), pp. 211–225; and SIPRI, *The Arms Trade with the Third World*, (Stockholm: Almquist and Wiksell, 1971), pp. 86–100.

3. United Nations, General Assembly, 31st Session, First Committee (A/C.1/31/L.20), November 22, 1976. How this question has been dealt with at the United Nations is discussed in Andrew J. Pierre, "International Restraints on Conventional Arms Transfers," in Jane M. O. Sharp, ed., *Opportunities for Disarmament: A Preview of the 1978 United Nations Special Session on Disarmament* (New York and Washington: Carnegie Endowment for International Peace, 1978), pp. 47–60.

4. See Lincoln P. Bloomfield and Harlan Cleveland, *Disarmament and the U.N., Strategy for the United States* (Aspen Institute for Humanistic Affairs, 1978), p. 30; and Lewis B. Sohn, *Approaches to Arms Control and Disarmament*, Twenty-Fourth Report of the Commission to Study the Organization of Peace, November 1976, p. 17.

5. Statement to the Conference of the Committee on Disarmament by U.K. Minister Lord Goronwy-Roberts, July 1, 1976 (mimeographed). See also the speeches of U.S. representatives Joseph Martin, Jr., on April 10, 1975, and Director of ACDA Fred C. Iklé on July 29, 1976.

6. U.S., Department of State, "Prospects for Multilateral Conventional Arms Transfer Restraints" (unpublished paper) 1976.

7. "Eight Latin American Governments Sign Declaration Aimed at Limiting Armaments," *U.N. Monthly Chronicle* (March 1975), pp. 54–57.

8. "Feud in Administration Said to Endanger Talks on Arms Sales Pact," *New York Times*, December 20, 1978; "Policy Shift Puts Arms Sales Talks in Doubt," *Washington Post*, December 19, 1978; "Conventional Arms Sales in the Carter Administration: An Interview with Leslie Gelb," *Arms Control Today* (September 1980); and interviews.

9. This section is drawn from my "Multilateral Restraints on Arms Transfers," in Andrew J. Pierre, ed., *Arms Transfers and American Foreign Policy* (New York: New York University Press, 1979), pp. 308–314.

10. Michael Gordon, "Competition with the Soviet Union Drives Reagan's Arms Sales Policy," *National Journal*, May 16, 1981.

11. New forms of consultations for dealing with political and security problems in the Third World are discussed in *Western Security: What Has Changed? What Should Be Done?*, a report prepared by the directors (with the assistance of an advisory group) of the Council on Foreign Relations (New York), the Royal Institute of International Affairs (London), the Institut Français des Relations Internationales (Paris), and the Forschungsinstitut der Deutschen Gesellschaft für Auswärtige Politik (Bonn), 1981.

12. Lawrence G. Franko, "Restraining Arms Exports to the Third World: Will Europe Agree?," *Survival* (January-February 1979).

13. For an excellent discussion of how rules of the game might reduce the risks and moderate the effects of Soviet-American rivalry in areas of instability, see Robert Legvold, "The Super Rivals: Conflict in the Third World," *Foreign Affairs* (Spring 1979), pp. 755–778. See also Alexander L. George, *Towards a Soviet-American Crisis Prevention Regime: History and Prospects*, Center for International and Strategic Affairs, University of California, Los Angeles, 1980. For a skeptical view see Robert W. Tucker, "The Purposes of American Power," *Foreign Affairs* (Winter 1980–1981), pp. 259–260.

14. U.S., Congress, Senate, Committee on Foreign Relations, *Prospects for Multilateral Arms Export Restraint*, Staff Report, 96th Cong., 1st sess., April 1979, p. 41.

15. International Institute for Strategic Studies, *The Military Balance 1979–1980*, pp. 101–103.

16. U.S., Congress, House, Committee on International Relations, *Issues concerning the Transfer of United States Defense Technology: Co-Production, Manufacturing Licenses, and Technical Assistance Agreements*, 95th Cong., 1st sess., June 30, 1977.

17. ACDA, *World Military Expenditures and Arms Transfers 1969–1978*, p. 21.

18. See M. A. Husain, "Third World and Disarmament: Shadow and Substance," *Third World Quarterly* (January 1980), pp. 76–99.

19. Permanent Mission of Singapore to the United Nations, Statement of the Minister for Foreign Affairs before the United Nations, General Assembly, 31st session, September 29, 1976.

20. "Arms and Dependence," in Sharp, ed., *Opportunities for Disarmament*, pp. 2–3.

21. See Albrech Ulrich, Ernst Dieter, Peter Lock, and Herbert Wulf, *Rüstung and Unterentwicklung* (Hamburg: Reinbek, 1976).

22. United Nations, General Assembly, *Final Document of the Tenth Special Session (S-10/2)*, June 30, 1978.

23. "Désarmement," *Le Monde*, May 27, 1978.

24. "Arms Sales: Blind Spot of a Generation," *Observer*, June 18, 1978.

INDEX

A-4 aircraft, 55
A-7 aircraft, 55, 222
A-10 aircraft, 28, 56
Abdullah, Prince, 179
Abu Dhabi, 238
ACDA, *see* Arms Control and
  Disarmament Agency
Aérospatiale, *see* Société Nationale
  des Industries Aérospatiale
Afghanistan (Kabul), 20, 147, 210,
  230; Soviet role in, 14–15, 21, 67,
  79, 82, 118, 175–76, 195, 207,
  223–25, 228, 230, 250, 261, 289,
  297, 303
Africa (sub-Saharan), 13, 20, 36, 91,
  167, 187, 210, 255, 267–68, 277,
  298; Soviet/Cuban role in, 19, 75–
  79, 82, 187, 244–45, 256–61, 263–
  64, 268–70, 277, 288; transfers to,
  9 (fig 2), 13, 23, 75–76, 110, 122,
  134–35, 161, 255–62, 277, 288;
  weapons restraint in, 268–71, 288–
  89, 303, 306, 309–10. *See also*
  Horn of Africa; individual countries
Airborne Warning and Control
  System, *see* AWACS
aircraft carriers, 294
aircraft production, 55, 59, 60, 71, 91,
  103, 121, 125, 171, 216, 238, 266,
  304; in Asian countries, 10, 55, 59,
  117, 124–25, 165–66, 213, 216–18,
  222, 224–27, 243; in European
  countries, 25, 60, 77, 87–88, 94,
  97–98, 121; in Israel, 156, 161–63;

in Latin American countries, 125,
  238, 243. *See also* individual
  countries; individual models
aircraft transfers, 10, 12 (tbl 2), 121,
  165–66, 187, 222, 245
  to African countries, 91, 257,
  260, 262, 266
  to Asian countries, 28, 55–56,
  60, 67, 213, 216, 219–23, 227–
  28
  to Israel, 10, 16, 22, 55–56, 66,
  80, 124, 137, 156, 162–63, 168–69,
  184–85, 305
  to Latin American countries, 67,
  234, 239–41, 244–45, 248, 285
  to Middle East countries, 10, 12
  (tbl 2), 56, 75, 84, 95, 141, 173–74,
  188, 190–91, 193–94, 197; Egypt,
  16, 21–22, 56, 165–66, 168–70,
  184, 207; Iran, 48, 56, 148, 153,
  181; Saudi Arabia, 10, 20, 22, 55–
  56, 66, 143, 153, 158, 168–69, 176,
  181–85, 207
  by Soviet Union, 10, 12 (tbl 2),
  75, 141, 188, 190–91, 193, 197,
  213, 221, 223–24, 240, 244, 257,
  262, 285
  by United States, 10, 12 (tbl 2),
  16, 21, 28, 30, 48, 55–56, 60, 65–
  67, 80, 137, 143, 145, 148, 165,
  173, 181–85, 188, 213, 219–21,
  223, 228, 240–41, 248, 260
  by West European countries, 10,
  22, 84, 87, 91, 95, 97, 98, 110, 113,

337

aircraft transfers (*cont.*)
166, 194, 197, 222, 227, 234, 240–41, 245, 266, 285.
See also individual countries; individual models
Algeria, 75, 79, 133 (tbl 3)
Ali, Kamal Hassan, 168
Allen, Lew, 169
Allende, Salvador, 31, 240, 242
Alouette helicopter, 222, 240, 267
Alpha Jet aircraft, 94, 113, 125, 165–66, 171
Alvarado, Juan Velasco, 240, 284
American Motors Corporation, 171
Amin, Idi, 20, 23, 106, 199
AML armored vehicle, 266
AMX-30 tank, 79, 84, 98, 240, 243
AN-12 aircraft, 77
Andean Pact, 135, 310. *See also* Declaration of Ayachucho
Angola, 24, 65–66, 75–77, 187, 199, 257, 260–61, 264, 269; Soviet/Cuban role in, 19, 76–77, 187, 244, 257–59, 261, 264, 269–70, 277
Antarctica, 235
anti-aircraft weapons, 12, 15, 56, 75, 91, 104, 113–14, 117, 141, 148–49, 156, 165, 168, 173, 197, 207, 211, 221–22, 226–27, 266; air-to-air, 65–66, 137, 154, 161, 168, 180, 184, 217, 226
anti-submarine weapons, 117, 228, 243
anti-tank weapons, 10, 21–22, 28, 56, 66, 98, 113, 117, 125, 156, 165–66, 171, 180, 192, 196, 211, 223, 226, 227, 294
AOI, *see* Arab Organization for Industrialization
Arab countries, 15, 28, 110, 137, 162, 177–78, 188, 238
and Israel, 15, 20, 22, 28, 136–37, 156–60, 176, 199, 209, 216, 305. *See also* 1947–49 war; Six

Day War; Yom Kippur War
weapons production plans of, 125, 170–72, 179–80.
See also individual countries
Arab League, 188
Arab Military Industrial Organization, 125, 170. *See also* Arab Organization for Industrialization
Arab Organization for Industrialization (AOI), 170–72, 179–80. *See also* Arab Military Industrial Organization
Arabian-American Oil Company, 180
Argentina (Buenos Aires), 66–67, 235, 332n; and human rights issues, 33, 55, 65, 241–42, 249–54; transfers to, 55, 95, 133 (tbl 3), 161, 233, 243–44; weapons production by, 124, 233, 243
Arieh aircraft, 163
Armaments Development and Production Corporation (South Africa), 266
armored vehicles, 12 (tbl 2), 84, 88, 91, 95, 102, 104, 112, 114, 117, 125, 137, 168, 180, 196, 197, 221, 238, 248, 266, 298, 304
arms control, *see* transfer restraints
Arms Control and Disarmament Agency (ACDA), 25, 46, 48, 60, 125, 183, 210, 212, 282, 287, 296, 313n
Arms Export Control Board, 58
artillery, 12 (tbl 2), 59, 88, 137, 179, 214, 219, 240, 266
ASEAN (Association of Southeast Asian Nations), 218, 221, 310
Asia, 9 (fig 2), 12, 36, 55, 135, 210, 218, 277, 288–89. *See also* individual countries
Assad, Hafaz, 141, 189–93
Australia, 52, 111
Austria, 121

338

Aviation Week and Space Technology, 64, 149
AWACS (Airborne Warning and Control System), 21, 169; proposed transfer to Iran of, 10, 56, 148, 153; proposed transfer to Saudi Arabia of, 18, 65, 158, 176, 181, 184–85, 207
Aziz, Prince Bin Abdul, 171

B-52 aircraft, 169
Bakhtiar, Shapur, government of, 153
Bandeirante aircraft, 238
Bangladesh, 210
Barre, Mohammed Siad, 187, 260
bases, *see* military bases
Bazargan, Mehdi, government of, 144, 153
Begin, Menahem, government of, 159–60, 174
Belgium, 86, 112, 123, 179, 219, 245, 261, 266, 270
Belize, 235
Bell helicopter, 217
Benson, Lucy W., 59
Bermudez, Francisco Morales, 240
Biafra (Nigerian civil war), 106, 111
Bialer, Seweryn, 73
Bin Zayed, Khalifa, 171
Blechman, Barry, 296
Bofers anti-aircraft gun, 121
Bolivia, 235, 244, 284, 332n
Brandt Commission, 36
Brazil, 4, 67, 132, 235, 237, 243, 244, 253–54, 284; and human rights issues, 33, 55, 249, 252; transfers by, 197, 238–39, 242, 248; transfers to, 133 (tbl 3), 233, 237; weapons production by, 13, 124–25, 233, 237–38, 304
Brezhnev, Leonid, 224, 228, 286
bribery, 29, 48–49, 89, 211
British Aircraft Corporation, 166
British Leyland, 103

Brown, Harold, 138, 158, 167, 181, 230, 289
Brussels Act, 281
Brussels Treaty, 110
Brzezinski, Zbigniew, 132, 223, 260, 288–89
Buckley, James L., 62, 66, 246
Burma, 112
Burt, Richard R., 66

C-130 Hercules aircraft, 165, 228, 230
Cactus surface-to-air missile, 91, 266
Callaghan report, 34
Cambodia, 22, 210, 219, 230
Campins, Luis Herrera, 246
Canada, 123; weapons transfers by, 13, 233, 265
Canberra aircraft, 240
Carstens, Karl, 111
Carter, Jimmy, administration of, 142, 152, 211, 259–61; and Asian countries, 28, 30, 118, 211–13, 215–16, 222–24, 229–30; and Latin America, 242–43, 249–53; and Middle East, 16, 138, 142, 149, 152, 160, 165, 168, 174–75, 183–84, 188, 206; transfer policy of, 30–33, 45, 49, 52–68, 183, 237, 285–97, 309
Cascavel armored vehicle, 238
Castro, Fidel, 74, 244, 248, 258
Castro, Raoul H., 251
CAT, *see* Conventional Arms Transfer
CATR, *see* Conventional Arms Transfer Restraints
Central America, 245, 247–48, 253
Central Treaty Organization (CENTO), 190, 221
Centurian tank, 161, 173, 267
Chad, 95–96, 255, 263
Chamanand, Kriangsak, 219
Chariot tank, 161

Ché Guevara, Ernesto, 244, 258
Cheysson, Claude, 95
Chieftain tank, 104, 111, 149, 175, 196
Chile (Santiago), 66–67, 93, 95, 233, 235, 239, 241–43, 253, 284, 332n; and human rights issues, 31–32, 65, 95–96, 106, 244, 249–51; transfers to, 20, 112, 133 (tbl 3), 161, 232–33, 238, 240–42
China (PRC, Beijing), 55, 61, 67, 104, 111, 165–66, 210, 214, 218–19, 225–27, 230, 288; and Africa, 263–64; and Soviet Union, 14–15, 67, 74, 81–82, 214, 225, 228–30, 256, 263–64, 280, 288, 303; transfers by, 13, 165–66, 222; transfers to, 74, 225–31, 279–80; and United States, 14, 28, 66, 215–17, 228–30, 289
Chiraq, Jacques, 194
Clark Amendment, 65, 260, 269
Clausewitz, Karl von, 5
Clements, William P., Jr., 24, 182
Clifford, Clark, 224
Cobra helicopter, 66, 238
COCOM, 231, 279
Colombia, 235–36, 244–46, 332n
COMECON (Council for Mutual Economic Assistance), 194
Commission Interministérielle pour l'Etude des Exportations de Matériels de Guerre (France), 89–90
Communist states, see Warsaw Pact
Concorde aircraft, 98
Confédération Française Démocratique du Travail (CFDT) (France), 93
Confédération Générale du Travail (CGT) (France), 93
Congo (Brazzaville), 76, 82, 255, 258, 264. See also Zaire

Congress: role in transfers, 31–32, 45, 48–52, 56, 64–65, 165, 169, 173, 180–84, 188, 207, 216, 247–48, 250, 260, 283
Conventional Arms Transfer (CAT), 286–90, 303–304
Conventional Arms Transfer Restraints (CATR), 293–96
co-production agreements, 4, 10–11, 53, 55, 59, 91, 112, 117, 124–25, 162, 171, 212–13, 217, 218, 222, 224, 238, 243, 266–67, 295, 300, 305
Council for Mutual Economic Assistance, see COMECON
Council on Foreign Relations, 50
Critchley, Julian, 107
Crotale anti-aircraft missile, 222, 227, 266
Cuba (Havana), 232, 240, 242, 246, 284, 302
    foreign activities of, 187, 233, 239, 241, 244–45, 247, 253; in Africa/Angola, 19, 74, 76–78, 187, 244–45, 256–58, 269
    and Soviet Union, 19, 21, 74, 76–78, 232, 244–45, 256–58, 278, 302
    transfers to, 19, 74, 232–34, 244, 277
Cyprus, 17, 21
Czechoslovakia, 123; weapons transfers by, 13, 139, 190, 203, 219, 257, 285

Dassault-Breguet, 88, 96–98
de Borchegrave, Arnaud, 148
Declaration of Ayacucho, 135, 233, 254, 283–84, 306, 310. See also Latin America, restraints in
Defence Sales Organization (DSO) (Great Britain), 103–105, 114
Defense Security Assistance Agency, 68

de Gaulle, Charles, 90-91, 161
Délégation Générale pour
l'Armement (DGA) (France), 87-
90, 114
Délégation Ministérielle pour
l'Armement (France), 86
Deng Xiaoping, 226
Denmark, 86, 281
destroyers, 48, 117, 149, 153, 214,
240, 243
developing world, see Third World
Dirección General de Fabriacaciones
Militares (Argentina), 243
Djibouti, 260, 263
Dragon anti-tank missile, 180
Draken aircraft, 121
Duarte, Jose Napoleon, 247

Eagle aircraft, see F-15
·economic development and weapons
trade, 36-38
Economist, 120
Ecuador, 55, 162, 235, 240-41, 284-
85, 332n
EEC (European Economic
Community), 84
Egypt (Cairo), 113, 123, 125, 132,
137, 139-41, 156-58, 164, 172,
177-78, 186, 189, 191, 201, 207-
208, 276-77, 285, 309; and Soviet
Union, 12, 16, 75-76, 78, 82, 139-
43, 154, 164-65, 169-70, 191, 193,
203, 205, 258, 285, 302; transfers
to, 12, 16, 21-22, 56, 91, 133 (tbl
3), 137-39, 164-70, 184, 203, 207,
285, 325n; and United States, 16,
21, 46, 56, 133 (tbl 3), 137-38,
141-43, 165-70, 184, 207, 325n.
See also Six Day War; Yom
Kippur War
Eisenhower, Dwight D.,
administration of, 173
Eland armored vehicle, 266

electronics, 48, 56, 88, 96, 103, 117,
162, 170, 224, 265
Elf-Aquitaine Company, 96
El Salvador, 24, 66, 235, 246, 247, 250
employment in weapons industries,
24, 26-27, 68-71, 85, 87, 94, 96,
102-103, 110, 113, 124, 161, 170,
222, 304
Empresa Brasileira de Aeronautica,
238
Equatorial Guinea, 257, 264
Eritrea, see Ethiopia
Ethiopia (Addis Ababa), 133 (tbl 3),
178, 199, 245, 263; and Eritrean
conflict, 178, 199, 257; and
Somalia/Ogaden conflict, 5, 57, 76,
187, 255, 257-61, 269; and Soviet
Union, 5, 33, 75-79, 178, 257-59,
269, 277; and United States, 5, 20,
23, 33
Euromissile consortium, 113
Europe, East, 194, 198, 240, 247. See
also Warsaw Pact; individual
countries
Europe, West, 32, 34-35, 84, 94, 136,
152, 199, 256, 262; as weapons
supplier, 12 (tbl 2), 26, 41, 60, 166,
229, 231, 234, 237, 256, 262, 270,
279, 290, 296-300, 305. See also
NATO; individual countries
European Economic Community, see
EEC

F-1 aircraft, see Mirage F-1
F-4 Phantom aircraft, 10, 55, 80, 117,
148, 162, 168-69, 195, 216
F-4G Wild Weasel aircraft, 55
F-5 aircraft, 22, 55, 60, 71, 148, 168,
173, 182, 195, 221, 234, 240-41,
248, 260
F-5E aircraft, 16, 29, 56, 59, 168,
180, 184, 188, 213, 214, 216-17,
219-20, 222, 238

F-5G aircraft, 60, 216, 223
F-6 Shenyang aircraft, 166
F-7 Shenyang aircraft, 226
F-12 aircraft, 227
F-14 Tomcat aircraft, 60, 153, 182, 195; and Iran, 48, 145, 148, 153–54
F-15 aircraft, 59–60, 117, 145, 168–69, 187, 218, 221, 228, 246; and Israel, 10, 16, 22, 56, 66, 80, 137, 156, 168, 184–85, 305; and Saudi Arabia, 10, 20, 56, 66, 143, 153, 158, 168, 176, 181–85, 207
F-16 aircraft, 25, 30, 55–56, 60, 66–67, 86–87, 98, 148, 153, 169, 182–83, 213, 221, 223, 228, 246; and Egypt, 21, 138, 168–69, 170, 207; and Israel, 124, 137, 162–63, 184, 305
F-16/79 aircraft, 60, 216
F-18 aircraft, 60, 182
F-18L aircraft, 49, 55
F-55 aircraft, 216
F-86 Sabre aircraft, 10, 110, 181, 234, 241
F-104 aircraft, 173, 214
F-404 engine, 163
Fagen, Richard R., 249
Fahd, Prince, 183
Figueiredo, Joao Baptista, 237
Finland, 121
Fitter C aircraft, *see* SU-22
FNLA (National Front for the Liberation of Angola), 264
Ford, Gerald, administration of, 46, 48–50, 58, 145, 182, 261
Foreign Assistance Act, 222, 242. *See also* Clark Amendment; Symington Amendment
Foreign Military Sales and Military Assistance Facts, 314n
Foreign Policy Association, 72
France (Paris), 4, 25–27, 35, 102, 114, 121, 164–65, 179, 201, 203,
206, 261, 270, 285–86, 298, 310, 321n
   transfer policy of, 19, 31, 83–96, 100, 108, 113–14, 231, 279, 310; oil and, 24, 84, 96, 194, 196
   transfers by, 8 (fig 2), 10, 13, 42, 84–85, 91, 97–98, 133 (tbl 3), 210, 219–22, 225, 227, 238, 279–80, 315n; to African countries, 91, 95, 256, 262–63, 265–66; to Middle East countries, 22, 24, 84, 91, 95–96, 114, 125, 148–49, 153, 166, 174, 179, 192, 194–197; to Latin American countries, 234, 240–41, 244, 248, 285
   weapons industry of, 25–27, 83–88, 94, 96–99, 102, 112–13, 299–300
Franco, Francisco, 111
Freedman, Lawrence, 228
frigates, 112, 214, 245, 267
FX aircraft, 60–61, 216–17, 220, 223

Gabriel surface-to-surface missile, 161, 217, 267
Galley, Robert, 92
Gamassy, Abdel-Gany, 166
Gandhi, Indira, 224
Gazelle helicopter, 166
Gelb, Leslie, 61, 286, 288–89
General Act for the Repression of the African Slave Trade (Brussels Act), 281
General Dynamics Company, 86–87, 153, 216
General Electric, 55, 162–63
Geneva Committee on Disarmament, 41, 281–82, 309
Germany, East, 110, 187, 257
Germany, West, 26, 33, 109, 121, 125, 179, 192, 206, 225, 228, 243, 251, 300; weapons industry of, 94, 110, 112–15; weapons transfer policy of, 110–16, 120, 165;

weapons transfers by, 8 (fig 2), 13, 109–112, 133 (tbl 3), 148–49, 179, 194, 219, 233, 241, 243–45, 256
Gespard anti-aircraft vehicle, 114
Ghana, 82, 255, 263
Giscard d'Estaing, Valéry, 88–89, 94–95, 201, 310
Glubb, Sir John Bagot, 172
Goodpaster, Andrew J., 250–51
Goronwy-Roberts, Lord, 282–83
Great Britain (United Kingdom, London), 4, 25–26, 35, 121, 125, 145, 161, 164–65, 171–73, 181, 198, 203, 282–83, 285, 300
    transfer policy of, 31, 100–108, 114, 242
    transfers by, 8 (fig 1), 10, 13, 42, 100–106, 111, 133 (tbl 3); to African countries, 19, 256, 262–63, 265; to Middle East countries, 104–105, 114–15, 148–49, 153, 166, 173, 175, 179, 194–95, 201, 219–22, 225, 245, 315n
        weapons industry of, 25–27, 94, 100–103, 107–108, 112
Greece, 17, 91, 93, 109
Grumman Company, 182
Guatemala, 66, 67, 235, 247–48, 250, 253
Guinea, 75, 82, 112, 245, 257, 259, 264
Guinea-Bissau, 76, 257

Haig, Alexander, 216, 230, 301
Hallstein Doctrine, 110
Harpoon anti-ship missile, 149
Harrier STOL aircraft, 222, 227
Hawk aircraft, 165
Hawk anti-aircraft missile, 15, 117, 168, 173
Healey, Denis, 103
helicopters, 12 (tbl 2), 66, 91, 95, 97, 117, 149, 166, 171, 173, 192, 196, 217, 222, 230, 238, 240, 247–48, 267, 298

Hercules aircraft, see C-130
Hernu, Charles, 95
Honduras, 235, 247
Horn of Africa, 5, 23, 76, 151–52, 204, 207, 259–60, 264, 268–70. See also Ethiopia; Somalia
Hot anti-tank missile, 113, 192, 227
hovercraft, 148–49
Hua Guofeng, 226
Huey helicopter, 248
Hughes weapons control system, 154
human rights and transfers, 7, 16, 31–34, 95–96, 120, 241–42, 294; U.S. policy on, 17, 31–34, 54–55, 65, 67, 72, 150, 152, 211, 220, 223, 232–33, 237, 242, 247–53, 316n. See also individual countries
Hunter aircraft, 240
Hussein, King of Jordan, 15, 143, 172–75, 196
Hussein, Saddam, 195

Iceland, 231, 279
IL-76 aircraft, 77
India (New Delhi), 15, 55, 132, 165, 222, 225, 282, 285; and Pakistan, 20, 30, 67, 147, 210, 221, 223–25, 285; transfers to, 15, 20, 75, 79, 110, 133 (tbl 3), 221–24; weapons production by, 13, 123–25, 222, 304
Indonesia, 124, 133 (tbl 3), 210, 212; and Soviet Union, 15, 75, 78, 81–82, 219, 302
Industria de Material Belico do Brasil, 238
Inoki, Masamichi, 118
International Institute for Strategic Studies (Great Britain), 282, 304, 314n
International Security Assistance and Arms Export Control Act, 32, 50, 69, 242
International Traffic in Arms Regulations (ITAR), 58

Iran (Teheran), 4, 20, 26, 32–33, 38,
    61, 107, 111–12, 132, 136, 144–54,
    155, 163, 176–77, 181, 186–87,
    194–96, 207, 251, 276, 288–89,
    309; transfers to, 12, 16, 24, 46, 95,
    104–105, 110, 133 (tbl 3), 148–49,
    153–54; and United States, 16–18,
    32, 46, 48–49, 55–56, 133 (tbl 3),
    142, 148–54, 181, 196
Iraq (Baghdad), 20, 22, 84, 91, 133
    (tbl 3), 157, 171, 177, 188–89,
    194–95, 276, 309; and Iran, 91,
    147, 177, 193, 195–97; and Kurds,
    22, 147, 194; nuclear program of,
    22, 194–95; and Soviet Union, 12,
    19, 22, 24, 75–76, 79, 82, 137,
    139–42, 189, 191–98, 205, 213
Iraqi Petroleum Company, 195
Irish Republican Army, 199
Israel (Jerusalem), 4, 10, 12, 21–22,
    28, 30, 55, 91, 110, 115, 121, 156–
    64, 168–70, 195–96, 199–209, 216,
    276, 309
    and Arab states, 15–16, 20–22,
    136–38, 143, 156–60, 167–68,
    172–76, 181, 184–85, 189–90,
    195–96, 305. See also 1947–49
    war; Six Day War; Yom Kippur
    War
    transfers by, 66, 125, 161–62,
    214, 217, 233, 240, 242–43, 247–
    48, 266–67, 305
    and United States, 16, 22–23,
    46–48, 52, 55–56, 66, 80, 124, 133
    (tbl 3), 137, 157–60, 162–64, 184–
    85, 190, 206–207, 240
    weapons industry of, 13, 123–26,
    156, 161–64, 304–305
Israeli Aircraft Industry, 161
Israeli Military Industry, 161
Italy, 48–49, 110, 112, 123, 125, 165,
    195, 238; transfers by, 13, 133 (tbl
    3), 179, 194, 233 (tbl 3), 245, 266
Ivory Coast, 259, 263

Jaguar aircraft, 94, 165, 222
Japan (Tokyo), 26, 48–49, 109, 115–
    20, 210, 225, 231, 279, 281–82,
    298; transfers to, 19, 52, 111;
    weapons production/co-production
    of, 10, 59, 116–20, 218
Jones, Thomas, 49
Jordan (Amman), 15, 157–58, 172–
    75, 178, 188, 207–208, 267, 276–
    77, 309; transfers to, 15, 66, 133
    (tbl 3), 173, 175, 177, 196; and
    United States, 15, 66, 173–75, 196

Kaldor, Mary, 308
Kassem, Abdul Karim, 193
Kawasaki company, 117
Kennedy Amendment, 31–32, 242
Kennedy, Edward, 145
Kennedy, John, administration of,
    234
Kenya, 20, 21, 110, 255, 260–61, 263
Kfir aircraft, 55, 66, 156, 161–63,
    185, 216, 240
Khalid, King of Saudi Arabia, 16, 95,
    183
Khomeini, Ayatollah, 23, 187, 195–96
Khrushchev, Nikita, 74
Kiran aircraft, 125
Kissinger, Henry, 16, 32, 46–50, 137,
    145, 160, 181–83, 260, 283
Korea, 118, 210, 212, 265, 276, 303
    North (Pyongyang), 19, 198,
    211–14, 263
    South (Seoul), 28–29, 132, 179,
    212, 219, 225, 288, 298; transfers
    to, 19, 28–29, 33–34, 55–56, 66,
    67, 133 (tbl 3), 210, 213, 251;
    weapons production of, 13, 59, 67,
    124, 212, 304
Kosygin, Alexei, 193
Krauss-Maffer company, 111–12
Krupp industries, 111
Kurds, 22, 147, 194
Kuwait, 133 (tbl 3)

labor unions, 93, 113
Laird, Melvin, 46
Lance surface-to-surface missile, 137
Laos, 210
Latin America, 15, 16, 20, 36, 38, 74, 82, 107, 232–36, 253–54, 258, 298; disputes within, 232, 234–36, 239, 245, 247, 254; and human rights, 16, 31–33, 55, 232–33, 237, 242, 247–53; transfer restraints in, 135, 162, 232, 254, 283–85, 288–89, 306, 309; transfers to, 9 (fig 2), 13, 15, 55, 67, 75, 96, 112, 134–35, 161, 210, 232–34, 244, 277; weapons production in, 13, 233. *See also* individual countries
Lavi aircraft, 163
League of Nations, 281
Leahy, O. A., 181
Lebanon, 22, 123, 158, 178, 190–91, 199
Le Monde, 65, 321n
Leopard tank, 111–12, 243
Leopard-2 tank, 114, 179
Leopardino tank, 112
L'Estoile, Hugues de, 86
Le Theule, Joel, 97
Libya (Tripoli), 20, 106–107, 133 (tbl 3), 166, 171, 189, 196–99, 238, 345, 309; and France, 84, 91, 95–96, 197; and Soviet Union, 12, 24, 27, 75–76, 79, 139, 142, 167, 197–98, 213
Lightning aircraft, 182
Lockheed Corporation, 48, 117, 228, 230
Lumumba, Patrice, 77
Lynx helicopter, 166, 171

McDonnell Douglas Corporation, 117, 182
MacMillan, Harold, 106
McNamara, Robert, 103

M-16 rifle, 212
M-47 tank, 173
M-48 tank, 173, 174, 212
M-60 tank, 173, 175, 196–97
Malaysia, 119, 220
Mali, 75–76, 257
Malta, 281
Mao Tsetung, 226
Marcos, Ferdinand, 17, 34, 220
Marder armored vehicle, 114
market-sharing, *see* transfer restraints
Marten armored vehicle, 112
Marty, François, 92
Marut aircraft, 222
Marwan, Ashraf, 170
Matra Company, 88, 96–98
Mauritania, 22
Mauroy, Pierre, 95
Maverick air-to-surface missile, 137, 168, 180
Mayer, Pierre, 89
Mendelevich, Lev I., 287
Mengistu, Haile-Mariam, 257
Méry, G., 90
Mexico, 248–49, 284
Middle East, 21, 28, 36, 94, 97, 115, 118, 136, 138, 156, 169, 172, 276, 296; conflicts in, 134, 136–37, 155, 192, 197, 199–201; transfer restraints in, 155–56, 199–209, 285, 297, 303, 308–309; transfers to, 9 (fig 2), 10, 12–13, 19–20, 42, 46, 75–76, 84, 112, 122, 134–35, 201–206, 285, 362n. *See also* Persian Gulf; individual countries; individual wars
MiG aircraft, 227, 244
MiG-15 aircraft, 193
MiG-17 aircraft, 10, 226
MiG-19 aircraft, 166, 221, 226
MiG-21 aircraft, 10, 22, 80, 165–66, 169, 188, 190–91, 193, 197, 213–14, 221, 222, 224, 226, 240, 245, 257, 262

MiG-23 aircraft, 10, 67, 75, 80, 141, 165–66, 177, 191, 193, 197, 213, 223, 224, 244
MiG-25 aircraft, 197–98, 224
Miki, Takeo, 117
Milan anti-tank missile, 113, 192, 227
military advisers/training, 15, 18, 66, 180, 210–11, 264; Soviet/Cuban, 16, 23, 76–78, 82, 140–41, 177, 187, 191, 198, 239, 241, 244–45, 257–58
military bases: and transfers, 16–17, 20–21, 41, 57, 76, 102, 169; for Soviet use, 16, 21, 74, 76, 82, 139–41, 154, 177, 187, 191, 198, 257–58; for U.S. use, 17, 20–21, 34, 57, 198, 261
Mirage aircraft, 22, 84, 87–88, 91, 96–97, 197, 228, 240–41, 285
Mirage F-1 aircraft, 10, 84, 86, 91, 95, 125, 165, 171, 174, 194, 196–97, 240, 266
Mirage 5 aircraft, 234
Mirage 4000 aircraft, 98, 196
Mirage III aircraft, 91, 166, 197, 222, 238, 245, 266
Mirage 2000 aircraft, 25, 98, 171, 196, 227
missile boats, 12 (tbl 2), 95
missiles, 48, 59, 88, 91, 96–97, 110, 125–26, 162, 170, 179–81, 194, 212, 214, 304, 313n; air-to-air, 65–66, 137, 154, 161, 168, 180, 184, 217, 226; air-to-surface, 137, 168, 180; anti-ship, 149; anti-tank, 10, 28, 56, 66, 98, 113, 117, 125, 156, 165–66, 171, 180, 192, 196, 211, 227, 294; surface-to-air (anti-aircraft), 12 (tbl 2), 15, 56, 75, 91, 104, 113, 117, 141, 156, 165, 168, 173, 197, 207, 211, 222, 226–27, 266; surface-to-surface, 47–48, 137, 161, 202, 217, 267, 294

Mitsubishi company, 117–18
Mitterrand, François, 93–96
Mitterrand, Jacques, 95
Mobutu, Sese Seko, 261, 270
Mondale, Walter, 45, 49, 160, 286
Moro National Liberation Front, 199
Morocco (Rabat), 22, 56, 66, 133 (tbl 3)
Mozambique, 75, 199, 257, 264
MPLA (People's Movement for the Liberation of Angola), 76, 244, 257–58, 264
Mugabe, Robert, 264
multilateral management, see transfer restraints

Namibia, 65
Nasser, Gamal Abdul, 164, 170, 189, 203, 285
National Front for the Liberation of Angola, see FNLA
national liberation movements, 4–5, 15, 42, 73, 76, 120, 139, 199, 256, 263, 268
NATO countries, 17, 34–36, 85–86, 118, 138, 297–98; transfers by, 13–14, 42, 231, 279, 315n; transfers to, 9 (fig 2), 12, 15, 19, 52, 98, 109, 111, 148. See also Europe, West; individual countries
naval vessels, 98, 110, 148–49, 157, 179–80, 194, 244, 313; aircraft carriers, 294; construction of, 25, 87, 103, 112, 117, 125–26, 212, 246, 304; destroyers, 48, 117, 149, 153, 214, 240, 243; frigates, 112, 214, 245, 267; missile boats, 12 (tbl 2), 95; patrol boats, 95, 117, 121, 149, 212, 266, 267, 304; submarines, 12 (tbl 2), 107, 112, 149, 197, 204, 214, 219, 243, 245, 266, 294
Near East Arms Coordinating Committee, 203, 285

Nelson Amendment, 50
Netherlands, 13, 48–49, 86, 214, 240
New Zealand, 52, 111
Nicaragua, 161, 247
Nigeria, 75, 106, 110–12, 132, 261–63
Nike-Hercules surface-to-air missile, 56, 211
1947–49 war (Israel War of Independence), 164, 203
1967 war, see Six Day War
1973 war, see Yom Kippur War
Nixon Doctrine, 145, 181
Nixon, Richard, administration of, 24, 46, 48–49, 145, 241. See also Kissinger, Henry
Nkomo, Joshua, 264
Northrop Corporation, 48–49, 60, 71, 216
North Atlantic Treaty Organization, see NATO
Norway, 86
nuclear programs, 6, 22, 29–31, 85, 67–68, 102, 132, 194–95, 223–25, 237, 243, 251, 277–78, 293; and conventional weapons, 4, 29–31, 67–68, 224–25, 278

Oerlikon-Buehrle (Switzerland), 122
Ogaden conflict, see Ethiopia
Ohira, Masayoshi, 119
oil: and military expenditures, 17, 24, 26, 36, 46, 75, 79, 115, 132, 134, 139, 151, 178–79, 193, 197–98, 248; and transfer policy, 17, 18, 21, 26, 28, 32, 36, 42–43, 56, 84, 96, 113, 115, 118, 136, 138–39, 143–46, 150–51, 162, 175–79, 181, 185, 193–94, 199, 216, 235, 245–46, 305. See also OPEC
Oman, 21, 147, 261
OPEC (Organization of Petroleum Exporting Countries), 17, 26, 136, 150, 162–63, 179. See also oil

Organization of African Unity (OAU), 271, 310
Organization of American States (OAS), 284, 310
Organization of Petroleum Exporting Countries, see OPEC
Orion aircraft, 117
OV-10 aircraft, 56

P-3C aircraft, 228
Pakistan (Islamabad), 20, 55, 125, 147, 198, 222–23, 263, 285; and India, 20, 30, 67, 147, 210, 221–25, 285; nuclear program of, 29–30, 67–68, 223–25; transfers to, 20, 29–30, 65–68, 110, 133 (tbl 3), 221–23
Panama, 332n
Panhard-Levassor company, 84, 88, 266
Park Chung Hee, 28–29, 211
patrol boats, 95, 117, 121, 149, 212, 266, 267, 304
Pax Christi movement, 92
People's Movement for the Liberation of Angola, see MPLA
Perez, Carlos, 284
Peron, Juan, 242
Pershing surface-to-surface missile, 48
Persian Gulf, 20, 21, 97, 115, 227, 261, 297, 309; transfers to, 12–13, 19, 24, 48–49, 107, 134–35. See also Middle East; individual countries
Peru (Lima), 20, 67, 235, 239–41, 244, 284, 322n; and Soviet Union, 15, 75, 77, 78, 82, 232, 239–40, 285; transfers to, 133 (tbl 3), 232–34, 239–40, 245
Phantom aircraft, see F-4
Philippines, 17, 33–34, 199, 220, 251; U.S. bases in, 17, 20, 39, 220
Phoenix air-to-air missile, 154
Pinochet, Augusto, 240, 242, 251–52

PLO, 174, 178, 199; and Soviet
  Union, 139, 142, 191
Pol Pot, 219
Poland, 188, 230, 257
Polaris submarine, 102, 204
Polisario, 56, 66
Portugal, 91, 258
Presidential Directive 13, 52
Pucara aircraft, 243

Qaddafi, Muammar, 23, 75, 95, 167,
  189, 197–99
Qatar, 125, 170–71

Rabin, Yitzhak, 160
Rajaratnam, S., 307
Rattlesnake armored vehicle, 197
Reagan, Ronald, administration of:
  proposed transfers by, 30–31, 65–
  67, 169, 181, 184, 213, 216, 223,
  246–47; transfer policies of, 45, 61–
  68, 211, 242–43, 253, 269
Redeye anti-tank missile, 180, 294
regional status, 3–4, 6, 11, 124, 132,
  135, 277
Reshef missile patrol boat, 267
Réunion, 263
Rhodesia (Zimbabwe), 111, 117, 264
Roland anti-aircraft missile, 113,
  227
Rolls Royce, 166, 227
Roosevelt, Franklin Delano, 20

Saab aircraft, 121
Sabah conflict, see Philippines
Sabre aircraft, see F-86
Sadat, Anwar, 16, 56, 138, 141–42,
  164–70, 186, 198, 202, 208
Sahara conflict, see Morocco
sales promotion of weapons, 24, 48–
  49, 53–54, 86–89, 103, 114
SALT II, 268, 286
SAM missiles, 12 (tbl 2), 141, 221.
  See also missiles, surface-to-air
Sampson, Anthony, 311

Sandinista, 247
Sato, Eisaku, 116
Saudi Arabia (Riyadh), 12, 22, 115,
  125, 157–58, 166, 168, 170–71,
  175–80, 186–88, 195, 208, 276,
  309; and Europe, 22, 24, 84, 95,
  114–15, 166, 179; and Iran, 20,
  147, 176–77, 186–87; military
  expenditures by, 84, 95, 125, 133
  (tbl 3), 171, 173, 178–79, 181,
  187–88, 260; oil of, 18, 24, 84,
  175–79, 181, 185–86, 216; and
  United States, 10, 15–16, 18, 20,
  46, 65, 115, 137, 143, 158, 165,
  176, 179–88, 207
Schmidt, Helmut, 111, 114–15
Scorpion tank, 149, 179
Scud missile, 75, 193, 197
Seahawk aircraft, 110
SEATO (Southeast Asian Treaty
  Organization), 221
Sella, Amnon, 204
Senegal, 259, 263
Sense About Defense, 108
Shaba conflict, see Zaire
Shafrir air-to-air missile, 161, 217
Shah of Iran, 16, 20, 32, 104–105,
  144–52, 176, 186; and United
  States, 16–17, 32, 48–49, 56, 145–
  46, 150–52, 251
Shenyang aircraft, 166, 226
ships, see naval vessels
Shir tank, 104–105
Sidewinder air-to-air missile, 65–66,
  168, 180, 184, 217
Singapore, 119, 132, 219–20, 307
Six Day War (1967 war), 16, 139,
  141, 161, 173–74, 190, 195, 207
Smith, Gerard, 251
Société Nationale des Industries
  Aérospatiales (SNIAS) (France),
  87–88, 95, 97–98
Société Nationale d'Etudes et de
  Construction de Moteurs d'Avions
  (SNECMA) (France), 87

348

Société Nationale de Poudres et
  Explosives (SNPE) (France), 87
Somalia (Mogadishu), 5, 21, 56–57,
  66, 187, 199, 260, 264, 270; and
  Ethiopia, 5, 57, 76, 187, 255, 257,
  259–61, 269; and Soviet Union, 5,
  19, 21, 23, 75–76, 187, 258–60,
  302
Somoza, Anastasio, 161, 247
South Africa, 4, 30, 91, 93, 106, 111,
  133 (tbl 3), 161–62, 217, 240, 242,
  255, 263, 265, 268, 304; embargoes
  against, 31, 91, 95–96, 106, 116,
  161, 265–67, 285; weapons
  production by, 13, 124, 266–67,
  304
South America, see Latin America
Southeast Asia Treaty Organization,
  see SEATO
Soviet Union (USSR, Moscow), 13,
  23–24, 27, 42, 60, 67, 73–81, 118,
  121, 136–37, 146, 154, 175–77,
  190–91, 203–205, 218, 224, 228–
  30, 247, 250, 256, 278, 286–90,
  301–303, 305, 314n
  and African countries, 19, 20,
  75–79, 82, 187, 244–45, 256–61,
  263–64, 277; Horn (Ethiopia/
  Somalia), 5, 19, 21, 23–24, 33, 75–
  79, 187, 204, 257–60, 269–70, 277,
  302
  and Afghanistan, 14–15, 21, 67,
  79, 82, 118, 175–76, 195, 207,
  223–25, 228, 230, 250, 261, 289,
  297, 303
  and Arab countries, 10, 15, 22,
  75–77, 79, 133 (tbl 3), 139–42,
  167, 175–77, 187–89, 201–206,
  326n; Egypt, 12, 16, 75–76, 78, 82,
  138–42, 154, 164–65, 169–70, 191,
  193, 203, 205, 258, 285, 302; Iraq,
  12, 19, 22, 24, 75–76, 79, 82, 133
  (tbl 3), 137, 139–42, 189, 191–98,
  205, 213; Libya, 12, 24, 27, 75–76,
  79, 139, 142, 167, 197–98, 213;

Syria, 12, 19, 21, 75–76, 82, 133
  (tbl 3), 137, 139, 141–42, 174, 189,
  190–93, 198, 205, 213
  and China, 14–15, 67, 74, 81–
  82, 214, 225, 228–30, 256, 263–64,
  280, 288, 303
  and Cuba, 19, 21, 74, 76–78,
  232, 244–45, 256–58, 277, 302
  and Latin American countries,
  242, 247, 250–54; Peru, 15, 75,
  77–78, 82, 232, 239–40, 285
  military advisers/personnel of,
  16, 23, 76–78, 82, 140–41, 177,
  187, 191, 198, 239, 241, 257–58
  and military bases, 16, 21, 74,
  76, 82, 139–41, 154, 177, 187, 191,
  198, 257–58
  political aims of, 4, 15–16, 19,
  21–22, 27, 73–79, 81–82, 102, 132,
  146, 167, 175–77, 193–94, 204–
  206, 222, 224–25, 228–30, 256–59,
  264, 277, 296, 302
  transfers by, 8 (fig 1), 12–13,
  19–24, 42, 66, 73–80, 133 (tbl 3),
  213, 221–24, 240–41, 257–58, 285,
  314n, 315n, 320n, 326n; aircraft,
  10 (tbl 2), 75, 141, 188, 190–91,
  193, 197, 213, 221, 223–24, 240,
  244, 257, 262, 285
Spain, 20, 111, 248, 258
Sparrow air-to-air missile, 168
Spica patrol boat, 121
Spruance destroyer, 48, 149, 153
Stalin, Josef, 74
standardization of weapons, 34–36,
  300
Stockholm International Peace
  Research Institute (SIPRI), 282,
  313n
Stokes, Sir Donald, 103
SU-7 aircraft, 190
SU-22 (Fitter-C) aircraft, 240
submarines, 12 (tbl 2), 107, 112, 149,
  197, 204, 214, 219, 243, 245, 266,
  294

Sudan, 56, 66, 110, 112, 167, 178, 257–58, 260, 263–64
Suffield, Sir Lester, 104
Sukarno, 81, 219
Sultan, Prince, 178
Sun, Y. S., 217–18
Super Frelon helicopter, 192, 267
Suzuki, Zenko, 119
Sweden, 13, 55, 101, 109, 111, 120–22, 281, 291
Swingfire anti-tank missile, 166, 171
Switzerland, 13, 109, 111, 122, 251, 291
Symington Amendment, 65, 222
Syria (Damascus), 22, 113, 133 (tbl 3), 141, 157–58, 171, 172, 177–78, 188–90, 192, 196, 198, 207–208, 276, 298, 309; and Soviet Union, 12, 19, 21, 75–76, 82, 133 (tbl 3), 137, 139, 141–42, 174, 189, 190–93, 198, 205, 213

T-54 tank, 188
T-72 tank, 192, 197, 224
Taiwan, 30, 55, 60, 61, 124, 179, 188, 210, 214–18, 225, 228–29, 267, 304–305; and United States, 133 (tbl 3), 214–17
TAM tank, 243
tanks, 12 (tbl 2), 28, 79, 84, 98, 102, 104–105, 111–12, 114, 117, 125, 149, 161, 173–75, 179, 188, 192, 196–97, 212, 224, 240, 243, 267. See also individual models
Tanzania, 20, 110, 264
technology transfer, 4, 73, 79, 112, 124, 162, 293, 305, 307
Thailand, 112, 119, 133 (tbl 3), 210, 218–19
Thatcher, Margaret, government of, 104–105, 242
Thieu, Nguyen Van, 17
Third World, 3–4, 10–11, 36–38, 42, 81, 111, 131–34, 197, 237, 258, 282, 290, 297–98, 301, 307–308

military expenditures by, 5, 11 (tbl 1), 13, 36, 133 (tbl 3), 134
and Soviet Union, 12 (tbl 2), 13, 73–81, 247, 256
transfer restraints in, 35–36, 43, 277–80, 306–11
transfers to, 3, 8, 9 (fig 2), 10, 12 (tbl 2), 13–14, 46, 60, 74, 190, 275–77; by West European countries, 12 (tbl 2), 84, 87, 94, 96, 104, 110–11, 113, 121
weapons production/export of, 8 (fig 1), 11, 13, 123–27, 132, 303–305, 315n.
See also individual countries; individual regions
Thomson-Hotchkiss-Brandt company, 88, 96
Tito, Josef, 165
Togo, 238, 263
Tomcat aircraft, see F-14
Toufanian, Hassan, 149
Touré, Sékou, 259
TOW anti-tank missile, 10, 28, 56, 180, 196
Tracked Rapier surface-to-air missile, 104
transfer restraints, 3, 6–7, 41–44, 49–50, 135; market-sharing in, 298–300; multilateral management of, 6–7, 14, 35, 43, 108, 126–27, 231, 278–86; negotiations on, 285–90, 302–303; obstacles to, 6–7, 43, 291–92, 299, 307, 309; proposals on, 291–302, 306–11. See also individual regions
transfers of weapons, 3–7, 8 (fig 1), 9 (fig 2), 12, 42–43, 133 (tbl 3); data sources on, 313–314; economics of, 24–27, 36–37, 125, 298–99; expenditures on, 5–6, 10, 13, 21, 23, 33, 36–37, 74–75, 79, 132, 133 (tbl 3); growth of, 3, 5–6, 9–10, 13, 36, 41, 131–34, 276–77; hazards

of, 3, 5, 7, 16–24, 28–29, 110–11, 144–45, 153–56, 170, 196–97; politics of, 3, 14–19, 154, 275–77; rationales for, 3, 14–27, 41, 43. *See also* individual countries; individual weapons

transportation of weapons, 77–78, 257

Trident submarine, 204

Tripartite Declaration, 164, 203

Truman, Harry, 142

TU-22 aircraft, 75, 197

Tunisia, 66

Turkey, 17, 21, 66, 109

Uganda, 20, 75, 106, 199, 255, 257

UN Association of the USA, 50

United Arab Emirates, 20, 125, 170–71

United Kingdom, *see* Great Britain

United Nations, 72, 117, 120, 195, 265, 281–82, 285, 307–308, 310

United States (Washington), 16–19, 22, 26, 28–29, 34, 84, 116, 118, 121, 136, 198, 250–51, 257, 277–78, 298, 305

and African countries, 21, 23, 33, 56, 65, 110, 187, 256–57, 259–62, 265, 268–70, 288

and China/Taiwan, 14, 28, 66, 214–17, 228–30, 289, 133 (tbl 3)

and Egypt, 16, 21, 46, 56, 133 (tbl 3), 137–38, 141–43, 165–70, 184, 207, 325n

and Iran, 10, 16–18, 32, 46, 48–49, 55–56, 133 (tbl 3), 142, 148–54, 181, 196

and Israel, 16, 22–23, 46–48, 52, 55–56, 66, 80, 124, 133 (tbl 3), 137, 157–60, 162–64, 184–85, 190, 206–207, 240

and Jordan, 15, 66, 173–75, 196

and Korea, South, 19, 28–29, 33–34, 55–56, 66–67, 133 (tbl 3), 210–13, 251, 288, 298

and Latin American countries, 16, 31–33, 55, 65–67, 162, 232–37, 240–43, 246–53, 288, 298

military bases for, 17, 20–21, 34, 57, 198, 261

and Saudi Arabia, 10, 15–16, 18, 20, 46, 65, 115, 137, 143, 158, 165, 176, 179–88, 207

transfer policies of, 24, 28–29, 31–32, 45–68, 132, 203–204, 206, 222, 242, 260, 265, 269, 278–79, 285, 296; Congress and, 31–32, 45, 48–52, 56, 64–65, 165, 169, 173, 180–81, 183–84, 188, 207, 216, 247–48, 250, 260, 283; human rights and, 17, 31–34, 54, 55, 65, 67, 72, 150, 152, 211, 220, 232–33, 237, 242, 247–53, 316n

transfers by, 8 (fig 1), 9 (fig 2), 9–10, 12–13, 20–21, 23, 25–26, 29–30, 45, 56–57, 65–66, 74–75, 102, 133 (tbl 3), 143, 187, 201, 218–20, 265, 314n; of aircraft, 10, 12 (tbl 2), 16, 21, 28, 30, 48, 55–56, 60, 65–67, 80, 137, 143, 145, 148, 165, 173, 181–85, 188, 213, 219–21, 223, 228, 240–41, 248, 260; rejections of, 21, 54–55, 124, 162, 169, 216, 222–24, 228–29, 234, 240–41, 246; value of, 10, 45–47, 56–57, 65, 74, 80, 314n

weapons industry of, 26, 68–71. *See also* individual administrations; individual countries; individual regions

USSR, *see* Soviet Union

Uruguay, 33, 55, 250

Uzi submachine-gun, 162, 267

Vance, Cyrus, 22, 230, 260, 286, 288

Venezuela, 66–67, 124, 233, 235–36, 244–46, 254, 322n

Videla, Jorge Raphael, 161, 242–43, 250–52

Vietnam, 12, 17, 19, 21–23, 75, 78, 118, 132, 133 (tbl 3), 155, 210, 218–21, 226, 263
Viggen aircraft, 55, 121
Vijayanta tank, 125
Vinnell Corporation, 180
Vosper-Thorneycroft, 166

Walters, Vernon D., 247
War of the Pacific, 235, 239
Warsaw Pact, 9 (fig 2), 12–15, 19, 74, 80, 279
weapons quality, 10–11
weapons standardization, 34–36, 300
weapons transfer restraints, see transfer restraints
weapons transfers, see transfers of weapons
weapons transport, 77–78, 257
Weizman, Ezer, 158
Western European Union, 110
Westland Aircraft company, 166
Wild Weasel aircraft, see F4-G
Wilson, Harold, 103
World Military Expenditures and Transfers, 313–14n

World Military and Social Expenditures, 314n

Xavante aircraft, 125, 238

Yamani, Ahmed Zaki, 18, 185
Yazdi, Ibrahim, 144
Yearbook of World Armaments and Disarmament, 313–14n
Yemen, North, 178, 187–88
Yemen, South, 21, 76, 133 (tbl 3), 139, 142, 167, 176–77, 188, 196, 245; and Soviet Union, 176–77, 187, 189
Yew, Lee Kuan, 220
Yom Kippur War (1973 war), 10, 16, 22, 23, 84, 91, 139, 141, 156–57, 160–61, 166, 169, 173–74, 190–92, 204
Yugoslavia, 165

Zaire (Congo), 22, 77, 187, 255, 261–62, 270
Zambia, 264
Zia, ul-Haq, 223
Zimbabwe, see Rhodesia

ABOUT THE AUTHOR

ANDREW J. PIERRE is a Senior Fellow at the Council on Foreign Relations. He was educated at Amherst College, the Institut d' Etudes Politiques in Paris and Columbia University from which he received a Ph.D. in Political Science. Before joining the Council in 1969, Dr. Pierre had been with the Brookings Institution and the Hudson Institute. He has been an Adjunct Professor at Columbia University and has lectured widely in universities and military academies in the United States and abroad. From 1962 to 1964 he was with the Department of State, first in Washington working on United Nations matters and then at the American Embassy in London dealing with politico-military affairs. He has been a consultant to the State and Defense departments as well as other U.S. government agencies.

Dr. Pierre's work has covered a wide range of foreign policy issues, including East-West relations, European-American relations, defense policy and arms control, nuclear proliferation, conventional arms transfers and international terrorism. *The Global Politics of Arms Sales* was begun when he was a Rockefeller Foundation Fellow in its program on Conflict in International Relations, and it was also supported by a grant from the Ford Foundation and a NATO Research Fellowship. Among his other writings are *Nuclear Politics: The British Experience with an Independent Strategic Force 1939–1970, Nuclear Proliferation: A Strategy for Control, Arms Transfers and American Foreign Policy* (editor and contributor), and he played a key role in the drafting of *Western Security: What has changed? What should be done?* issued by the Council on Foreign Relations and three comparable institutes in Europe. Dr. Pierre has contributed chapters to a number of volumes and is the regular book reviewer for *Foreign Affairs* of the section on military, science, and technology. He has written articles for many publications including *Foreign Affairs, Foreign Policy, Survival, International Security, Orbis, Survey, Atlantic Community Quarterly, Political Science Quarterly, Parameters, New Scientist, Armed Forces and Society, Politique Internationale, The World Today, Europa-Archiv,* and has also published in the *Washington Post* and the *New York Times.*

Library of Congress Cataloging in Publication Data

Pierre, Andrew J.
    The global politics of arms sales.

    "A Council on Foreign Relations book."
    Includes bibliographical references and index.
    1. Munitions—Political   aspects.   2. Armaments—Political   aspects.
3. Firearms industry and trade—Political aspects.   4. World politics.
I. Title.
HD9743.A2P5   382'.4535582   81-15895
ISBN 0-691-07635-9   AACR2
ISBN 0-691-02207-0 (pbk.)